RIOTS AND POGROMS

Also by Paul R. Brass

CASTE, FACTION AND PARTY IN INDIAN POLITICS,
   Vol. I: Election Studies, Vol. II: Faction and Party
ETHNIC GROUPS AND THE STATE
ETHNICITY AND NATIONALISM: Theory and Comparison
FACTIONAL POLITICS IN AN INDIAN STATE: The Congress
   Party in Uttar Pradesh
THE INDIAN NATIONAL CONGRESS AND INDIAN SOCIETY
   1885–1985: Ideology, Social Structure, and Political Dominance
   (*with Francis Robinson*)
LANGUAGE, RELIGION, AND POLITICS IN NORTH INDIA
THE POLITICS OF INDIA SINCE INDEPENDENCE, 2nd edition
   Vol. IV:i of the New Cambridge History of India
RADICAL POLITICS IN SOUTH ASIA (*with Marcus Franda*)
SCIENCE, POLITICS, AND THE AGRICULTURAL
REVOLUTION IN ASIA (*with Robert S. Anderson, Edwin Levy and
   Barrie M. Morrison*)

Riots and Pogroms

Edited by

Paul R. Brass
Professor of Political Science and South Asian Studies
University of Washington

NEW YORK UNIVERSITY PRESS
Washington Square, New York

First published in the U.S.A. in 1996 by
NEW YORK UNIVERSITY PRESS
Washington Square
New York, N.Y. 10003

Library of Congress Cataloging-in-Publication Data
Riots and pogroms / edited by Paul R. Brass.
p.   cm.
Includes bibliographical references and index.
ISBN 0–8147–1274–6 (cloth). — ISBN 0–8147–1282–7 (pbk.)
1. Racism—Case studies.   2. Communalism—Case studies.
3. Violence—Case studies.   4. Riots—Case studies.   5. Pogroms–
–Case studies.   6. Ethnic relations—Case studies.   7. Race
relations—Case studies.   I. Brass, Paul R.
HT1521.R56   1996
305.8—dc20   96–12916
                                                       CIP

Printed in Great Britain

Contents

To All Human Rights Workers

Notes on the Contributors

Paul R. Brass is Professor of Political Science and South Asian Studies at the University of Washington, Seattle. He is the author of *The Politics of India Since Independence* (Cambridge University Press, 1994, 2nd ed.) and *Ethnicity and Nationalism: Theory and Comparison* (Sage, 1991), among other works. He has just completed a book on incidents of public violence in India, called *Theft of an Idol*, to be published by Princeton University Press in 1996.

Edward Taehan Chang is Director of the Center for Asian Pacific America (CAPA) and Assistant Professor of Ethnic Studies at the University of California, Riverside. He has co-edited two volumes on the Los Angeles civil unrest: *Los Angeles: Struggles toward Multiethnic Community* (University of Washington Press, 1995) and *Building Multiethnic Coalitions in Los Angeles* (Institute for Asian American and Pacific American Studies at CSULA, 1995).

Gyaneshwar and **Jayati Chaturvedi** are, respectively, Chairman and Senior Lecturer in the Department of Political Science, St. John's College, Agra. Jayati is the author of *Indian National Movement: A Critical Study of Five Schools* (MG Publishers, Agra, 1989).

Yen Le Espiritu is Associate Professor or Ethnic Studies and Sociology at the University of California, San Diego. She is the author of *Asian American Panethnicity: Bridging Institutions and Identities* (Temple University Press, 1992) and *Filipino American Lives* (Temple University Press, 1995).

Roger Friedland and **Richard D. Hecht** are respectively professors of Sociology and Religious Studies at the University of California, Santa Barbara. Their ethnographic study of the religion and politics of Jerusalem, *To Rule Jerusalem*, is to be published by Cambridge University Press (1996). Their historical analysis of the contests over sovereignty and sacrality in the city will also be published by Cambridge as *Jerusalem: The Profane Politics of a Sacred Place*, in 1997.

Leonidas E. Hill is Professor of History at the University of British Columbia. He has edited books and articles in German and English on Ernst von Weizsäcker, notably *Die Weizsäcker Papiere 1900–1932* (Berlin, 1982), and

viii   *Riots and Pogroms*

has published several articles as well on German foreign policy, resistance to the Nazi regime, and the Holocaust.

Peter van der Veer is Professor of Comparative Religion and Director of the Research Centre Religion and Society at the University of Amsterdam. He is the author of *Gods on Earth* (Athlone Press, 1988) and *Religious Nationalism* (University of California Press, 1994) and the editor of *Nation and Migration* (University of Pennsylvania Press, 1995) and *Conversion to Modernities* (Routledge, 1995), among other works.

Virginia Van Dyke has just completed the field work in India for her Ph.D. dissertation in the Department of Political Science, University of Washington, on the subject of Religious Specialists in Political Mobilization in North India.

Robert Weinberg is Associate Professor of History at Swarthmore College. He is the author of *The Revolution of 1905 in Odessa: Blood on the Steps* (Indiana University Presss, 1993) and is currently writing a history of Birobidzhan, the Jewish Autonomous Region in Russia.

Preface

This volume originated in the Seminar of the program in Comparative Studies in Ethnicity and Nationality (CSEN) at the University of Washington, held in the Spring Quarter, 1991, under the sponsorship of the Jackson School for International Studies. Earlier versions of all but two of the papers were presented at that seminar. Seven of the original papers were selected for publication and have been substantially revised since then while two new contributions were solicited as well, one from Gyan and Jayatai Chaturvedi on communal tension in Agra in 1990 and 1992 and the other by Virginia Van Dyke on the anti-Sikh massacres in New Delhi in 1984. All but one of the contributions, that by Robert Weinberg, are being published for the first time in this volume.

Riots and Pogroms provides comparative studies of public violence in the twentieth century in Russia, Germany, Israel, India, and the United States, with a comparative, historical, and analytical introduction by the editor. This is the first comparative and historical study done on the subject of riots and pogroms. A common framework has been provided by the editor, parts of which have been addressed by each of the contributors depending upon their relevance to each case. All the contributions in turn provide original material on particular occurrences of public violence, which illustrate the general argument.

The book departs from the conventional social science search for the causes of public violence to focus upon the struggle which takes place afterwards to gain control over the right to interpret it. The concern of the editor and contributors is with the contest to capture the meaning of riotous events, for the right to represent them properly. This conflict encompasses their labelling, the making of judgments concerning their causes, the determination of the social composition and motives of rioters and "pogromists," the degree of organization and/or spontaneity involved in riots and pogroms, the reasons why members of particular groups are selected for violent assaults, and the degree of implication in them of the state and its agents. Finally, the settlement upon a particular interpretation of major incidents of public violence, particularly when they occur simultaneously or in rapid sequence in a particular country, involves the assessment of blame: which groups or which social problems "explain" their occurrence adequately. The assignment of causes and the assessment of blame in turn have significant implications for public policies to prevent their repetition.

Although we have generally avoided the search for causes of particular riotous events, our focus upon the subsequent interpretive process has led to an important conclusion concerning the persistence of riots in societies in which they have been at times endemic, namely, that the very search for causes itself may contribute to their perpetuation. The general argument is that three discourses, ostensibly oriented towards the determination of the causes and the search for solutions to public violence, have been in fact implicated in their persistence. The so-called "Jewish question" provided the starting point for most discussions of inter-ethnic violence between Jews and other groups and for pogroms against the Jews in late nineteenth-century Europe, particularly in Russia. Similarly, racism has for long provided a general rubric for framing an explanation concerning the persistence of inter-group riots involving Blacks and for Black violence directed against white-owned property. Likewise, "communalism," that is, the tendency for Hindus and Muslims in India to define themselves politically as members of one or the other religious group and to see their political interests as different from that of the other group, to see the other group as either unpatriotic or seeking to dominate or as privileged or pampered, and to sustain feelings of hostility towards the other provides the backdrop for explanations of most incidents of violence involving Hindus and Muslims in India. Communalism in turn is but one manifestation of the many forms of contemporary ethnic and religious nationalism, of which the political violence between Arabs and Jews in Jerusalem provides yet another example in our volume. In fact, all three discourses – the "Jewish question," racism, and communalism – have flourished under the protection of the modern nation-state, itself born in violence and the ultimate source of internal war in deeply divided societies.

The bulk of the introductory chapter was written in the summer of 1994, then revised and completed in the Spring, 1995. Parts of it were presented during the past year at the Center for International Affairs Seminar, Harvard University, in February, 1995 and at a lecture at the University of Jerusalem in March, sponsored by the Truman Institute and the Leonard Davis Institute for International Relations, Hebrew University. I am grateful to my hosts on these two occasions, Ashutosh Varshney at Harvard and Reuven Kahane at Jerusalem, for their own comments on my paper and for the lively and helpful discussions which followed after my lectures in both cases. I am also appreciative of the critical comments made by students and colleagues who read the first version of the chapter: Barry Ames, Kenneth Cummings, Allen Kornmesser, Amelie Rorty, Amnon Sella, Stanley Tambiah, Virginia Van Dyke, and Pierre van den Berghe. Final revisions on the chapter were made at the end of my stay as a Fellow at the Woodrow Wilson International Center for Scholars in Washington, DC. I want to take this opportunity, therefore, to acknowledge my appreciation of the wonderful environment for research and collegial interchange provided by that Center, by its Director, Charles Blitzer, and by its staff. Of course, neither the Center nor any of my students and colleagues are responsible for the opinions and arguments expresssed in that chapter.

Finally, thanks and acknowledgments are due to Cambridge University Press for permitting the publication in this volume of an abridged and somewhat revised version of Robert Weinberg's contribution to it, which originally appeared under the title, "The pogrom of 1905 in Odessa: a case study," in John D. Klier and Shlomo Lambrozo (eds), *Pogroms: Anti-Jewish Violence in Modern Russian History* (Cambridge: Cambridge University Press, 1992).

Paul R. Brass
Seattle, Washington
September 11, 1995

1. Introduction: Discourses of Ethnicity, Communalism, and Violence

Paul R. Brass

TEXT AND CONTEXT

Increasingly in the twentieth century, though the process began in the nineteenth, the power to define and intepret local incidents of violence, to place them in specific contexts based on local knowledge, has been removed from the local societies in which they occur. Ideologies of protest from Marxism to contemporary feminism and the simultaneous spread of systems of psychiatric, psychological, criminological, and sociological systems of "knowledge" have all produced "authorities" who claim to know better than the people themselves the reasons for acts of common or uncommon violence in everyday life. Events which occur in isolated villages and hamlets or on the city streets have become subject to placement in categories and contexts previously not known to or incidental to the lives of those who experience them.

In modern times, local acts of violence have also been commonly placed in political contexts depending upon the ethnic identities of the persons involved in them. Indeed, inter-ethnic relations have become such a pervasive concern in contemporary societies that the interpretation of virtually any act of violence between persons identified as belonging to different ethnic groups itself becomes a political act. But the interpretive process is not only political, it also generates competing systems of knowledge concerning inter-ethnic relations, the sources of tension between members of ethnic groups, the causes of discrimination and prejudice, their social and economic bases, and the like.

The focus of this book is on the interpretive process which follows after the types of violence which are known as riots and pogroms, rather than on the search for their causes. The question asked here is how do we get different narratives about particular riots at different times and in different places. Our concern is primarily with the struggle for control over the meaning of riotous events, for the right to represent them properly. It is my argument that this struggle takes place among forces operating at many levels: at the local and

1

the supra-local levels, between spokesmen for particular ideological interpretations, between competing political groups, between academics, on the
one hand, and journalists and politicians, on the other hand, and within
academia between spokesmen for different social scientific disciplines.

Although the focus here is on the aftermath of riotous events, it is not possible
to avoid some discussion of the issue of causation, most particularly because
the struggle for control over the representation of riots is in large part a struggle
to "explain" them satisfactorily, to establish politically as well as scientifically their "causes." At the same time, it is part of my purpose to demonstrate
that this very search for causes, whether undertaken by academics, journalists, or politicians is in no way free from the struggle to represent riots
properly, that it is not possible to present a causal theory of riots that is neutral
to the interests of those seeking to capture its meaning. Most important, it
is also questionable whether it is possible to develop a causal theory of ethnic
riots separate from the discourses which encompass them, free from the
pressures of the prevailing ideological and social scientific paradigms and
the master narratives into which they are so often placed. Finally, it is the
purpose of this introduction to suggest that the very tendency to place
particular kinds of riotous events into a pre-framed context involves mis-
placement, which in turn contributes to the distribution and persistence of
those events in space and time.

The issue focused upon here is not simply one of identifying the multiple
contexts in which violence occurs because it can occur anywhere and can
be organized or random, premeditated or spontaneous, directed at specific
persons, groups, or property or not. While these aspects of violence must be
identified insofar as possible in our descriptions of particular events, we need
also to examine the discourses of violence, the ways in which participants
and observers – local and external, media, politicians and authorities, journalists and academics – seek to explain incidents of violence.

Consider what is probably the most widely quoted and respected article
on the subject of riots written in the past two decades, that of Natalie
Zemon Davis. In this famous article, Davis is concerned to establish two
points. The first is to rescue studies of crowd violence from the hands of
those who have considered it as arising largely from the unplanned actions
of lower class mobs, whose purpose, if there is any, is loot and plunder.
The second is to rescue these studies from the hands of economic deter-
minists, who grant rationality and purpose to violent crowds, but explain
their motives primarily in economic terms. To this interpretation, Davis
responds by emphasizing the religious motivations of the rioters she has
studied in sixteenth-century France.

> Clearly, [she says], some riotous behaviour, such as the extensive pillaging done by both Protestants and Catholics, cannot be subsumed under these heads [defending true doctrine or ridding the community of defilement]; but just as the prevalence of pillaging in a war does not prevent us from typing it as a holy war, so the prevalence of pillaging in a riot should not prevent us from seeing it as essentially religious.[1]

The problem with such an argument is that there is no evident reason for disregarding the facts of loot, pillage, and plunder and granting a privileged place to the rationales of priests, preachers, and generals for the wars and riots they lead – or justify if they do not actually lead them. While the fact of "extensive pillaging" also does not necessarily mean that some, many, or most of the rioters were not religiously motivated, it cannot be disregarded or arbitrarily relegated to a secondary place.

Consider also the multiplicity of interpretations and the sequencing of them which followed upon the first outbreaks of anti-Jewish pogroms after 1871 in Russia. Confining ourselves to Odessa, which has occupied a central place in the history of Russian pogroms and of scholarly accounts of them, Klier notes that the 1871 pogrom and its successors have been variously inter- preted ever since their occurrence. The authorities and the press under their "supervision" wished to preserve "the honor of the city" by minimizing "the significance of the disorders" of 1871, which they did by emphasizing "the high spirits of the holiday crowd and the traditional antipathy of Greeks and Jews" as well as the use of liquor stolen "from taverns and warehouses" once the pogrom got underway.[2] Recent scholarly accounts of this pogrom, however, have attributed it and other less serious ones which preceded it to "economic competition between Greeks and Jews." However, Greenbaum has argued, as has Davis in her account of Catholic–Protestant riots, that "the religious factor [in this and other Russian pogroms of the nineteenth century] is not always given its due weight by twentieth-century historians."[3]

But the religious factor was not the one that came to be stressed in later interpretations of both the pogroms that followed and in retrospective analyses of the 1871 pogrom by Russian commentators. What Klier calls a "paradigm" for the Russian pogroms in general grew up among "Russian intellectuals" who explained "pogrom violence" in terms of "Jewish exploita- tion, religious intolerance, [and] the low cultural level" of the masses.[4] Once this paradigm came into existence, it provided a ready context in which both to place the next pogrom and to reinterpret all previous ones.[5] It became in effect what Pandey has called a "master narrative," one often impervious to other facts, interpretations, and explanations.[6] In the hands of the authorities, it also became a convenient tool to blame the Jews for their own misfortunes and to displace blame from their own complicity or incompetence.

Quite the opposite occurred in the interpretation of the Black ghetto riots of the 1960s in the United States where manifest violence committed by Blacks against white-owned properties was nearly uniformly treated by the national media, official inquiry commissions, and scholars as the justified rage of an oppressed people, subjected to virtually universal discrimination, absence of economic opportunites, and police harassment. These riots which on their face seemed to arise in the majority of instances out of incidents of actual or perceived police harassment, were placed in complementary contexts by white liberals and Black activists. White liberals saw them as legitimate responses to discrimination, even as insurrections or rebellions against white domination and exploitation, while Black activists developed "a riot ideology" which gave them the political purpose of revolt against the oppression of Blacks in America.[7]

By 1992, however, when both the liberal consensus and Black political activism had faded, the Los Angeles riots could be observed from a number of angles through a multiplicity of accounts, some of them foolish or tendentious, others half-true. Nor has any consensus emerged about the Los Angeles riots. For most Americans, white and Black, the riots were an aspect of white–Black relations in American society, a reflection of either Black response to continuing police harassment and their inability to get justice or of the Black tendency to violence and attacks on whites when given a chance. Some of the media, however, adopted a more sophisticated view and focused on Black–Korean American conflicts – which had nothing to do with Rodney King and Black–police relations – and the way they were played out in these riots. However, largely neglected was the fact that "nearly half the looters arrested were Latinos,"[8] for whose behavior not much evidence or explanation has been offered.

In the paper by Espiritu in this volume, we are provided with an analysis of a single incident which did not and could not lead to an inter-ethnic riot if only because the sizable, juxtaposed, hostile populations necessary to produce one were not available. Yet, this paper is of particular interest because of its focus on a single incident of a type which, in many other circumstances, might very well have produced a riot. Even with a single incident of this type, however, Espiritu has found it virtually impossible to reach a definitive conclusion concerning the character of the incident leading to the killing by a white man of a Chinese man, Vincent Chin, that is to say, whether or not the killing was inspired by racial hatred against Chinese or Asians in general or whether it was simply the aftermath of a barroom brawl.[9]

The struggle among competing groups in society to capture the meaning of a violent incident or a riot, that is, for the right to *represent* it properly is far from a merely verbal game. It is also a struggle over resources and policy. If it is accepted that Russians attack Jews because Jews exploit them and because Jews set themselves apart, then measures need to be taken to prevent "Jewish exploitation" and to either promote their assimilation or separate them completely from contact with Russians by keeping them in the Pale of Settlement. Conversely, if Black ghetto violence is interpreted as justified rage against discrimination in white society, then policies and resources must be devoted to eliminating discrimination. If a riot is seen to arise out of justified mass resentment against a minority's exploitation of the majority or out of its alleged disloyalty to or betrayal of the country as in the case of Muslims in India, then measures to curb the minority's rights or demands and to put its members in their place will be the preferred response. Alternatively, if Hindu–Muslim riots are seen as a consequence of provocation of a harassed minority by militant Hindu nationalists, then measures to protect the minority and constrain militant Hindu groups are in order.

The struggle to control the representation of riots is also one to cast and divert blame.[10] If the people are responsible, the government is not to blame. If the government is not to blame, the argument can also be made that its powers and authority need strengthening in order to prevent further such events. If the police are to blame, then the politicians are saved. If the politicans are blamed, then the police may be freed from blame and their hands and those of their supporters strengthened in state and society. It is, in fact, one of the most astonishing features of riots that the very process of casting blame widely, of justifying, explaining, and interpreting riots contributes to the failure to prosecute the perpetrators of violence even when their identities are well known. While the air is full of charges and counter-charges, journalistic and social scientific analyses, reports of inquiry commissions, and pious proclamations of all types, known killers and looters and their patrons, whose pictures may even have appeared in the newspapers or their acts filmed in videos go free. The same is true, perhaps even more true for the police who take sides and do their own share of beating and killing.

Some ethnic and communal rioting also has international aspects, enlarging still further the universe of potential meanings which can be attributed to them. Hindu–Muslim violence in India cannot escape efforts to place it within the context of India–Pakistan relations. The status of the two mosques atop the Temple Mount in Jerusalem is, of course, the best-known example of an issue between two peoples with the broadest possible international ramifications. The 1929 and 1991 riots here could hardly escape massive international coverage and placement in not just specific religious and national contexts, but in "a geo-political context"[11] as well. It needs also to be stressed that such violence as that associated with Hindu–Muslim and Jewish–Muslim riots in India and Israel may be perpetrated deliberately by many of the participants with full knowledge of their consequences for themselves and with the intent to insure that they are properly understood and represented thereafter.[12]

Three discourses are prominent in the contributions to this volume – the "Jewish question," communalism, and racism. They constitute highly generalized and categorical explanations for particular events that often disguise and certainly always simplify, covering a variety of personal and political behaviors. They are grand constructions created in the battle of discourses in deeply divided societies. These discourses have also been used to structure inter-ethnic relations: to define minorities and majorities, to differentiate the loyal from the disloyal, the weak from the strong, those that are privileged and those that are disadvantaged, and to distribute rewards and punishments, benefits, services, and quotas. The discourses of ethnicity, communalism, and violence used to represent riots and pogroms are never neutral to the events. On the contrary, most – and especially the larger interpretations, the grandest constructions – are implicated in the perpetuation of the violence they claim to deplore. Therefore, the selection of a form and level of explanation for riots and pogroms, a context in which to place the discourses of violence – for scholars as well as journalists and politicians – is a serious political act.

TIME, TIMING, AND TRIGGERS: IMMEDIATE, REMOTE, AND PRECIPITATING CAUSES

While there are many different kinds of approaches to the study of riots and pogroms – comparative and particular, descriptive and statistical – most are in search of general explanations for their timing, that is, the particular moment in which they occur, for the historical times in which they occur, and for the triggers which precipitate them or, in social scientific terms, for the immediate, remote, and precipitating causes. There is a very strong tendency in this literature towards objectification, best represented in the nearly universal metaphor in which riots are seen as conflagrations which are ignited by a spark upon a bed of combustible material.

This metaphor has had serious circumscribing effects in the study of riots and pogroms, ignoring two sets of contributing factors in particular. On the one hand, it ignores the contribution of discursive formations to the historical timing of particular types of riots and pogroms. On the other hand, the comparative approaches in particular, but even some of the studies of specific riots as well, fail to focus adequately on the dynamics of riots, and especially on the specific individuals, groups, and forces which act as intermediaries in the conversion of triggering incidents into full-scale riots.

The metaphor of combustion in the literature on riots and pogroms, therefore, raises very serious problems of dealing with agency and responsibility. The approach offered in this section and throughout the remainder of this introduction seeks to deal with the problem of agency and responsibility in three ways. First, in the focus on the critical importance of discourse, it recognizes a diffuse and general responsibility for the endemic character of riots and pogroms in certain historical periods in particular countries and world regions. Second, however, where it is evident that specific individuals, groups, and forces are engaged in activities whose effects are to promote riots and pogroms – even where "intentionality" cannot be proved – I believe it is important to so indicate. Third, in the focus on the representation of riots and pogroms, I argue that here we see most clearly the interests that are served and the power relations that are predominant in societies not only in the capturing of the meaning of riots and pogroms, but in maintaining the conditions for their very persistence.

Triggers

Weinberg, in this volume, notes that "anti-Jewish pogroms occurred in waves." In 1905, he argues, "they were connected with the revolutionary events of that year." The specific occasion for the outbreak of the pogrom in Odessa itself was a "patriotic procession" connected with those "revolutionary events," which had been preceded by clashes between Tsarist loyalists and Jews celebrating the October Manifesto in the streets and "carrying desecrated portraits of the tsar and waving red flags" in demonstrations and processions of their own.[13]

However, earlier riots in Odessa, like those in sixteenth-century France, were associated with religious rather than patriotic processions. Klier notes that "scuffles and fights" were common between Jews and Greeks in the early and mid-nineteenth century at the time of Easter processions or when Easter and Passover rituals coincided because of the location of "the principal Greek Orthodox Church" in close proximity to the Jewish quarter.[14]

Hindu–Muslim riots in India in the twentieth century have also occurred in "waves." Such waves occurred in the aftermath of Gandhi's non-cooperation movement in the early 1920s, massively after the Partition of 1947, and most recently in the aftermath of the destruction of the mosque at

Ayodhya which in turn was preceded by several mass mobilizations of Hindus. In these and many other such waves of Hindu–Muslim violence, a specific incident in a particular locality in one part of the country triggered a riot event, news of which was then alleged to lead to retaliatory attacks by members of one community against the other in different parts of the country. In fact, however, it is often the case that patterned provocations are repeated in one town after another, as during the movement to consecrate bricks and bring them to Ayodhya at the end of 1989, when faithful Hindus in numerous towns in northern, central, and western India set off in processions for Ayodhya or marched through other towns in processions, precipitating riots in their wake.[15]

Atmosphere

Yet, Klier tells us, the early and mid nineteenth-century riots and pogroms in Odessa "remained local events," which did not extend in "waves" across the Empire to other cities and towns. They remained local, he argues, because of the "lack of rapid communications and the absence of a national press," on the one hand, and because "the Jewish Question" had not yet "burst into the consciousness of public opinion."[16] The "Jewish Question" in nineteenth-century Europe was a discourse in which discussion revolved around opposite sides of the position that various social, economic, and political problems of European societies could be somehow attributed to the presence and activities of Jews.[17]

Thus, the 1881 pogroms in the Russian Ukraine were, it is said, preceded by the development of a "psychological atmosphere" "marked by mutual suspicion [between Ukrainians and Jews] and resentment, and occasionally even outright hatred."[18] Weinberg also remarks that the Odessa pogrom of 1905 was preceded by the propaganda activities of "organized anti-Semitic groups" who deliberately "engaged in 'fomenting a pogromist atmosphere' by stirring up 'anti-Jewish sentiments'" and explicitly calling for the beating of Jews.[19]

Palpable increases in tensions have been often noted in Indian cities and towns before the outbreak of Hindu–Muslim riots. Such increases in tension have sometimes been attributed to generalized, public behavior on the part of one community, usually the Muslims, involving increased "spending on religious and semi-religious activities such as construction of more mosques, madrasas and maktabs," resented by Hindus as evidence of increased wealth in the community or suggesting a "flow of Arab money into India to strengthen the Muslim fundamentalists." Secular activities such as increased real estate purchases by Muslims also may have a similar effect. The augmented wealth among Muslims may also intensify their "political aspirations," leading to still further resentment among Hindus.[20]

However, many, if not most, observers who have noted the existence of a particular kind of atmosphere before most riots or pogroms do not consider the "atmosphere" itself as a cause of riots, but only a kind of precondition. The atmosphere itself is produced by other factors such as "economic competition."[21] The "communal atmosphere" then becomes an intermediate cause of riots behind which lies economic competition between "two communities," which in turn "leads to social tensions which can be easily turned into communal tension by exploiting certain situations on the occasion of religious festivals, etc."[22] Similarly, although Grimshaw emphasizes the importance of what he calls violations of the "sacred" norms of white supremacy, including the inviolability of the white Southern woman, as precipitating incidents in Southern race riots, he is certain that "a broader analysis of background factors in social tension would ... reveal more 'secular' sources of economic competition."[23] The assumption behind such reasoning clearly is that people do not act solely on their mean prejudices, but in response to genuine and understandable grievances, the "real causes."

Ecology

If historical or other general explanations fail to satisfy, some social scientists also have despaired of finding the causes of riots at particular times and specific places through rigorous comparative and statistical analyses of the demographic, ethnographic, and economic conditions of cities and towns where riots have occurred and where they have not. Attempts to focus on unemployment, among the principal reported "causes" of the 1981 and 1985 riots in Great Britain have foundered.[24] Rather, as in the Black urban riots in the United States in the 1960s, unemployment turned out to be only an important background or "conditioning" factor in which the foreground was occupied by relationships of "confrontation" between ghetto residents and the police, which played "a central role in explanation of the events of 1981"[25] as of the events of 1966–9 in the United States.

Many observers have in fact dismissed the whole idea that riots, even non-ethnic riots – that is, riots which appear more closely related to economic than to ethnic conflicts – can be at all correlated with general factors such as are found in "census statistics" and unemployment data.[26] Factors such as unemployment, which are almost invariably associated in ghetto communities with other sub-standard conditions in housing, education, and crime rates, create only "a general potential for violence," but the "root cause" for many observers is "racial discrimination."[27] Another observer has maintained "that riots are caused more by particular events than by general conditions." While "conditioning factors" such as "unemployment, poor housing conditions and so on" may be important, in this view it is "the relationship of groups to each other" that is critical.[28]

We are thus faced with interpretations which are virtual polar opposites. On the one hand are those who say racial hostilities, predispositions, and resentments are only background factors whereas economic factors are primary. On the other hand are those who say the economic factors constitute only the background whereas group relations are the critical conditions.

Competition and Exploitation

There are yet other approaches which link public prejudices and economic competition, which see the former as genuine – not false consciousness – but at the same time as a kind of smokescreen behind which specific, iden- tifiable persons and interests pursue particularistic economic ends.[29] A further type of competition which intrudes into many social science expla- nations is political competition, sometimes seen as either related to economic competition or as a variable in its own right. Engineer, for example, sees the "communal phenomenon" as political in origin. The "tensions" associated with that phenomenon arise "as a result of the skilful manipulation of the religious sentiments and cultural ethos of a people by its elite which aims to realise its political, economic and cultural aspirations by identifying these aspirations as those of the entire community."[30] The competitive mobiliza- tions which follow such manipulation can easily lead to violent confrontions between members of rival communal groups. Here the blame is clearly laid upon elite manipulators as the creators of tension and communal violence rather than on the people themselves.

Sometimes, the question of economic "exploitation" also is mentioned as a source of riotous behavior, but this term has a subjective element, for exploita- tion may be a matter of perception rather than material reality. Alleged economic exploitation by Jews was obviously a common element in popular stereotypes in nineteenth- and twentieth-century Europe. But the argument is also made that exploitation of a minority group, such as Blacks in the United States, explains their rage against white shopkeepers and their riotous behavior and looting in Watts and other places in the late 1960s.[31]

On this question, as of all others pertaining to the origins of riots, it is necessary to ask whose interests, doctrines, and values are best served by the adoption of a particular interpretation. Interpretations which stress an atmosphere of hostility, fear, and resentment between ethnic, communal, and religious groups, caused or intensified by economic competition, displace blame from the authorities, politicians, the police, and the church except insofar as they too are seen to be "conditioned by popular prejudices and social stereotypes."[32]

Such interpretations also sometimes partially mitigate public responsibility as well because the hostilities, fears, and resentments are either not considered to be endemic, but instilled by instigators, organizations, and agencies or, even if public sentiments and prejudices are considered to be latent, they are seen to require fanning or stressful economic and environmental changes to make them manifest and violent. Even "pervasive prejudices ... do not of themselves produce pogroms and riots"; they constitute rather "latent antagonisms" which are mobilized and erupt in violence under stressful conditions of change in "urban environment[s]."[33] There is neither agency nor responsibility here. In fact, these social science theories which emphasize economic competition and/or exploitation in effect cast no blame at all, but make public violence a kind of understandable response, however misguided or misdirected, to objective circumstances under no one's particular control or, at most, under the control of an objectified capitalist or bourgeois class in the case of the Marxists.

At its worst, the exploitation argument may be used by the authorities to justify a pogrom, such as that in Odessa in 1871, by defining it as "a popular protest against dishonest exploitation" and "hatred elicited by the Jews' economic domination."[34] As noted above, this explanation became a virtually generic catch-all one for countless pogroms perpetrated in Russia and elsewhere in Europe thereafter, fed by the press and used by the authorities to avoid any blame for their own failures to prevent them or for their very complicity in them.[35]

The "exploitation" argument has also been used to explain Black riots in American cities in the 1960s, characterized as "a strategy or solution to end the problems of segregation, exploitation, and subordination"[36] rather than as an expression of controlled or uncontrolled rage at white shopkeepers for their particular exploitation of Blacks. Although, in the latter case, the writer's remarks are sympathetic rather than hostile to the "exploited" group, the exploitation argument, nevertheless, is a tainted one which ought to be discarded altogether by social scientists. It is tainted not only because of its susceptibility to misuse by government officials and others who seek to displace blame from perpetrators to victims. It is also a term that can in no way be defined objectively separately from the perceptions of the participants in the alleged relationships of exploiter and exploited or from ideological preconceptions concerning what in fact constitutes exploitation.[37]

The "Value-Added" Model

The emphasis in the surveyed literature on time, timing, and the triggering mechanisms which precipitate riots is largely on the background factors which make of inter-group relations a kind of tinder-box, the social tensions, hatreds, antipathies, and latent animosities which are supposed to "explain" how one incident, often a trivial one, can lead to a major conflagration. Among the most sophisticated analyses of this type in the literature of collective behavior is the sequential or "value-added" model of Smelser[38] in which a set of "conditions" pile on to one another "into a sequence of increasing determinacy – structural conduciveness, strain, generalized beliefs, precipitating factors, and mobilization."[39]

Although such factors as leadership and organization are included in Smelser's model, its emphasis is on "objective factors," which take on a life of their own, flowing somehow out of general tendencies in human behavior, particularly the aggressive tendency. Intent and agency, therefore, have a rather limited role in this model. Missing from such analyses is an adequate appreciation of the intermediary factors which transform an incident into a riot.[40] The common explanation, a simplistic one, is that the response to the triggering incident is spontanous mass anger, a "hostile outburst." The view taken here, however, is that other factors and forces are at work that need to be examined more closely if one is to explain how and why it is that similar triggering incidents lead to major riots in some places and to only minor riots or none at all in other places.

INSTITUTIONALIZED RIOT SYSTEMS

The kinds of violence that are committed in ethnic, communal, and racial "riots" are, I believe, undertaken mostly by "specialists," who are ready to be called out on such occasions, who profit from it, and whose activities profit others who may or may not be actually paying for the violence carried out. In fact, in many countries at different times in their histories, there have been regions or cities and towns which have developed what I call "institutionalized riot systems," in which known actors specialize in the conversion of incidents between members of different communities into ethnic riots. The activities of these specialists are usually required for a riot to spread from the initial incident of provocation.

Who are these specialists? They certainly include criminal elements and members of youth gangs, but the organizers, in different times and places, often come from local militant group leaders, politicians, businessmen, religious leaders – Catholic priests, *ulama*, rabbis, and itinerant preachers of all sorts – and college and university professors. Pamphleteers and journalists also make their contribution, deliberately spreading rumors and scurrilous propaganda against a particular group or as part of what they perceive to be the legitimate and honest pursuit of their profession. Such specialists range from the generic category of "armed thugs," who helped spread the pogrom in Odessa in 1905;[41] to the "athletic clubs" which "formed definite nuclei for crowd and mob formation" in the Chicago riot of 1919;[42] to Nazi SA hooligans seeking to generate "spontaneous" mass violence against Jews in Germany; to the English "football hooligans" of today, who translate their joy in the experience of violence, in setting off violent brawls between English and other national crowds, into a kind of ethnonational and racial antagonism;[43] to local communal political elites in contemporary India who deliberately set out to mobilize support in particular communities by taking their followers to the "brink" of violent conflict by inciting feelings of hostility against another group. In many such cases, both in the events preceding and in the "crowd action" during a riot, internal observations or interviews with observers and participants often reveal a "riot," such as the St. Pauls Riot of 1980 in Bristol "to have been a highly structured event, in which there was a clear pattern to crowd action."[44]

At the center of such institutionalized riot systems in many cities and towns in contemporary India where large numbers of both Hindus and Muslims and social tensions between them have existed for some time, or have been fostered recently, are individuals and organizations which take as one of their purposes the protection of the status, pride, and interests of one community against presumed threats to them from another. These individuals and organizations are always on the alert for instances of such threats or violations and will report them to other members or leaders of their organizations or to the authorities. In the latter case, they will present their efforts as designed to preserve the peace against a natural and spontaneous outburst of group anger at such a threat or violation and urge the police and the civil administration to act to punish the offenders in order to prevent such an outburst.

In such situations, one cannot say that the persons and organizations involved wish at a particular moment either to prevent or to create a riot. Rather, such networked actions have two persisting purposes – or at least consequences. One is to keep the members of the rival community cowed and to enlist the support of the authorities in doing so. The second is to keep the members of one's own community always ready and alert for mobilization, for crowd action, and for violence if necessary should it be considered desirable for political or other reasons to enlarge an incident into an occasion for a riot or pogrom. Such a state of readiness obviously also builds communal identity, which in turn makes the community generally more accessible to communal political parties and organizations for non-violent political uses as well.

To describe the environment in which riots are most likely to develop as "institutionalized" does not mean that spontaneity is absent. Crowds may very well form in the aftermath of an incident in which a person from one group or community is killed or hurt or harassed by the police or a member of another group and some kind of crowd action may develop on the spot, a small riot. In riot-prone areas, however, there are likely to be persons and groups whose specialty is the conversion of small riots into larger ones.

It seems to me that some such institutionalized riot systems must have also been in operation in late nineteenth-century Russia and that they have existed in both the United States and Great Britain during riot periods in their histories as well. In the latter two cases, moreover, it is evident also that a climate of hostility exists not only or perhaps not even between members of two communities, but between one community and the police. Nor is it a climate only, but as Keith has shown,[45] a situation in which police–public incidents are recurring events. Such events can be turned into riots either through the mobilizing activities of local militants or through the actions of police officers who, for example, feel it is time to show the Blacks their place.

Moreover, it is not always the case that underlying hostilities between groups precede the outbreak of a riot or pogrom. The massacre of the Sikhs in Delhi in November, 1984 was, no doubt, preceded by an increasingly violent conflict in the Punjab between the Indian state and groups of militant youth. On the face of it, the triggering incident for these massacres was the assassination of Mrs Gandhi by her two Sikh bodyguards, themselves enraged, like most Sikhs, by the Indian army's assault in June, 1984 on militants who had turned the Golden Temple into a military fortress.

However, in the face of all this, one still cannot say that, at this time, there was underlying hostility between the Sikh and Hindu populations, particularly in the national capital of the country where the massacres took place. In fact, these massacres, improperly labelled as "riots," had to be instigated, fomented, planned, and directed. Obviously, the riot engineers did not believe that the funeral procession for Mrs Gandhi in which hundreds of thousands of Indians participated and hundreds of thousands more watched on TV would be a sufficient triggering event to precipitate riotous assaults on Sikhs in the city, for rumors had to be deliberately spread that Sikhs were dancing in the streets to celebrate the assassination, "setting off firecrackers, and distributing sweets," in order "to incite" among Hindus " a spirit of revenge."[46] Even this would not have been enough to cause the massacres of thousands of innocent Sikhs living in slums; crowds of murderers had to be brought in trucks by Congress politicians to do the killings for money, whiskey, and loot. Moreover, once the attacks on the Sikhs had begun, further rumors "were spread in order to 'prevent or remove any kind of sympathy or compassion' that every burnt 'gurdwara was an arsenal,' that the Sikhs were gathering and would 'attack at night' or would kidnap children."[47] Rumors are sometimes said to spread like wildfire. It is more likely that here too riot specialists assist the process.

The last stage in a riotous event is its placement in an explanatory or interpretive context. It then becomes a mediated event in which the attitudes toward it taken by local politicians and local representatives of state authority and its further reinterpretation by the press and extra-local politicians and authorities transform it into an event with a "meaning." Such riot events often also conclude sooner or later after the violence has subsided with an "official" interpretation that finally becomes universally accepted, but which is often, if not usually, very far removed, often unrecognizable, from the original precipitating events. Such interpretations are frequently embedded in a broader discourse into which incidents involving persons from groups presumed to be hostile towards each other can be easily fit no matter the actual nature of the dispute. Nineteenth-century Europe produced the discourse on the "Jewish question," post-Civil War America the discourse of racial conflict,[48] and modern India in the twentieth century the discourse of Hindu–Muslim conflict, all of which proved to be convenient frameworks into which intergroup incidents and riots could be placed and readily explained in such a way that any dispute between Jews and Christians, whites and Negroes, Hindus and Muslims instantly became an example of a broader "problem" of the society as a whole.

In short, the sequence from social antagonisms to processions to precipitating incident to riot which prevails in most of the literature discussed in the preceding section needs to be replaced by another kind of sequence. It is a much more diverse and complex one which may or may not begin with existing social prejudices. Sometimes, those prejudices need to be created first where none existed before, as in the case of Hindus and Sikhs. The second step is the politicization of those differences. The third is the selection or development of sites where it is politically advantageous to allow or disadvantageous to prevent the proliferation of riot specialists and of institutionalized systems of riot promotion. The fourth, which follows as it were naturally, is the transformation of the environment in which all these events are taking place into a social problem. The media may be the first to promote this process either by inciting its further development or deploring its existence, but in either case magnifying it. This stage also requires the intervention of other kinds of specialists: social workers, psychologists, communications and public relations specialists, commissions of inquiry, large social science research projects funded by government or philanthropic agencies, and the like. The ultimate end of this process is the creation of an object of inquiry which allows society and its "anti-riot" specialists to focus their gaze, dissect the social body, open it up to fuller view, expose the prejudices in our very hearts, and create a "knowledge" of the social processes at work which, somehow, has little or no provable discernible effect upon them.[49]

PARTICIPATION: ON THE QUESTION OF THE SOCIAL COMPOSITION AND MOTIVES OF RIOTERS AND "POGROMISTS"

Riot studies in virtually all times and places have sought to identify the social composition and motives of the actual participants in riot events, not just the riot specialists but the larger bodies of people as well, who constitute the crowds or mobs. Broadly speaking, the conclusions of such studies divide into two quite sharply opposed points of view. One is the "riff-raff" theory that, whether approved or condoned by the better elements in society, the authorities, and the police or not, the actual looters and killers come from the poorest elements of society, the unskilled laborers, the unemployed, criminals, vagrants, and hoodlums of all types. Moreover, their motives are contained in the riot acitivity itself or arise out of instinctive or instilled prejudices and hostilities to "targeted" groups rather than being goal-directed towards the achievement of some kind of new order. Rioting is a merely destructive and profitable activity for the rioters. The opposing point of view is that rioters often, if not generally, come from respectable segments of society, that the social composition of rioters is frequently not significantly different from that of the general population from which the rioters come, and that the participants are well-informed persons, upholders of a faith, believers in a cause, expressing rage against an old order and calling for a new one to which their riot acitivites are consciously directed. Examination of numerous riot studies provides support for both points of view.

Davis argues against the view that "urban rioters" come primarily from the "miserable, uprooted, unstable masses." On the whole, Davis found that the Catholic and Protestant crowds in sixteenth-century France, like the movements from which they were drawn, "cut vertically through the social structure," leaving out only "the most vulnerable of the urban poor ... the unskilled, the day labourers and the jobless," all the favorite elements of the "riff-raff" crowd theory.[50] On the contrary, these crowds included "artisans" and "other men from the lower orders" at times, but their "social composition ... extended upward to encompass merchants, notaries and lawyers, as well as the clerics." Youths, "teenaged boys" were also prominent in these crowds and so were "city women."[51]

The "riff-raff" theory has nevertheless persisted, notably in studies of the Russian pogroms of the nineteenth and early twentieth centuries and of Hindu–Muslim and anti-Sikh riots in contemporary India. Weinberg in this volume has remarked that "unskilled, non-Jewish day laborers, perhaps more than any other group ... filled the ranks of the mobs which attacked Jews and destroyed property."[52] He notes further "that many Odessans, particularly those responsible for anti-Jewish pogroms, lived marginal lives."[53] These marginalized Odessans, especially "unemployed, unskilled Russian workers" found "an outlet for their frustrations and problems" in attacks on Jews.[54] Their "frustrations and problems"arose at least in part from objective conditions of economic competition between them and Jewish "day laborers" for scarce jobs "at dockside and in the railway depots, where thousands of unskilled workers vied for employment during the peak season of commercial activity." This "job competition" was not, however, merely seasonal for it "acquired even larger dimensions during the off-season or periods of slump and recession, when over half of all dockworkers were unemployed."[55] At the same time, Weinberg argues that "many day laborers and dockworkers" engaged in such attacks on Jews for "vodka and money."[56] Moreover, Weinberg also notes that the October riots in Odessa were preceded by numerous incidents in which right-wing, that is, pro-Tsarist groups organized attacks on Jews during which "Jewish workers and revolutionaries retaliated" in kind,[57] which indicates the involvement of, if not pre-planning by, persons other than *lumpen* elements.

Van Dyke gives an account similar to Weinberg's for Odessa of the groups involved in the massacre of the Sikhs in Delhi in 1984, whom she identifies as marginalized, displaced urban villagers, coming from castes designated as "backward" and from the lowest castes as well, accustomed to living outside the law and to engaging in criminal activities, who were "provided with liquor" and paid to carry out their work in the lower class Sikh residential areas of Delhi.[58] However, in contrast to the observers of Russian pogroms against the Jews, she denies that these massacres constituted "communal" riots at all.[59]

Looking at the organization of the SA in Germany, whose members were clearly specialists in the production of violence for which the term "riots" may be a misnomer,[60] studies of its leadership and social composition indicate that both "riff-raff" and more stable elements of German society were part of it. On the whole, despite "a relative underrepresentation of workers," Bessel found the most striking fact concerning the social composition of the SA in eastern Prussia to be the "remarkable degree of social heterogeneity which characterised the organisation." Although, therefore, the SA provided a haven and a source of activity for many unemployed youth,[61] the murderous young men who joined the SA came from the same broad social groups which joined the Nazi party as a whole, who presumably joined it for ideological, economic, and other reasons rather than for the excitement of participating in acts of violence.[62]

Studies of American race riots also have sought to identify the social composition of the crowds which participated in acts of violence. The most notorious race riot in American history and one of the worst urban riots which has occurred anywhere in the modern world, the New York draft riots of 1863, arose in a context of job competition between "unskilled Irish labor" and "black labor" when Irish laborers felt they were being drafted into a war for the emancipation of blacks who were taking their jobs in the city.[63]

The East St. Louis riot of 1917 also was said to have arisen out of competition between unemployed white workers suddenly confronted with an influx of 10,000 Negroes "imported" from the South by "the railroads and the manufacturing establishments" to fill the jobs they themselves sought.[64] However, in the Chicago Riot of 1919, observers reported that the violent crowds consisted mostly of "boys between fifteen and twenty-two" and that the lead in "many attacks" was taken by boys from "athletic clubs," whose existence and names were known to the authorities.[65]

The rioters in Detroit in 1943 came entirely from unskilled or "semi-skilled" or unemployed persons – at a time when jobs were readily available at the peak of wartime industrial expansion.[66] Most had police records.[67] Studies of persons arrested for alleged involvement in the urban riots in England in the summer of 1981 indicate that the arrested came mostly from "the young, the black, the unemployed, the male and those with police records,"[68] all of whom were disproportionately represented "in relation to the total population."[69]

On the other hand, the evidence from the American riots of the 1960s in Detroit, Los Angeles, and other places is that "the most active participants ... were likely to be employed rather than unemployed." In direct contrast with earlier American riots, there is "little evidence ... that the rioters were newly arrived persons." Moreover, studies indicated that there was "widespread" support for the violence from those who did not themselves necessarily participate in it.[70]

In both Detroit and Newark in 1967, such studies found no significant "differences in unemployment between the rioters and the noninvolved."[71] The rioters were "more likely to feel dissatisfied with their present jobs than were the noninvolved" and to attribute their inability "to obtain the kind of job they wanted" and the low wages for which they therefore had to work to "racial discrimination."[72] The Detroit and Newark rioters were reported also to "have strong feelings of racial pride" as well as feelings of "intense hostility toward whites."[73] They were also "better informed than the noninvolved"[74] and "more likely to be involved in activities associated with Negro rights."[75] However, consistent with findings for all other American riots, most of the 1967 Detroit "rioters were late teenagers or young adults."[76]

Nevertheless, Fogelson and Hill find that the evidence on the whole thoroughly contradicts the "riff-raff" theory. On the contrary, the available evidence demonstrated to their satisfaction "that many working- and middle-class blacks joined in the looting and assaults" and "that many who did not themselves participate tacitly supported the rioters anyway."[77] The rioters did not come primarily from hoodlums and criminal elements but "were fairly representative of the ghetto communities," a substantial minority or sometimes a majority of whom "sympathized with the rioters."[78]

Although the evidence from Fogelson and Hill is persuasive, it is far from overwhelming. As in virtually all riot studies, there is evidence of mixed participation of all kinds of elements from teenagers to unskilled laborers to middle-class political activists. The emphasis on widespread Black participation downplays the heavy involvement of teenagers and the possibility that their motives might have been less political and more for the rush that comes with violence and the gains from looting. There is also not much doubt that the emphasis accords with the writers' own sympathies. The Negro rioting of the 1960s was not to be seen as the action of rootless, irresponsible, "juvenile, unskilled, unemployed," and "criminal" elements or of "outside agitators"[79] out to exploit the poverty of the American Negro ghetto population, but rather the understandable, if not legitimate expression of educated, informed, politically active persons rebelling against racial discrimination which keeps the black population in permanent subjection.

Fogelson and Hill also argue that their findings are consistent with those of Rudé, who showed that European rioters in the eighteenth and nineteenth centuries also did not come primarily from "riff-raff" or "criminal" elements. Clearly also their findings are consistent with those of Davis. Obviously, therefore, they are not consistent either with the interpretations given to them by "French and British officials during the eighteenth century and nineteenth century European riots"[80] or with "the prevailing view of riot participation" in twentieth-century America.[81] The "riff-raff" theory is, therefore, seen to be a myth held by officials and dominant elements in a society who seek comfort and reassurance in the face of riotous and murderous disorders that the latter are the work of marginal elements in the society rather than justifiable reactions to illegitimate authority or to an unjust and discriminatory social order.

However, it is not so easy to read Fogelson and Hill's intepretation
backward or Rudé's and Davis' forward to the earlier American riots
attributed primarily to job competition between blacks and whites in northern
cities. Why do we have an interpretive consensus on the American riots in
northern cities from the 1860s to the end of World War I which attributes
them to economic factors and an interpretive consensus for the 1960s which
attributes them to racial hostilities in a discriminatory society? Why are the
Irish in New York in the draft riots seen equally with blacks as victims rather
than as rampant racists as were the unspecified "whites" (but mostly Polish
Americans) in Chicago during the civil rights movement of the 1960s?
Clearly, in fact, both elements were present in both periods: economic competition and racial hostilities. Moreover, there cannot be the slightest doubt
that "riff-raff," criminal elements, and youth gangs almost invariably come
out in riots in all times and places. None of the evidence cited from these
various riot studies is clear enough to eliminate not only different, but
opposed interpretations of them. What is clear enough is that an interpretation which emphasizes the role of *lumpen* and youth elements in riots serves
authority and the dominant elements in society better than alternative explanations which justify or legitimize riots as arising from the rage of the
people.

However, it is not always obvious that a particular interpretation serves
only one set of interests. It is not so clear, for example, that an interpetation
which stresses poverty or job competition among unskilled laborers rather
than racial hostilities arising out of discrimination and prejudice favors
authority and the dominant. The former is consistent with a Marxist or trade
union perspective which seeks to place the blame on the authorities and the
economic order and displace blame from ordinary people whose racial
prejudices are seen to be a consequence of job competition, instilled by the
authorities and dominant classes to keep the workers divided. The second,
the emphasis on racial hostilities, may lead to proposals which seek to
reform the hearts and minds of the dominant groups and classes in society
as well as to dismantle and reform all the institutions which permit and promote
racism in the belief that the opportunities then opened to the minorities will
lead to the removal of their poverty and economic grievances. Although the
ultimate aims of proponents of both these interpretations may be the same,
provision of economic opportunities for Blacks and elimination of racial hostilities, the policy implications of these interpretations are different.

One must ask, therefore, not what is "the central trend in the disorders"[82]
called riots, but whose ideals, interests, and purposes are served by

propagating a belief in the existence of such a "central trend" and in achieving a consensual interpretation of a riot event which itself is multifarious in its manifestations and effects and, therefore, open to a multiplicity of interpretations, none of which can hope to arrive at the "truth" of the event. In this case, it is probable that the Fogelson and Hill interpretation, which was the dominant sociogical interpretation of the time, reflected also in the extremely influential Kerner Commission report, and which soon became the consensual one in American society for some time thereafter, achieved more for the civil rights of Blacks in the next decade under the political leadership of Lyndon Johnson than any available alternative. It is, however, a matter of dispute how much it accomplished for their economic advancement.

It also needs to be noted that theories which suggest the involvement of heterogeneous elements of a population in riots rather than simply "riff-raff" also often serve the purposes of the authorities. While the authorities may sometimes be pleased with interpretations which emphasize the involvement of only marginal elements, who do not threaten the overall peace and stability of the state, at other times the argument for general group involvement in attacks on another group may displace blame from the authorities onto – not the attackers – but the victims, who are said to have instilled in the attackers a justifiable desire for "retribution" against an allegedly economically dominant group, such as Jews in Russia.[83]

VICTIMS AND TARGETS

Riot studies refer to those persons killed by rioting mobs in different ways. Two terms are favored: victims and targets. The labels used partly reflect theoretical issues, partly the sympathies of the writers. The term targets is used especially by those who see riot crowds as organized and motivated, whether by noble or base motives, acting purposefully rather than randomly. The term victims is used more often by those who see crowds as disorganized, chaotic, and leaderless, moved by passions, hatreds, antipathies, striking out aimlessly at persons of whatever rank, status, sex, or age from a group seen in stereotypical images.[84]

In fact, most riots contain elements of organization and of randomness and most crowds are either led or generate leaders from their midst. Most riots also begin with some purpose and some targets. The larger the crowds become, the more diverse and random their goals and targets also become until a point is reached when "all hell breaks loose" or, as Bill Buford's thugs put it, when a city "goes off."[85]

New York, considered by some to be the world's greatest city, also produced one of the world's greatest riots, in 1863, which still stands in the awesomeness of the crowds produced, the destruction wreaked, and the persons killed in a special class. The New York draft riots of 1863 began, according to the published record, with a purpose, which – as much or more than those described by Davis and others – many considered to be soundly based in moral and legal principle, namely, opposition to the right of the government to draft its citizens, a free people, to fight in a war. Every Marxist, indeed every person on the Left would also have to agree that the draft itself was unjust and discriminatory in allowing the rich to buy substitutes and leaving the poor no option but to go to war – and that to one for which they had no sympathy. In its early stages, moreover, the riot was directed against the buildings and records pertaining to the draft and those, such as the *Tribune*, which supported the war and the draft: the targets were clear and the purpose evident, to stop the draft.

However, as the crowd swelled to enormous proportions, divided also into numbers of separate mobs, its purpose became different, namely, to kill any Negro who could be found on the streets. Although the persons and property of those in authority continued to be attacked, most of the crowd engaged in the destruction of property in Negro areas and the killing of Negroes. One segment of the mob even directed its efforts to the destruction of a Colored Orphan Asylum. At this point, one of the riot's most eloquent chroniclers sought, with dark humor, to understand the logic of the crowd, which he described in the following terms:

> There would have been no draft but for the war – there would have been no war but for slavery. But the slaves were black, ergo, all blacks are responsible for the war. This seemed to be the logic of the mob, and having reached the sage conclusion to which it conducted, they did not stop to consider how poor helpless orphans could be held responsible, but proceeded at once to wreak their vengeance on them.[86]

Even if one adds to the original anti-draft purpose of the riot a further "cause," namely resentment on the part of Irish laborers who would be drafted to fight for Negro emancipation while the Negroes in New York took their jobs, that is to say, if one adds an explanation based on job competition between Irish and Negroes, the logic of an attack on a Negro orphanage would have to be equally twisted.[87] There is no moral justification which can be produced for such an attack, for describing the persons endangered and forced to flee it as anything but victims.

Although the size of the New York draft riots was unusual, its course was not. Moreover, its course makes clear the futility of ascribing "cause" and overall logic to the incidents which occur once a riot expands. It is possible to find for many, if not most, individual incidents particular reasons, such as local personal enmities or economic rivalries settled under the cover of chaos. But cause, reason, and logic in an abstract sense, of the kind that underlies social science theories on the subject, all disintegrate in the face of the heterogeneity of motivations which impel large crowds to loot, destruction, and murder. Again, Headley's description of the actions of the New York mob at its height puts the matter well:

> Mobs springing up everywhere, and flowing together often apparently by accident, each pursuing a different object: one chasing negroes and firing their dwellings, others only sacking a house, and others still, wreaking their vengeance on station-houses, while scores, the moment they got loaded down with plunder, hastened away to conceal it – all showed that the original cause of the uprising had been forgotten.[88]

Sometimes, persons killed or hurt in riots are described not only as victims but as "innocent" persons. This qualifier is especially frequently used when passersby or mere onlookers are injured, fatally or otherwise, by police use of force to disperse a rioting mob. The penchant for uniformed forces to use their weapons, to become themselves killers of "sometimes innocent persons,"[89] is so great that every society based on law has strict provisions to govern their use of force in riotous situations which they are called upon to control. These measures are not designed only to protect the law-abiding public, but to protect the authorities from the inevitable charges, with politically damaging consequences for them, that instead of saving the targeted victims of riotous mobs, the police or the military have themselves created "innocent victims."

A special situation arises when the targeted victims defend themselves against rioting mobs or against the police and troops, whom they see as enemies rather than as their protectors. In Odessa and other parts of Russia in the late nineteenth and early twentieth centuries as in post-Independence India, reports sometimes appeared that Jews and Muslims, respectively, counterattacked, "injuring or killing" persons from rioting mobs or even the police.[90] In both cases also, anti-Semites in Russia and anti-Muslim elements in India have called for the disarming of the potential targets or victims and for searches of their quarters to find arms. Again, in both cases, the tables were semantically turned and the victims blamed for the riots directed against them or for actions leading to riotous situations in which mostly Jews or Muslims were killed.[91]

Sometimes, moreover, the very act of self-defence may transform a riot into a pogrom, in which "the intended victims" are victimized "by those charged with their protection." In Gomel in Russia in 1903, where the Jewish Bund's "armed fighting squads" – created in the aftermath of previous pogroms to protect Jews from becoming victims – were particularly active, Russian troops used the very act of Jewish self-defence as a justification for teaching the Jews and their armed squads "a lesson." A quarrel between "a Jewish tradeswoman and her customer," which escalated into a riot calling for the use of troops, was then turned into a pogrom.[92]

Jews were considered not only exploiters by Russian authorities but as "responsible" for much political "unrest" directed against the government and the Tsar.[93] When riots followed political unrest for which the Jews were blamed, they were then considered to have "provoked [their own] bloodshed."[94] Those Russians who killed Jews on such occasions were considered "patriotic," acting to punish Jews for their "treasonous behavior." In short, from the point of view of the city governor responsible for quelling the 1905 riots in Odessa, "Jews were responsible for the trouble, and the pogrom was retribution."[95] In effect, the Russian authorities attributed to Russian killers of Jews the same moral authority and legitimacy which Davis attributes to her sixteenth-century French rioters.

The Sikhs in India in 1984 were also blamed by very considerable segments of upper caste Hindus in north India for their own massacres, particularly in Delhi, but also in several other cities and towns in the north. They were accused of having brought the massacres upon themselves for failing to criticize "the terrorists in Punjab," for "not loudly condemning the assassination" of Mrs Gandhi, and for reports that some Sikhs in India and abroad had danced in the streets and distributed sweets when the news of her assassination was broadcast.[96] The latter charge was particularly emphasized by a local Congress leader who has been accused by civil liberties groups of organizing the massacres.

Often, violence against a targeted group is sanctioned by rumors that the authorities themselves desire it. Such was the case during the 1881-2 Russian pogroms when Jews were blamed for the killing of the Tsar. The rumor was then spread that the "Tsar's son now permitted, or even ordered" vengeance against the Jews.[97] The "Imperial Manifesto of 18 February 1905 which called on loyal Russians to unite against their foreign and domestic foes" was taken as a license to kill Jews.[98] Similar rumors accompanied the massacres of the Sikhs in Delhi, namely, that Mrs Gandhi's son, Rajiv, who had become the new Prime Minister of India, himself desired vengeance against the Sikhs.

Once a pattern of victimization of a particular group has been established, acts of violence against its members may not require rumors that the authorities desire such acts as revenge or just punishment. In the absence of any state authority, as in the Ukraine in 1919-20 during the Russian Civil War, Jews were simply considered by "White commanders" as "fair game for loot, for 'contributions,' revenge, or bloody sport."[99] However, where there is established authority, no matter how weak, rumors that the authorities desire punishment of a targeted group commonly appear to sanction the violence and reassure its perpetrators that they will have a free hand. Whether or not "a strong state power" committed to ending victimization and "terrorizing of minorities" is required to prevent pogroms, as Rogger argues,[100] is a more debatable matter which will be taken up below.

The height of hypocrisy on this matter of blaming the victims was reached in the aftermath of *Krystallnacht,* which was followed by the "big lie" that the Jews themselves had been "responsible for the pogrom," for which they were required to pay a huge fine.[101]

Occasionally, a defensive riotous response to racist provocations is accepted by the broader public and the authorities as justified. Such at least was the case with the Southall riots in England in 1981 when "Asian residents" declined to become either targets or victims of racist attacks "by violent skinhead youths" and responded instead with violence of their own.[102] However, in Brixton and Toxteth in the same year, there was no such consensus that Blacks had rioted with good cause.[103]

The use of the term victims becomes problematic also when the response of a targeted group is not merely "defence," but rather when rioting groups are attacking each other. For then the "victims" may have themselves been "assailants," as Chang reports for the Los Angeles riots of 1992. In fact, the traditional portrayal of Blacks as victims of a racist society in general became partly transformed in both New York and Los Angeles as a consequence of the boycotts of Korean American stores by Blacks. Blacks considered themselves victims of Korean racism in general and of the shooting of individual Blacks in Korean stores in particular. Korean merchant shops then became targets in the Los Angeles riots as had white shops before in Watts. However, some of the media reversed matters and accused Black "boycotters" of racism and of victimizing Korean merchants.[104]

In India also, although most persons killed in Hindu–Muslim riots until recently were Muslims, it is a standard explanation by militant Hindus and by many in authority as well that the Muslims always start the riots, that they attack first, and that they are mostly killed by the police rather than by Hindu rioters. This argument is not entirely false, but it is a gross distortion of some of the facts, particularly with regard to the provocations which impel Muslims into the streets, among other matters. There is, however, sufficient factual support for the explanation to make it problematic in such situations to distinguish "victims" and "assailants" in the abstract or in any categorical sense, though it is possible to go round to the sites of particular incidents and make a judgment in particular cases that certain persons killed were indeed relatively defenceless and harmless victims.

A further problem arises when a general pattern of "racial victimization" exists in a society, such as that of "Asian Americans" in the United States. When a particular group is considered responsible, however irrationally, for a set of ills affecting an entire society, in this case unemployment attributed to unfair Japanese trade practices with the United States, any incident in which an Asian is beaten or killed by whites may be considered by Asian Americans as part of a general pattern of "racial victimization."[105] It matters not to the group which identifies with the "victim" whether a particular incident began as a barroom brawl or whether the racist attitudes of the whites involved were representative or not of white society as a whole.

Group members who see themselves as victimized by prejudice and discrimination in a broader society tend, therefore, to place any incident in which another member of the group has been hurt or killed as part of the broader pattern of prejudice and discrimination in the society as a whole. The police, however, often prefer to define local incidents of violence, whether between members of different ethnic groups or not, simply as crimes and to treat them as such, that is, to localize and confine them. Such localization, however, becomes more difficult when isolated incidents of inter-ethnic violence become transformed into something broader, a "riot" involving large numbers of massed persons from opposing ethnic groups engaged in assaults on persons, lives, and property. In such situations, the police may themselves take sides; even when they do not, they are often accused of doing so, particularly by the side which emerges with the greater losses. Some ethnic "riots" do not even involve two ethnic groups, but only one community and the police, with the latter perceived or described by spokesmen for the rioting community as responsible for the precipitating incidents leading to the "riot." When it can be proved that the police and the state authorities more broadly are directly implicated in a "riot" in which one community provides the principal or sole victims, then, of course, one is confronted with a pogrom, in which the victims were targeted by the state itself or its agents.

THE STATE AND ITS AGENTS

The degree of implication of the state in riots is one of the most controversial subjects in their study. At one extreme is the view that the state itself often creates and promotes riotous conflicts for its own purposes. When the victims of such conflicts are mostly members of a single ethnic group or religion, and especially when their deaths occur mostly as a consequence of actions taken by the police or other state security forces, then the supposition is that the term pogrom is more suited to describe them. *Kristallnacht*, of course, stands as the most extreme example of its type in the twentieth century. Destruction over an entire country aimed at a single group was carried out "with the encouragement of the regime or upon direct order."[106]

It is also sometimes argued that even when the state is not directly implicated in such actions, it creates the conditions for them in the first place by the ways in which it defines the nature of the interactions between and the rights of different communities to have access to public space or contested sacred sites.[107] Between these two points of view on the continuum of state involvement in riotous conflicts are a variety of assessments which deny the partiality of the state authorities as a whole, while taking note of the fact that state agencies, particularly the police and other armed forces, are often participants in riotous conflicts or deliberately fail to control them or are simply incompetent and inefficient, failing thereby to perform the elemental state function of protecting the lives of citizens/subjects.

Whether as participants in or controllers of riotous outbreaks, the armed forces of the state, police and soldiers, often are responsible for many of the deaths and frequently for the majority of them. Scholarly controversy nevertheless differs on the meaning to be attributed to these facts. There is first of all the issue of whether and to what extent such deaths caused by agents of the state constitute a legitimate use of force to protect the public peace as opposed to intervention by the police and military on one side or another in a public conflict. Second, even where there is no doubt that the police have engaged in the illegitimate use of force or have failed to use force when innocent persons are being killed by rioters, the question still arises whether inappropriate police action or inaction reflects the design of the state authorities or is merely misconduct on the part of the police or incompetence. Third, sometimes well-known politicians in government or opposition are involved in organizing killings: recruiting the killers, providing lists of targets, conveying them to the designated sites, and supplying them money and whiskey for their work while the police stand by. Does this situation come under the head of state involvement or police dereliction of duty?

The most tortuous academic controversy concerning the role of the state in riots and pogroms has involved the interpretation of the Russian pogroms of the late nineteenth and early twentieth centuries. In the case of the 1905 pogrom where Weinberg has documented substantial involvement of the police in assaults on Jews and suspects as well "the culpability of certain local officials,"[108] he has emphasized that there was no "plot by top-ranking local authorities"[109] as well as the fact that "when the military did act to stop public disorders, ... the attacks did stop."[110] In other words, whatever the culpability of the local authorities and the police, the Russian state acted to stop the pogrom, a fact which Weinberg uses to contradict the "conventional wisdom" that the Tsarist government "planned and executed the first two waves of pogroms in order to discredit the revolutionary movement and deflect popular hostility away from itself toward a helpless scapegoat."[111]

The issue of responsibility remains central in contemporary polemical and academic discussions of ethnic and communal riots in contemporary India as well. Van Dyke, in her paper on the Sikh massacres in Delhi in 1984, raises questions similar to those discussed by Weinberg for the Odessa pogrom of 1905. Like Weinberg, she acknowledges that the highest state authorities in India probably did not actually order "the killings as part of a conspiracy," but at the same time she does not relieve those authorities from responsibility. She argues rather "that the riots were organized for the government by forces which the government itself had created."[112]

As in Odessa, the police in Delhi "were actively involved in the carnage."[113] As in Odessa, the deployment and effective use of the army were delayed while the killings were in full progress[114] and while the Home Minister of the Government of India – now (1995) its Prime Minister – sat comfortably in his home in New Delhi, fully informed of events. How does it matter, therefore, whether or not orders were given and a conspiracy mounted? The responsibility of the state authorities is no less in either event. Van Dyke, therefore, arrives at "two inescapable conclusions": the massacres were "prearranged and preplanned" and, whether or not the highest authorities in the land gave the orders, "a pre-existing 'technology of terror'" – the creation of a corrupt, bureaucratic, and partly criminalized state apparatus – "was already in place" to implement the massacres to teach the Sikhs a lesson.[115]

If there is much evidence as well as disagreement about varying degrees of police incompetence, inefficiency, and misbehavior during riots, there is on the contrary a broad consensus that nothing is so important to the control of riots as appropriate and judicious police action, including the use of force when required. It is quite astonishing, in fact, to listen to highly respected, competent, and efficient administrative officers in India deputed to particular districts notorious for their riotous history to say boldly: "There will be no riots on my watch." Yet, the political leaders in the provincial governments in India all know who these officers are and, when they themselves are determined to prevent riots, it is these men whom they depute to sensitive spots. Similarly for the United States, Lieberson and Silverman have remarked on the basis of comparative studies of the outbreak and control of riots in American cities in the 1960s: "Prompt police action can prevent riots from developing; their inaction or actual encouragement can increase the chances of a race riot."[116] The even stronger proposition that riots only occur in situations where the police are incompetent, inefficient, and biased has also been made both in India and in the United States.[117]

The historical record confirms these perceptions, repeated in numerous scholarly, journalistic, and commission reports on riots everywhere. Rogger, whose own views are however different, reports that "Jewish commentators and a governmental commission agreed that whenever and wherever during 1881-2 local administrators had shown determination and energy, they had been able to stifle or altogether to prevent pogroms."[118] The *New York Times* summed up its views on the Chicago Riot of 1919 as follows:

> To remove the causes of race riots is a matter that will require a good deal of thought and a good deal of time, if it can ever be done at all, but to repress the outbreaks of rioting nothing seems to be needed but officials with courage to use the force that they have in hand.[119]

Grimshaw gives equal place to police inefficiency as to social tensions as a cause of the outbreak of riotous violence.[120] The National Advisory Commission on Civil Disorders, in its comments on the successful control of the Detroit riots of 1967 by paratroopers brought in for the purpose, remarked that their success supported the "view that the key to quelling a disorder is to saturate an area with 'calm, determined, and hardened professional soldiers.'"[121]

Thus, it seems that the misbehavior of the police is seen as the critical factor in explaining the outbreak of riots and the proper behavior of police and other armed forces as the critical factor in the control of riots. Indeed, with only rare exceptions in American history, the praise for the disciplined and impartial behavior of troops called in to aid the civil authorities in urban race riots has been as universal as have been the criticisms of the police.[122] The same situation prevails in post-Independence India where the police, in the vast majority of riot situations, are roundly criticized, the Provincial Armed Constabulary in the state of Uttar Pradesh is considered an anti-Muslim force, but the army is nearly always praised for its prompt, decisive, and disciplined action in supressing riots with a minimum of actual use of force.

There is, therefore, a quite wide consensus in contemporary riot studies in different parts of the world on three points related to the role of the state and its agents in the eruption and control of racial and communal rioting. The first is that the differential role played by the police is critical in both respects. The second is that the military usually, though not always, acts consistently in a decisive, unprejudiced, and effective manner in controlling riots that have gone beyond the abilities of the police. The third is that the application of disciplined, decisive, overwhelming force will always bring rioting to an end with fewer injuries and fatalities than more cautious approaches. These three conclusions together would seem to free the state itself from culpability. Its local police agents may be incompetent, corrupt, inefficient, biased, and ultimately responsible for the occurrence or non-occurence of riots, but the federal or central government's neutrality is almost invariably demonstrated by the behavior of its troops when they are finally called out.

The often contradictory roles of central and provincial or local authorities should not, however, divert attention from the substantial body of evidence accumulated from studies of riots which have occurred around the world during the last century and more that the state authorities – and not just the police – bear a substantial share of responsibility for the occurrence and control of riots and pogroms. The range of state action includes undoubted deliberate instigation, as in Nazi Germany; deliberate inaction or turning of a blind eye either for narrow political purposes or to avoid an undesired political reaction for suppression of a riot; conflicting actions or inaction by local, state, and national authorities; and the deliberate and cynical manipulation of riot situations once they have occurred for political advantage in party and electoral competition. Yet, all this evidence to the contrary notwithstanding, strong voices continue to insist that excessive responsibility has been placed on the state authorities for planning, organizing, and conspiring to bring on riots and pogroms. In Rogger's view, on the contrary, these are merely comforting explanations for those who believe in the goodness of ordinary people, attempts to "absolve ... the people of guilt for the injustices committed by their rulers."[123]

On the contrary, in Rogger's account, while government action may have varied in its response to the outbreak of pogroms against Jews in Russia and other parts of Europe in the nineteenth century under efficient or inefficient administrators, "monarchical and republican regimes," in the cities and in the countryside, "in times of peace, war, and revolution,"[124] the one common denominator was the hatred of the people, particularly the rural peasants, for the Jews, and their willingness to take out their hatred against them in violent actions when the opportunity arose to do so. Nowhere in Europe did Rogger find "deliberate, much less careful, organization" in the outbreak of attacks on Jews. "Only in conditions of near anarchy, of ethnic and civil war ... can wholesale assaults upon Jews be said to have originated in the license consciously given to armed men to cleanse their country of its external and internal foes. Even then," Rogger wonders how much of "the brutality" may be attributed to "the brutalization and ill-discipline of the perpetrators" and how much to "the direction and permissiveness of their superiors and betters."[125]

However, "in most places and in normal times," whatever prejudices "policemen and soldiers, officers and officials" had against Jews, they did "their duty" in trying to prevent attacks upon them.[126] Insofar as the pogroms of 1881–2 are concerned, Rogger argues that the latest evidence, having shown that "all suspicions of official, semi-official, or unofficial preparation and orchestration" are "unfounded, spontaneity must be listed above all others in the hierarchy of proximate causes."[127] Even where Rogger acknowledges that "administrators or officers" may have delayed or been too restrained in defending Jews against mob violence because of their "lack of sympathy for [an] unpopular minority," he has some sympathy himself for their "genuine reluctance to shoot into unarmed crowds."[128] Rogger does not explain how so many Jews could have been killed in these pogroms by "unarmed crowds." In those cases where Rogger acknowledges that officials and police "sympathized and drank with looters, accepted stolen goods from them and sometimes released those they had caught," he insists that "such behavior and outright dereliction of duty ... were most fequent among the lowest level of officialdom and the woefully undermanned, ill-paid, and poorly trained provincial police units."[129]

Indeed, Roggers' sympathy for the police is repeatedly made clear. Insofar as 1905 is concerned, for example, he notes that the first actions "against Jews and others" was "largely the work of policemen and soldiers." However, their action seems almost justified in his account or, as it were, some kind of involuntary manslaughter, as suggested by the following citation:

> Exasperated and demoralized, outnumbered and under almost constant stress, taunts, and attacks, they went on rampages against their presumed tormentors, sometimes quite aimlessly, especially in the non-Russian borderlands.[130]

This quote is, moreover, passing strange, for these soldiers and police, who are under "almost constant stress, taunts, and attacks" must go on "rampages against their presumed tormentors." Does this mean that the soldiers and police, taunted and attacked, could not recognize their "tormentors"? Were they so stressed? Or were they being taunted by the Jews whom they massacred? Or did they presume that somehow those who were taunting and attacking them were not their real tormentors?

Further on 1905, Rogger is constrained to acknowledge that "some governors, higher local officials, and military commanders ... welcomed or tolerated such violence as part of the battle against revolution; a few abetted it." He assures us, nevertheless, that "one cannot speak of the pogroms of 1905 as government-sponsored or arranged; not if by government are meant the ruler, the appointed head (Sergei Witte) and members of his cabinet."[131]

One must wonder at such a narrow definition of government action, as at this view of a Tsar and his councillors, any one or several of whom might perhaps, like Henry VIII and his Becket, have been heard to mutter aloud at times if they would ever be rid of these revolutionaries and Jews. But we have no tapes to give evidence of their mutterings, only the sense to suspect the likelihood of their occurrence.

However, once all authority has been removed, as in the Civil War years in Russia and the Ukraine, Rogger finds no difficulty in assuming pre-planning and assigning blame. It is no longer soldiers and police hitting out aimlessly, "but sizable detachments of armed men who descended upon Jewish communities and decimated them." "Men and officers, including the higher White commanders" joined equally in the massacres.[132] Clearly, the Jews did not realize how lucky they were under the tsars and would soon be again once authority was re-established in the Soviet Union. For, "it required the reimposition of a strong state power, ruthless consistency in its application, as well as compelling practical and ideological reasons to end Jewish victimization."[133] In authority is peace. The stronger the authority the better for the Jews ... up to a point. That point is when the state itself, as under Hitler and Stalin as well in his later years, organizes systematic attacks on Jews. However, Rogger denies the name of pogrom to these attacks, to which he gives no name. A pogrom for Rogger is what happens to Jews and minorities under weak authority or no authority.[134]

Even on the question of crowd control once a riot has begun, Rogger argues a dissenting position against the prevailing consensus described above. Assuming both a strong state and "an energetic and impartial use of force by the police, or military," he does not believe, as do most students of riots and present-day Indian administrators, that such a "use of force ... can carry the day quickly at all times, and in all circumstances, against crowds that form, melt away, and reform in unpredictable patterns."[135] We cannot allow all the qualifiers attached to this statement, which render it meaningless, to detract from the meaning intended: riots are the product of irrational crowds acting spontaneously out of racial hatreds, which cannot necessarily be controlled even by the best-intentioned state and its agents.

RIOT OR POGROM?

The Oxford English dictionary is clear on the distinction between a riot and a pogrom. The former refers to "violence, strife, disorder, tumult, *esp.* on the part of the populace" and of "a violent disturbance of the peace by an assembly or body of persons: an outbreak of active lawlessness or disorder among the populace."[136] A pogrom is defined as "an organized massacre in Russia for the destruction or annihilation of any body or class," but used in the English-speaking world since 1905-6 "chiefly" to apply "to those directed against the Jews." Klier notes as well that, "in the West," the term pogrom has also come to connote "official planning or collusion."[137] It is noteworthy – and also associated clearly with the legal use of the term riot, as in the Riot Act – that a riot is defined as an outbreak among the people in violation of the laws and order of the state. A riot is not defined, except in what the OED characterizes as an archaic use of the term, as a hostile attack, though clearly many riots, past and contemporary, have involved violent attacks by one ethnic group against another or mutual attacks between two or more ethnic groups.

In fact, neither the term riot nor pogrom effectively captures the dynamics of most violent occurrences involving large crowds, which tend to share features of both definitions. In practice, there are virtually always some elements of organization and planning before riots as well as pogroms.[138] Moreover, much of the organization and planning which does go on is designed both to give the appearance of spontaneity and to induce spontaneous actions on the part of the populace. In states such as Tsarist Russia or contemporary India, whose authority over its subjects or citizens is relatively feeble or insecure or under threat, there is often outright complicity or abetment on the part of the state authorities or its agents. However, even in states with more secure structures of authority, such as the United States and Great Britain, institutional racism, involving endemic and systematic discrimination against and subordination and stereotyping of a racial group may provide a general climate which makes both state and society complicit indirectly or directly in riotous events.[139]

It is quite fruitless in such situations to seek to define a situation precisely as either a riot or a pogrom. While there are many instances of large-scale violence in which a consensus might well be reached by outside observers that one was a riot, the other a pogrom, in many, if not most cases, the boundary lines are blurred – and almost always deliberately by either or both the instigators and the state authorities. Pogroms might indeed best be defined as attacks upon the persons and property of a particular ethnic, racial, or communal group in which the state and/or its agents are implicated to a significant degree, but which are given the appearance, by design of the authorities or otherwise, of a riot.

In fact, much of the political strategy surrounding crowd violence revolves around labelling. The winning side is not only the one which inflicts the most damage and suffers the least from crowd violence, but the one which succeeds in labelling it a riot. The losing side may gain sympathy and political support if it succeeds in demonstrating that what in fact occurred was a pogrom. Interestingly enough, in the United States and Great Britain, the term pogrom is not even available. In those countries, all acts of crowd violence are classed as riots, which indicates not that pogroms have not occurred in them, but that the "political formula" in both countries is so strong that it is virtually unthinkable to use such a term, which implies that the state/government, elected by the people, could be directly at fault for such heinous acts.

STATE AND SOCIETY

A fundamental flaw runs through most of the arguments on both sides of the debate concerning the complicity of the state and its agents in the fomenting of riots and pogroms, namely, the persisting belief in the existence of a dichotomy between state and society. This belief can be used equally well by scholars and polemicists on both sides of the issue. If the state is responsible for riots and pogroms, then the people are relieved of responsibility; if the people are responsible, then the state and its leaders are free of blame. The first argument also supports demands for greater state accountability to the people, the second for greater state authority over the people.

Those in the camp of the state, which usually includes most of the media in all societies, have a ready explanation for riots everywhere. They are the product of "ancient hatreds" between peoples, a phrase used day-in and day-out by the *New York Times* and most other media to "explain" the murderous conflict in ex-Yugoslavia and many other places, or, as in India, "the 'centuries old' hostilities of Hindus and Muslims." These ancient hatreds and hostilities express themselves from time to time in "mob fury"[140] when economic or political or social conditions ignite the pre-existing antagonisms between peoples or in times of breakdown of authority such as in the disintegration of states. Thus, Rogger sees the Russian pogroms as expressions of "social turbulence and mass rage, the blind destructiveness which might strike out in any direction" and against which the powers of the Russian state were limited.[141] The "virulence of popular Judaeophobia" was so great in nineteenth-century Europe "that it was under the protective shelter of the state that Jews were most likely to find tranquility and well-being."[142]

At the same time, it is difficult to see how such "protective shelter" could have been comforting to Jews in Russia, a state in which, Weinberg tells us, "bureaucrats and police alike revealed the extent to which they were conditioned by popular prejudices and social stereotypes."[143] Rogger, however, has a ready answer to such doubts. Though he acknowledges that "policemen and soldiers, officers and officials" "harbored" the same prejudices as ordinary people, "in most places and in normal times, that is, when structures and lines of authority were intact," their prejudices "did not keep them from doing their duty" during outbreaks of anti-Jewish violence.[144]

Donald Horowitz has taken this argument to its extreme limits, positing a common "antipathy" between peoples juxtaposed to each other, who also frequently engage in mutual comparisons in which one group almost always appears more advanced than another. Such comparison generally leads to doubts concerning the worthiness of the group and its members, which are then taken out in acts of hostility, rage, and ultimately the violence of riots against the more advanced group, to whom aggressive motivations are imputed as a justification for the violence committed.[145] This kind of argument generalizes and takes to a deep psychological level arguments commonly made by the authorities, especially in developing countries, and by theorists of the plural society,[146] who both argue that conflicts in multi-cultural societies are likely to be organized on the basis of pre-existing differences and hostilities between peoples. Theorists of the plural society argued that these differences were so great as to make unattainable the aspi-rations of the leaders of anti-colonial movements for viable independent states based on the existing colonial boundaries. Leaders of the nationalist movements and post-colonial regimes which followed dismissed these arguments, but then acted as if they also believed them by insisting upon the necessity of a strong centralized state to prevent the diverse peoples within them from killing each other and destroying the new states.

Moreover, such explanations have been commonly used as well by the organizers, instigators, and perpetrators of such violence as the pogrom against the Jews in Germany in 1938 or the massacres of the Sikhs in Delhi in 1984. Hill points out, of course, that "Goebbels' attempt to make [the pogrom] appear spontaneous," that is, an expression of the natural and justifiable hatred of Germans for Jews, had completely failed.[147] However, the somewhat less obvious planning of the organizers of the massacres of the Sikhs did not completely fail to mask itself behind the appearance of spontaneity.

Van Dyke's paper, however, shows clearly that the idea that the massacres arose out of spontaneous "grief and anger" was nothing but a cover to hide "the blatantly planned and well directed nature of the violence."[148] Even more to the point, there has never been any mass "antipathy" between Sikhs and Hindus in India nor any riots except those organized by thug politicians aided or abetted by the police. The very idea that Sikhs and Hindus are in hostile competition with each other hardly exists in India, as Van Dyke makes clear in her paper. "The fostering of antipathy"[149] against the Sikhs was part of a political strategy for mobilizing Hindu votes for a governing party for whom such "riots" provided a politically useful demonstration of its determination to preserve the unity of India in the face of alleged threats from recalcitrant minorities.[150]

When we come, however, to the matter of Hindu–Muslim relations and riots in India, the situation is rather different. Here indeed there are prejudices instilled in children from birth against the members of the opposite group. Here also more than a century of political competition between Hindu and Muslim elites has enlarged those prejudices.

Until recently, the Indian state stood forth as the protector of Indian minorities, which meant in effect mostly Muslims, against communal Hindus. At the same time, the resentments against Muslims fostered by the partition of the country, the belief that Muslims were not truly loyal Indians at heart, and the political use by the governing party of its "protection" of the Muslims as a device to maintain a hold on Muslim votes laid the basis for the massive political mobilization of Hindus in the Ayodhya movement in the 1980s and early 1990s. In the course of this movement, it became clear that many Hindu magistrates, officials, and police sympathized with it[151] and held anti-Muslim sentiments themselves and that the leaders of the Indian National Congress also were no longer willing to risk their own political positions by forcefully suppressing a broad-based movement of Hindu religious-political mobilization. In such a situation, it becomes rather difficult to conceive of a dichotomy between state and society, for most of Hindu society and most Hindu employees of the Indian state, including its police, hold either hostile or ambivalent feelings towards Muslims.[152]

At the same time, yet another set of values persists in India both alongside and separate from anti-Muslim sentiments, namely, an ideology of Indian nationalism in which the preservation of the unity and integrity of the Indian state constitutes the ultimate value. Those who hold to this ideology, that is to say, virtually all Hindu and most non-Hindu Indians as well, divide into two broad groups: those who feel that the preservation of a strong Indian state depends upon maintaining its neutrality in relation to Hindu–Muslim conflicts and those who feel that the state must become a Hindu state. But it by no means follows from the fact that such an ideology of state neutrality exists that the state itself is in fact neutral. On the contrary, the idea of the neutrality of the state is itself a political ideology in competition with another which seeks to replace it, that of militant Hindu nationalism.[153] There is, therefore, no state on one side nor civil society on the other but two ideologies occupying both state and society in which minorities must choose either to ally with those who uphold an ideology of state neutrality or fight against the state.

In fact, the idea of the neutral state standing above the conflicts – ethnic or otherwise – in a secular or multi-cultural society is a liberal idea associated especially with Western democracies and most especially those which conceive their societies as founded upon a union of individuals rather than as an expression of the unity of a people. Ideologies of nationalism which developed in Europe in the nineteenth century and spread to other parts of the world thereafter emphasize the latter. The state becomes for these ideologies an instrument of a people imagined to be united in their determination to achieve specific goals. Thus it is with Hindu nationalism in India and with militant Jewish nationalism in Israel where its ideologues imagine a "'real Israel' ... fully embodied in the state," "a whole nation."[154] The goals of such nationalisms are not to create or work within a state that mediates between Muslims and Hindus or Muslims and Jews in their conflicts over sacred space, but to create a state based on an imagined nation which defines those who are not part of the "nation" as "minorities" who must accept a secondary position within the state.

It is within this broad discourse of the modern state and national unity that one must look for an explanation for the persistence of that most pernicious and violence-producing "sub-discourse" of Hindu–Muslim confrontation in South Asia. The latter, though subordinate to or embedded within the former, is a discourse in the full Foucauldian sense of that term. It is grounded within a set of institutions which promote its persistence: communal organizations, political parties, peace committees, and the like. It includes a set of practices and behaviors as well: communal postures, secular counterpostures, appointments of commissions of inquiry to analyze riots, appointments of minority commissions to report on incidents of communal tension of all sorts, funding of social science research institutes to examine the causes of Hindu–Muslim communalism and riots. The latter in turn are engaged in a so-called search for the "truth" of communalism and violence, which is often found – in the best liberal tradition of the search for truth – within the innermost beings of Indian selves. While this search for the truth of communalism goes on decade after decade, the roll of the dead which, if one counts the violence of partition in 1947, now numbers in the hundreds of thousands, increases year by year.

A similar search for the "truth" of racism in the United States and Great Britain has taken place as scholars, journalists, and policy makers have sought to explain the various forms of both Black–white and the more recent Black ghetto riots. The former occurred only in the United States and mostly in the nineteenth and early to mid-twentieth centuries. The predominant explanations for such riots, including lynchings, has, as was shown earlier, emphasized mostly factors of economic dislocation, relatively sudden and rapid migrations of Blacks from South to North, job competition, and political controversies, among other factors settling upon local societies in which "racial hatred" was already endemic, providing thereby the spark to ignite such hatred in violent, riotous confrontations.[155]

Another type of explanation, however, has been required for that rather different form of rioting in the Black ghettos of both countries, directed primarily against white-owned property within the ghettos themselves. That is, the riots in the United States in the 1960s and in Great Britain in the 1980s were not primarily or even substantially race riots at all in the same sense that Hindu–Muslim riots in India or earlier riots in the United States involved searches for and attacks against the persons as well as the properties of another group in areas both within and outside one's own home locality. In both cases also, as we have seen, the majority of these riots were touched off by confrontations with the police or were generally interpreted as reactions to some form of genuine or perceived police harassment of Black persons.

Much scholarship concerning Black rioting in the United States and Great Britain discounts utterly the idea that such rioting represents mere "mob fury" or "blind rage." On the contrary, insofar as the United States is concerned, T. M. Tomlinson, for example, uses the term "outrage" rather than "rage," to describe the attitudes of Blacks over the discrimination against them and the consequent limitations on their life opportunites, and argues further that few Negroes raised their voices or did anything to counter rioting in Los Angeles in 1965 from within "the Negro community" because so many considered "the riot ... a justifiable protest" against their condition.[156] On the other side, closer to the "mob fury" view is the argument that all rioting emerges "on the basis of a pre-existing hostile belief system" which may or may not bear a close relation to reality. Anti-Catholic rioters in nineteenth-century America actually "believed that the Pope, in Rome, was trying to take over the country." In the case of black rioters in the 1960s, the belief system in question is one that accepts "the malevolence of white society, its duplicity, and its basic commitment to oppressing Negroes."[157] "Judeophobia" presumably would fall into a similar category of "a pre-existing hostile belief system" which erupted into anti-Jewish violence in nineteenth and early twentieth-century Europe and Russia.[158] So would the stereotyping of Tamils by Sinhalese in Sri Lanka "as privileged" and therefore a legitimate target for the rage of the "lumpen proletariat" elements among them against their "condition."[159]

In all three situations under discussion here – European and Russian anti-Semitism; anti-Muslim prejudices or Hindu–Muslim hostilities in India and Tamil–Sinhalese conflicts in Sri Lanka; and racism in the US and Great Britain – we are referring to widely held prejudices and beliefs endemic in societies from which state agents are hardly immune. In the first two cases, minorities become scapegoats for the ills of society and the failures of the state authorities to promote the well-being of their subjects or citizens. In the third case, Blacks are seen as responding to the "racism" of British or American society and particulary to racism at the point where it is most keenly felt, from the police.[160]

At the same time, Keith argues strongly and persuasively in his superb and extraordinary study of the 1980s riots in Britain that it is a mistake to single out the police to bear the brunt of the blame for British racism. Rather, drawing on the American social science term, "institutional racism," often used to describe Black–white relations in the US, he argues that police racism must be seen "alongside the institutional racism of all other facets of British society," manifested in "a series of policies which have sustained the systematic racial subordination of one class of British citizens, have become built into the daily routine of British policing, and yet are understood as a normal facet of daily life."[161] Keith argues that it is not a few policemen but the actions of a racist police force in a racist society that lie behind the outbreaks in Bristol and London in the 1980s and "that the police force as an institution and police officers as individuals are no worse and no better than the society from which they are drawn."[162] Finally, just as many academic observers of Black rioting in American cities in the 1960s saw it as a "justifiable response" to the discrimination against Blacks and their mistreatment by white police officers, so Keith argues that Black response to racist mistreatment of them by the police took many forms, of which "rioting" was "merely one of several alternative expressions" of an ongoing conflict between Blacks and the police.[163]

VIOLENCE AND POLITICS AND THE POLITICS OF VIOLENCE

Inter-personal violence is an aspect of everyday life in virtually all societies, inter-ethnic violent confrontations are endemic in most multi-ethnic urban areas, and police violence and harassment of ethnic minorities and other vulnerable groups are commonplace practically everywhere. What makes violence in civil societies appear exceptional is the transformation of everyday acts of violent and near-violent confrontations into specialized forms through the labelling of them as riots, pogroms, insurrections, revolts, rebellions, and the like, developing categories defined as more serious or threatening to civil order and state authority, and fitting particular incidents or events into these categories. Once such a process of labelling and categorization takes place, then the exceptional also soon becomes general as more and more of the violent acts and incidents of everyday life are fitted into them. The end result of this process of objectification of violence may become the institutionalization of specific forms of violence as methods of purification of society, which in turn become methods of purifying oneself through a ritual of fire.

The process of objectification and glorification of violence began with Marx's category of *revolution*. Before long a band of Marx's heirs, most of them not even *Marxist*, but bourgeois academics, arose to chronicle the onward march of *revolution*, to define it more precisely – though usually in terms derived from Marx's emphasis on that other reification known as *class* – and to survey all the instances of uprisings among the poor, the disadvantaged, and the exploited to see which ones fit the grand category and which deserved only a lesser designation such as insurrection, rebellion, or riot.

Riots and pogroms have at last come into their own as ethnicity and nation have displaced class as the preferred categories into which to place all the peoples of the world. Feeding this process of categorization further has been the state itself which, through its censuses, has placed its peoples into categories defined by caste, language, religion, and "national" origin. Moreover, the state everywhere in the nineteenth and twentieth centuries has created that new category of persons known as *minorities*. Every state in today's world now has its counterpart to "the Jewish Question," which is its minority question: the "problem" of the Muslim minority in India, of the disadvantaged minorities in the United States, of the Black and East Asian minorities in Great Britain, and so on.

A great further change in this direction came in the mid-twentieth century as every former territory ruled by a European colonial power experienced some form of nationalism and aspired to a state of its own based on the European idea of the unity of state and nation. Since that idea of unity of state and nation was a falsehood from its inception in Europe and an even greater one in post-colonial Asia and Africa, its practice in contemporary developing societies also meant the adoption of the European doctrine of state exaltation, which defined the state as the supreme value and the supreme authority over the peoples in its territory.

However, states everywhere in the late twentieth century, even the older, well-established states of Europe and America have had to redefine themselves in relation to the ethnic groups which are contained within them because of the spread of ethnic movements demanding rights and privileges according to their group affiliations and disadvantages in relation to those groups alleged to be politically dominant and economically privileged. These tendencies have been further strengthened as the older imperial countries of Europe, the presumed bastions of the nation-state, have been in turn colonized by immigrants from their former imperial domains, introducing further elements of cultural diversity to break the facade of the unity of state and nation.

With these old and new diversities encompassed within the falsehood of the nation-state and its self-defeating categorization of all those who do not fit into its definition as *minorities* have come new conflicts and new interpretations of old conflicts under the general heading of riots and pogroms. Riots, once clearly defined as disturbances of public order and dangers to the state authorities, have now become transformed into expressions of mass inter-group sentiments, prejudices, and hatreds which the state must struggle to keep under control for the sake of the safety of its own citizens and subjects. Behind this facade also sits another lie, one that classifies the violence of the state and its agents against its citizens and subjects, which takes the form of the pogrom or some masquerade of it, as a "riot."

Behind these facades and wars of words and definitions in turn lie the continuing reality of the persistence of violence in everyday life even in the states considered the most stable and economically powerful. Amidst that violence, which has multiple purposes large and small, the calls to arms are the labels placed upon incidents and the definition of the initial perpetrators as Blacks, whites, police, Muslims, Jews. The general rubrics are anti-Semitism, communalism, and racism, useful terms to encompass myriad acts, to mask other forms of power relations, and to displace responsibilty. The climactic outbursts known as riots or pogroms, which occur from time to time or in waves or chains are merely episodes in a continuing warfare. These episodes in turn may be used either to demonstrate some "truth" such as the need for increased state authority or, where they shock a society and/or threaten sufficiently the state authorities, they may be used to justify policy changes designed to reduce the level of intensity of the struggle between groups or between groups and the police and the state.

It is a well-known axiom that all states have been created in violence. In the process of state formation in the contemporary world, violence between ethnic groups with or without the direct implication of the state authorities, is essential to that process as it has been defined, that is, the creation of a homogenous nation-state. One of the most curious aspects of the process is the extent to which competing elites in these states proclaim a message of secularism while mobilizing ethnic groups around symbols of religion, language, and ethnicity. Riots between ethnic groups, sometimes deliberately fomented by politicans or by the state authorities themselves, are an ongoing part of the political processes so generated.

Though they have other aspects as well, race and ghetto riots in the United States and Great Britain also bear a relationship to the question of national identity. The imperfect integration of whites and Blacks in the United States has been a persistent failure in American self-definition of the United States as a Republic of free and equal citizens. For Great Britain, the post-colonial immigration of Blacks and Asians has also challenged the English/British sense of national identity.

Riots and pogroms open windows into the broader realities of violent and near-violent ongoing conflicts in contemporary states. Economic competition, especially job competition, conflicts between criminalized and other marginal elements in society and the police, local political mobilizations which make use of ethnic differences, quarrels between small groups and individuals on many matters, youth gangs out for fun, all reveal themselves at one time or another and sometimes all at once in the larger riotous events. But there is a tendency with regard to the latter, already pointed out, to frame them within or reduce them to particular constructions. The argument here is that there is a still larger frame, that of the modern nation-state, whose everyday operations – of self-definition, of preserving its order and maintaining or enlarging its territory, of defining and creating crimes against its order and authority – generate violent conflicts. But the state does not operate independently of its citizens and subjects, who are themselves implicated in these conflict-generating processes through their upbringing, education, socialization, reading of newspapers, submission to media representations and misrepresentations of reality, and aspirations for economic advancement and political influence.

Rather than generate typologies of violent incidents, placing them into categories such as riots, pogroms, feuds, vendettas, and the like, all of which are but manifestations of broader forms of conflict in societies, we would do better to categorize the conflicts themselves and the conditions which make them endemic, which allow them to persist, and out of which come the variously named incidents from time to time. Historians of the Russian pogroms have labored greatly to decide whether or not the pogroms were state-initiated or spontaneous expressions of Jew-hatred. They have all also mostly rejected the work of its first chronicler, Dubnov, who, according to Greenbaum, "saw the entire 1881–1917 period as one long war by the authorities against the Jews."[164] But surely these pogroms were something more than mere expressions of popular hostility even if they were not all instigated by the state authorities. What made them all possible was assuredly something more encompassing, a discourse available to rulers and public alike, to those suffering from economic insecurities and those wishing to make political use of them, a discourse so pervasive that even Lenin, like Marx, made use of anti-Jewish rhetoric and polemic in his political analyses while at the same time condemning anti-Semitism as such.

Such a discourse has arisen also in modern India, known as Hindu–Muslim communalism, which has taken two centuries to come to full political fruition. The British began the process by their assiduous categorization of the peoples of India into these two fundamental categories, the distribution of political benefits and disadvantages according to them, and at times deliberate attempts to enlarge them in order more easily to rule over the sometimes recalcitrant peoples of the subcontinent. Nationalist elites, both Hindu and Muslim, far from overturning these categories in a broad movement to overthrow the British, made use of them for their own purposes to the extent even of deliberately provoking demonstrations they knew would lead to Hindu–Muslim riots or fomenting them outright. The process continued, at times with many added subtleties and nuances, throughout the post-Independence period until it reached a new peak in the post-Ayodhya riots in India in December–January, 1992–3. These riots and their thousands of predecessors before and since Independence, sometimes mislabelled as such rather than as pogroms or massacres, have been studied in their particularity and must be so studied if they are to be understood at all. However, at the same time, one must also not fail to note that it would be a mistake to explain them all away by their particularities or to fail to consider how their persistence is fostered by a discourse which perpetuates them, drawing popular prejudices taught from childhood into a social construction that justifies them, and linking state and society, authorities, politicians, police, and people in a common net which enlarges while it is functionally useful for influential elites and political groups and contracts when it is not.

There is, however, a fundamental difference among states and societies in the uses which are made of violence and in the extent to which the state authorities are implicated in them. At one extreme, as always, is "the politics of Nazism," which Bessel describes as "the politics of hatred, struggle and violence."[165] Ultimately, of course, with the victory of the Nazis over all their political rivals, it became state-directed violence against the Jews above all, but against other ethnic groups as well.

While the extent of implication of the state apparatus and of the German public as a whole in a system of routinized violence and murder remains unprecedented in world history, the connection between routine politics and "violent outbursts" exists in most societies known for their riotous propensities. In societies such as India or, for that matter, Russia in the nineteenth century, violence was merely one form in which broader conflicts often displayed themselves. Violence in these societies has been a continuation of everyday politics by other means.

Nor are there any grounds for smugness in these matters in the great Western democracies including the United States and Great Britain, where historically and in the present, a kind of intermittent and, in some places, endemic warfare has been waged against Blacks. In London in 1981, as Keith has pointed out, the violent outbursts which took place in various parts of the great city were but incidents in an ongoing warfare between the police and Blacks.[166] And, in American cities today, where it is unthinkable to use the cruder political methods of fomenting Black–white disorders such as occurred in East St. Louis in 1917, the victimization of Blacks nevertheless continues on a national level in the "war against drugs" and in the enlargement of the police forces to control the crimes generated by this war as well as the building of new prisons to house the increasing numbers of its largely Black victims.

Here we have another grand discourse, like that of the nation-state, ostensibly deployed for noble purposes, but whose main effects are otherwise. A moral crusade, launched by not the "welfare" state but the "pastoral" state, which is designed to protect and nurture the lives of every American, to ensure that none shall suffer from "substance" abuse or any other kind of abuse, becomes transformed into a vehicle for the creation, definition, and elaboration of a list of crimes, which in turn expands the potential criminal population of the country into a very large percentage of its citizens, creates opportunities for criminals to make large amounts of money quickly, which in turn requires increased police forces to catch and prisons to house the populations of criminals so created, which in turn promotes the warfare on the city streets between a criminalized population and the police, which finally, from time to time, explodes in "violent outbursts" known as riots.

It should finally be noted that the discourses which perpetuate violence, whether they focus on the building of nation-states or on the care and moral purification of citizens, help to maintain relations of dominance and subordination in societies and the deployment of economic resources which sustain them. They allow developing countries to build showcase steel mills, nuclear power plants, and huge military establishments while neglecting the welfare of their populations and creating vast new urban slums and violence-prone populations within them. They allow the Western democracies to allocate billions of dollars for similar purposes including space exploration, wars on drugs and myriad other moral crusades. The latter, of course, involve creating huge bureaucracies manned by whole new classes of professionals: psychologists, social workers, scientists quantifying the precise physical and psychological consequences in statistical terms of various forms of substance abuse or child abuse, public relations specialists to spread the propaganda, *etcetera* while avoiding the allocation of resources which might go to the direct benefit of affected populations through creating educational and job opportunities.

THE STRUGGLE TO CONTROL THE
INTERPRETATION OF VIOLENCE

We have tried in this volume to go beyond analyzing the process of violence and the violent political struggle to investigate as well the struggle to interpret the violence, the attempts to govern a society or a country through gaining not a monopoly on the legitimate use of violence but to gain control over the interpretation of violence. We need to view the contest for gaining control over the interpretation of violence as at least as important and probably more important than the outcome of specific violent struggles themselves. The struggle over the meaning of violence in each society may or may not lead to a consensus or a hegemonic interpretation. It will certainly not lead to the truth, but at most to a "regime of truth" which will give us a pre-established context into which to place future acts of a superficially similar type into the same context as well as a context for reinterpreting previous acts of violence in the history of a country.

Examples of both consensus and dissensus in the interpretation of riots abound in all societies in which they have occurred in large numbers or in which they have become endemic and have been discussed above. A reading of the literature on Black–white violence in the late nineteenth and early twentieth centuries in the northern part of the United States reveals a consensus that they reflected job competition among unskilled Black and white workers in a context of racial animosities. A much stronger, hegemonic consensus was reached concerning Black riots in the 1960s in the US that they reflected the justified anger and rage of an oppressed and disadvantaged minority for whom the time had at last come to rectify their condition by eliminating the sources of their rage in discrimination and victimization by the white majority. In contrast, the meaning of the Los Angeles riot of 1992 has been contested and no consensus has emerged, with some continuing to discern its source in the plight of Blacks in our society, others seeing it as a consequence of the decline of family values, still others seeing it as an opportunity for playing out Black–Korean enmity, and so on. In fact, none of these interpretations are *true* or perhaps all of them are true, but it matters less to discover the truth of these riots than to uncover the relations of power/knowledge which establish or fail to establish a consensus within a regime of truth about violence and riots.

Certainly white racism and the institutional racism of white-dominated American society became the general, all-purpose rubric for explaining Black rioting in the 1960s. So too has "communalism" become the general explanation for all riots in India involving a number of Hindus and Muslims on opposite sides. So too was the "Jewish Question" the starting point for all discussions of the causes of pogroms in nineteenth and early twentieth-century Russia. With the last example especially – which by its very title implies that the victims themselves are the problem – is it clear how the very search for "causes" and explanations itself contributes to the perpetuation of the violence for which it claims to seek solutions? For this very search for causes is either futile or a smokescreen. It is futile because it objectifies a series or multiplicity of events into a single large event which, as such, can have no "cause," only a multiplicity of explanations depending upon the observation point of the analyst or chronicler. It is a smokescreen also because individuals, gangs, groups, politicians, the media, and state agencies, among whom there are usually easily identified culprits – promoters, fomentors, and instigators of violence – most often not only escape prosecution but often themselves join the phalanxes of those seeking causes and the chorus of moaners for the dead.

A more profitable enterprise is the task of examining the uses of violence, considering how violence becomes isolated as an object of study and our own implication in the discourses of violence by the ways in which we write about, hold seminars on the subject, and even contribute to national commissions of enquiry to report on particular riots and sequences of riots. In other words, we might do well to stop the talk about violence and consider alternative ways of exposing it more clearly to view by painting its picture in words. We might listen to all the interpretations of violence, especially from those on site, who have seen it, participated in it, or somehow been close to it. Above all, we should resist absolutely any single causal explanation or consensus on the causes and courses of riotous, and other violent events.[167] At the same time, we should not avoid exposing to view the perpetrators of violence: the specific persons and groups and the gains they make from it. Finally, we should ask what specific interests and relations of power are served by the perpetuation of violence.

NOTES

1   Natalie Zemon Davis, "The Rites of Violence: Religious Riot in Sixteenth-Century France," *Past & Present*, LIX (May, 1973), 65.
2   John D. Klier, "The Pogrom Paradigm in Russian History," in John D. Klier and Shlomo Lambroza (eds), *Pogroms: Anti-Jewish Violence in Modern Russian History* (Cambridge: Cambridge University Press, 1992), pp. 24–5.
3   Avraham Greenbaum, "Bibliographical Essay," in Klier and Lambroza, *Pogroms*, p. 376.

4 Klier, "The Pogrom Paradigm," p. 34.
5 See, for example, Hans Rogger, "Conclusion and Overview," in Klier and Lambroza, *Pogroms*, p. 334, who shows how the element of "Jewish exploitation" emphasized in 1871 "was repeated almost in its entirety" in an official "account" of the 1881 pogroms.
6 Gyanendra Pandey, *The Construction of Communalism in Colonial North India* (Delhi: Oxford University Press, 1990), especially ch. 2. Thus, in India, another paradigm or what Pandey calls a "master narrative" of Hindu–Muslim "communalism" exists to explain all riots in which both Hindus and Muslims have been involved and quite a few in which no trace of "communalism" can be found in the historical record of particular incidents.
7 T. M. Tomlinson, "The Development of a Riot Ideology among Urban Negroes," in Allen D. Grimshaw (ed.), *Racial Violence in the United States* (Chicago: Aldine, 1969), p. 230.
8 Chang chapter, this volume, p. 235.
9 Espiritu chapter, this volume, p. 221.
10 See the Van Dyke chapter, this volume, on this use of the representation of riots in the case of the massacres of the Sikhs.
11 Friedland and Hecht chapter, this volume, p. 134.
12 Van der Veer chapter, this volume and Friedland and Hecht chapter.
13 Weinberg chapter, this volume, p. 66.
14 Klier, "The Pogrom Paradigm," pp. 16–17.
15 Van der Veer chapter, p. 169.
16 Klier, "The Pogrom Paradigm," p. 18.
17 Indeed, "the Jewish Question" became such an all-pervasive topic of discussion and an explanation for everything under the sun in the nineteenth century that jokes about it were commonplace and continue up to the present, though most people today would not understand, for example, the joke about the necessity for a study of, say, "The Elephant and the Jewish Question."
18 Michael I. Aronson, "The anti-Jewish Pogroms in Russia in 1881," in Klier and Lambroza, *Pogroms*, p. 49.
19 Weinberg chapter, p. 61.
20 Ashgar Ali Engineer, "The Causes of Communal Riots in the Post-Partition Period in India," in Asghar Ali Engineer (ed.), *Communal Riots in Post-Independence India* (Hyderabad: Sangam Books, 1984), p. 40.
21 Engineer, "The Causes of Communal Riots," p. 40.
22 Engineer, "The Causes of Communal Riots," pp. 36–7.
23 Allen D. Grimshaw, "Three Cases of Racial Violence in the United States," in Grimshaw, *Racial Violence*, p. 113.
24 Ceri Peach, "A Geographical Perspective on the 1981 Urban Riots in England," *Ethnic and Racial Studies*," IX, no. 3 (July, 1986), 397; John Benyon, "The Riots, Lord Scarman and the Political Agenda," in John Benyon (ed.), *Scarman and After: Essays Reflecting on Lord Scarman's Report, the Riots and their Aftermath* (Oxford: Pergamon Press, 1984), p. 12.
25 Peach, "A Geographical Perspective," pp. 407–8.
26 Peach, "A Geographical Perspective," p. 408 and E. P. Thompson, "The Moral Economy of the English Crowd in the Eighteenth Century," *Past & Present*, L (February, 1971), 77.

27   Stan Taylor, "The Scarman Report and Explanations of Riots," in Benyon, *Scarman and After*, p. 27.
28   Peach, "A Geographical Perspective," p. 408.
29   Engineer, "The Causes of Communal Riots," p. 36.
30   Engineer, "The Causes of Communal Riots," p. 34.
31   Raymond J. Murphy and James M. Watson, "Ghetto Social Structure and Riot Support: The Role of White Contact, Social Distance, and Discrimination," in Grimshaw, *Racial Violence*, pp. 248–9.
32   Weinberg chapter, p. 62.
33   Rogger, "Conclusion and Overview," pp. 360–1; *cf.* also Weinberg's statement that "a reversal in Odessa's economic fortunes at the turn of the century strengthened anti-Jewish sentiments among its Russian residents"; Weinberg chapter, p. 60.
34   Klier, "The Pogrom Paradigm," pp. 29–31.
35   Klier, "The Pogrom Paradigm," p. 33, notes how this explanation used for the 1871 Odessa pogrom was trotted out "quickly ... in the midst of the pogroms of 1881." Aronson observes that the Russian government adopted the "explanation" for the 1881 pogroms as "a spontaneous otuburst of popular anger against Jewish exploitation"; Aronson, "The anti-Jewish Pogroms," p. 46. Rogger records how the authorities in Russia in 1881 and 1905 at first sought to blame "some outside agency" for the pogroms, but then resorted to "the more comforting explanation of popular resentment at Jewish exploitation; Rogger, "Conclusion and Overview," p. 317.
36   Murphy and Watson, "Ghetto Social Structure and Riot Support," p. 249.
37   The last two sentences were stimulated by the comments of an anonymous reviewer who raised the following query: "Does this [the recommendation that the exploitation argument be discarded by social scientists] not imply that exploitation can never be objectively defined (as segregation is)? Should a purported cause be thrown out for consideration because it has previously been used to blame the victims?" My answers are given above, but it should be evident that there is a distinction between a term such as segregation which can be observed independently of the perception, ideological predispositions, and feelings of observers and observed and exploitation which cannot.
38   Neil J. Smelser, *Theory of Collective Behavior* (New York: The Free Press, 1962), p. 253.
39   Smelser, *Theory of Collective Behavior*, p. 269.
40   Smelser's model and others of its type have also been effectively criticized by McAdam, who developed a political process model to replace the older sociological sequential and ecological approaches. Applying his model to the Black riots of the 1960s, he interpreted them as extensions of an historic insurgent movement, whose ups and downs, violent and non-violent manifestations related more to the state of internal organization among Blacks and the fluctuations in external political opportunities than to the state of societal strains between Blacks and whites. However, McAdam's model does not help us to interpret particular riots either in the United States in the 1960s or elsewhere because it eliminates the question altogether of why a riot occurred in one city and not another, why it was more severe here than there, what interests were served in particular incidents and how they relate to the broader goals of Black insurgency. See Doug McAdam, *Political Process and the Development*

of *Black Insurgency, 1930–1970* (Chicago: University of Chicago Press, 1982).

41 Weinberg chapter, p. 67.

42 Chicago Commission, "The Negro in Chicago," pp. 103–4.

43 Bill Buford, *Among the Thugs* (New York: W. W. Norton, 1992).

44 Stephen Reicher and Jonathan Potter, "Psychological Theory as Intergroup Perspective: A Comparative Analysis of 'Scientific' and 'Lay' Accounts of Crowd Events," *Human Relations*, XXXVIII, No. 2 (1985), 176.

45 Michael Keith, *Race, Riots and Policing: Lore and Disorder in a Multi-Racist Society* (London: UCL Press, 1993).

46 Van Dyke chapter, p. 208.

47 Van Dyke chapter, p. 209.

48 *Cf.* Grimshaw, "Lawlessness and Violence in America and Their Special Manifestations in Changing Negro–White Relationships," in Grimshaw, *Racial Violence,* p. 21.

49 I do not see this as a "causal" sequence but more as a kind of ideal typical description which combines broad social, ideological, and scientific – developments in social "knowledge" – changes in societies with specific conditions which may or may not develop at specific sites. It is of course still open to social scientists who find the argument concerning "institutionalized riot systems" worth testing to undertake comparisons which seek to determine the ecological and other characteristics which exist at sites where they have developed. From the point of view of both predictive and practical considerations, however, my response would be that this is a waste of time, which would be better spent simply in identifying the sites where they exist and gaining a more detailed knowledge of the dynamics of riot production and of the potential variations in those dynamics. In places where riots are endemic, the local authorities usually understand those dynamics very well and know the individuals and groups who are at the center of them, though they would not use a fancy term such as "institutionalized riot systems" to describe them. The law of the self-denying prophecy unfortunately is also at work in such places and will work even more ingeniously as soon as such knowledge spreads widely, leading to the development by "riot specialists" of new techniques.

50 Davis, "The Rites of Violence," pp. 80–1.

51 Davis, "The Rites of Violence," pp. 85–6.

52 Weinberg chapter, p. 76.

53 Weinberg chapter, p. 77.

54 Weinberg chapter, p. 78.

55 Weinberg chapter, p. 76.

56 Weinberg chapter, p. 79.

57 Weinberg chapter, p. 61.

58 Van Dyke chapter, p. 202. However, see Tambiah, who drew on some of the same sources as Van Dyke, but interprets the information differently, emphasizing the diversity of participation and the involvement of ordinary people in the riots; Stanley Tambiah, "Presidential Address: Reflections on Communal Violence in South Asia," *Journal of Asian Studies*, XLIX (November, 1990), 746–7.

59 Van Dyke chapter, p. 214.

60 It is certainly a misnomer from 1933 onwards, once the Nazis were in power, when actions against the Jews, notably in *Kristallnacht*, were surreptitiously state-sponsored and state-directed. However, I think it is a misnomer also before this time, for the term "riot" presumes a certain amount of spontaneity whereas the SA violence was planned and the responses, particularly by their targets on the left, also involved prepared defensive actions. These acts of violence, therefore, constitute to my mind fights in which the SA were aggressors.

61 Richard Bessel, *Political Violence and the Rise of Nazism: The Storm Troopers in Eastern Germany, 1925–1934* (New Haven: Yale University Press, 1984), p. 51.

62 Bessel, *Political Violence and the Rise of Nazism*, p. 44.

63 Grimshaw, "Lawlessness and Violence in America," p. 20.

64 Ben Johnson *et. al.*, "East St. Louis Riots: Report of the Special Committee Authorized by Congress to Investigate the East St. Louis Riots," in Grimshaw, *Racial Violence*, pp. 62-3.

65 Chicago Commission, "The Negro in Chicago," p. 100.

66 Elmer R. Akers and Vernon Fox, "The Detroit Rioters and Looters Committed to Prison," in Grimshaw, *Racial Violence*, p. 302.

67 Akers and Fox, "The Detroit Rioters," pp. 302–3.

68 Peach, "A Geographical Perspective," p. 407.

69 Peach, "A Geographical Perspective," p. 405; also pp. 399, 402.

70 Murphy and Watson, "Ghetto Social Structure and Riot Support," p. 236.

71 The National Advisory Commission on Civil Disorders, "The Riot Participant," in Grimshaw, *Racial Violence*, p. 309.

72 National Advisory Commission, "The Riot Participant," p. 310.

73 National Advisory Commission, "The Riot Participant," pp. 310–11.

74 National Advisory Commission, "The Riot Participant," p. 311.

75 National Advisory Commission, "The Riot Participant," pp. 311–12.

76 National Advisory Commission, "The Riot Participant," p. 306.

77 Robert M. Fogelson and Robert B. Hill, "Who Riots? A Study of Participation in the 1967 Riots," in Grimshaw, *Racial Violence*, pp. 314–15.

78 Fogelson and Hill, "Who Riots?", p. 316.

79 Fogelson and Hill, "Who Riots?", pp. 313–14.

80 Fogelson and Hill, "Who Riots?", p. 315fn.

81 Fogelson and Hill, "Who Riots?", p. 314.

82 The National Advisory Commission on Civil Disorders, "Patterns of Disorder," in Grimshaw, *Racial Violence*, pp. 330–1.

83 Klier, "The Pogrom Paradigm," p. 22.

84 However, see Veena Das, who sees no contradiction in studying crowds from both perspectives simultaneously; "Introduction: Communities, Riots, Survivors – The South Asian Experience," in Veena Das (ed.), *Mirrors of Violence: Communities, Riots and Survivors in South Asia* (Delhi: Oxford University Press, 1990), p. 28.

85 Buford, *Among the Thugs*.

86 J. T. Headley, *Pen and Pencil Sketches of the Great Riots: An Illustrated History of the Railroad and Other Great American Riots* (New York: E. B. Treat, 1882), pp. 169–70

87 Smelser provides a general statement on this phenomenon of illogical violence, where he remarks that, once a large-scale disturbance begins, crowds become

diverse, as do their grievances, and "it attracts many potentially deviant and destructive persons in the population"; *Theory of Collective Behavior*, pp. 260–1. Such a general statment, however, cannot succeed in dispelling wonder at the nature of such attacks as that on an orphanage. In my own work in India, I have come across incidents of this type, including an attack by Hindus on a Muslim orphanage in a small town in north India in the midst of a riot.

88 Headley, *Pen and Pencil Sketches,* pp. 213–14. For a thorough analysis of these riots and a discussion of its causes, which includes also the political and economic history of the city in the period before their occurrence, see Iver Bernstein, *The New York City Draft Riots: Their Significance for American Society and Politics in the Age of the Civil War* (New York: Oxford University Press, 1990).

89 Government of Gujarat, Home Department, *Report on the Police Firing at Village Parthampura, District Baroda, on 14th August, 1972*, by Shri K. M. Satwani, District and Sessions Judge Ahmedabad (Rural), Narol, Commission of Inquiry (Gandhinagar, 1975), pp. 18–19.

90 Weinberg chapter, p. 61.

91 Weinberg chapter, pp. 61–62 and personal interviews by the editor at riot sites in India.

92 Rogger, "Conclusion and Overview," p. 341.

93 Weinberg chapter, p. 62.

94 Weinberg chapter, p. 75.

95 Weinberg chapter, p. 72.

96 Van Dyke chapter, p. 208.

97 Rogger, "Conclusion and Overview," p. 337.

98 Rogger, "Conclusion and Overview," p. 347.

99 Rogger, "Conclusion and Overview," pp. 350–1.

100 Rogger, "Conclusion and Overview," pp. 351, 359.

101 Hill chapter, this volume, p. 107.

102 Benyon, "The Riots, Lord Scarman and the Political Agenda," p. 6.

103 Benyon, "The Riots, Lord Scarman and the Political Agenda," pp. 7–8.

104 Chang chapter, this volume, pp. 244, 249.

105 Espiritu chapter, this volume, p. 227.

106 Hill chapter, p. 108.

107 Das, "Introduction," p. 10.

108 Weinberg chapter, p. 70.

109 Weinberg chapter, p. 72.

110 Weinberg chapter, p. 69.

111 Weinberg chapter, p. 69.

112 Van Dyke chapter, p. 206 citing Gananath Obeyesekere on the Sri Lankan riots of 1983.

113 Van Dyke chapter, p. 210.

114 Van Dyke chapter, p. 212.

115 Van Dyke chapter, p. 213.

116 Stanley Lieberson and Arnold R. Silverman, "The Precipitants and Underlying Conditions of Race Riots," in Grimshaw, *Racial Violence*, pp. 368–9.

117 Although Grimshaw himself does not go to the extent of blaming the police for the occurrence of riots, he notes that "the claim has been made that major racial violence in the United States has occurred only when the police have

been corrupt, partisan, ineffective, or some combination of these three characteristics"; Grimshaw, "Factors Contributing to Color Violence," p. 257.

118   Rogger, "Conclusion and Overview," p. 316.

119   Editorial, *New York Times*, July 31, 1919, in Grimshaw, *Racial Violence*, p. 88.

120   Grimshaw, "Lawlessness and Violence in America," in Grimshaw, *Racial Violence*, p. 27. *Cf.* his reference to police misbehavior as an "alleged ... precipitating cause of the riots" in Chicago in 1919; Grimshaw, "Actions of Police and the Military in American Race Riots," p. 270.

121   The National Advisory Commission on Civil Disorders, "Detroit," in Grimshaw, *Racial Violence*, p. 219.

122   Grimshaw, "Actions of Police and the Military in American Race Riots," p. 277.

123   Rogger, "Conclusion and Overview," p. 317.

124   Rogger, "Conclusion and Overview," p. 325.

125   Rogger, "Conclusion and Overview," p. 326.

126   Rogger, "Conclusion and Overview," p. 327.

127   Rogger, "Conclusion and Overview," p. 329; Rogger's view that the 1881 pogrom was not officially sponsored is now the generally accepted view among historians and is strongly supported in the same volume by Aronson, "The anti-Jewish Pogroms in Russia in 1881," p. 51

128   Rogger, "Conclusion and Overview," p. 330.

129   Rogger, "Conclusion and Overview," p. 331.

130   Rogger, "Conclusion and Overview," p. 347.

131   Rogger, "Conclusion and Overview," p. 345.

132   Rogger, "Conclusion and Overview," pp. 350–1.

133   Rogger, "Conclusion and Overview," p. 351.

134   Rogger, "Conclusion and Overview," p. 359.

135   Rogger, "Conclusion and Overview," p. 359–60.

136   The numbers of persons whose assembly is required to define a riotous mob varies in law from country to country and from time to time. In the United States, the numbers required have historically been defined as "three persons or more, assembling together at their own authority, with the intent mutually to assist one another against all who shall oppose them, and afterward putting the design into execution in a turbulent and violent manner, whether the object in question be lawful or otherwise." Bryon L. Bargar, *The Law and Customs of Riot Duty: A Guide for National Guard Officers and Civil Authorities With Commentaries on Federal Aid* (Columbus, Ohio: By the author, 1907), p. 46, citing various state court decisions.

137   Klier, "The Pogrom Paradigm," p. 35fn2; Rogger, however, in his crusade to blame the people and save the state from responsibility insists on virtually the opposite connotation of "pogrom": "Social turbulence and mass rage, the blind destructiveness which might strike out in any direction, were always implict in the word [pogrom]"; Rogger, "Conclusion and Overview," p. 315. Somehow, it does not seem to trouble him that his view is the same as that of the Russian state which, as Aronson points out in connection with the 1881 pogroms, "adopted an explanation of the pogroms ... in line with its traditional view of the Jewish Question, namely, that the riots were a spontaneous outburst of popular anger against Jewish exploitation"; Aronson, "The anti-Jewish Pogroms in Russia in 1881," p. 46. Aronson notes a few pages on as well that "the evidence

argues against a view of the pogroms as simply a spontaneous outburst of peasant hostility towards the Jews"; p. 49.

138   Once again, of course, Rogger is quite on the opposite side: "Evidence from Germany in 1819, as well as from other times and places, indicates that large and small eruptions were rarely, if ever, the result of prior planning or coordination"; Rogger, "Conclusion and Overview," p. 326.

139   Keith describes the background to the riots in Britain as "a series of policies which have sustained the systematic racial subordination of one class of British citizens, [which] have become built into the daily routine of British policing and yet are understood as a normal facet of daily life; Keith, *Race, Riots and Policing*, p. 6.

140   Das, "Introduction," p. 7.

141   Rogger, "Conclusion and Overview," pp. 315–16.

142   Rogger, "Conclusion and Overview," pp. 321–2.

143   Weinberg chapter, p. 62.

144   Rogger, "Conclusion and Overview," p. 327.

145   Donald Horowitz, *Ethnic Groups and Conflict* (Berkeley: University of California Press, 1985), pp. 179–90. Horowitz's arguments are rooted in "frustration-aggression theory," in connection with which see also his "Direct, Displaced, and Cumulative Ethnic Aggression," *Comparative Politics*, VI, No. 1 (October, 1973), 1–16.

146   For an analysis and critique of the ideas on this subject of the principal theorists of the plural society, namely, J. S. Furnivall, M. G. Smith, Pierre L. van den Berghe, and Arendt Lijphart, see Paul R. Brass, *Ethnic Groups and the State* (London: Croom Helm, 1985), ch. 1.

147   Hill chapter, p. 103. He does not, however, by any means absolve the German people as a whole for these acts, for he remarks that, although "most actions took place with the encouragement of the regime or upon direct order, ... individual acts were revealing of popular mentalities"; p. 108.

148   Van Dyke chapter, p. 201.

149   Van Dyke chapter, p. 205.

150   *Cf.* Ashish Nandy, "The Politics of Secularism and the Recovery of Religious Tolerance," in Das, *Mirrors of Violence*, p. 85: "The anti-Sikh riots which took place in Delhi in November 1984" as well as "anti-Muslim riots in Ahmedabad in 1985" and "anti-Hindu riots in Bangalore in 1986 – all were associated not so much with religious hatred as with political cost-calculations and/or economic greed."

151   The Chaturvedis note how, during the various phases of the Ayodhya movement, it became clear that "be it the beat constable in a riot situation, the DM Faizabad or SSP Faizabad," more and more "Hindu agents" of the state in India "are finding it more and more difficult to stifle what they see as their own conscience and render unquestioning obedience to the dictates of an increasingly alien state"; Chaturvedis chapter, this volume, p. 190.

152   *Cf.* Ashish Banerjee, "'Comparative Curfew': Changing Dimensions of Communal Politics in India," in Das, *Mirrors of Violence,* p. 56: "Lower personnel of the State Reserve Constabulary, at least in north India, have usually been communally biased on account of the social class from which they are recruited and the predominant religious group to which they belong. But in recent years this has worsened. This is largely explained by the fact that often

senior officials themselves are not secular." See also Engineer, "An Analytical Study of the Meerut Riot," pp. 274–5, who recounts incidents of public respect shown by two senior police and administrative officers in Meerut, "notorious for their anti-Muslim bias," to the head of the anti-Muslim, Hindu communal organization, the RSS. These were also the "officers who ordered firing on Muslims" during the riot in that city in September–October, 1982.

153   It is an issue in contemporary polemical controversy in India whether a Hindu state in power would necessarily be on the side of Hindus in every conflict. The BJP, the principal party of militant Hindu nationalism, declares that there will be no riots under its administration. Only one relatively small riot occurred during the less than two-year administration of the BJP in the largest Indian state, Uttar Pradesh, between 1991 and December 6, 1992. However, the direct complicity of the state chief minister and his cabinet in the destruction of the mosque at Ayodhya and, therefore, in the horrendous riotous consequences which followed is widely believed in India and by this writer.

154   Friedland and Hecht chapter, p. 132.

155   See, for example, Lee E. Williams, II, *Post-War Riots in America, 1919 and 1946: How the Pressures of War Exacerbated American Urban Tensions to the Breaking Point* (Lewiston: The Edwin Mellen Press, 1991), pp. 101–2 on "the Omaha lynching and rioting" of 1919.

156   Tomlinson, "The Development of a Riot Ideology," p. 230.

157   Spiegel, "Hostility, Aggression and Violence," p. 333; see also Smelser, *Theory of Collective Behavior*, ch. 8, in whose model of the development of "hostile outbursts," "hostile beliefs" play an important role.

158   Weinberg, for example, refers to the existence of "popular prejudices and a Judeophobia prevalent among many gentile Odessans," p. 58. Rogger, "Conclusion and Overview," p. 349 refers to violence against Jews during the Russian Civil War as arising out of "the need and wish to see the Jews as authors of the nation's misfortunes."

159   Tambiah, *Sri Lanka*, pp. 56–7.

160   *E.g.*, see Peach, "A Geographical Perspective," pp. 396–7 where it is argued that Black rioting is a response to the "pervasive racism in British society, particularly in its manifestation in the relationship between the police and Afro-Caribbean youth."

161   Keith, *Race, Riots and Policing*, p. 6.

162   Keith, *Race, Riots and Policing*, pp. 22, 24.

163   Keith, *Race, Riots and Policing*, p. 25.

164   Greenbaum, "Bibliographical Essay," p. 377.

165   Bessel, *Political Violence and the Rise of Nazism*, p. 75.

166   Keith, *Race, Riots and Policing*.

167   In effect, I am arguing *contra* Peirce that insofar as the social and human sciences are concerned, there are occasions when doubt should be preserved rather than resolved through the search for a consensus, for the fixing of belief through rigorous hypothesis-testing. Of course, one response might be that the questions asked about these events known as riots and pogroms are not sufficiently precise and that the framing of more precise questions might lead to a cumulation of answers concerning their causes, which would constitute a consensus about them. My reply would be that we might very well arrive at a consensus on particular aspects of such large-scale events, for example, on the nature of the

immediate precipitating incident, on the precise roles played by organized groups or what I have called "riot specialists" in converting such incidents into a large-scale riot, on the behavior of the police, and the like. However, it is no good to say that, if our inquiries could be continued to the end, we would arrive at an understanding of the whole picture through such cumulations. In practice, the room left after all such inquiries will leave substantial areas of doubt about particular events and sufficient grounds for varying interpretations depending upon the weight placed upon particular incidents and factors in contributing to the whole. Indeed, it is necessary to go further and say that the grounds for doubt ought to be greatest concerning such events just when a consensus has been reached. On Peirce's notions concerning the "fixation of belief," see Charles S. Peirce, *Selected Writings (Values in a Universe of Change)*, ed. Philip P. Weiner (New York: Dover, 1958), ch. 5 (pp. 91–112) and C. J. Misak, *Truth and the End of Inquiry: A Peircean Account of Truth* (Oxford: Clarendon Press, 1991).

2. Anti-Jewish Violence and Revolution in Late Imperial Russia: Odessa, 1905

Robert Weinberg

Towards the end of the nineteenth century, Russian anti-Semitism turned savage as Jews became the targets of unprecedented attacks resulting in thousands of casualties and property damage in millions of roubles. Anti-Jewish pogroms occurred in waves: the first started in the wake of the assassination of Tsar Alexander II in 1881 and petered out several years later, while the second began in 1903 and peaked in the fall of 1905, at the height of Russia's first revolution. Violence against Russian Jews again reared its ugly head in the aftermath of 1917, when peasant rebels and anti-Bolshevik armies roamed the countryside and massacred tens of thousands of Jews during the Civil War.[1]

In the weeks following the publication of Tsar Nicholas II's Manifesto of October 17, 1905, which granted fundamental civil and political liberties, violent attacks on mainly Jews but also non-Jewish students, intellectuals and other national minorities occurred throughout urban and rural Russia, resulting in deaths and injuries to thousands of people. In the port city of Odessa, the police reported that at least 400 Jews and 100 non-Jews were killed and approximately 300 people, mostly Jews, were injured, with slightly over 1,600 Jewish houses, apartments and stores incurring damage. These official figures undoubtedly underestimate the true extent of the damage, as other informed sources indicate substantially higher numbers of persons killed and injured.[2]

This essay focuses on the tragic events that transpired in Odessa in October 1905 in an effort to understand the dynamics of anti-Jewish pogroms in late Imperial Russia. As the fourth largest city in the Russian Empire at the turn of the twentieth century, Odessa's 403,000 residents experienced as much social and political unrest as any other city during 1905, and its Jewish inhabitants, numbering nearly 140,000, were victims of the most vicious and bloody pogrom in that year. I am particularly concerned here with exploring the timing of the pogrom, analyzing the social composition and motives of the pogromists, and examining the connection between the eruption of ethnic conflict and the revolutionary events of 1905.

The pogrom that ravaged Odessa Jewry in 1905 grew out of developments specific to Odessa as well as the general political crisis confronting the autocracy in 1905 and the unrest that marred the urban landscape of Russia in that revolutionary year. The pogrom must also be examined in the context of the strains contributing to the social and political instability of late Imperial Russia. Finally, the particular events that triggered the pogrom need to be placed against the backdrop of anti-Semitism in the city, the structure of Odessa society, and the course of the 1905 revolution in Odessa.

I have therefore divided the essay into several sections. Taken together, they form a multi-layered explanation of the pogrom that proceeds from the general "environmental" factors to the proximate causes of the violence. The first part of this essay is an overview of Odessa society on the eve of 1905, with particular emphasis on how the position of Jews in the local economy and the nature of Jewish–gentile relations provided fertile soil for anti-Semitic violence. It is followed by a discussion of the revolutionary events and the process of political polarization in Odessa that preceded the pogrom and served as catalyzing agents. I then analyze the events that triggered the pogrom, evaluate the problems of organization, premeditation and culpability, and offer my reflections on the social basis of pogromist behavior and the consequences of the unrest. Finally, I conclude the essay with a brief comparison of events in Odessa with the pogrom in the nearby city of Ekaterinoslav in order to highlight the implications of ethnic violence for our understanding of late Imperial Russian society and politics.

THE JEWISH POPULATION AND ANTI-SEMITISM IN ODESSA

Founded in the last decade of the eighteenth century, Odessa emerged as a significant commercial, financial and cultural center during the nineteenth century. It ranked as Russia's number one port for foreign trade by 1900, handling the shipment of nearly all the wheat and more than half the other grains exported from Russia. Odessa's meteoric growth was facilitated by the fact that the government did not inhibit but rather encouraged all residents – Russians, non-Russians, foreigners, and Jews alike – to participate actively in the life of the city. Odessa was an open, enlightened and cosmopolitan city by Russian standards: it tolerated diversity and innovation, welcoming persons of all nationalities who could contribute to its development. Greeks, Italians and Jews helped set the tempo of economic life in Odessa and assumed active roles in the city's cultural affairs. Jews were especially welcome in Odessa and were exempt from many of the onerous burdens and restrictions that coreligionists in other areas of the Pale of Settlement endured.

Unfortunately, this receptive environment clashed with popular prejudices and a Judeophobia prevalent among many gentile Odessans. During the nineteenth century Jews fell victim to anti-Semitic violence in Odessa on numerous occasions: pogroms in which Jews were killed and wounded, and Jewish houses and businesses suffered substantial damage occurred in 1821, 1859, 1871, 1881, and 1900. Apart from these dramatic outbursts, anti-Jewish sentiment among Odessa's non-Jewish population manifested itself in other ways. Gangs of Jewish and Russian youths often engaged in bloody brawls, and every year at Eastertime rumors of impending attacks circulated through the city's Jewish community. The appearance after the turn of the century of militantly chauvinistic and pro-tsarist organizations that engaged in Jew-baiting and other anti-Semitic activities fueled apprehension and fear among Odessa's Jews.[3]

Popular anti-Semitism in Odessa was rooted in socio-economic and political realities as perceived by gentile Odessans who tended to harbor exaggerated fears of Odessa Jewry as a danger to the well-being of society. Over the course of the nineteenth century, religious hatred, which was the traditional base of anti-Semitism, was supplanted by social and economic concerns as a source of anti-Jewish sentiments. The increasing prominence of Jews in the commercial life of the city, particularly their success in the grain trade, played no small role in fueling resentment of Jews and fomenting anti-Jewish violence. In a society which considered agricultural pursuits productive and commerce exploitive, it is not surprising that Jews, who were heavily involved in trade as middlemen and brokers, were regarded as parasitic members of society who made their livings at the expense of non-Jews.

The growing visibility of Jews enhanced the predisposition of Russian residents of Odessa to blame Jews for their difficulties. According to some Russians, exploitation by and competition with Jews figured prominently as the causes of the 1871 pogrom. Some insisted that "the Jews exploit us," while others, especially the unemployed, blamed increased Jewish settlement in Odessa for reduced employment opportunities and lower wages.[4]

As elsewhere in Russia and Western Europe, many non-Jews in Odessa perceived Jews as possessing an inordinate amount of wealth, power and influence. As evidence they could point to the steady growth of the city's Jewish population during the nineteenth century – from approximately 14,000 (total population of 100,000, or 14 percent) in 1858 to nearly 140,000 (total population 403,000, or 35 percent) in 1897.[5] The increasingly prominent role played by Jews in the commercial and industrial life of the city after mid-century also contributed to resentment against Odessa's Jewish community. By 1910 Jewish firms handled nearly 90 percent of the export trade in grain products. By century's end Jews also occupied prominent positions in manufacturing; even though Jews in 1887 owned 35 percent of all factories, these firms produced 57 percent of the total factory output (in roubles) for that year.

Despite the outstanding success of some Jews in economic pursuits, the common perception that the growing Jewish presence threatened to result in total Jewish domination had little basis in reality. The bulk of wealth in Odessa still remained in the hands of non-Jews, and the number of gentiles involved in commerce and manufacturing counterbalanced the economic role played by Jews. According to the 1897 census, thousands of Russians and Ukrainians were engaged in commercial activities of some sort, especially the marketing of agricultural products, and comprised approximately a third of the total number of individuals listed as earning their livings from trade. On the eve of 1905 approximately half the licenses granting permission to engage in commercial and industrial pursuits were given to non-Jews, and in 1910 non-Jews owned slightly under half the large stores and trading firms and 44 percent of small shops. On the eve of World War I foreigners and Russians, many of whom employed primarily Russian workers, owned the majority of enterprises under factory inspection in Odessa. Jews in 1910 owned only 17 percent of real estate parcels in the city, down from 20 percent a decade earlier, while gentiles controlled about half of all large commercial enterprises.[6]

Thus, contrary to popular perceptions prevalent among non-Jews in both Odessa and throughout Russia, Odessa was not controlled by Jews. Wealthy Jews could not translate their wealth into political influence and power. Only a handful of Odessa's Jews lived from investments in land, stocks and bonds, or worked for the Imperial government, the judiciary or the municipal administration. This was due in part to the 1892 municipal reform which made it more difficult for Jews to occupy government posts and stripped Russian Jewry of the right to elect representatives to city councils. That year the responsibility for appointing Jewish city councillors was assigned to a special municipal bureau.[7]

In contrast to the wealthy and influential stratum of Jews, which never constituted more than a fraction of the total Jewish population, the vast majority of Odessa Jews eked out meager livings as shopkeepers, hawkers, salesclerks, *shmata* (rag) dealers, domestic servants, day laborers, workshop employees, and factory hands. Poverty was a way of life for most Jews in Odessa, as it was also for most non-Jewish residents. Isidor Brodovskii, in his study of Jewish poverty in Odessa at the turn of the century, estimated that nearly 50,000 Jews were destitute and another 30,000 were poverty-stricken.[8]

Despite the disparity between popular perception and the reality of Jewish wealth and power, a reversal in Odessa's economic fortunes at the turn of the century strengthened anti-Jewish sentiments among its Russian residents. Russia entered a deep recession as the great industrial spurt of the 1890s faltered. In turn, Odessa's economy suffered a setback due to the decrease in the demand for manufactured goods, the drop in the supply of grain available for export, and the drying up of credit. Conditions continued to deteriorate as the year 1905 approached, due to the outbreak of war between Russia and Japan in 1904. Trade, the mainstay of Odessa's economy, declined even further and the city's industrial sector, which had grown dramatically since 1890, entered a period of retrenchment.[9]

THE YEAR 1905 IN ODESSA

Let us now turn our attention to the year 1905 itself since the pogrom needs to be understood within the context of both empire-wide political developments and the emergence of a radicalized Odessa labor movement in 1905. In that year the Romanov dynasty faced a crisis of major proportions as a political movement of peasants, workers, white-collar employees, professionals, intellectuals, soldiers, and even noble landowners challenged the time-honored prerogatives of autocratic government. Through widespread political agitation, urban strike actions and rural rebellions, the various strands of the opposition movement nearly brought the government to its knees.

As elsewhere in urban Russia, Odessa workers played a crucial role in the effort to reform the autocracy. During the first half of the year, they engaged in a series of work stoppages that began initially as efforts to win improved working conditions but slowly evolved into a movement that demanded political concessions from the regime. Workers capped their campaign to win rights of citizenship with the formation of trade unions and a Soviet of Workers' Deputies in late 1905.

Sporadic strikes in March and April grew into massive walkouts in May and a general strike in June.[10] On June 13 Cossacks shot several workers from metalworking and machine-building factories who had been on strike since the beginning of May. The next day workers retaliated by walking off their jobs and paralyzing life in the city. Odessa became the scene of popular disorders: pitched battles between workers and government forces ensued as the workers, helped by children and teenagers, erected barricades from overturned trams and uprooted telephone poles. Civilians ambushed policemen and soldiers on patrol, disarming and savagely beating them, sometimes fatally.

The police had a busy day arresting persons whom they caught on the streets with guns, ammunition and bombs, but they were helpless to restore order.

The battleship *Potemkin* (memorialized in Sergei Eisenstein's 1927 film), whose crew had mutinied and murdered its captain and officers, arrived in Odessa's harbor in the early morning hours of June 15 night and diverted the workers from further confrontation with their employers and the government. That day thousands of Odessans, instead of intensifying the strike, jammed the port district in order to view the battleship and rally behind the mutinous sailors. By late afternoon some members of the crowd began to ransack warehouses and set fire to the harbor's wooden buildings. Although available sources do not allow a precise determination of the composition of the rioters, partial arrest records reveal that non-Jewish vagrants, dock-workers and other day laborers comprised the majority. To suppress the unrest, the military cordoned off the harbor and opened fire on the trapped crowd. By the next morning well over a thousand people had died, victims of either the soldiers' bullets or the fire which consumed the harbor. Economic life returned to normal several days later as stores reopened and workers returned to work, although some 20,000 soldiers patrolled the streets.

These events are important not only for what they tell us about the heightening social and political tensions in the city but also for what they reveal about the state of Jewish–gentile relations, which grew more ominous during these tumultuous times. Anti-Jewish feelings ran particularly high throughout Russia during the first half of 1905, with pogroms occurring in several cities. In Odessa anti-Semites became more vociferous in their attacks on Jews in the spring, when two militantly patriotic and pro-tsarist groups, later accused by the mayor of fomenting a pogromist atmosphere, launched an effort to stir up anti-Jewish sentiments. Their newspapers were frequently distributed free throughout the city, especially in the harbor and workers' districts. Beginning in late January 1905 leaflets circulated blaming Georgians, Poles, Armenians, but especially the Jews for anti-government opposition. They called upon Russians to "beat the Jews, students and wicked people who seek to harm our Fatherland" and rid Russia of Jews who "are the cause of evil and grief." There were no outbreaks of ethnic violence at this time, however.[11]

During the June disorders right-wing agitators and pogrom-mongers once again took to the streets. They accused Jews of instigating the current disorders and encouraged gentiles to attack them. In several incidents Jewish workers and revolutionaries retaliated against these provocations by either injuring or killing some of the rabble-rousers.[12] On June 20, an anonymous, virulently anti-Semitic, four-page broadside entitled *Odesskie dni (Odessa Days)* appeared. It blamed the Jews for the recent disorders and the tragedy at the port. Accusing Jews of instigating the unrest and enlisting the support of unwitting Russians, the author of the broadside stated that Jews initiated the shootings on June 14 and 15 and were responsible for setting fire to the port. The tract ended with a call to hold the Jewish community of Odessa collectively responsible for the destruction and demanded that Jews compensate gentiles who suffered property damage and personal loss. In addition, it called for the disarming of all Jews and suggested a general search of all Jewish apartments in the city.[13] Though *Odesskie dni* did not call for acts of anti-Jewish violence and its diatribes did not lead to any known attacks on Jews, its appearance graphically illustrates how in times of social unrest and political uncertainty anti-Semitism could come to the fore.

The accusations expressed in *Odesskie dni* found their way into the reports of government officials who held Odessa Jewry responsible for the June unrest. Gendarme chief N. M. Kuzubov wrote that the instigators of the disorders and arson were "exclusively Jews," and Count A. P. Ignat'ev, the fiercely reactionary chairman of a government commission set up in 1905 to address the issues of state security and religious minorities, seconded this conclusion in his report on the June disorders. Even the British Consul in Odessa believed Jews were behind the recent disorders.[14] These reports highlight the emotionally charged atmosphere of Russian–Jewish relations in Odessa and the extent to which government officials were hard-pressed to make nuanced assessments. In their search for simple explanations and their unwillingness to dig deeper into the root causes of the turmoil in Odessa, bureaucrats and police alike revealed the extent to which they were conditioned by popular prejudices and social stereotypes. In doing so they were following a tradition of accusing Jews for initiating the trouble in Odessa.

While many reports of Jewish revolutionary activity were exaggerations or even fabrications, Jews did play a role in the opposition to the autocracy. Jewish workers figured prominently in the ranks of the various social democratic organizations operating in Odessa, and several dozen Jews were included in the list of 133 revolutionaries either considered politically unreliable, arrested or exiled after the June Days. During the summer not only did the police arrest several Jews for making and stockpiling bombs, but a leaflet distributed throughout the city urged Jews to arm themselves, struggle for civil and political freedom and overthrow the autocracy.[15] Like others throughout the Empire, Odessa's university became the locus of anti-government activity after August when the tsar granted administrative autonomy to Russia's universities and thereby removed them from the jurisdiction of the police. Jewish youths, students and workers filled the ranks of the crowds that attended the rallies at the university in September and October. Jews also actively participated in the wave of work stoppages, demonstrations and street disorders that broke out in mid-October. On October 16, a day of major disturbances, 197 of the 214 persons arrested were Jews.[16] Two days later Jews eagerly celebrated the political concessions granted in the October Manifesto as the first step in the civil and political emancipation of Russian Jewry. Their fervor terrified those Odessans who believed that the Jews were eager to destroy the Orthodox faith and place a Jew on the throne. These events confirmed many high-ranking police and other officials in the belief that Jews were indeed a seditious element.

One more aspect of Odessa society and politics contributed to an atmosphere conducive to pogroms and served as a remote causal explanation of the 1905 pogrom. This is the impact of official discrimination against Jewry and governmental tolerance and at times sponsorship of anti-Jewish organizations and propaganda. As Leonidas Hill suggests in his piece on *Kristallnacht* in this volume, government policies and pronouncements could set a tone that fostered popular acceptance of violence against Jews as an appropriate form of behavior. In similar fashion, the legal disabilities and mistreatment endured by Russian Jewry since the late eighteenth century engendered an attitude that did not look askance at anti-Jewish prejudices and actions and may have also signaled to anti-Semites that authorities in Odessa would perhaps countenance violence against Jews.

Thus fertile soil for a pogrom existed in Odessa. The fear of Jewish domination, the legacy of anti-Jewish violence, economic resentment, and alarm at the visible role Jews were playing in the opposition to the regime provided the necessary psychological and material preconditions for the outbreak of anti-Jewish violence. Nonetheless, the fact that longstanding ethnic tensions mixed with short-term political developments such as the revolutionary events of 1905 created a situation ripe for a pogrom should not lead us to the conclusion that ethnic violence was inevitable. Indeed, it was the events themselves during the several days prior to the October pogrom that hold the key to understanding the timing of the anti-Jewish disorders, the intensity of the pogrom, and the failure of those officials responsible for maintaining law and order to suppress the pogromists.

THE OCTOBER POGROM

In the wake of the June disorders, the labor movement in Odessa entered a period of remission for the duration of the summer, much as elsewhere in the Empire where the strike movement reached its nadir of the year in August and September. The next wave of labor unrest started in September and swelled to a peak of the year in October when at least 481,000 workers went on strike.[17] The re-emergence of mass unrest in urban Russia crystallized in conjunction with several other developments that affected political stability: the signing in August of the Treaty of Portsmouth which marked Russia's humiliating defeat at the hands of Japan; the radicalization of the liberal movement after Nicholas II announced in August plans for elections to the country's first national legislative assembly; the rising up of peasants and national minorities; an outbreak of military mutinies; and the revival of student radicalism after the granting of university autonomy. The movement against the autocracy culminated with a general strike that forced Nicholas to issue the October Manifesto, which established a popularly elected legislative assembly and guaranteed fundamental civil liberties. The revival of the revolution and the government's timely concessions set the stage for confrontation between the forces of revolution and reaction. Militant right-wing organizations and patriotic student groups consolidated their ranks, while radical student groups reinforced the organized revolutionary parties already active in Odessa.

Public order in Odessa had been breached with the outbreak of bloody confrontations between the populace and the government several days before the pogrom began on October 19. On October 15, a day after the police had injured several high school students who were boycotting classes in sympathy for striking railway workers, rallies attracting thousands of concerned Odessans were held. Radical students and revolutionaries appealed to workers to start a general strike, collected donations for guns and ammunition, and made the rounds of factories and workshops. Odessa was a powderkeg ready to explode, and on October 16 groups of students, youths and workers, without any signs of leadership, direction and coordination, roamed the streets of Odessa, building barricades and engaging the police and military in combat. Government troops encountered fierce resistance when they took action to restore order and dismantle the barricades. Greeted with rocks and gunfire as they approached, soldiers retaliated and returned fire. Military patrols were also targets of snipers positioned in apartments and on rooftops. The shooting continued throughout the afternoon of the sixteenth, but by early evening the army had secured the streets of Odessa. The police disarmed and arrested scores of demonstrators, systematically bludgeoning some into unconsciousness. The exact number of casualties is difficult to determine, with officials reporting nine civilians killed and approximately 80 wounded, and seven soldiers and policemen injured.[18]

Monday, October 17 passed without any serious disturbances, though tensions remained high. The military continued to patrol the city, but life did not return to normal. Schools and many stores remained closed and, even though not all workers responded to the appeal for a general strike, at least 4,000 workers – many of whom were Jewish – walked off their jobs. Groups of workers congregated outside those stores open for business and passed the time singing and drinking vodka. Officials feared that the relative peace of October 17 was only the calm before the storm.

When the storm broke on October 18, events had gone way beyond the control of local officials. The all-nation struggle against the autocracy had succeeded in winning significant concessions from the regime in the form of the October Manifesto. News reached Odessa by the morning of October 18 and prompted thousands of Odessans to celebrate in the streets. For Jews living in the Russian Empire, the promised reforms heralded the initial blow against the legal disabilities which they had endured for well over a century. But Jews were not the only ones to welcome the concessions of October 17 with open arms; Russians and other non-Jewish national minorities also eagerly celebrated the Manifesto as the first step in the long-awaited restructuring of Russian society and politics.

Indeed, thousands of Odessans, drunk with the victory symbolized by the Manifesto, celebrated the tsar's capitulation by unfurling red flags and banners with antigovernment slogans. Shouts of "Down with the Autocracy," "Long Live Freedom" and "Down with the Police" pierced the morning air. Apartment dwellers draped red carpets and shawls from balconies and windows, and groups of celebrants forced passersby to doff their hats or bow before the red flags. In the city council building, demonstrators ripped down the portrait of the tsar, substituting a red flag for the Imperial colors and collecting money for weapons. Throughout the day orators delivered impromptu speeches on street corners, and thousands of people from all over Odessa assembled in front of the city council building. Excited by all that was transpiring and hoping to inspire the populace to strike a death blow to the autocracy, revolutionaries urged their audiences to continue the struggle for full political freedom and called upon Odessans to arm themselves.[19]

At first the crowds were peaceful, but the mood of the demonstrators grew angry as the day wore on. Celebrants – primarily Jewish youths according to official accounts – viciously attacked and disarmed policemen and began shooting at troops patrolling the city. By mid-afternoon city governor Dmitrii Neidhardt had received reports that 2 policemen had been killed, 10 wounded and 22 disarmed, with many others abandoning their posts in order to avoid injury.[20]

The attacks were not limited to policemen, however. Nor were Jews the sole culprits. During the course of the day tensions between those Odessans heralding the Manifesto and those disapproving of the concessions granted by Nicholas and resenting the flagrant disrespect shown by the Manifesto's celebrants reached a breaking point.

Most accounts of the October pogroms assert that they began when members of organized patriotic processions, intent on teaching Jews a lesson, clashed with celebrants of the Manifesto as a prelude to a full-scale attack on Jews and their property.[21] In Odessa, however, confrontation between Jews and Russians began spontaneously on October 18, the day before a pro-government march occurred. Armed clashes between Jews and Russians originated on the eighteenth near the Jewish neighborhood of Moldavanka. The fighting started when a group of Jews carrying desecrated portraits of the tsar and waving red flags to celebrate the October Manifesto tried to force a group of recalcitrant Russian workers, outraged by the sight of the portraits, to doff their caps. Harsh words were exchanged, a scuffle ensued and then shots rang out. Both groups scattered, but quickly reassembled in nearby streets and resumed fighting. The clashes soon turned into an anti-Jewish riot, as Russians indiscriminately attacked Jews and began to vandalize and loot Jewish homes and stores in the neighborhood. The troops which were summoned to quell the disorders were met by gunshots and were equally vigilant in their efforts to restrain both Russians and Jews. They restored order by early evening but not before four Russians had been killed, dozens of Russians wounded – including policemen – and twelve Russians arrested. The number of Jews injured or arrested is unknown.[22]

Thus what began as as a fray between two groups with opposing political views almost immediately transformed itself into an ethnic and religious battle: the Russians did not vent their hostilities against other Russians celebrating in the streets, but rather soon turned on Jews as the source of Russia's current problems. But the fact that the rioters also initially attacked policemen and troops summoned to quell the disorders suggest that on the eighteenth they were not yet fully focused on Jews. Moreover, the actions of the military and police prove that local officials at this point did not welcome the disorders and tried to prevent the outbreak of anti-Jewish violence.

The situation deteriorated the next day when the fighting degenerated into a full-scale bloodbath. At mid-morning on October 19, hundreds of Russians – children, women and men – gathered in various parts of the city for patriotic marches to display their loyalty to the tsar. Like other rallies organized throughout Russia by extreme, right-wing organizations such as the Black Hundreds, this procession enjoyed the tacit blessing of local authorities and was used by advocates of an unreformed autocracy to bolster the government and undermine the concessions of October. Day laborers, especially those employed at the docks, comprised a major element of the crowd that assembled at the harbor. They were joined by Russian factory and construction workers, shopkeepers, salesclerks, workshop employees, other day laborers, and vagrants.[23] The main contingent of marchers assembled at Customs Square at the harbor, where the procession's organizers distributed flags, icons and portraits of the tsar. Plainsclothes policemen reportedly handed out bottles of vodka, along with money and guns.[24] Onlookers and passersby joined the procession as the demonstrators made their way from the port to the city center. Singing the national anthem and religious hymns and, according to some reports, shouting "Down with the Jews" and "They need a beating," they stopped at the city council building and substituted the Imperial colors for the red flag that demonstrators had raised the previous day. They then headed toward the cathedral in central Odessa, stopping en route at the residences of city governor Neidhardt and military commander Aleksandr Kaul'bars. Kaul'bars, fearing confrontation between the patriotic marchers and left-wing students and revolutionaries, asked them to disperse. Some heeded his request, but most members of the procession continued their march. Neidhardt, on the other hand, greeted the patriots enthusiastically and urged them to hold a memorial service at the cathedral. After a brief prayer service, the procession continued to march through the streets of central Odessa.[25]

The march was soon marred by a round of gunfire that left dead a young boy carrying an icon. Although most accounts of the incident assert that the shots came from surrounding buildings, probably from the offices of a liberal-leaning newspaper, the evidence regarding this incident is not conclusive, and we cannot determine with certainty who fired first. In any case, the immediate consequence of the shooting was panic as members of the patriotic procession sought to avoid the shots that rang out from rooftops, balconies and apartment windows. The gunfire was soon joined by homemade bombs thrown by revolutionaries and self-defense units organized by students and Jews. The stepped-up violence triggered a chain reaction: convinced that Jews were responsible for the shootings, members of the patriotic demonstration began to shout "Beat the Kikes" and "Death to the Kikes" and went on a rampage, attacking Jews and destroying Jewish apartments, houses and stores.

The course of events was similar in many other parts of the city, as radicals and government supporters engaged in fierce fighting. Though it is unclear who started the trouble in the city center, in the outlying factory district of Peresyp, where no patriotic procession took place, the pogrom started only after armed thugs from the city center arrived and began to incite local residents. Mob violence against the Jews was difficult to contain or control once it started. By mid-afternoon a brutal and savage onslaught against Jews had developed, and the looting, pillage and murder raged until October 22.[26]

For several days Russians savagely and relentlessly beat, mutilated and murdered defenseless Jewish men, women and children. They hurled Jews out of windows, tore people's eyeballs from their sockets, discharged guns inside the mouths of victims, raped and cut open the stomachs of pregnant women, and slaughtered infants in front of their parents. In one particularly gruesome incident, a woman was hung upside down by her legs and the bodies of her six dead children were arranged on the floor below.[27] Frightened Jews huddled together in their apartments and waited for marauding gangs to break in and set about their business of murder and pillage.

The lurid details of the savage atrocities perpetrated against the Jews, the likes of which had never been seen in Odessa, sent shock waves throughout Russia and the international community. The viciousness of the pogromists was intensified in part by the refuge of anonymity afforded by large rampaging crowds; the Russians engaged in a collective act of national or ethnic self-affirmation. As Daniel Brower has written in general terms about ethnic violence in late Imperial Russia, "The rioters were acting out a communal drama of ethnic hatred (Christians versus Jews)."[28]

The pogrom's unrestrained violence and destructive excesses were in large measure made possible by the failure of authorities to adopt measures to restore law and order. Low-ranking policemen and soldiers refrained from interfering and in many instances participated in the looting and killing. At times policemen, seeking to avenge the attacks of October 16 and 18 on their colleagues, provided protection for pogromists by firing on the self-defense units formed by Jews, students and revolutionaries and hindering the efforts of first-aid groups and the Red Cross. For their part, soldiers, concluding from the actions of the police that the attacks on the Jews were sanctioned by higher authorities, stood idly by while civilians looted stores and murdered unarmed Jews. Such reasoning accords with views of the 1881 pogroms in which rumors, such as that the tsar commanded people to attack Jews as punishment for their revolutionary inclinations, incited pogromist activity.[29] Eyewitnesses also reported seeing policemen directing crowds of Russians to Jewish-owned stores or Jews' apartments, while steering them away from the property of non-Jews. As the correspondent for *Collier's* reported, "Ikons and crosses were placed in windows and hung outside doors to mark the residences of the Russians, and in almost every case this was a sufficient protection." Indeed, *Odesskii pogrom and samooborona* (*The Odessa Pogrom and Self-Defense*), an emotional account of the October tragedy published by Labor Zionists in Paris, argues that the police more than any other group in Odessa were responsible for the deaths and pillage.[30]

Some evidence indicates that policemen acted (or failed to act) with the knowledge and tacit approval of their superiors. Neither Neidhardt nor Kaul'bars took any decisive action to suppress the disorders when they erupted. Consequently, these two officials must be held accountable for dereliction of duty. As the head of the Odessa gendarmes reported, the military did not apply sufficient energy to end the disturbances. In fact, the rioters would greet soldiers and policemen with shouts of "Hurrah" and then continue their rampage and pillage without interference.[31] It was not until the evening of October 20 that Kaul'bars ordered his troops to shoot at pogromists as well as self-defensists. Until then soldiers and police had shot at only self-defensists. Whether this directive helped restore order is unclear, but it is hard to ignore the fact that the pogrom began to peter out the next day when pogromists met with resistance from the military. Of course, the return to calm may have been due more to the exhaustion of the mobs than to any military directive and action. Yet it bears stressing that when the military did act to stop public disorders, as it did on October 18 and again on October 21 and 22, the attacks did stop. More immediate and vigorous action by the military, which had some 20,000–25,000 soldiers garrisoned in the city, might have prevented the disorders from assuming such monstrous proportions.

Kaul'bars and Neidhardt defended the behavior of the police and military, arguing that attacks by student and Jewish militias hampered efforts of policemen and soldiers to contain the violence. After all, they maintained, self-defense brigades shot not only at Russian civilians, but also at police, soldiers and Cossacks. The police and military were undoubtedly targets of civilian militias and rightly concerned about their own safety and security. Yet as the pogrom gathered momentum and degenerated into a massacre, one can hardly blame members of self-defense brigades for continuing to shoot at soldiers and policemen, many of whom were actively participating in the violence. Neidhardt and Kaul'bars reacted as if civilian militias were the only groups involved in the disturbances, conveniently ignoring how the actions of policemen and soldiers might provoke Jews and others to defend themselves. Had the police and military genuinely applied their energies to halting the unrest, the need for self-defense would have been reduced and attacks on soldiers and policemen would have dropped accordingly. Neidhardt and Kaul'bars were basically attempting to shift blame for the failure of the authorities to perform their basic law enforcement functions to the victims.

THE QUESTION OF THE RESPONSIBILITY OF THE AUTHORITIES

Conventional wisdom posits that the autocracy planned and executed the first two waves of pogroms in order to discredit the revolutionary movement and deflect popular hostility away from itself toward a helpless scapegoat which had been the traditional target of popular and official discrimination. As the eminent historian Salo Baron concluded about the 1905 pogroms, "the government itself instigated public disorders." Similarly, Simon Dubnow asserted that these attacks "had been engineered by the authorities."[32]

In recent years historians have debunked the traditional interpretation, with its emphasis on governmental conspiracy and complicity. Inspired by the path-breaking work of Hans Rogger, these scholars have reached consensus that the central government did not promote pogroms as deliberate policy. Nor did tsarist officials conspire with anti-Semitic organizations in organizing and executing them. As the author of one recent study of anti-Jewish violence during the years 1903–6 has concluded, "Upon closer inspection, theories that the government followed a conscious and deliberate 'pogrom policy' are unconvincing."[33] Even the central leadership of the most militant and anti-Semitic of political groups in early twentieth-century Russia, the Union of Russian People, did not conspire to organize and lead pogroms.[34]

Nonetheless, given what we know about the actions of the police and military, the culpability of certain local officials is less easy to dismiss. Many contemporaries blamed civilian and military authorities, specifically Neidhardt, for fostering a pogromist atmosphere and conspiring to unleash the attack against the Jews. City council members and journalists were angered by Neidhardt, who accused Odessa's Jews, students, liberals, and radicals of provoking the violence and therefore deserving what they suffered. They placed full responsibility for the bloodletting on the city governor and stressed his decision to remove the police from their posts on October 18 as the catalyst for the unrest. One national Jewish paper published in St. Petersburg called for a judicial investigation in order to reveal Neidhardt's "criminal responsibility." Neidhardt's dismissal several days after the violence subsided did not satisfy demands for his head.[35]

Despite the accusations lodged against Neidhardt, the Odessa pogrom was not a plot hatched by him and other high-ranking officials in the city. But neither was it a spontaneous riot. Politically motivated pogrom-mongers and rabble-rousers preyed upon the prejudices and anxieties of gentile Odessans and sought to channel their anger into attacks on Jews and other perceived enemies of the state. Leonidas Hill points out in reference to *Kristallnacht* that direct commands are not needed to inspire and prompt pogroms. Certain, unidentified local officials may have played an active role in promoting the pogrom as well. The government inquiry into the Odessa pogrom itself collected evidence that points to the involvement of low-ranking members of the police force in the planning and organization of the patriotic counter-demonstration and the pogrom. It stopped short, however, of suggesting that Neidhardt, as head of the police force, had planned the disorders.[36] According to the testimony of L. D. Teplitskii, an ensign in the army, as early as October 15 and 16 policemen were proposing to use force against Jews who were seen as "culprits ... in the various disorders." As one policemen told Teplitskii, "Jews want freedom – well, we'll kill two or three thousand. Then they'll know what freedom is." Teplitskii also testified to meeting a group of day laborers on the morning of October 18 who told him they had just received instructions at a police station to attack Jews that evening.[37]

Teplitskii's account is supported by additional testimony gathered by the government inquiry. An army captain stated that a policeman had told him that his superiors had given their permission for three days of violence because Jews had destroyed the tsar's portrait in the city council. In working-class neighborhoods policemen and pogromists went from door to door. After spreading rumors that Jews were slaughtering Russian families, they urged Russian residents to repel the Jews with force. Policemen reportedly compiled lists of Jewish-owned stores and Jews' apartments to facilitate attacks. One Jewish newspaper asserted that documents existed revealing how plain-clothes policemen, upon instructions of their superiors, paid pogromists from 80 kopecks to 3 roubles per day.[38]

Unfortunately, no evidence has surfaced indicating which police officials were responsible for these directives. Nor is there conclusive evidence linking Neidhardt to pogrom agitation. This is understandable: as a government official entrusted with maintaining law and order, it would have been foolhardly for Neidhardt to organize a major public disturbance. Reluctance to sanction any kind of unrest for fear of events getting out of hand would undoubtedly have been heightened in the midst of the turmoil then engulfing Odessa.

Although Neidhardt may have known about the patriotic procession and even welcomed it, this does not warrant the conclusion drawn by many Odessans that the city governor knew that the pro-government march was intended as a prelude to violence. Indeed, he took a few steps to avoid the outbreak of bloodshed between regime loyalists and their opponents. In the morning of October 19 he requested that Kaul'bars cancel permission for a planned funeral procession commemorating the deaths of protesters on October 16 in order to avert violence between the mourners and the patriotic counter-demonstration. And soon after he received news of the initial clashes on October 19 the city governor called upon the military commander to adopt measures to prevent the outbreak of a pogrom and appealed to Odessans to calm down.[39] Neidhardt was a conscientious defender of law and order: his actions prior to October indicate that he would not tolerate violations of public peace. Neidhardt possessed a strong disciplinarian streak and was willing to use the stick as well as the carrot to maintain calm.

And yet, once the pogrom began Neidhardt did not order his men into action. How can we account for his (as well as Kaul'bars's) failure to take vigorous measures to suppress the disorders as soon as the pogrom began in full force on the nineteenth? The conspicuous failure of police and soldiers to stop the pogrom stands in stark contrast to the quickness with which Neidhardt and Kaul'bars coordinated efforts on October 16 and October 18 to suppress street disturbances.

Part of the explanation may have to do with Neidhardt's underlying sympathy with the pogromists. Even though Neidhardt had made sure that anti-Semitic activities stopped short of open anti-Jewish violence prior to October, he nonetheless attended meetings of right-wing, anti-Semitic organizations where he presumably approved of the speeches condemning "cosmopolitanism and other socialist teachings" and advocating that "In our country the Russians should consider themselves masters."[40] In the midst of the October disorders, Neidhardt reportedly told a delegation of Jewish leaders, "You wanted freedom. Well, now you're getting 'Jewish freedom'."[41] From his perspective, Jews were responsible for the trouble, and the pogrom was retribution. Thus, although Neidhardt did not plan the pogrom and did not welcome public unrest, he may have viewed attacks on Jews as an effective method of squelching the revolution, which he believed was due to the machinations of Jews and other revolutionaries. Neidhardt's actions support in modified fashion the notion that officials hoped pogroms would deflect popular hostility and resentment away from the government and its policies. However in the case of Odessa, the violence against the Jews was not the result of a plot by top-ranking local authorities. The willingness of Neidhardt and Kaul'bars to tolerate the disturbances occurred only *after* the violence erupted and points out their inability both to prevent and suppress the pogrom.

The report of the government inquiry particularly castigated the city governor for withdrawing all police from their posts in the early afternoon of October 18 and waiting until October 21 before ordering his staff back to work. According to the report, Neidhardt had left Odessa defenseless by not ordering the police patrols to take vigorous action to prevent trouble and suppress the disorders.[42] The absence of police ready to maintain law and order on October 18 and 19 made for an explosive situation and allowed pogromists to have free reign of the streets. Neidhardt also deserves blame for not preventing his men from participating in the looting and pillaging. His callous refusal to heed the pleas of Jewish victims, including a rabbi and bank director who begged him to intercede, highlights his indifference to the tragic consequences of the unrest.[43]

At the same time, he may simply have been unable to control his recalcitrant police force, which was demanding higher wages and then refused to heed his order to return to duty on October 21. According to Aleksandr von Hessberg, the police force's second in command to Neidhardt, the police had decided to strike for higher wages.[44] Neidhardt may have realized that he could not depend on a severely underpaid, understaffed and disgruntled police force to maintain order in the city. The Odessa police resembled most municipal police forces throughout the Empire in its reputation for corruption. But unlike many others, the Odessa police frequently failed to obey orders and directives.[45] I do not wish to exonerate Neidhardt; these comments are meant simply to bring to the fore some of the concerns that might have limited a more vigorous response on his part, though the problem of whether he *wanted* to do so cannot be determined.

Kaul'bars also shares the burden of responsibility for not acting more promptly to restore order. His failure is not surprising, since he had a reputation for performing poorly during times of crisis. Curiously, the military commander was not censured by the government inquiry, despite the fact that his troops were already in position to act against pogromists. Kaul'bars not only discounted reports that his troops were participating in the disorders as "unsubstantiated" rumors, but like Neidhardt, he waited several days before ordering his troops to combat pogromists.[46] Defending his inaction before a delegation of city councillors on October 20, Kaul'bars stated that he could not take more decisive measures because Neidhardt had not explicitly requested the use of force to stem the disorders. Kaul'bars took action to confront the pogromists only in the evening of the twentieth, after Neidhardt reiterated a day-old request to adopt measures to prevent the outbreak of anti-Jewish violence. Evidence suggests that Kaul'bars did not act until compelled by his superiors.[47]

One question that the government inquiry attempted to answer centered around who had ultimate responsibility, Neidhardt or Kaul'bars, in suppressing the disorders. In their respective defenses, Neidhardt and Kaul'bars bitterly accused each other of dereliction of duty and claimed that the other was responsible for maintaining order. According to the chain of command, civil authorities were to request the assistance of military units when the police concluded that they were unable to maintain control. Thus, the prerogative to determine whether force should be employed resided with the city governor. But once he made such a decision, the military commander assumed independent control until the end of operations. As one historian has recently written, "This law on the use of force seemed designed to permit both civilians and the military to pass the blame for shedding Russian blood to one another. Arms could not be used without civilian authorization, but orders to fire must come from the troop commander."[48] In Odessa the military commander claimed he lacked authorization to deploy his troops; at the same time, the city governor asserted that he had in fact given Kaul'bars the green light to use arms. In an ironic bureaucratic stalemate, both men were adamant that they had followed regulations to the letter.[49]

The government inquiry ruled that Neidhardt was at fault for not following proper procedures when requesting military assistance; he accused the city governor of failing to make a determination on whether the situation required the use of arms. Thus, the report concluded that Neidhardt remained responsible for ensuring law and order in Odessa, and Kaul'bars was justified in looking to the city governor to command the troops.[50] Yet Kaul'bars's claim that he could not interfere in "civilian administration" was a feeble and self-serving excuse for his inaction, as was Neidhardt's half-hearted abdication of responsibility to the military.

The sad truth of the matter is that both police and troops were in position to act. That soldiers and police used their weapons on the side of the pogromists is a fact that the government inquiry conveniently ignored in its assessment. The bloody excesses of the pogrom were in large measure due to the poor communication between the two men responsible for law and order in the city. The tragic consequences in terms of human life make the dispute over jurisdiction and responsibility into a mockery of bureaucratic procedure and legal formalism. Conflicting lines of command may have confused Neidhardt and Kaul'bars, but this does not absolve them of their guilt for not taking more vigorous measures. Since October 19, when Neidhardt had written Kaul'bars a note asking him to take measures to prevent a pogrom, the military commander should have directed his troops to restore order. As we have seen, Kaul'bars had responded promptly to the city governor's prior requests for military assistance, but this time he did nothing to prevent the unrest. Such inaction hints at a joint decision by the police and military to let the pogrom run its course, but no evidence has been uncovered to confirm this suspicion.

Like Neidhardt, Kaul'bars was torn between his personal views and official duties. On October 21 he remarked to an an assembly of Odessa policemen that "all of us sympathize in our souls with the pogrom." But he tempered his remarks by acknowledging that neither his personal sentiments nor those of the police and military relieved them of the responsibility to maintain law and order and protect all civilians, including Jews.[51] Unfortunately, his remarks came after almost two full days of unrestrained violence and savagery. This conflict between personal values and official duty, between sympathy for the pogromists and the obligation to preserve social peace, helps account for the failure of Kaul'bars and Neidhardt to act more decisively. Undoubtedly they were galled at the prospect of ordering their men to restrain the perpetrators of the anti-Jewish violence who, in their eyes, were the only loyal subjects of the autocracy in Odessa. How could they justify shooting defenders of the tsar? Such logic and attitudes led both men to shirk their duties and allowed Odessa's Jews to fall victim to pogromist mobs.

Like many other government reports, the pogrom inquiry concluded that the Jews themselves had provoked the bloodshed since the pogrom "was only the sad consequence of the armed struggle of revolutionaries trying to seize power." It attributed previous incidents of anti-Jewish violence to economic exploitation by Jews and national hatreds. But the October disorders, according to its report, were the result of Jews "playing the dominant role in the revolutionary movement" and insulting "the national sentiments of the Russians." For government officials, then, patriotic Russians were justified in punishing Jews for such treasonous behavior as desecrating portraits of the tsar and forcing bystanders to pay tribute to revolutionary flags. They had trouble condemning those participants in the patriotic processions who tried to incite other Odessans by appealing to age-old fears and suspicions that Jews contaminated the social fabric, threatened the purity of Russian Orthodoxy, and subverted the political order. The inquiry characterized the pogrom as an unplanned offshoot of the patriotic procession; its "horrible dimensions" resulted from Neidhardt's failure to adopt adequate countermeasures.[52]

Such tortuous reasoning of blaming the victims for their suffering dated back to the 1880s when government apologists seeking to explain the anti-Jewish disturbances of 1881–2 also blamed the Jews. To the government they were exploiters of the peasantry as well as visible members of the revolutionary movement.[53] Given the course of events in Odessa in 1905, it is not surprising that officials were predisposed to view Jews as the source of the troubles besetting the autocracy. As we have already noted, the actions of certain Odessa Jews, particularly during the summer and fall, fueled the belief among conservative circles that Jews were spearheading a revolutionary assault on the autocracy. As the Okhrana chief stated, Jews were attempting to establish their "own tsardom" and were therefore responsible for the pogrom.[54] Rumors abounded among some supporters of autocracy that Jews were planning to subjugate non-Jews by establishing a "Danubian–Black Sea Republic" with Odessa as the capital and ruled by Jews who would seize land for themselves.[55]

THE ROLE OF NON-JEWISH DAY LABORERS AND DOCK WORKERS

The government inquiry was essentially correct to note the connection between the outbreak of the pogrom and revolutionary events: had there been no patriotic procession, which was a consequence of the revolution, there would have been no pogrom. But politics alone do not explain the motives of many participants in the ethnic violence. Examination of the social composition of the pogromist mobs reveals why so many Odessans joined the ranks of the pogromists. Available sources do not allow a precise determination of the composition of those responsible for the killing and looting, but they do reveal that unskilled, non-Jewish day laborers, perhaps more than any other group (including the police), filled the ranks of the mobs which attacked Jews and destroyed property.

Competition for employment between Jewish and gentile day laborers assumed special importance at dockside and in the railway depots, where thousands of unskilled workers vied for employment during the peak season of commercial activity, which began in spring and lasted well into the fall. According to the 1897 census, slightly over 16,000 workers were unskilled day laborers without permanent jobs and specific occupations, but who supplemented the city's sizable work force of dockworkers, porters and carters during the busy season. Precise data do not exist, but most estimates of the number of dockworkers in Odessa at the turn of the century range from 4,000 to 7,000, with one estimate placing the number at 20,000. Approximately half of these dockworkers were Jews, and at least 9,000 other Jews found employment as unskilled laborers elsewhere in the city by century's end. Thus, somewhere between 11,000 and 12,500 Jews worked as day laborers.[56]

Even during peak periods of port activity, operators of shipping lines, brokerage firms and warehouses did not require the services of all dockworkers looking for work. In the summer few dockworkers worked more than fifteen days a month; job competition acquired even larger dimensions during the off-season or periods of slump and recession, when over half of all dockworkers were unemployed. It is estimated that between 1900 and 1903 at least 2,000 dockworkers were unemployed at any given time.[57] Unemployment for longshoremen had increased dramatically in the late 1890s and early 1900s when the labor market began to constrict as a result of crop failures, economic recession, the Russo–Japanese War, and Odessa's declining share of the export trade in grain. The constricting labor market heightened job competition between Jewish and gentile dockworkers and led shipowners, city authorities and longshoremen to establish a quota system for Jewish and non-Jewish dockworkers after 1905.

Dependent on the activity of the port for their livelihood, day laborers in general and dockworkers in particular were usually the first workers to feel the impact of downturns in the economy. During such times, lacking even the few kopecks that night shelters charged, they often slept under the nighttime sky or in open barrels at dockside.[58] Hunger was such a constant factor in the day laborers' lives that they used a broad range of colorful phrases to express its intensity.[59] In the words of one observer, day laborers, dock-workers in particular, "perpetually curse and are dirty, ragged, drunk, and have almost lost human appearance. ... Life has passed them by; they have no hope for a better future and are concerned only with finding a piece of bread and a corner in a flophouse."[60]

Recent research on Russian labor casts doubt on the view held by many tsarist authorities and members of the radical intelligentsia that migrant workers and other members of the laboring population, as "strangers and outsiders" to Russian cities, were more prone than other urban residents to engage in public disorders and violence.[61] It is not my intention to argue that social uprootedness determined such behavior, but it bears noting that many Odessans, particularly those responsible for anti-Jewish pogroms, lived marginal lives. Though some day laborers had lived in Odessa for years and enjoyed the relative comforts and security afforded by permanent housing and fairly steady work via membership in a work gang, others had never developed family and social roots and existed on the margins of urban society.

In fact, day laborers in general and dockers in particular enjoyed a reputation throughout Russia and Western Europe as rabble-rousers and troublemakers prone to acts of public disorderliness. They constituted one element of the swelling social underbelly of Odessa society. An undercur-rent of tension and discontent existed, sometimes manifesting itself in public disturbances.

The events of October were neither the first nor the last time that day laborers and dockworkers engaged in violent behavior. But Jews were not always their targets. In 1900, at the height of the Boxer Rebellion, dockworkers, resentful that soldiers were being assigned the task of loading ships destined for the Far East, reacted by attacking not only Jews and their property but also by looting and destroying stores owned by gentiles.[62] And in June 1905, when day laborers and dockworkers participated in the unrest that led to the burning down of the port, Jews were not singled out. Quite clearly then, these workers were not inherently predisposed to anti-Jewish behavior; sometimes their actions acquired class coloration as they attacked persons possessing wealth and property regardless of ethnic or religious background. Nor did dockworkers follow a consistent conservative, pro-government line. Like other Odessa workers in 1905, they were involved in the movement to achieve improved working conditions. In May, for example, several hundred dock-workers conducted an orderly and successful strike for higher wages and shorter workdays, and in November dockworkers again struck over working conditions and the right to select deputies who would have the final say in the levying of fines. In mid-1906 these same workers would again announce demands for increased pay, an eight-hour day, free medical care, and employee participation in the determination of dismissals and fines.[63]

The domination of the grain trade by Jewish merchants and competition with Jews for work at the harbor, however, predisposed many gentile dock-workers and day laborers against Jews, whom they conveniently saw as the source of their troubles, especially during 1905 when unemployment ran exceptionally high. Consequently, when unemployed, unskilled Russian workers sought an outlet for their frustrations and problems, they generally focused on Jews. The words of one Marxist activist speaking about the labor movement in 1903 also apply to the situation in 1905: some workers feared that "they would be replaced by Jews and left without work" in the event of revolution.[64] But without taking into account the hostile, anti-Jewish atmosphere in Odessa and the acceptance of anti-Jewish violence as an appropriate way to vent anger, we cannot understand why Russian day laborers at times of economic distress chose not to attack other Russian workers who competed with them for scarce jobs or Russian employers. Instead, they indiscriminately lashed out at *all* Jews, regardless of whether they were job competitors. Thus, the pogrom was a result of the dynamics of labor protest, the politics of resentment, and ethnic tensions.

Although anti-Jewish sentiments in Odessa usually remained submerged, many residents feared that Russian–Jewish hostilities could explode in a matter of hours given the right combination of factors. During major labor demonstrations or strikes, organizers often felt compelled to exhort workers not to direct their anger at Jews, but to present a united front of Jew and gentile against employers. Employers also understood that religious animosities could be used to hinder worker solidarity; owners of the few enterprises with ethnically mixed labor forces sometimes encouraged Russian workers to direct their anger at Jewish coworkers.[65] Despite the common exploitation that both Russian and Jewish workers experienced as wage laborers, ethnic loyalties of Russians to each other could overshadow their class affinities to Jews.

But economic problems alone do not explain why these financially strapped Russian workers decided to attack Jews in October 1905. Otherwise, we might expect them to have turned on Jews in June, when material conditions were not all that different from those in the fall. What had changed since the June disorders was the political atmosphere; in October it had become more polarized. The breakdown of government authority and the apparent success of the revolution created a power vacuum that left Odessans of all social and political stripes unsure as to whether the new political arrangement had altered class and social relations. The revolutionary climate of mid-October allowed the airing of all sorts of social, economic and political resentments in a relatively unrestrained atmosphere. It enabled what Paul Brass aptly calls "riot specialists" to take advantage of the confusion brought on by revolution and made it more likely for anti-Jewish violence to emerge. Economic insecurity and political turmoil were transformed into anti-Jewish violence due to a combination of factors rooted in the particular circumstances of Odessa both before and during 1905.

To be sure, many day laborers and dockworkers were less interested in the political turn of events than the vodka and money that the police reportedly offered. They may have welcomed the pogrom simply because it afforded them the opportunity to vent some steam and, perhaps, acquire some booty. Not all pogromists consciously stood on the extreme right of the political spectrum. For the politically apathetic and unaware workers, the struggle between revolution and reaction played a secondary if not negligible role; they were simply caught up in the general tenor of events and behaved in a manner reminiscent of their actions during the destruction of the harbor in June. At the height of the pogrom, even non-Jewish property fell victim to the onslaught of the mobs.

These pogromists were clearly not acting with malice aforethought; rather they were behaving in a spontaneous manner to events that tended to channel their violence toward Jews. For them violence, regardless of whether it was directed against Jews, the police or employers, was an expression of fundamental social and economic antagonisms. In short, some participants in the unrest may not have intended to assault Jews, but the shooting and bombthrowing on October 18 and 19 provoked them to anti-Jewish violence and goes a long way to explaining the virulence and intensity of the attack. Though a cross-section of the Russian work force participated in the pogrom, it is clear that certain categories of Russian workers tended to stay clear of the violence and did all they could to help Jews and combat the pogromists. Many Russian workers enlisted in self-defense units, while others sheltered their Jewish neighbors and friends during the terror. Russians from a variety of enterprises patrolled the harbor to protect Jewish property, seized pogromists and organized self-defense units. After the pogrom Russian self-defensists provided financial aid to pogrom victims and took vigorous action to punish pogromists and ensure that another round of anti-Jewish violence would not occur.[66] Significantly, many of the Russian self-defensists were skilled workers from metalworking and machine-construction plants that supplied the workers active in the organization of strikes and the formation of district and city strike committees, trade unions and, in December, the Odessa Soviet of Workers' Deputies.

One reason for the reluctance of these workers to join ranks with pogromists had to do with the simple fact that skilled metalworkers and machinists did not face serious employment competition with Jews, who rarely worked in these industries. Despite the fact that Jews comprised a third of Odessa's population, Jews and Russians rarely worked in the same factory or workshop, or even as members of the same work gang at dockside. In fact, Jews and Russians were generally not employed in the same branch of industry, with the major exception being unskilled day labor. Perhaps more important was that many of the factories employing skilled workers had a history of labor activism and a tradition of political organization and awareness, particularly of Social Democracy. The presence of political organizers and propagandists may have muted the anti-Jewish sentiment of the Russian workers in these plants and imparted an appreciation of worker solidarity that transcended ethnic and religious divisions.

PREMEDITATION AND SPONTANEITY

In sum, the social composition of the work force helped determine the make-up of the pogromist ranks. At one end of the occupational spectrum stood the unskilled day laborers who were wont to engage in campaigns of violence and destruction. At the other end were the skilled, more economically secure Russian metalworkers and machinists who tended not to participate in the pogrom and were more inclined than the unskilled to channel their protest and discontent in an organized fashion. The unrest that often accompanied strikes by skilled workers, as in June, could radicalize the participants and pose a revolutionary threat. But worker militance and social unrest also had reactionary consequences when Jews became the object of the workers' outrage and hostility.

It is a commonplace that the most politically militant and radical of workers in both Western Europe and Russia during the late nineteenth and early twentieth centuries were generally not found among the poorest and most disadvantaged segments of the work force. Yet the unskilled and least integrated workers were very prone to violence – perhaps to a much greater extent than the better skilled and politically aware and mobilized workers – and this violence could unintentionally contribute to or impede the revolutionary cause. In June a riot by the unskilled posed a serious threat to the authorities, but in October protest by these same workers effectively undercut the force and power of the revolution. The pogrom unwittingly served the purposes of the threatened regime because it helped defuse the revolutionary situation; the counter-revolutionary cause was strengthened when the target of the workers' wrath was no longer the autocracy but the Jews, an object of popular hatred and resentment. The October 1905 pogrom in Odessa illustrates how ethnic hostility was a potent force in workers' politics and served as a centrifugal force that diminished the capacity of Odessa workers to act in a unified fashion.

The Odessa pogrom occupied a middle ground between premeditated violence and a spontaneous riot. The pogromists did not respond to government orders but were provoked into action impetuously, inflamed by the attack on the patriotic procession. The actions of individual police and soldiers as well as the negligence of Neidhardt and Kaul'bars underscore the conclusion that arms of the state did intervene and choose sides once the violence erupted. The details of the Odessa pogrom resemble other incidents of ethnic violence (particularly between Muslims and Hindus in India) in many respects. The events that triggered the Odessa pogrom were not inherently ethnic in nature, but the violence quickly acquired ethnic coloration because of social and political circumstances. In addition, competition for scarce jobs pitted members of different ethnic groups against each other and was a significant factor in explaining pogromist behavior. More importantly, ethnic violence served the purposes of the state, notwithstanding the fact that many pogromists had no conscious political purpose in mind when they set out on their rampage. The pogrom enabled the regime to weather the political crisis of 1905 because it diverted the energies of workers, liberals and revolutionaries from the offensive against the regime to dealing with the pogrom and its aftermath.

THE OCTOBER 1905 POGROM IN EKATERINOSLAV

A very brief examination of the October 1905 pogrom in Ekaterinoslav, where events closely parallelled those in Odessa, will drive home this point about the political function of ethnic violence in late Imperial Russia as well as buttress my argument that pogroms were intimately connected to the dynamics of revolution and labor protest. My remarks are based on the excellent work by Charters Wynn, and do not do justice to his nuanced argument concerning the 1905 Revolution in Ekaterinoslav and the pogrom.[67] Ekaterinovslav (known today as Dnepropetrovsk) was located some 200 miles northwest of Odessa in the heart of the coalmining Donbass Region and was known for its metallurgical enterprises. Having a total population of some 113,000 at the end of the nineteenth century, Ekaterinoslav resembled Odessa in terms of having a large presence of Jews (35 percent of the population). Jews found employment as artisans or owned small retail shops and factories, and peasant migrants of Great Russian or Ukrainian stock worked in the mines and factories of the region, where resentments and frustrations built up over the last quarter of the nineteenth century as a result of horrible working and living conditions. Ekaterinoslav's history was also speckled with incidents of anti-Semitic violence that tended to emerge during times of labor unrest.

As in Odessa, the precipitating events of the pogrom were the street celebrations after the announcement of the October Manifesto and the patriotic counter-demonstration designed to blunt the impact of the regime's concessions. Groups of demonstrators – some in favor of the revolution, others opposed to the dilution of autocratic power – competed for public space and the opportunity to express their views. In striking similarity to events in Odessa, the prelude to the pogrom in Ekaterinoslav occurred when the patriotic marchers found themselves the target of a Jewish self-defense group which opened fire. Once the blood began to flow, the military and police also did very little to restore order. Indeed, the police went on strike and some individual policemen egged on the pogromists. Workers and members of Ekaterinoslav's urban underclass were heavily involved in the pogrom, and their participation was in large measure conditioned by their reaction to the revolution and labor movement of 1905.

In 1905 workers in Ekaterinoslav successfully struck for higher wages and other material concessions, but they became disillusioned with the October general strike because it did not result in economic improvements and had imposed additional financial hardships. They blamed the revolutionaries for diverting their struggle for bread-and-butter issues into the campaign for political reform, and when the general strike did not deliver the goods, workers in Ekaterinoslav turned their backs on the revolution and lashed out at revolutionaries whom they had trusted to win better working and living conditions. And as in Odessa, Ekaterinoslav workers displayed their anti-political, indeed anti-intellectual sentiments, by targeting Jews, many of whom were prominent in the revolutionary movement.

Compounding the workers' frustration with politics was the perception that Jews were responsible for their economic problems. Workers in Ekaterinoslav were also experiencing a politics of resentment that was fueled by political developments and economic difficulties. The violent attack on the Jews was very much the result of the dynamics of labor protest and the revolution itself. As Wynn concludes:

> Pogroms were part of the basic dynamic of the 1905 Revolution, inextricably linked with revolutionary events. ... In the politicized atmosphere of the years surrounding the 1905 Revolution, pogroms largely took the form of a mass backlash, a somewhat organized reaction against the failure of the general strikes and of the revolutionary movement to fulfill the expectations of the many Donbass workers. ... Donbass pogromist

activity did not develop independently of the general strike movement, but rather in conjunction with the radicalization of labor.[68]

In conclusion, anti-Jewish violence in late Imperial Russia developed in tandem with the polarization of politics and was part of the process of revolution and labor protest. In both Odessa and Ekaterinoslav the pogromist backlash undercut the enthusiastic reception of the October Manifesto and diverted the energies of the revolutionaries, thereby enabling the regime to weather the crisis of 1905. The pattern of pogromist behavior that emerges from our examination of Odessa and Ekaterinoslav reveals that ethnic tensions tended to assume violent and ugly forms during times of political uncertainty, particularly when the government was on the retreat.

ABBREVIATIONS

TsGAOR SSSR (Central State Archive of the October Revolution of the USSR)
TsGIA SSSR (Central State Historical Archive of the USSR)
TsGVIA SSSR (Central State Military Archive of the USSR)

NOTES

1   See John Klier and Shlomo Lambroza, eds, *Pogroms: Anti-Jewish Violence in Modern Russian History* (Cambridge: Cambridge University Press, 1991) for the most recent research on pogroms in Russia.
2   For example, city governor Dmitrii Neidhardt estimated the number of casualties at 2,500, and the Jewish newspaper *Voskhod* reported that over 800 were killed and another several thousand were wounded. See A. Linden (L. Motzkin), "Die Dimensionen der Oktoberpogrome (1905)," in *Die Judenpogrome in Russland*, vol. 2, p. 130; *Voskhod*, November 11, 1905, p. 16; *Materialy k istorii russkoi kontr-revoliutsii*, vol. 1, *Pogromy po offitsial'nym dokumentam* (St. Petersburg, 1908), pp. clxvi-clxvii and 201 (hereafter cited as Kuzminskii Report); S. Iu. Witte, *Vospominaniia*, vol. 3 (Moscow, 1960), p. 615; Maxim Vinaver, "La situation à Odessa," at the Archives of the *Alliance Israélite Universelle*, Dossier: URSS IC-1. Odessa; Viktor Obninskii, *Polgoda russkoi revoliutsii*, vyp. 1 (Moscow, 1906), p. 44.
3   See Steven Zipperstein, *The Jews of Odessa: A Cultural History, 1794–1881* (Stanford: Stanford University Press, 1985), pp. 114–28 and Lambroza, "The Pogrom Movement in Russia," in Klier and Lambroza, *Pogroms*, pp. 275–7.

4 *Opisanie odesskikh ulichnykh bezporiadkov v dni sv. Paskhi 1871 goda,* pp. 10–11.

5 A. A. Skal'kovskii, *Zapiski o torgovykh i promyshlennykh silakh Odessy* (St. Petersburg, 1865), p. 12; *Pervaia vseobshchaia perepis' naseleniia Rossiiskoi Imperii, 1897 g.,* vol. 47, *Gorod Odessa* (St. Petersburg, 1904), pp. 2–3.

6 A. P. Subbotin, *V cherte evreiskoi osedlosti* (St. Petersburg, 1890), pp. 212–30; "Odessa," *Evreiskaia entsiklopediia,* vol. 12 (St. Petersburg, 1910), pp. 59–62; G. Bliumenfel'd, "Torgovo-promyshlennaia deiatel'nost' evreev v Odesse," *Voskhod,* nos 4 (April 1884), pp. 1–14 and 5 (May 1884), pp. 1–14; Patricia Herlihy, "Greek Merchants in Odessa in the Nineteenth Century," *Harvard Ukranian Studies,* III–IV, 419; "Odessa," *The Jewish Encyclopedia,* vol. 9 (New York, 1905), pp. 378–80; *Pervaia vseobshchaia perepis' naseleniia Rossiiskoi Imperii, 1897 g.,* vol. 47, pp. 134–49.

7 *Pervaia vseobshchaia perepis' naseleniia Rossiiskoi Imperii, 1897 g.,* 47: 134–49; *Voskhod,* January 29, 1904, pp. 23–6, February 5, 1904, pp. 1–5 and January 27, 1905, pp. 15–16.

8 I. Brodovskii, *Evreiskaia nishcheta v Odesse* (Odessa, 1902), pp. 5–6; *Iuzhnoe obozrenie,* March 22, 1905.

9 See Robert Weinberg, *The Revolution of 1905 in Odessa: Blood on the Steps* (Bloomington: Indiana University Press, 1993), chap. 1.

10 For a discussion of events in Odessa during the first half of 1905, particularly the June disorders, see Weinber, *The Revolution of 1905,* chaps. 4 and 5.

11 *Vedomosti Odesskago gradonachal'stva,* March 1, 1905 and April 28, 1905; *Voskhod,* February 5, 1904, pp. 26–7, March 17, 1904, pp. 25–6 and January 22, 1905, p. 20; *Posledniia Izvestiia,* December 3/November 20, 1903, p. 4, December 17/4, 1903, pp. 2–3, April 6/March 24, 1904, p. 1, March 11/February 26, 1905, p. 6, June 3/May 21, 1905, pp. 1 and 6, and July 10/June 24, 1905, p. 1; *Iskra,* February 10, 1904, May 1, 1904, October 5, 1904, March 10, 1905, and April 18, 1905; *TsGIA,* f. 1284, op. 194, d. 69, pp. 2–2 ob., d. 53, 1905, p. 5 and f. 1405, op. 530, d. 110, pp. 60–1 ob.; *Khronika evreiskoi zhizni,* April 10, 1905, p. 24 and May 8, 1905, pp. 25–7; TsGAOR, f. 124, op. 43, d. 298, 1905, pp. 1–2 and f. 102, OO, d. 5, ch. 4, lit. B, pp. 3–8.

12 TsGAOR, f. 102, OO d. 106, chl. 1905, pp. 4–5; *Poslednie izvestiia,* July 17/July 4, 1905, p. 2 and July 25/July 12, 1905, pp. 4–5; *Iskra,* July 1, 1905; *Proletarii,* July 10/June 27, 1905, p. 12 and July 3/June 20, 1905, p. 11.

13 *Odesskie dni* can be found in the Bakhmeteff Archives at Columbia University, Zosa Szajkowskii Collection, Oversized Folders.

14 TsGAOR, f. 102, 7th delopr., d. 3769, 1905, pp. 16 ob. and 24 and f. 124, d. 3115, p. 80; TsGIA, f. 1101, op. 1, d. 1033, p. 4; Richard Hough, *The Potemkin Mutiny* (New York: Pantheon Books, 1960), p. 100.

15 At the empirewide level, Jews by 1900 constituted 30 percent of persons arrested for political crimes. See the 1986 University Lecture at Boston University by Norman Naimark, "Terrorism and the Fall of Imperial Russia," p. 4. For the leaflet see TsGAOR, f. 102, OO, d. 5, ch. 4, 1905, pp. 193–4. On the role of Jews in the revolutionary movement, see Weinberg, *The Revolution of 1905,* especially chaps. 3 and 6.

16 Kuzminskii Report, p. cxxv.

17 Abraham Ascher, *The Revolution of 1905: Russia in Disarray* (Stanford: Stanford University Press, 1988), p. 138.

18 For an extended discussion, see Weinberg, *The Revolution of 1905*, chap. 6.

19 Some of the more relevant sources on the events of October 18 are: Kuzminskii Report, pp. cxxxiv–cxxxv, 110–11, 138–9, 186, and 196–8; TsGAOR, f. 102, OO, d. 1350, ch. 30, lit. A, 1905, pp. 42, 45 ob. and 83, op. 233, d. 1350, ch. 30, 1905, pp. 60–1 and op. 5, d. 3, ch. 49, 1905, pp. 63 ob. and 123 ob.–124; Osip Piatnitskii, *Memoirs of a Bolshevik* (London, 1930), pp. 84–5.

20 TsGAOR, f. 102, OO, d. 1350, ch. 30, lit. A, 1905, p. 45 ob.; Kuzminskii Report, pp. 126, 168, 177–80, and 198.

21 See, for example, Louis Greenberg, *The Jews in Russia: The Struggle for Emancipation, vol. 2, 1881–1917* (New Haven: Yale University Press, 1951), p. 76.

22 TsGAOR, f. 102, OO, d. 1350, ch. 30, lit. A, 1905, p. 42 ob.; Kuzminskii Report, pp. cxlvii and 104; *Izvestiia Odesskoi gorodskoi dumy,* (February 1906), p. 312.

23 On the large number of dockworkers, day laborers, and vagrants in the procession, see N. N. Lender (Putnik), "Revoliutsionnye buri na iuge. ('Potemkin' i oktiabr'skaia revoliutsiia v Odesse)," *Istoricheskii vestnik* 104, no. 6 (1904): 894; Kuzminskii Report, pp. cxlvii–cxlviii, 128 and 158; *Kommercheskaia Rossiia,* November 25, 1905; S. Semenov, "Evreiskie pogromy v Odesse i Odesshchine v 1905 g.," *Puti revoliutsii,* no. 3 (1925), pp. 119–20.

24 Kuzminskii Report, p. 105.

25 Kuzminskii Report, pp. cxlviii–cl, 105, 111, and 129; TsGVIA, f. 400, 16th otd., op. 15, d. 2641, 1905, pp. 35–35 ob.; TsGAOR, f. 102, OO, op. 5, d. 3, ch. 49, 1905, pp. 59 and 64 ob., op. 233, d. 1350, ch. 30, 1905, pp. 60 ob.–61 and d. 1350, ch. 30, lit. A, 1905, p. 47; *Khronika evreiskoi zhizni,* November 11, 1905, p. 19.

26 TsGVIA, f. 400, 16th otd., op. 15, d. 2641, 1905, p. 35 ob.; TsGAOR, f. 102, OO, op. 5, d. 3, ch. 49, 1905, p. 125 ob. and f. 124, op. 49, d. 294, 1911, p. 58 ob.; Kuzminskii Report, pp. cl–cli, 152–3 and 170–1; *Odesskii pogrom i samooborona* (Paris, 1906), pp. 46–7.

27 Semenov, pp. 115–35; D. Hurvits, *Der blutiger pogrom in Odessa* (Odessa, 1905); A. Malavich, *Odesser pogrom* (London, 1906); *Khronika evreiskoi zhizni,* October 28, 1905, pp. 11–14 and November 11, 1905, p. 20; *Voskhod,* October 27, 1905, p. 29, November 11, 1905, pp. 16–29 and February 9, 1906, pp. 14–15.

28 Daniel Brower, *The Russian City between Tradition and Modernity, 1850–1900* (Berkeley and Los Angeles: University of California Press, 1990), p. 204.

29 I. Michael Aronson, *Troubled Waters: The Origins of the 1881 Anti-Jewish Pogroms in Russia* (Pittsburgh: University of Pittsburgh Press, 1990), pp. 82–3.

30 Kuzminskii Report, pp. cliii–clvi, 4, 10, 112, 115, and 137; N. Osipovich, "V grozovye gody," *Kandal'nyi zvon,* no. 3 (1926), p. 66; TsGVIA, f. 400, 16th otd., op. 15, d. 2641, 1905, p. 38; Semenov, pp. 118 and 123; TsGAOR, f. 102, OO, d. 2540, 1905, p. 94; T. Forre, "Vospominaniia sestry miloserdiia ob oktiabr'skikh dniakh 1905 goda," in *1905 god. Revoliutsionnoe dvizhenie v Odesse i Odesshchine* (Odessa, 1926), 2: 233–4; *Odesskii pogrom i samooborona* pp. 64–65; *Collier's,* December 9, 1905, p. 13.

31 TsGAOR, f. 102, OO, op. 5, d. 3, ch. 49, 1905, pp. 65–65 ob.

32 Salo Baron, *The Russian Jews under Tsars and Soviets,* 2nd ed. rev. (New York: Macmillan Publishing Co., Inc., 1976), p. 57; Simon Dubnow, *A Short History*

of the Jewish People, trans. D. Mowshowitch (London: M. L. Cailingold, 1936), p. 282.

33   Lambroza, "The Pogrom Movement in Tsarist Russia, 1903–1906," p. 300.

34   Donald Rawson, "The Union of the Russian People, 1905–1907: A Study of the Radical Right" (Ph.D. dissertation, University of Washington, 1971), p. 195.

35   *Odesskie nosvosti*, November 2, 1905, November 16, 1905 and November 17, 1905; *Voskhod,* December 1, 1905, p. 39 and December 30, 1905, pp. 25–7; Greenberg, pp. 76–8; *Khronika evreiskoi zhizni*, November 11, 1905, pp. 19–20 and 22 and December 23, 1905, p. 44; Kuzminskii Report, pp. cxlv, clxi and clxxi; *Izvestiia Odesskoi gorodskoi dumy*, (March 1906), p. 768.

36   Kuzminskii Report, pp. cxlviii–cxlix, clxxi and 3–4.

37   Kuzminskii Report, pp. 100–1. An American correspondent reported recognizing "a police inspector in plain clothes" engaged in "Jew-baiting." *Collier's*, December 9, 1905, p. 13.

38   *Khronika evreiskoi zhizni*, November 11, 1905, p. 22; G. Achkanov, "Vospominaniia o revoliutsii 1905 goda," in *1905 god. Revoliutsionnoe dvizhenie v Odesse i Odesshchine*, vol. 2 (Odessa, 1926), pp. 199–200; S. Semenov, "Evreiskie pogromy v Odesse i Odesshchine v 1905 g., "*Puti revoliutsii*, no. 3 (1925), pp. 116–17; Kuzminskii Report, pp. cliii–cliv and 112.

39   Kuzminskii Report, pp. 3–4, 39, 47, and 187–9; *Vedomosti Odesskago gradonachal'stva*, October 19, 1905.

40   TsGIA, f. 1284, op. 194, d. 69, pp. 2–2 ob., d. 53, 1905, p. 5 and f. 1405, op. 530, d. 110, pp. 60–61 ob.

41   S. Dimanshtein, "Ocherk revoliutsionnogo dvizheniia sredi evreiskikh mass," in M. N. Pokrovskii, ed., *1905: Istoriia revoliutsionnogo dvizheniia v otdel'nykh ocherkakh*, vol. 3, *Ot oktiabria k dekabriu. Revoliutsionnoe dvizhenie natsional'nostei i okrain* (Moscow–Leningrad, 1927), p. 171.

42   Kuzminskii Report, pp. cxxxviii–cxliii, clxxiv–clxxvii, clxxxviiix–cxc, cxcvi–cci, 6–13, 18–22, 40–4, 120–1, 128–30, 169–70, 172, 177, and 182–6. See also TsGAOR, f. 124, op. 49, d. 294, 1911, pp. 81 ob. and 167–167 ob.

43   Kuzminskii Report, pp. 123 and 156–7.

44   Kuzminskii Report, p. 155.

45   TsGIA, f. 23, op. 20, d. 1, p. 174; Kuzminskii Report, pp. cxlv–clxvi, 69–71, 74, 128, 155, and 186; Herlihy, *Odessa: A History, 1794–1914* , p. 290; *Vedomosti Odesskago gradonachal'stva*, October 25, 1905.

46   TsGVIA, f. 400, 16 otd., op. 15, d. 2641, 1905, p. 38.

47   Kuzminskii Report, pp. 175–6 and 190.

48   Richard Robbins, *The Tsar's Viceroys: Russian Provincial Governors in the Last Years of the Empire* (Ithaca: Cornell University Press, 1987), pp. 196–7.

49   TsGAOR, f. 102, OO, d. 1350, ch. 30, lit. A, 1905, p. 71; TsGVIA, f. 400, 16th otd., op. 15, d. 2641, 1905, p. 37; Semenov, pp. 125 and 130; Kuzminskii Report, pp. clvi–clix, clxi–clxii, clxxix, clxxxi, cci, 9–11, 27, 31, 39, 43–4, 47, 68, 82–90, 115, 123–4, 175–6, and 191–2, and *passim*.

50   Kuzminskii Report, pp. 43–4.

51   Kuzminskii Report, pp. clxv and 123–5; William C. Fuller, Jr, *Civil–Military Conflict in Imperial Russia, 1881–1914* (Princeton: Princeton University Press, 1985), p. 211; M. Vinaver, "La situation à Odessa."

52 Kuzminskii Report, pp. cv–cvi, cxlviii, ccxv, 4, and 17; TsGAOR, f. 102, OO, op. 5, d. 3, ch. 49, 1905, pp. 66 ob. and 124 ob. and. d. 1350, ch. 30, lit. A, 1905, p. 85 ob.; TsGVIA, f. 400, 16th otd., op. 15, d. 2641, 1905, p. 35.

53 Shlomo Lambroza, "Jewish Responses to Pogroms in Late Imperial Russia," in Jehuda Reinharz, ed., *Living with Antisemitism: Modern Jewish Responses* (Hanover and London: University Press of New England, 1987), pp. 258 and 268.

54 TsGAOR, f. 102, OO, op. 5, d. 3, ch. 49, 1905, p. 124 ob.

55 P. Almazov, *Nasha revoliutsiia (1902–1907)* (Kiev, 1908), pp. 586–7; A. I. Elishev, *Oktiabr'skoe vooruzhennoe vosstanie v Odesse* (Moscow, 1908), p. 19; TsGAOR, f. 102, OO, op. 233, d. 1350, ch. 30, 1905, pp. 60–1.

56 By 1884 there were over 1,700 Jewish dockworkers in Odessa; in some categories, such as those who weighed sacks of grain, Jews filled a majority of positions. Zvi Halevy, *Jewish Schools under Czarism and Communism: A Struggle for Cultural Identity* (New York: Springer Publishing Co., 1976), p. 21; TsGIA, f. 23, op. 20, d. 1, p. 173; TsGAOR, f. 102, d. 2409, 1903, p. 74 and 4th delopr., d. 84, ch. 12, t. 12, 1907, p. 279; *Pervaia vseobshchaia perepis' naseleniia Rossiiskoi Imperii, 1897 g.*, 47: 88–131 and 134–49; I. A. Adamov, "Rabochie i moriaki odesskogo porta v revoliutsionnom dvizhenii XIX i nachala XX stoletii" (Candidate of Historical Science dissertation, Odessa University, 1940), p. 59; Ia. M. Shternshtein, *Morskie vorota Ukrainy* (Odessa, 1958), p. 19; V. K. Vasil'evskaia, "Polozheniia portovykh rabochikh v Odesse," *Trudy Odesskogo otdela Russkogo obshchestva okhraneniia zdraviia*, vyp. 4 (1904), p. 37; M. Tsetterbaum, *Klassovye protivorechiia v evreiskom obshchestve* (Kiev, 1905), p. 27; A. P. Subbotin, *V cherte evreiskoi osedlosti* (St. Petersburg, 1890), p. 230; N. Vasil'evskii, *Ocherk sanitarnogo polozheniia g. Odessy* (Odessa, 1901), p. 6.

57 One observer of the Odessa port stated that dockworkers worked an average of 120 days per year. N. Shelgunov, *Ocherki russkoi zhizni* (St. Petersburg, 1895), p. 470.

58 Z. V. Pershina, "Nachalo rabochego dvizheniia. Pervye marksistskie kruzhki v Odesse (1883–1895 gody)," in K. S. Kovalenko, ed., *Iz istorii odesskoi partiinoi organizatsii. Ocherki* (Odessa, 1964), p. 9.

59 *Kommercheskaia Rossiia*, February 8, 1905.

60 G. G. Moskvich, *Illiustirovannyi prakticheskii putevoditel' po Odesse* (Odessa, 1904), p. 177.

61 See especially Brower, *The Russian City*, pp. 203–4.

62 *Iskra*, (December 1900); "Khronika vnutrennei zhizni," *Russkoi bogatstvo*, (August 1900), pp. 159–62.

63 TsGAOR, f. 102, OO, d. 4, ch. 19, lit. A, 1905, pp. 213–14; *Kommercheskaia Rossiia*, November 27, 1905 and December 1, 1905; TsGIA, f. 1405, op. 530, d. 400, p. 52; *Iuzhnoe obozrenie*, June 29, 1906 and July 9, 1906; Elishev, p. 37.

64 Godlevskii, "Kishinev, Odessa, Nikolaev. (*Iz istorii s.-d. dvizheniia 1895–1903 g.g.*) Vospominaniia." *Letopis' revoliutsii*, no. 2(7) (1924), pp. 131.

65 *Kommercheskaia Rossiia*, November 2, 1905; *Proletarskoe delo*, October 10, 1905.

66 Kuzminskii Report, pp. 130–1; *Kommercheskaia Rossiia*, October 28, 1905, October 30, 1905, November 1, 1905, November 3, 1905, November 5, 1905, November 8, 1905, November 13, 1905 and December 6, 1905; *Odesskii listok*,

October 29, 1905, November 18, 1905 and November 26, 1905; *Odesskie novosti*, November 2, 1905, November 3, 1905, November 6, 1905, December 2, 1905 and December 6, 1905; *Iuzhnoe obozrenie*, October 30, 1905 and November 11, 1905.

67 Charters Wynn, "Russian Labor in Revolution and Reaction: The Donbass Working Class, 1870–1905" (Ph.D. dissertation: Stanford University, 1988) and *Workers, Strikes, and Pogroms: The Donbass to Dnepr Bend, 1870–1905* (Princeton: Princeton University Press, 1992).

68 Wynn, "Russian Labor in Revoluton and Reaction," pp. 320 and 331.

3. The Pogrom of November 9–10, 1938 in Germany

Leonidas E. Hill

Interpretation of the pogrom of November 9–10, 1938 from an ethnic perspective must begin with some remarks on the applicability of the concept of ethnicity to the Jews in Germany. Then it will be necessary to explain the long-term background, the environment of the year 1938, the development of the pogrom itself, and some of its larger purposes. My re-examination of these themes is based above all on a reading of a collection of nearly 250 largely unpublished autobiographies of Germans and Austrians, mostly in German and of greatly varying lengths, written for the "My Life in Germany" prize contest sponsored by three Harvard professors in 1939. A high proportion of those who submitted essays were Jews, and they wrote for posterity about the frightful treatment they had endured. These autobiographies illuminate vividly the premonitions of the victims and their interactions with the perpetrators, who expressed their violent or murderous intentions and fantasies with a complete lack of restraint.*

DEFINING THE JEWS

There were two very different groups, 500,000 German Jews and nearly 100,000 foreign Jews, most of the latter designated as *Ostjuden* (eastern Jews), 56,480 from Poland, almost 5,000 from Austria as well as from Czechoslovakia, and nearly 20,000 stateless Jews, most of whom were originally from old Austria–Hungary or the Soviet Union.[1] The different characteristics of their ethnicity can be examined together under the headings of language, religion, residence, communal affiliation, Nazi "racism" and Nazi legislation.

First, there is the question of whether the ethnicity of these two groups of Jews could be defined linguistically. For the most part, the Jews of German nationality were German speaking and were not distinguished from their fellow citizens by accent or vocabulary. They had long been linguistically assimilated. This was not true of the *Ostjuden*, most of whom spoke Polish, Czech, or Yiddish, and whose German was frequently accented. Many Germans, including Jews, were unsympathetic or antagonistic toward the *Ostjuden* because of xenophobic nationalism. German Jews also feared the attention that the foreignness of the *Ostjuden* attracted to Jews in general,[2] but at first thought the Nazis would only pursue *Ostjuden*, not themselves. One German Jew remembered that he even thought the deportation of *Ostjuden* who had come to Germany since 1918 was appropriate.[3] The *Ostjuden* provided material and stereotypes for the arguments of anti-Semites, and undermined the efforts of German Jews to be as much like other citizens as possible.

A second obvious criterion was the religious affiliation of the Jews. Connected with this was their appearance. Most German Jews apparently dressed the same as other Germans and had the beards, mustaches and haircuts of the period. They had deliberately adopted the mores of the larger society during the nineteenth century and especially after removal of restrictions on their rights and citizenship at the time of unification.[4] A considerable number of Jews were very secular and no longer practiced their religion at all, or very little, whereas those who attended synagogues were thereby distinguished from Christian Germans. The sense of this religious difference was still very strong in much of the Christian German population and was a powerful source of Catholic and Protestant antipathy to the Jews. This often virulent dislike of Jews fed particularly off the much more marked distinguishing external appearance of the *Ostjuden*, whose attire and facial hair identified them. Some of these aspects of their appearance were connected to religious practice, but others derived from their national antecedents. In both groups there were considerable numbers who ate Kosher food, thus shopped for this in Jewish stores, and of course observed different religious holidays from the Christian population.

Third is the question whether Jews in Germany were defined by what some political scientists call ethnoterritoriality.[5] Probably many of us unfamiliar with the look of German cities in the 1930s might imagine that Jews resided in a Jewish quarter resembling a ghetto. This is because we assume these cities were still quaintly medieval. Thus we might think of the Jews as having been concentrated in a particular area, separate or distinguished from the rest of the German population and because of that an obvious target for ethnic antagonism. This was not the situation and the reasons why will be obvious if we reflect for a moment on some important changes during the late nineteenth and early twentieth centuries. The populations of cities grew enormously as they became centers of industry, commerce, and finance. They acquired modern plans, green belts, parks, suburbs, streets suitable for automobiles, transportation facilities (streetcars, railways), power plants, electric grids, lighting, telephones, sewers, water systems, new stone, glass and steel buildings, highrises and department stores serviced by elevators. Indeed, many of these cities were redesigned and rebuilt on a grand scale to improve their appearance and expanded to accommodate their vast new populations. Thus the Jews became distributed unevenly in space in these cities and did not stand out by location. Nevertheless, in many of these cities a *Judengasse* might still be found, with a synagogue on it or near it, and possibly a Jewish old people's home. These were usually located in the poorer parts of the city while most of the Jews lived elsewhere. The exception to this picture was the location of the living quarters of many of the *Ostjuden*, who did tend to be concentrated in special areas in a few cities, such as the Scheunenviertel in Berlin.

Fourth, there were, of course, communal ways in which many German Jews were distinguished from other Germans, such as by their membership in Jewish organizations or their subscription to Jewish newspapers and magazines. The Jews had their own telephone book in Berlin. Since there was such a strong consciousness in the German population of the differences between Jews and Christians, the latter were reluctant to admit Jews to public office, private clubs, Christian society, and so on. Jewish children of practicing parents attended classes to educate them in their religion and its observances, too. Because of these differences and the somewhat traditional and stiff mores of German society, still strongly stamped by their equivalent of the outlook of the Victorian era, most people were highly conscious of the religious and cultural affiliations of their neighbors. This not only resulted in a kind of segregation in Germany, but also in North America, in both the United States and Canada, in this period.

Fifth, it is necessary to remember that the chief grounds for the singling out of the Jews in Germany by their tormentors, the Nazis, were supposed "racial" criteria. The reason that one must refer to "supposedly 'racial'" criteria is that these were wholly unscientific, indeed pseudo-scientific. Some of the Nazi writings on the subject had the appearance of science but they ignored genetics. Nazi "racism" was based on classification of body and facial types as well as skin color. Nazis believed in the superiority of "Aryan" man, whose existence cannot be scientifically verified. They asserted that the Jews constituted a "racial" type, with a number of outstanding and easily identifiable characteristics, the stuff of caricatures based on old stereotypes. Only towards the end of the nineteenth century were these caricatures assimilated to modern pseudo-scientific "racism," which became central to anti-Semitism. There is no Semitic race: the gene pool of the Semitic peoples in the Middle East and their ancestors elsewhere has become so mixed that a separate race of Semites no longer exists, if it ever was a "race" in the distant past. The Nazis also made much of "blood" as a distinguishing characteristic of supposed Jewish inferiority, but this was a purely rhetorical device, was utterly unscientific, and had nothing to do with a legitimate typology of blood.[6]

Just as Social Darwinism had been coupled with eugenics in the late nineteenth century, so also the two strains of thought together reached their nadir of primitivity in Nazi ideology and propaganda, which emphasized the inferiority of Jews to "Aryans." In a frequently used biological metaphor Jews were described as parasites and vermin.[7] Thus killing them was not just permissible but desirable. For example, in 1932 Goebbels wrote "Fleas, too, are exterminated."[8] As an "inferior race," Jews were classified with others characterized as inferior by the eugenics movement, such as the retarded, or psychiatric and physically handicapped inhabitants of asylums. The Nazis passed laws to sterilize them, then implemented the laws in such a way that people who were not retarded but had limited intelligence were also sterilized. The Nazi leadership anticipated that when the population was distracted by war this entire group of undesirable human beings could be secretly murdered.[9] This is indeed what the Nazis undertook as soon as the war commenced in September 1939.[10] Thoughts of this kind about the Jews were more frequently expressed by Nazis as war approached in 1938 and helps explain the murderousness and murders during the pogrom in November.

Melded with the "racism," Social Darwinism, and primitive eugenics were a number of mythological beliefs about Jews. These ranged from the original xenophobic antipathy of ancient times, through the Christian myth of the Jews' murder of Christ, the early modern legend that Jews controlled the purse strings of monarchs and fomented wars, to the modern assertions of their dominance in high finance and international organizations, as well as their conspiratorial ties with one another as depicted in the "Protocols of the Elders of Zion."[11] During the Wilhelmine and Weimar eras German Jews had sought to counter these often libelous stereotypes, and their legal actions against publicists sometimes resulted in successes. They used libel laws in court actions to counter the vilification of Jews by the Nazis, among others.[12] Obviously this ceased when Hitler assumed power.

Finally, the chief means by which the Nazis defined Jewish ethnicity were action and legislation. Only a few months after their assumption of power, the Nazis introduced laws against them, temporarily boycotted Jewish stores, searched their houses, frequently confiscating or stealing silver, jewelry, papers and books, and destroyed what they liked, arrested many Jews for 8, 14 or 30 days,[13] and physically attacked numerous Jews in what amounted to a mini-pogrom. A policeman said to a Jew under arrest in a cell: "You deserve to be hanged; we must exterminate the Jews."[14] Radical words were more frequently expressed by average Nazis. Especially communist and socialist Jews, but soon many others too, burnt their books and papers, such as membership cards, address books, letters and diaries, lest the Nazis use them against them.[15] In May the Nazis burnt books publicly, and one Jew reflected that at least instead of burning Jews as in the Inquisition, now it was only books.[16] A census in 1933 helped identify the Jews; special card files for all Jews were created in 1935–6, and they had to carry an identification card after July, 1938.[17] The Nazis periodically increased the pressure on Jews during the entire period leading up to the pogrom of November 1938, but one of the most important stages was signalled by the introduction of the Nuremberg laws in 1935.

These laws were certainly not improvised[18] and made a thorough attempt to define legally who was a Jew, which depended on ancestry rather than the practice of religion or affiliation with Jews.[19] Some Jews who were entirely secular and assimilated, thus not Jews in religion, or by other obvious ethnic criteria, were nevertheless designated as such by the Nazi laws. Some parents had completely concealed their family's Jewish ancestors from their children, who now were identified as Jews by the government and suddenly treated as pariahs in schools and society.[20] These very elaborate laws went a long way towards defining exactly the status of those the Nazis called "Mischlinge," the children of mixed marriages. To the nearly 500,000 identified as German Jews in 1933 were added 100,000 defined as such by the new laws.[21]

Because of the dangers posed by being a Jew or associated with one, engagements were broken and marriages dissolved, in some cases tragically, in others demeaningly.[22] A university professor's daughter who was accused of having relations with a Jew was paraded through the streets, then thrown out by her family, and emigrated to the US.[23] The Nazis did not solve all their problems of defining Jews with these laws and were still discussing the issue at the Wannsee Conference in January 1942 and afterward. Yet the essential point is that after 1935 these laws defined, separated and distinguished Jews from other Germans. The situation encouraged other Germans to report Jews for any violations so as to gain advantages for themselves, and many Jews feared that someone would exploit the possibility.[24] The result was that by 1938 the Nazis had identified Jews according to this law and could make them suffer for their antecedents. Jews lost the most elementary rights of citizenship: many towns had signs saying that Jews could not enter, and as residents they could not walk in the parks, swim in pools or at beaches, get their cars repaired, ride on public transport, attend concerts or the theater, eat in public restaurants, attend schools or universities, practice their professions, buy goods from or sell them to other Germans.

One family on vacation at Arendsee in a health spa for Jews in 1936 suddenly found their provisions stopped and the spa attacked by rowdies shouting that they would burn the house and hang all the Jewish children.[25] Of course these threats terrified them. Assimilation seemed to have suffered a "100% collapse."[26] Jewish cemeteries were desecrated. Jews were isolated and segregated as well as robbed of their livelihoods. Not surprisingly, Jews suffered breakdowns, exhibited nervous symptoms, and committed suicide in record numbers. They feared for their lives, suffered from what was called arrest-psychosis, and could not sleep.[27] The Nazis had for years been pressing Jews in an attempt to make them leave Germany, but at the same time impeded their departure by complicated bureaucratic requirements, a crass contradiction which some Jews noticed.[28] One young woman in a long line asked an official why the Nazis made it so hard to leave if that was what they wanted. In response the official asked her who had told her that they wanted the Jews to emigrate. "We want you to perish; it is all one to us whether you perish here or abroad."[29] Jews had to obtain a visa from some other country of destination, and were forced to forfeit virtually all of their belongings and wealth to the Nazis before they could depart. As a result of this many Jews found it impossible, or inordinately difficult, or too painful to leave, and because of their virtually complete assimilation to German society would not believe that things might get worse. In 1938 their situation worsened enormously and the Nazi bureaucracy became an even more hideously complicated and time-consuming obstacle. Nazi officials obviously took sadistic pleasure in seizing passports; police took equally sadistic pleasure in catching Jews jaywalking or doing anything else that would give them a record and disqualify them from emigration.[30]

Obviously the Nazis as perpetrators had made extraordinary efforts since 1933 to define and isolate their Jewish victims. The government at all levels was blatantly permissive toward mistreatment and even murder. A vicious ideology empowered not only the Nazi Party members, the Hitler Youth, SA, SS and various forms of the police, but also average citizens to convert hatred into action. The Jews suffered a devastating reversal of their fortunes in a five year span.

NAZI RESTRAINT

If the Nazis were so strongly disposed to attack the Jews physically and to destroy their homes, shops and synagogues, why was this assault so long delayed? If Dr Erich Schultze is to be believed, it was not for lack of intention. In February 1933 Heydrich visited him in hospital and related that Hitler had told a small inner circle of his "secret plan...[that] inside of five years there should be no more free Jews in Germany. And inside of a further five years no more Jews alive."[31] But their actions in 1933 provoked a strong reaction from much of the western world and Hitler concluded that they would have to wait until they were in a stronger position before they could resume their efforts to fulfil that part of their program. After the Enabling Act, the Nazis were preoccupied with their consolidation of power, and in 1934 they were absorbed with the internal struggle with the SA that culminated in the blood bath of June. They reeled from the attributions of responsibility for the assassination of Dollfuss and the attempted coup in Austria, then wanted calm so as not to imperil the plebiscite in the Saar at the beginning of 1935.

Nevertheless, during 1934 the Nazis had pressed Jews to give up their shops. In February and March 1935 they attacked Jewish businesses, dwellings and synagogues. They also mistreated individuals. After the Parteitag in 1935, speaking to a small group, Hitler said of the Jews: "Out of all the professions, ghetto, imprisoned in a territory where they can disport themselves according to their nature, while the German people looks on as one watches wild beasts."[32]

Hitler was absorbed with foreign affairs, including the Naval Agreement with Great Britain in 1935, thereafter with the risky reoccupation of the Rhineland and engagement on Franco's side in Spain during 1936. Evidence of Hitler's caution as well as of a long term intention to carry out a violent pogrom against the Jews dates from the aftermath of the assassination of the leader of the Swiss branch of the Nazi party's *Auslandsorganisation*, Wilhelm Gustloff in Davos, Switzerland on February 4, 1936 by a Jewish medical student from Yugoslavia, named David Frankfurter. Hitler and his minions considered using this as justification for a pogrom against the Jews but then decided that damage to Germany's relations with other countries must be avoided in view of the approaching Olympic Games during the summer of 1936.

In August 1936 Hitler's preoccupation with the economic preparations for war resulted in a rare memorandum from his own hand on the Four Year Plan. One of the two laws he wanted from the Reichstag would make "the whole of Jewry liable for all damage inflicted by individual specimens of this community of criminals upon the German economy, and thus upon the German people."[33] Here was one source of the confiscatory disposition evident in the huge fine imposed on the Jews after the November 1938 pogrom.

In January 1937 an official in the Jewish division of the SD headquarters had "recommended 'popular anger' as the 'most effective means' to accelerate 'a solution to the Jewish Question.'"[34] This view was not confined to his office. The question of action still arose in connection with the trial of

Frankfurter. Consequently, in a speech to party leaders on April 29, 1937
Hitler confronted these demands and said that he would await the right day.

> Then: the final aim of our whole policy is quite clear for all of us. Always
> I am concerned only that I do not take any step from which I will perhaps
> have to retreat, and not to take any step that will harm us. I tell you that
> I always go to the outermost limits of risk, but never beyond. For this you
> need to have a nose more or less to smell out: "What can I still do?" Also
> in a struggle against an enemy. I do not summon an enemy with force to
> fight, I don't say: "Fight!" because I want to fight. Instead I say "I will
> destroy you! And now, Wisdom, help me, to maneuver you into the corner
> that you cannot fight back, and then you get the blow right in the heart."
> That's it.[35]

Nazis accepted the restraint and understood that they were at one with their
leader about the goal.

Efforts to consolidate an effective coalition of powers with an ideological affinity, Italy and Japan, dominated a part of 1936 and 1937, at the end
of which in the famous November 7, 1937 Hossbach Conference Hitler
described his long term objectives.[36] The resistance he encountered to them
culminated in the Blomberg–Fritsch crisis and his appointment of Joachim
von Ribbentrop as Foreign Minister. At the same time, a crisis over Austria
resulted in Anschluß and immediate, radical, public mistreatment of the
Jews there.

Thus the explanation for the Nazis' relative restraint in their treatment of
the Jews from 1933 to 1938 lies in the exigencies of their domestic and foreign
policies. During that period there were occasions when the Nazis physically
attacked and mistreated Jews, also when leading Nazis expressed a desire
to stage a pogrom, for example after the assassination of Gustloff. They were
held back. But in 1938 Germany suddenly acquired a much stronger position
and the Nazis sought external war or as a substitute for it, a pogrom.

AUSTRIA AND CZECHOSLOVAKIA

Anschluß with Austria took place without any resistance from the Western
powers or from within Austria, and resulted in an important accession of
territory and population as well as a greatly improved strategic position
toward Czechoslovakia. Many Austrian Jews and people of the left reacted
to Anschluß as their brethren had to Hitler's appointment in 1933: they
burnt their diaries, correspondence, membership cards, address books, all
socialist literature, and authors such as Tucholsky.[37] The Nazis showed a

new arrogance toward the world and an overt viciousness first in their treatment of Jews in Austria, then too in Germany.What happened to the Austrian Jews at Anschluß amounted to a pogrom, which provided precedents for the November pogrom in Germany. Suddenly the Jews of Austria were publicly subjected to savage physical punishment, humiliation, and gigantic robbery, as well as imposition of the entire array of prohibitions and discriminations already in place in Germany.

The Jews had expected the worst and experienced it from some Austrian Nazis who had long been awaiting the day. A long-time Party member in Vienna had in 1935 composed a list of Jews he found "unsympathetic" and wanted to massacre on the day the Nazis seized power.[38] Much of the action against the Jews in the "Anschluß" pogrom was spontaneous, carried out by average people, more often than not quite young, and many of them as members of or in conjunction with the SA. Whether in uniform or in civilian clothes and wearing a Nazi armband, SA men, Nazis, and robbers pretending to be one or the other invaded homes and "requisitioned" everything valuable – money, jewellery, silverware, furniture, carpets – that they could lay their hands on. They frequently destroyed the furniture and furnishings, beat or even killed the inhabitants. They stole their automobiles. Soon Jews were afraid of mistreatment on public transportation and took taxis.[39] The Nazis and others plundered businesses, including department and grocery stores, as well as small shops of every variety.

In the first nine months after Anschluß the Nazis sequestered 44,000 of 70,000 Jewish dwellings in Vienna. An agency directed by Adolf Eichmann eventually controlled these seizures; his work provided a model for such seizures in Germany later.[40] Party commissars took over 25,000 businesses in the first weeks, attempted to live off them, and in doing so frequently ruined them. Nazi physical mistreatment had been open during the first days, and then took place almost privately in homes or in cellars to which groups of arrested Jews were taken. On April 1 a first transport of 151 Austrians taken to Dachau under protective custody included 60 Jews. In May the Gestapo arrested 2,000 Austrian Jews and sent them to different concentration camps. This was hardly noticed by a world obsessed with Hitler's aggressive pressure on Czechoslovakia, and the successful deportations from Austria, designed to drive Jews out, constituted a precedent for a similar move in Germany after the November pogrom. The barbaric treatment they suffered in the concentration camps will be described in conjunction with that suffered by the German Jews after the November pogrom. Probably 600 to 700 of the 2,000 Austrians were murdered, died, or committed suicide.[41] Many of the rest did everything they could to leave Austria after they were released from the camps.

In Austria as in Germany they could not leave without relinquishing almost the entirety of their possessions and fortunes, probably 96 percent by 1939.[42]

The Nazis took further actions against Jewish physicians and lawyers during the year, especially through new restrictions on July 6, 1938. During the spring and summer, the example of Nazi activity in Austria seems to have stimulated attacks in Germany on Jewish businesses, dwellings and individuals. On June 8 Nazi authorities told the Jewish congregation of the largest synagogue in Munich to evacuate it within 24 hours. The Jews held a last service and removed all the sacred objects, whereupon the Nazis dynamited the synagogue on June 9. They paid perhaps a tenth of the value of the building for its expropriation, and within weeks a parking lot took its place.

Quite apart from hatred as a reason for the destruction of synagogues, and the desire to drive Jews out of Germany by loss of their places of worship, it also appears that city governments wanted prime properties for their own uses. On June 18 the government of Nuremberg ordered the expropriation of the chief synagogue, but the Jews would not allow its demolition. Consequently the government resorted to a law of October 4, 1937 concerning renovation of cities as a cover for the dispossession they effected. On August 10 the Nazis dynamited the synagogue. Three weeks later a synagogue in Dortmund was also wrecked. Synagogues were an increasingly popular target for the Nazis because of the property lust of city governments.[43]

A decree of April 22 threatened prison for anyone who concealed that a business was owned by a Jew. From June, finance offices and security police prepared a list of prosperous Jews. After July, Jews had to obtain specially stamped identity cards. Another decree of August 17 legislated that all Jews must take the names Israel or Sara. A decree of October 5 required that Jews obtain a "J" stamp in their passports. During an October 14 meeting Göring said that the Jews must be expelled from the economy.[44]

During the summer of 1938 Hitler drove towards war over the Sudetenland and there is strong evidence that he wanted such a war right up to the eve of the agreement consummated in Munich on September 29, 1938.[45] Immediately after Munich he expressed his increased contempt for the Western powers and his disappointment at not getting his war. As a true Social Darwinist he thought war was a higher experience that every young German man should enjoy. Yet he had noticed the German public's obvious aversion to war on the eve of the Munich conference. Since he still wanted and intended to drive Germany into war, he sought ways to stimulate enthusiasm for the adventure, to steel Germans to their fate. As he acknowledged in a speech to representatives of the German press on November 10, the murderousness and destructiveness loosed in the November pogrom was an ideal way to achieve this objective.[46]

The war that he sought would also provide a cover for actions against various kinds of "inferior" peoples: the Jews, inhabitants of asylums, Slavs. For example, in 1935 Hitler said "that if war came, he would pick up and carry out this question of euthanasia," which "could be put into effect more smoothly and readily," that is, there would be less opposition.[47] This was precisely what Hitler did immediately after the outbreak of war on September 1, 1939. The radical promise of the word was realized in action. Similarly, the prospect of the seizure of all of Czechoslovakia, which was one of Hitler's aims after the Munich Agreement, generated grandiose ambitions and visions of brutality against the Slavs of Czechoslovakia. Nazis had long discussed the relocation of the Czechs and Slovaks to Siberia, or South America, or Madagascar, so that Germans could settle Bohemia, Moravia and Slovakia.

After the annexation of the Sudetenland opened the remainder of Czechoslovakia to seizure, on October 15, 1938 a Sudeten German party official named Neuwirth reflected that although "military necessity" might justify "the greatest brutality," the "physical extermination of the Czech people [could] only be achieved to a limited extent . . . because even in the event of extermination of a third of the population four million would still remain." He also rejected such an attempt because it would constitute "a heavy moral-political burden for the [German] nation." Similarly, the Sudeten German Party representative Ernst Kundt argued that "Ausrottung und Aussiedlung"[48] were impractical because of the adverse effect their implementation would have on the other peoples in eastern and southeastern Europe. Important here is the fact that they discussed the "physical extermination" of the Czech and Slovak peoples.

Propaganda had long suggested the necessity of the extermination of the Jews as vermin and an inferior people. Some Nazis even said to Jews, usually while mistreating them in the streets, or prisons, or concentration camps, but sometimes almost casually and in ordinary circumstances, that they deserved to be burned alive or put in rooms and gassed. Such vivid images of the treatment that was meted out to millions of Jews after 1941 were widespread in 1938, a year in which gas masks were distributed to the population because of the fear of war, and considerable numbers of Jews committed suicide using gas in their homes or apartments, commencing in Vienna and then throughout Germany during the November pogrom.

Not long after Anschluß with Austria in March 1938 a young Jewish girl in Vienna had a nightmare in which Hitler came into her room, closed the windows and doors, then "wrote on the wall that every Jew must be anni-hilated, [and] fill[ed] the place with poison gas."[49] One of the Jews arrested and in a cell in Vienna predicted war but thought it would not last long, but during it there would be a danger of breathing a little poison gas.[50] Late in 1938 one close observer of the Third Reich, Konrad Heiden, had heard that upper echelon Nazis were "fond of using the term 'to push the button,' though their listeners are never quite sure whether the mocking tone should be taken seriously. Often they added the explanation – still in jocular vein: to assemble all Jews in a large hall and then to release the gas by pressing a button." [51]

In the last months of the year and in January 1939 Hitler talked a number of times about the extermination of the Jews.[52] Some scholars have recently claimed that this was merely verbal radicalism and anyway meant no more than robbing them of their material assets and ability to earn a living, rather than envisaging their wartime extermination.[53] There is quite enough evidence from a variety of sources to disqualify this interpretation and to support the claim that Hitler meant in the most extreme sense what he said.

The massively changed environment of 1938 facilitated harsher measures against the Jews of Austria and Germany. The spontaneous nature and apparently enthusiastic participation of considerable numbers in the attacks on Jews in Austria no doubt encouraged Nazis in Germany to believe that they could unleash something comparable there. Heightened aggressiveness and the drive toward war, boundless ambition for territory and ferocious visions of the extermination of the victims were expressed by leaders and led in the ranks of the Nazis. Almost a mirror image of this was what some Jews dreamt and others embraced, suicide with gas, as an escape from their apparently hopeless situations. In the midst of this crucible of dispositions, Nazi and Jewish, the pogrom of November 9–10, 1938 occurred.

PRELIMINARIES AND THE POGROM

Historians have found a variety of signs that seemed to point toward a pogrom, and because, quite obviously, one took place throughout the already greater German Reich, including Austria and the Sudetenland, they have probably read some of the signs credulously. But the historians who have rejected such an interpretation of all of them, have not been aware of all the evidence, some of which is new and yet dates from 1939–40. Recollections dating from a relatively short time after the events appear more credible than those from after the war.

A Berliner with good contacts in high places told a Jewish friend in mid-October, 1938 that if the Jews knew what was being prepared against them in Berlin, they would try to leave Germany in any way that they could manage. Before relating in more detail what he had heard, he asked that his friend swear not to tell anyone because being caught might mean his death. He then said that in a short time Jews were going to be required to give up a large part of their fortunes, that they would be confined to ghettos, that Jews below the age of 60 would be forced to perform hard labor in concentration camps, for which purpose barracks were being built. In addition all the synagogues were going to be closed.[54]

Apparently in mid-October, Streicher's anti-Semitic publication, *Der Stürmer* urged the destruction of the synagogues.[55] An informant told Konrad Heiden that an SA man of his acquaintance said the "orders for the pogrom had come through two weeks earlier – long before vom Rath was killed."[56] A Norwegian witness to the pogrom reported in the *Dagbladet* of Oslo that the pogrom had been long prepared but was supposed to be a spontaneous reaction to the exhibition "Der ewige Jude." Instead of waiting for the exhibit the regime had used the assassination of vom Rath to start it earlier.[57] Another story concerns two Jewish academics, both decorated veterans from World War I, who arrived in New York on October 30, 1938 and related that the head of their police district in Germany had said a campaign against Jews, without any consideration for their standing, had been planned.[58] Apparently, then, the Nazis did intend much sharper action against the Jews, and if they did not envisage a pogrom, they at least thought of measures that were part of the pogrom which took place a short time later.

What triggered the pogrom? At the beginning of 1938 Himmler "ordered the expulsion within ten days of all Jews in Germany who were Russian nationals, many of whom had been living in Germany since the Bolshevik Revolution."[59] Fearing a similar measure against its Jews in Germany, the Polish government in March 1938 suddenly decreed that Poles living abroad more than five years had to obtain a special stamp on their passport by October 31 or they would lose it and their citizenship. Some months later it was clear that most of the Polish Jews in Germany could not obtain this stamp and would become stateless persons in Germany. Consequently, the German Foreign Office commissioned the Gestapo to deport these Polish Jews. Poland stopped them at the border and Germany prevented their return. Approximately 17,000 of them were stranded in miserable conditions in no man's land at the border.[60] This first deportation of a large number of people by the Nazis was precisely what some police authorities and anti-Semites during the Weimar Republic had wanted to do to the *Ostjuden*.[61] Deportation of unwanted populations was an old idea whose time had apparently arrived again.

The desperate plight of these stranded Polish Jews stimulated the son of one of the families (his parents and two sisters) to retaliate against Germany. On November 7 Herschel Grynszpan,[62] a 17-year old who had become stateless in Paris because of the Polish measures, was admitted to the German embassy where he shot an official named Ernst vom Rath, who died two days later. This was the event for which the Nazis had been waiting. Whereas their opponents, thinking of the Reichstag fire in 1933, attributed the act to the Nazis, the Nazi propaganda apparatus immediately trumpeted that this assassination was part of the larger world Jewish conspiracy. They connected Gustloff's assassination by David Frankfurter in Davos with vom Rath's by Herschel Grynszpan in Paris, and asserted that Jewish control over the German economy exploited German citizens as well as that foreign Jews urged war against Germany. Consequently, the time had come for a major change in the treatment of the Jews. Germans would draw their own conclusions and act accordingly.[63] This they did. At meetings called in many small towns, local Nazi party leaders and mayors harangued crowds into action, so that it was impossible to distinguish clearly between Nazis and ordinary citizens in the actions taken against the Jews on November 8. First youths, then adults, destroyed some Jewish shops, beat Jews and set fire to a few synagogues.[64] These scattered and isolated attacks were not ordered or directed by party headquarters.

On the 9th, a day on which various Nazi organizations gathered to celebrate the memory of the failed Putsch of that date in 1923, they acted in a more organized way, separate from one another – SA, Hitler Youth, Nazi Party – and especially in districts where these were led by a radical anti-Semite. This was particularly true of the SA, which had lost large numbers of members and political power after the purge of its leaders in 1934, but always revived the memory of the struggle in 1923 with great fervor and was eager to show its ferocity against the Jewish "enemy." Thus the actions on that day had a slightly different character but still did not result from orders by the Nazi hierarchy.[65]

The leaders of the Nazi party had assembled in Munich as usual for their November 9 commemoration of 1923. Vom Rath died in Paris at 4:00 p.m. It is impossible to believe that Hitler was not informed immediately. Thus he must have known by the late afternoon or early evening at the latest, and presumably discussed then, or even before vom Rath died, exactly what should be done. Perhaps he talked then with Goebbels, if not directly at least on the telephone, and Goebbels would have had some time to consider the staging of the announcement of vom Rath's death, the content of his speech that evening, the orders for action that would be issued.

Between 7:00 and 8:00 that evening, during the Nazi meeting, a messenger staged a report that vom Rath had died of his wounds. Goebbels talked animatedly with Hitler; the two presumably discussed the details of their management of the action that they had already decided upon earlier when they knew that vom Rath was dead. At the end of their conversation Hitler was heard to say that the SA "should have its fling." After the meal, without delivering his usual address to his comrades, Hitler withdrew to his residence in Munich, and neither he nor Goebbels ever revealed the content of their conversation. Goebbels delivered a well considered anti-Semitic speech referring to the actions of the 8th and 9th, and said that although the Party was not to organize further actions, it was also not to prevent them where they spontaneously took place. He spoke so angrily against the Jews that his auditors understood that they were supposed to organize and carry out a pogrom but to conceal their responsibility. Because Goebbels related word and deed so subtly and judged so perfectly the mixture of emotionalism and calculation, it seems highly likely that he had composed it beforehand.

Thus Hitler almost certainly knew about this plan before the evening assemblage, and confirmed the details with Goebbels during their conversation. But Hitler wanted the action to appear spontaneous, and if it did not he wanted to avoid suffering any repercussions. So also did Himmler and Göring, who only learned shortly before midnight about what was being undertaken, and believed Goebbels was attempting to increase his power.

After Goebbels' speech, the SA's *Stabschef*, Viktor Lutze, assembled the SA leaders and followed Goebbels' example by making clear what should be done without issuing an explicit command. Yet he was supposedly not a fanatic[66] and left room for a passive reaction by his group leaders. The *Gauleiter* and *Gaupropagandaleiter* were inspired by the prospect of bloody rage and destruction against Jews, and between 11 and 12 that night, they telephoned commands to their Gau, whose officials then called the *Kreisleiter*, who called the *Ortsgruppen*. Ingenious Swiss and Dutch journalists established by interviewing the wives of SS men that their husbands were woken by telephone calls after midnight and received orders to don their civilian clothing and commence their destructive work. The wives saw their husbands examining the lists of Jews and their addresses before they departed.[67]

The SS and SD in the persons of Heydrich and Himmler only learned about all of this shortly before midnight. Heydrich contacted Himmler, who talked with Hitler, then later called Heydrich to say that the action was under Goebbels' command. The SS should stay out of it unless the Gestapo needed help. Heydrich made clear in commands to the Gestapo that it should protect non-Jews and their property, especially from the effects of burning synagogues. Unlike Goebbels, he, Himmler and Göring remembered what had happened in Vienna and worried about the economic losses that would be involved. The Gestapo should also arrest prosperous male Jews who were not too old and take them to concentration camps. In fact the Berlin Gestapo headquarters – without contact with Himmler or Heydrich – had already issued such an order an hour-and-one-half before for the arrest of 20–30,000 Jews. Apparently the official responsible, SS-*Standartenführer* Müller, had acted in accordance with a previously arranged plan.[68]

Late at night and during the next day the Party, SS, SA and Hitler Youth carried out violent actions on a grand scale against Jews in person as well as their homes, their shops, and synagogues. The SS did not stay out and were sometimes in uniform. The SA were very active, usually in civilian clothing. The Hitler Youth in uniform played a notable part in the destruction.[69] Efforts under the orders of Heydrich to limit the damage were not very effective. Massive destruction was wreaked: the 267 synagogues were in some cases torched by firemen, prepared with supplies of gasoline, collaborating with SS, SA or police, and sometimes in the presence of the mayor and the police-president.[70] Approximately 7,500 businesses and shops, as well as innumerable dwellings were destroyed.[71]

Gangs of young men, probably SA men, were active in most cities and towns, but in some areas there were reports that professors, teachers, and museum directors participated in the violence and destruction. Presumably they were Nazis who could not resist the action. The men engaged in looting frequently threw quantities of goods, such as clothing, from the stores, and women battled one another for the takings. Thus, although the larger part of the destruction was carried out by Nazi agencies under orders, there was some spontaneous participation and exploitation of the opportunity by men, women and children.[72] Ninety-one Jews were killed and many more beaten; 30,000 were assembled in various cities and towns and were taken to concentration camps, where approximately 1,000 were simply murdered or died after excruciating and brutal mishandling.

At Buchenwald an SS guard asked a Jew if he knew what being a Jew in the Third Reich signified and answered his own question "less than a piece of shit lying on the ground."[73] The camp commander said so all could hear that a dead Jew only provided material for the crematorium.[74] No one was tried for the murders; indeed, party courts sanctioned them because they were committed by party members who believed they were virtually following orders, as was indeed the case. These were obviously not the first murders committed by Nazis during the Third Reich, but because of their numbers they constituted a caesura in history.

Clearly the first actions against the Jews on the 8th and 9th were suggested in Nazi propaganda, thus partially precipitated by it. The suggestions worked upon popular mentalities prepared by years of indoctrination in Nazi "racism," Social Darwinism, eugenics, and anti-Semitism. But these widespread small scale attacks were also to a considerable degree spontaneous insofar as Nazis who were involved undertook the actions without orders from above and were joined by some of the citizenry. No doubt some of them were moved by sheer destructiveness, and visions of plunder.

The second and much larger wave of destructiveness on the 10th, which took place almost everywhere in Germany where Jews were to be found, was a result of orders from Munich followed by Nazi party and SA officials, who depended on their own troops in most places because the local citizenry was not easily moved to action. In one town the SA in civilian clothes on its way to carry out the pogrom was stopped by Nazi Party leaders in uniform. Some SA and party leaders were sent from one area to another to organize the action; in other cases 30–50 SA men arrived in trucks, stormed a synagogue, then moved on to destruction of Jewish shops and dwellings. In the countryside and small towns the political leader of the NSDAP played the largest part, whereas in the towns and cities the SA were highly organized in numerous troops that could be easily mobilized. Indeed, they thought in military categories and distinguished themselves so clearly from civilians that they sometimes even prevented them from participating in the pogrom. The SA were usually unrestrainedly brutal, stabbing, shooting and beating their victims, while the Party only in a few cases physically harmed Jews. Here and there the SS mistook their role and joined the NSDAP and SA; however, for the most part they followed orders and were passive.

In many cases, while synagogues burned the fire department stood by, in accordance with orders, to protect neighboring buildings.[75] The Nazis subsequently collected money from the Jewish community to tear down the remains of synagogues and carry away the stones, which the Nazis viewed as Jewish stones and would only use for street repair or similar purposes. They then forced the sale of the property for next to nothing, so that the whole operation amounted to confiscation.[76] The space was frequently used for parking. One Nazi Party official said he regretted that the higher authorities would not allow him to burn local Jews in a Baden-Baden synagogue.[77] That of course would be done in less than a year in Poland.

Nazis in Vienna considered throwing Jews tied together into the Danube so that they would drown.[78] The SA did drown some Jews in rivers and canals. They also invaded a few police stations and beat the Jews who had been brought there and placed in cells by the police or Gestapo. In the 3rd District of Vienna a number of Jews were taken to a cellar and shot.[79] The viciousness exhibited during the pogrom demonstrated that the word, which for a long time had emphasized that Jews could be treated as though they were not human, could fairly easily be converted into the deed. At the same time it is clear that the Nazis were organized for such an effort in order to carry it out as uniformly as they did.

The ability of the police and Gestapo to round up 30,000 Jews and then deport them to selected concentration camps so swiftly also indicates a high degree of organization. The lists of prosperous Jews prepared in the summer of 1938 were used for this purpose.[80] In Vienna 6,547 Jews were arrested and 3,700 of them sent to Dachau.[81] Some scholars have argued that the concentration camps were only capable of accommodating all of them because their facilities had been expanded during the summer of 1938 in anticipation of the pogrom.[82] But other scholars believe the expansion of the concentration camps was merely a response to the deterioration of their facilities and was not carried out in conscious anticipation of an impending pogrom.[83] The connection of the two was supposedly due to a confusion of memory on the part of Nazis and Jews later.

Certainly in the concentration camps the Nazis treated the Jews with unparalleled viciousness. They obviously had no qualms even about murder. The Jews were required to stand in the cold for 18 hours or more, or drill on the parade ground for 48 hours, and were not fed. Their clothing was thin and inadequate. Some suffered frozen ears, fingers and feet; one whose feet were amputated, died from poisoning.[84] At roll-call one day an SS block leader kicked a nearly dead but still breathing Jewish doctor on a stretcher and said loudly that "one should kill an entire block of Jews every day in this way." The Nazis drowned a few Jews in the latrine and others in a cement mixing machine.[85] They were whipped, beaten on their buttocks, and suspended by their arms tied behind their backs. In a special punishment, prisoners were incarcerated in a dark bunker for six weeks on half rations. In normal daily work they broke and carried stones, endured terrible thirst and nearly starved when their rations were halved in November. Sanitary conditions were frightful, some died of typhus, others committed suicide by fleeing or dying on the electric fences, and a number were executed.[86] The concentration camp authorities sent a card reporting the death in camp from a "heart attack" to the relatives, who first had to pay for the card and then for the urn containing the ashes.[87] The Nazis reportedly joked about even worse treatment: "the higher SS officers discussed among themselves whether they should not slaughter or burn some of the particularly fat Jews. This conversation was meant to be funny,"[88] according to its auditor. Clearly the Nazis enjoyed such brutality and murder for itself.

The most radical Nazis at all levels had long lusted for a pogrom. Nazi ideological indoctrination and propaganda had obviously prepared the way. The deportation of *Ostjuden* to Poland stimulated the assassination in Paris which triggered the pogrom. Nazi propaganda suggested the first outbreaks, which can in considerable measure be justifiably called spontaneous, but the second and much more extensive wave was ordered by Nazi Party and SA leaders. Local members of the Nazi Party and SA units were central to the actions, but some other Germans participated. However, because of the destructiveness of the pogrom and Nazi mistreatment of Jews, many Germans disapproved.[89] Virtually all Germans knew that the Nazi Party and SA had been chiefly responsible for these events; so did the outside world, whose diplomats and correspondents had not been deceived into believing that the pogrom had been spontaneous. Thus Goebbels' attempt to make it appear spontaneous had completely failed. The pogrom and the incarceration of 30,000 Jews in concentration camps for some weeks or months did not end this episode. It also had larger purposes.

THE ECONOMIC ASPECT

The pogrom was part of an escalation of action against the Jews to drive them out of Germany and Austria. At the same time the Nazis sequestered their dwellings, possessions and fortunes before allowing them to leave, if they could indeed arrange their departure. Legislation to strip the Jews of their positions in economic life and the entirety of their means had been implemented throughout 1938. In the aftermath of the pogrom, at a meeting on November 12 in the Air Ministry building to discuss economic problems, Göring proposed and had accepted an enormous fine of one billion marks on the Jews, who were held responsible for the pogrom. The idea of such a special tax for Jews dated back to Heinrich Claß, long-time leader of the Pan-German League, in 1912, which Hitler had revived and accepted on December 18, 1936 because of Gustloff's assassination. The law for this measure had been ready in June 1937, thus had merely to be implemented by Göring two years later.[90] As part of the fine, all of the insurance money for the destruction, 225 million marks, was seized by the Nazis.

Had the Nazis carried out the pogrom so as to seize remaining Jewish assets in Germany and Austria because they would make such a difference for their preparations for war? This certainly was the argument of East German historians.[91] However, the costs of rearmament from the beginning of 1935 to the end of 1938 were 40.5 billion marks. Jewish property in 1933 had been worth approximately 12 billion marks, and 5.1 billion in 1938, plus 3.4 billion in Austria, a total of 8.5 billion marks.[92] The East German thought the motivating factor was armaments cost, the West German that the Nazis expected to be saved by expansion rather than by the Jewish money. One can agree with the latter and still consider the sequestered money important.

At the end of this November 12 meeting Göring said that it was obvious that when Germany became engaged in war it would be time to complete the settlement with the Jews. In addition, as has been mentioned before, Hitler spoke more frequently with visiting diplomats or to the world about the impending annihilation of the Jews. This was part of increasingly warlike rhetoric associated with turning the screws on Poland.

CONCLUSION

This chapter has emphasized the bizarre form of ethnicity attributed to the Jews by Nazis, the intentional violence of word, law, and deed in the years from 1933 to 1938, and the degree of anticipation that precipitated the pogrom. Very little in the pogrom was truly spontaneous; most actions took place with the encouragement of the regime or upon direct order, but individual acts were revealing of popular mentalities. The regime tried but failed to conceal its responsibility. There is a much larger context which situates this pogrom as part of the history of the Holocaust, the extermination of the European Jews. The emphasis here has been on the victims as well as the perpetrators. The pogrom was a step on the way toward the escalation of violence into extermination during a war the Nazis desired against Jews and Slavs. The pogrom tested Nazi willingness to carry out extreme measures against their most hated foes. They passed the test. The pogrom also determined how much resistance the German people might offer to such actions. Clearly large numbers of Germans disapproved, but their resistance was minimal. The war itself would prove that "ordinary men" not only would fight dependably but could be relied upon to murder innocent civilians of all ages who were designated as the enemy.[93]

NOTES

* This collection is in the Houghton Library at Harvard. I have read all of them and am unaware of any other individual who has done so. I wish to dedicate this essay to the authors of the autobiographies.

1 Trude Maurer, "Ausländische Juden in Deutschland, 1933–1939," in Arnold Paucker (ed.), *Die Juden im Nationalsozialistischen Deutschland 1933–1943* (Tübingen: Mohr 1986) (Schriftenreihe wissenschaftlicher Abhandlungen des Leo Baeck Instituts Bd. 45), pp. 189–210; *idem*, "The Background for Kristallnacht: The Expulsion of Polish Jews," in Walter H. Pehle (ed.), *November 1938: From 'Reichskristallnacht' to Genocide* (New York: Oxford University Press, 1991), pp. 44–72.

2   Autobiography no. 207, Karl Schwab, p. 28; autobiography no. 219, Margot Spiegel, pp. 4, 21, in the "My Life in Germany" collection, The Houghton Library, Harvard University. Other biographies in the collection will simply be referred to by their number.

3   Autobiography no. 6, Martin Andermann, p. 106.

4   Reinhard Rürup, *Emanzipation und Antisemitismus. Studien zur "Judenfrage" der bürgerlichen Gesellschaft* (Göttingen: Vandenhoeck and Ruprecht, 1975).

5   Joseph R. Rudolph, Jr. and Robert J. Thompson (eds), *Ethnoterritorial Politics, Policy, and the Western World* (Boulder, CO: Lynne Rienner, 1989).

6   George L. Mosse, *The Crisis of German Ideology: Intellectual Origins of the Third Reich* (New York: Schocken, 1981).

7   Alexander Bein, "'Der judische Parasit'. Bemerkungen zur Semantik der Judenfrage," *Vierteljahrshefte für Zeitgeschichte* 13:2 (April 1965), pp. 121–49.

8   Konrad Heiden, *The New Inquisition* (New York: Modern Ages Books, 1939), p. 149.

9   Gisela Bock, *Zwangssterilisation im Nationalsozialismus: Studien zur Rassenpolitik und Frauenpolitik* (Schriften des Zentralinstituts für Sozialwissenschaftliche Forschung der Freien Universität Berlin, vol. 48) (Opladen:Westdeutscher Verlag, 1986); autobiography no. 163, Necheles, p. 26.

10   Ernst Klee, *"Euthanasie" im NS-Staat: Die "Vernichtung lebensunwerten Lebens"* (Frankfurt a.M.: Fischer Taschenbuch, 1989).

11   Norman Cohn, *Warrant for Genocide: The Myth of the Jewish World-Conspiracy and the Protocols of the Elders of Zion* (London: Eyre and Spottiswoode, 1967).

12   Udo Beer, "The Protection of Jewish Civil Rights in the Weimar Republic – Jewish Self-Defence through Legal Action," in *Leo Baeck Institute Year Book* XXXIII (London, 1988), pp. 149–76.

13   Autobiography no. 13, W.M. Citron; autobiography no. 227, Rudolf Steiner, p. 88; autobiography no. 239, Frederick Weil, pp. 5–6.

14   Autobiography no. 40, Paul Brüll, p. 76; autobiography no. 234, Richard Tischler, p. 35, relates a similar case of a friend arrested and taken to the Braunhaus, where he was forced to the wall, beaten, and told "Du Jude mußt jetzt sterben."

15   Autobiography no. 209, Ernst Schwartzert, p. 9; autobiography no. 251, Wolfgang Yourgran, p. 45.

16   Autobiography no. 249, Herman Wurzel, p. 73..

17   Götz Aly, Karl Heinz Roth, *Die restlose Erfassung: Volkszählen, Identifizieren, Aussondern im Nationalsozialismus* (Berlin: Rotbuch Verlag, 1984), pp. 8, 10, 57.

18   Reinhard Rürup, "Das Ende der Emanzipation: Die antijüdische Politik in Deutschland von der 'Machtergreifung' bis zum Zweiten Weltkrieg," in Arnold Paucker (ed.), *Die Juden im Nationalsozialistischen Deutschland 1933–1943* (Tübingen:Mohr, 1986), pp. 97–114.

19   Jeremy Noakes, "The Development of Nazi Policy towards the German–Jewish 'Mischlinge' 1933–1945," in *Leo Baeck Institute Year Book* XXXIV (London, 1989), pp. 291–354.

20   Autobiography no. 217, Charles Sorkin, p. 61; autobiography no. 219, Margot Spiegel, pp. 22–3; Ursula Büttner, "The Persecution of Christian–Jewish

Families in the Third Reich," In *Leo Baeck Institute Year Book* XXXIV (London, 1989), pp. 267–89.

21   Hermann Graml, *Reichskristallnacht: Antisemitismus und Judenverfolgung im Dritten Reich* (Deutsche Geschichte der neuesten Zeit vom 19.Jahrhundert bis zur Gegenwart) (Munich: Deutscher Taschenbuchverlag, 1988), p. 124; autobiography no. 217. I have followed Graml's recent volume, which brings up to date his excellent earlier *Der 9. November 1938: "Reichskristallnacht"* (Bonn: Bundeszentrale für Heimatdienst, 1957). See also Lionel Kochan, *Pogrom: 10 November 1938* (London: A. Deutsch, 1957); Rita Thalmann, Emmanuel Feinermann, *Crystal Night: 9–10 November 1938* (New York: Holocaust Library, 1974).

22   Autobiography no. 33, Hildegaard Bollmann (pseudonym); autobiography no. 158, Gerhard Miedzwinski, p. 15; autobiography no. 159, Hugo Moses, p. 6; autobiography no. 196, Arthur Samuel, pp. 39–40.

23   Autobiography no. 33, Hildegard Bollmann (pseudonym).

24   Autobiography no. 212, Hilda Sichel, p. 76; autobiography no. 250, Eva Wysbar, p. 22.

25   Autobiography no. 247, Annemaria Wolfram (pseudonym for Peine), pp. 15–16.

26   Autobiography no. 224, Herbert Stein, p. 266.

27   Autobiography no. 4, Henry Albert; autobiography no. 40, Paul Brüll, p. 80; autobiography no. 226, Margarete Steiner, p. 25; autobiography no. 227, Rudolf Steiner, p. 92.

28   Autobiography no. 232, Lore Tant, p. 108.

29   Autobiography no. 197, Karl Saas, p. 12.

30   Autobiography no. 160, Margaret Moses, pp. 38–41.

31   Record of interview by Prof. Harold Deutsch of Dr Erich Schultze in 1970, *Institut für Zeitgeschichte*. Dr Schultze, a Social Democrat, and his wife and child were badly beaten by the SS. See Harold C. Deutsch, *Hitler and his Generals. The Hidden Crisis, January–June 1938* (Minneapolis: University of Minnesota Press, 1974), pp. 54–5.

32   Graml, p. 162; translation from Lucy S. Dawidowicz, *The War Against the Jews 1933–45* (New York: Holt, Rinehart, Winston, 1975) p. 122, whose endnote quite rightly criticizes the translation in the English version of Krausnick, *Anatomy of the SS State*, p. 34.

33   *Documents on German Foreign Policy*, C, V, no. 490, p. 861.

34   Avraham Barkai, "The Fateful Year 1938: The Continuation and Acceleration of Plunder," in Pehle (ed.), *November 1938*, p. 109; Graml, p. 175.

35   Dawidowicz, pp. 124–5. The text of this speech is in Hildegard von Kotze and Helmut Krausnick, *Es spricht der Führer. Sieben exemplarische Hitler-Reden* (Gütersloh: S. Mohn, 1966), quoted in Helmut Krausnick, "Judenverfolgung," in H. Buchheim *et al.*, *Anatomie des SS-Staates* (Olten u. Freiburg i.Br: Walter Verlag, 1965), Bd. II, p. 326.

36   Jonathan Wright and Paul Stafford, "Hitler, Britain and the Hoßbach Memorandum," *Militärgeschichtliche Mitteilungen*, 2/87, no. 42, pp. 77–123.

37   Autobiography no. 130, Gertrude Lederer, p. 60; autobiography no. 224, Herbert Stein, p. 208.

38   Autobiography no. 238, Rudolf Walter, p. 3.

39   Autobiography no. 224, Herbert Stein, p. 271.

40   Gerhard Botz, *Wien vom "Anschluß" zum Krieg. Nationalsozialistische Machtübernahme und politisch-soziale Umgestaltung am Beispiel der Stadt Wien 1938/39* (Vienna: Jugen und Volk, 1978), Botz, pp. 243–54, 459–63; Götz Aly, Susanne Heim, *Vordenker der Vernichtung: Auschwitz und die deutschen Pläne für eine neue europäische Ordnung* (Hamburg: Hoffman and Campe, 1991), p. 33 ff.; *idem, Sozialpolitik und Judenvernichtung: Gibt es eine Ökonomie der Endlösung?* (Berlin Rotbuch Verlag, 1983), p. 20 ff.

41   This last number is from autobiography no. 16, Ernst Ballak; other accounts are in autobiography no. 238, Rudolf Walter; autobiography no. 239, Frederick Weil, pp. 80–104; see Eckart Früh, "'Erstarrt und erstorben...' Terror und Selbstmord in Wien nach der Annexion Österreichs," *Wiener Tagebuch* Nr. 3 (March 1988), pp. 15–19, Botz, pp. 98–105; Herbert Rosenkranz, *Verfolgung und Selbstbehauptung. Die Juden in Österreich 1938–1945* (Vienna: Herold, 1976); Konrad Kwiet, "The Ultimate Refuge – Suicide in the Jewish Community under the Nazis," in *Leo Baeck Institute Year Book* XXIX (London, 1984); Elisabeth Klamper, "Der schlechte Ort zu Wien: Zur Situation der Wiener Juden vom 'Anschluß' bis zum Novemberpogrom 1938," in *Der Novemberpogrom 1938: Die "Reichskristallnacht" in Wien* (Vienna: Historisches Museum, 1988); *idem,* "Der 'Anschlußpogrom,'" in Kurt Schmid and Robert Streibel (eds), *Der Pogrom 1938. Judenverfolgung in Österreich und Deutschland* (Vienna: Picus Verlag, 1990), pp. 25–33.

42   Konrad Kwiet, "To Leave or Not to Leave: The German Jews at the Crossroads," in Pehle (ed.), *November 1938*, p. 143.

43   For further details on these cases see Thalmann and Feinermann, *Crystal Night*, pp. 17, 19.

44   Graml, p. 173 ff.; Dawidowicz, pp. 129–30; Aly, Roth, *Die restlose Erfassung*, p. 53. These complicated edicts must have been prepared well before their introduction and application. See Avraham Barkai, "'Schicksalsjahr 1938'. Kontinuität und Verschärfung der wirtschaftlichen Ausplünderung der deutschen Juden," in Ursula Büttner (ed.), *Das Unrechtsregime: Internationale Forschung über den Nationalsozialismus. Festschrift für Werner Jochmann* (Hamburger Beiträge zur Sozial- und Zeitgeschichte, Bd. XXII) (Hamburg: Christians, 1986), Bd 2, pp. 62–63 and Avraham Barkai, *From Boycott to Annihilation: The Economic Struggle of German Jews, 1933–1943* (London: University Press of New England, 1989).

45   See Leonidas E. Hill, *Die Weizsäcker Papiere, 1933–1950* (Berlin: Ullstein Verlag, 1974) pp. 145, 170.

46   Graml, p. 176.

47   Dawidowicz, p. 122.

48   These two documents are in Vaclav Kral (ed.), *Die Deutschen in der Tschechoslowakei 1933–1947.* (Acta occupationis Bohemiae et Moraviae) (Prague: Nakl. Ceskoslovenské akademie ved, 1964), pp. 349–53, 357–62, cited by Stephan Dolezel, "Deutschland und die Rest-Tschechoslowakei (1938–1939) Besatzungspolitische Vorstellungen vor dem deutschen Einmarsch," in K. Bosl (ed.), *Gleichgewicht-Revision-Restauration. Die Außenpolitik der Ersten Tschechoslowakischen Republik im Europasystem der Pariser Vorortsverträge* (Munich: Oldenbourg, 1976), pp. 256–60.

49   Autobiography no. 9, Miriam Arrington, p. 28.

50   Autobiography no. 224, Herbert Stein, p. 323.

51 Heiden, *The New Inquisition*, pp. 148–9.
52 Graml, p. 186 ff; Dawidowicz, *The War Against the Jews* p. 142.
53 Martin Broszat, "Hitler und die Genesis der 'Endlösung.' Aus Anlaß der Thesen von David Irving," *Vierteljahrshefte für Zeitgeschichte* 25:4 (October 1977), English version "Hitler and the Genesis of the 'Final Solution.' An Assessment of David Irving's Theses," *Yad Vashem Studies* XIII (1979), pp. 73–125; Hans Mommsen, "Die Realisierung des Utopischen: Die 'Endlösung der Judenfrage' im 'Dritten Reich'," *Geschichte und Gesellschaft* 9:3 (1983), S. 392, Anm. 36; English version in Gerhard Hirschfeld (ed.), *The Policies of Genocide* (London:Allen and Unwin, 1986), pp. 134–5, fn. 36.
54 Autobiography no. 159, Hugo Moses, p. 9.
55 Autobiography no. 159, Hugo Moses, p. 11A.
56 Heiden, *The New Inquisition*, p. 79.
57 "National-Zeitung" (Basel), no. 542, November 21, 1938, p. 1.
58 Autobiography no. 256, Hubertus Flambo, p. 219.
59 Dawidowicz, p. 131.
60 Sybil Milton, "The Expulsion of Polish Jews from Germany, October 1938 to July 1939: A Documentation," in *Leo Baeck Institute Yearbook* XIX (London, 1984), pp. 169–99; Mauer, "The Background," in Pehle (ed.), *November 1938*; Dawidowicz, p. 133.
61 Maurer, *Ostjuden*, p. 355 ff.
62 See Gerald Schwab, *The Day the Holocaust Began: The Odyssey of Herschel Grynszpan* (New York: Praeger, 1990).
63 Graml, p. 13.
64 "National-Zeitung" (Basel) no. 522, November 9, 1938, p. 1.
65 This account of the events of 8–9–10 November is based entirely on Graml, p. 13 ff.
66 Graml, p. 20, says that he was not a fanatic. However, autobiography no. 29, Arthur Bluhn, p. 127, reports that Lutze said, "Don't speak to me about Jews. We have to hate and to exterminate them; and we will do so. We ignore any other considerations. Even I must obey."
67 "National-Zeitung" (Basel) no. 530, November 14, 1938, p. 2.
68 Graml, p. 22.
69 Heiden, *The New Inquisition*, *passim*, citing numerous newspaper reports; "National-Zeitung" no. 530, November 14, 1938, p. 2.
70 Heiden, *The New Inquisition, passim*.
71 Jonny Moser, "Depriving Jews of Their Legal Rights in the Third Reich," in Pehle (ed.), *November 1938*, p. 126 provides these figures. See also Graml, p. 32.
72 Heiden, *The New Inquisition, passim*.
73 Autobiography no. 199, David Schapira, p. 4.
74 Autobiography no. 239, Frederick Weil, p. 90.
75 Autobiography no. 247, Annemaria Wolfram (pseudonym for Peine), p. 5.
76 Autobiography no. 196, Arthur Samuel, pp. 24–5, 28.
77 Autobiography no. 239, Frederick Weil, p. 124.
78 Autobiography no. 226, Margarete Steiner, p. 24.
79 Autobiography no. 229, Fritz Stern, p. 53.
80 Graml, pp. 22, 177.

81   Elisabeth Klamper, "Der Anschlußpogrom," in Schmid, Streibel (eds), *Der Pogrom 1938*, p. 31; Gerhard Botz, "The Jews of Vienna from the Anschluß to the Holocaust," in Ivar Oxaal, Michael Pollak, and Gerhard Botz (eds), *Jews, Antisemitism and Culture in Vienna* (London: Routledge and Kegan Paul, 1987), p. 195.

82   Graml, p. 174.

83   Uwe Dietrich Adam, "How Spontaneous Was the Pogrom?" in Pehle (ed.), *November 1938*, pp. 81-3.

84   Autobiography no. 135, Joseph Levy, p. 75.

85   Autobiography no. 199, David Schapira, p. 7.

86   Autobiography no. 16, Ernst Ballak, pp. 32–63; autobiography no. 192, Karl Rosenthal, pp. 61–103; autobiography no. 199, David Schapira, pp. 1–7; autobiography no. 207, Karl Schwabe, pp. 73–82; autobiography 239, Frederick Weil, pp. 80–96; autobiography no. 247, Annemaria Wolfram (pseudonym for Peine), pp. 44, 48.

87   Autobiography no. 224, Herbert Stein, pp. 258, 277.

88   Heiden, *The New Inquisition*, p. 103.

89   William S. Allen, "Die deutsche Öffentlichkeit und die 'Reichskristallnacht' – Konflikte zwischen Werthierarchie und Propaganda im Dritten Reich," in D. Peukert and J. Reulecke (eds), *Alltag im Nationalsozialismus*, pp. 397–411.

90   Graml, pp. 161–2; see especially Barkai, *From Boycott to Annihilation*, pp. 114–15.

91   Kurt Pätzold, "Der historische Platz des antijüdischen Pogroms von 1938. Zu einer Kontroverse," *Jahrbuch für Geschichte* 26 (1982), pp. 193–216.

92   Graml, pp. 165–72.

93   See especially Christopher R. Browning, *Ordinary Men: Reserve Police Battalion 101 and the Final Solution in Poland* (New York: Harper Collins, 1992).

4. Divisions at the Center: The Organization of Political Violence at Jerusalem's Temple Mount/*al-haram al-sharif* – 1929 and 1990[1]

Roger Friedland and Richard D. Hecht

Carnage has come often to Jerusalem. At the city's sacred center, major collective violence has occurred twice in this century, first in August, 1929 and more recently in October, 1990. In this essay we examine the social organization of these violent encounters at the site which the Jews claim as the platform of their nation's ancient Temple and for Muslims the point from which the Prophet Muhammad leapt to Paradise. We analyze these episodes of violence at the center as a particular form of ritual politics, not just as irrational explosions of communal hatred.

NARRATIVE ACCOUNTS OF THE VIOLENCE OF AUGUST, 1929 AND OCTOBER, 1990

August, 1929

Shortly after mid-day prayer on Friday, August 23, 1929, thousands of Muslims streamed out of Jerusalem's *al-haram al-sharif* or "Noble Sanctuary" to begin what would become the most savage communal rioting of the less than decade-old British Mandate of Palestine. They had massed there at the call of the Mufti, Hajj Amin al-Husayni, Palestine's highest Islamic cleric to protect the site from an anticipated Jewish incursion. The mob moved through the Old City's narrow streets toward the Damascus and Herod's Gates where British police on horseback charged into the crowd trying to disperse them.[2] The mob continued north through Musrara and into Meah She'arim

114

where they attacked every Jew they could find. Stores were looted, buildings were torched.

On the following day, the rioting spread to the Jewish agricultural settlements of Motzah, Har-Tuv, Hulda and Be'er Tuvia outside Jerusalem. At Motza, an entire family was slaughtered, their property looted and their home set afire. In Hebron, the mobs went house to house, killing 66 Jews with knives and hatchets. More than 50 others were seriously wounded, one of the Jewish community's synagogues was desecrated and the hospital clinic at Bet Hadassah, which had served the health needs of both Jews and Arabs was completely ransacked. In several cases, Arabs protected the defenseless Jews by secreting them in their own homes[3]

On the 25th and 26th, there were more attacks in Tel Aviv, Jaffa and Haifa and on the 29th a ferocious attack was staged on the Jewish quarter of the Galilean town of Safed. Using reinforcements from Egypt and Malta, it took the British almost ten full days to restore order. In the end, 133 Jews had been killed and 339 wounded. British troops and police killed 116 Arabs and wounded 232.

October, 1990

On Friday, October 5, 1990, the sermon in al-Aqsa mosque included a special appeal for Muslims throughout Israel, the West Bank and Gaza to gather on *al-haram al-sharif* the following Monday. They were called to defend it against the attempt of a small Jewish group called "The Faithful of the Temple Mount" to enter the *haram* and to lay the foundation stone of the Third Temple. While the Israeli police banned the move, this small Jewish group immediately appealed. On Sunday, October 7, the Israeli High Court of Justice upheld the police action. Nonetheless, on the morning of October 8, as many as 3,000 Palestinians gathered on the *haram*, some of them arriving as early as 5:00 a.m. In the plaza below in front of the Western Wall of the Temple Mount, more than 20,000 Jews gathered for the Sukkot morning prayer and the *birkat ha-kohanim*, "the blessing of the priests" which follows the service on the intermediate days of the festival. At approximately 9:30 a.m., as the Sukkot service ended, the leader of the Faithful of the Temple Mount, Gershon Salomon, and about 50 followers attempted to enter the *haram* at the Mughrabian Gate above the Western Wall plaza. They were met by a contingent of Israeli Border Police and Municipal Police who told them that they could not enter. Salomon's group quickly left the Old City through the Dung Gate on their way to the Shiloah Pool in Silwan carrying a banner which proclaimed "Temple Mount – The Symbol of Our People is in the Hands of Our Enemies."

According to press reports filed that afternoon or on the following morning, the Palestinians, without provocation, began throwing rocks over the *haram*'s walls onto the Jews who were leaving the plaza of the Western Wall.

The media's initial sequence was later challenged by both Palestinian and Israeli civil rights groups. Border Police apparently broke through the locked and barricaded Mughrabian Gate to the *haram,* fearing that two of their officers were trapped within its precincts. [4] Storming into the *haram,* the Border Police began shooting with their weapons on automatic fire. Within a matter of minutes 17 Palestinians had been shot to death and more than 100 seriously wounded.[5]

Violence erupted in other parts of Jerusalem where buses and cars were stoned by young Palestinians. The army immediately clamped a curfew on much of the West Bank and Gaza hoping to avoid the kind of violent rioting that had taken place in 1982 after an Israeli soldier had shot up the Dome of the Rock, killing two Palestinians and wounding almost a dozen others. As in Hebron in 1929, Palestinians saved Israelis from the anger of their neighbors.[6]

One reporter described how a "cult of martyrdom" instantaneously enveloped the *haram.* Young people dipped their hands in the blood that had hardly coagulated on the *haram* and made palm prints on walls near where individuals fell or on the marble walls of the Dome of the Rock. Spent cartridges and tear gas canisters were put on display in al-Aqsa mosque and a display was hastily added in the nearby Islamic Museum for the blood-soaked clothing of the dead and wounded.[7]

VIOLENT PARALLELS

Contested Sacred Site

Separated by more than 60 years, these two violent explosions originated at a ritual center of overwhelming importance to both Jews and Muslims. For both traditions, the Temple Mount/*al-haram al-sharif* is simultaneously the center of time and space. The Jews refer to it as the *kotel ha-ma'aravi,* "the Western Wall," and *har ha-bayit,* "the Temple Mount." The Muslims refer to the very same space as *al-buraq,* "(the wall) of Buraq" and *al-haram al-sharif,* "the Noble Sanctuary." For Jews, the Temple Mount is the sacred center, the place where Abraham bound his son Isaac for sacrifice, where David united the confederation of ancient Israelite tribes and where his son, Solomon, constructed the first Temple, where the second Temple was reconstructed after the Babylonian Exile and later expanded by Herod the Great, and finally destroyed by the Romans in 70 C.E. The ritual of the Temple maintained the created order of the cosmos and bound heaven and earth. In the course of Jewish history, the reconstruction of the Temple and the reintroduction of its sacrificial ritual became normative components in speculation about the messianic end-time.

For Muslims, the *haram al-sharif* was identified after the Muslim conquest of Palestine as the location of Muhammad's *isra'* from the Qur'an's *al-masjid al-haram*, the mosque at Mecca, to *al-masjid al-aqsa* or "far distant mosque" (Sura 17:1). Still later perhaps, the traditions of the *mi'raj*, or the Prophet's ascension, were fused with the traditions of the *isra'*, or "night journey," so that as R. J. Zwi Werblowsky has observed: "There are no direct flights from Mecca to heaven; you have to make a stop-over in Jerusalem."[8] As in the Jewish tradition, the *haram al-sharif* is expected to play a crucial role in the drama of the end of time. On the day of judgment God will weigh the deeds of men in scales suspended from the arches which flank the Dome of the Rock.

Conflict over Ritual Rights

Both episodes of violence took place in a context where Jews were attempting to increase their ritual rights against Muslim opposition. The Muslims consider the Western Wall to be an inseparable part of the *haram al-sharif*, while the paved street below was part of a *waqf*[9] created by the Abu Madyan family in 1320, intended to provide housing and charity for Moroccan Muslim pilgrims.[10]

The Jewish ability to pray at the Western Wall of the Temple Mount dates from the mid-nineteenth century when Jews were granted a sultanic decree, or *firman*, to worship in the *al-buraq* alleyway. The *firman* curtailed the nature of their ritual rights in relation to times of prayer and what might be used in their rituals. At earlier periods the Jews worshipped at other areas of the surviving Herodian walls surrounding the *haram* on both the southern and eastern sides.[11]

Muhammad Ali of Egypt had issued an order in 1849 granting Jews permission to visit the Wall and to pray there. Muhammad Ali's order became part of the regulations governing various religious communities in Jerusalem's holy places, regulations which were comprehensively set out by Sultan Abdul Mejid's *firman* four years later. In 1911 and 1912 the Ottoman government of Jerusalem reconfirmed that while Jews might worship there, they could not bring chairs, tables or screens to divide male and female worshippers as required by *halakhah* or religious law. The Jews were not allowed to blow the *shofar* (the ram's horn) which is normally a part of the *Rosh ha-Shannah* and *Yom Ha-Kippurim* rituals.

The British sought to manage the potential for conflict between Jews and Muslims as well as between the diverse Christian communities of Jerusalem by retaining the entire series of Sultanic declarations awarding custody of the sacred places and times in them to one community or another. This body of *firmans* was widely known as the *Status Quo* in the holy places.

In 1929, Muslims believed that the Jews were intent upon rebuilding their Temple on the *haram*.[12] Mufti Hajj Amin al-Husayni held that the Jews would not be content with only the Western Wall, but desired the entire *haram* where they planned to construct the Third Temple. Hajj Amin insisted that the Jews were violating the *Status Quo* by bringing chairs and benches to the Wall. On September 28, 1925 he had written to the governor of Jerusalem that "you are undoubtedly aware of the fact that the Jews had on several occasions attempted to disregard the rules of the Wailing Wall by placing benches and wooden chairs [there]...Recently the Jews renewed this attempt publicly [and hence] the Muslim community was greatly annoyed."[13]

But, the Mufti was also making it increasingly difficult for Jews to worship at the Western Wall, even according to the *Status Quo*. The paved street used by the Jews, for example, was originally a quiet dead-end alley. The Mufti ordered the closed end of the ally to be opened, converting the street to a noisy public thoroughfare, where donkeys would sometimes defecate and bray at the backs of the Jewish worshippers.

In 1967, Israel achieved sovereignty over the entire Old City. Immediately after the Six Day War of 1967, the Israeli Knesset passed "The Law for the Protection of the Holy Places" which quaranteed free access to all holy places in Jerusalem, stipulated that the religious communities of each would administer them, and provided penalties for any violation of their sanctity. This law continued the language of Israel's Proclamation of Statehood stating that "the Holy Places shall be protected from desecration or any other harm, or anything which might affect the access of believers or their feelings for those places."[14] However, the Knesset's law failed to mention the *Status Quo* which had regulated the holy places from Ottoman times. Nor did it even make reference to the more oblique idea of "existing custom" in the holy places which had been used by the British after 1917 to stabilize relations between the competing religious communities.

In 1967, when the Israeli Army's rabbinical staff loaded their staff car to follow the paratroopers to the Western Wall, they packed a Torah scroll, a *shofar* and a bench to demonstrate that they would not abide by the *Status Quo*. When they arrived at the very narrow *al-buraq* alleyway, their first acts were to place the bench, hold up the Torah scroll and blow the *shofar*. Rabbi Shlomo Goren, then Chief Rabbi of the Israeli Army, was led by the rabbinical staff first across the *haram al-sharif* and then down to the Western Wall via the Mughrabian Gate.

The rabbi's actions were not just the acknowledgment of the providence of God in delivering the city, the Temple Mount, and the Western Wall to the Jews, nor devout ritual actions accompanying the return to the most sacred of places. They were also political acts announcing that the *Status Quo* was no longer the ruling paradigm for the governance of sacred space in Jerusalem. The state immediately decided to clear the Mughrabian Quarter of the Abu Madyan *waqf* to create a large plaza in front of the Western Wall. No longer would Jews be denied a place to worship.

Nonetheless, the Six Day War and the Knesset's "Law for the Protection of the Holy Places" created a central contradiction for Zionism. Jerusalem was united under Jewish sovereignty, but that sovereignty was not extended to the very site which symbolized and authorized the primeval unification of the ancient Israelites by King David almost three thousand years before. The state had chosen to extend full sovereignty over the *haram* without allowing Jews ritual access to Judaism's most sacred place, the Temple Mount itself.

The rabbis immediately began to debate the status of the Temple Mount. Does religious law, or *halakhah*, permit a Jew to enter the Temple Mount, regardless of its status within Israeli civil law? Shortly after the war, Goren had set up a small office on the *haram* where he carried out research on the Temple Mount to determine its exact precincts. In early August of 1967, Goren presented his findings to a group of army rabbis. At the end of their meeting Goren and the other rabbis made an extensive tour of the *haram* dressed in their military uniforms. Shortly afterward, Goren announced his intentions to pray on the Temple Mount later in the month on Tisha be'Av, the solemn fastday commemorating the Roman destruction of the Temple. On Tisha be'Av, which fell on August 15, Goren, other army rabbis and a group of students entered the Temple Mount carrying a Torah Scroll and a *shofar*. After their prayer service, Goren blew the *shofar*.

Defense Minister Moshe Dayan ordered Goren to desist from further efforts to pray on the Temple Mount. Then, in 1977, Goren's colleague, the Sephardic Chief Rabbi, Ovadia Yosef, ruled that it was improper to go there unless its precincts were indeed established and that no one was authorized by religious law to delineate those areas. Chief Rabbi Ovadia Yosef's opinion has held and therefore today a sign warning religious Jews is posted at the entrance to the Mughrabian Gate of the *haram*: "NOTICE AND WARNING – ENTRANCE TO THE AREA OF THE TEMPLE MOUNT IS

FORBIDDEN TO EVERYONE BY JEWISH LAW OWING TO THE SACREDNESS OF THE PLACE – the Chief Rabbinate of Israel."[15]

Nevertheless, Goren's efforts to pray on the Temple Mount triggered renewed fears among Jerusalem's Muslims that the Israelis were intent upon taking the entire *haram*. Almost immediately after Goren's prayer service on Tish be-Av, the Muslim religious authorities published a *fatwa* or religious pronouncement which stated that the question of the Western Wall had been fixed after the 1929 riots. The Western Wall was Muslim religious property, although Jews have the right to visit it. This they believed "ended the Jewish-Arab debate on the subject of this Holy Place...This debate should not be re-opened as it has been resolved through judicial means."[16]

Over the decades since Israel "unified" the city, as we shall see, there have been consistent efforts to repeal the Law for the Protection of Holy Places, to grant Jews the right to pray as individuals and to assemble on the *haram*. While they have all failed, the Muslim authorities of Jerusalem look fearfully at what has happened in Hebron. In Hebron, Abraham's family grave, equally revered by both Jews and Muslims, was until 1967 a mosque from which Jews were forbidden entry. Since 1967, in a city where Israel does not claim sovereignty, Jews have steadily expanded their ritual rights within the "mosque."

Moshe Dayan sought to make an arrangement in Hebron by which Jews would be able to visit, make pilgrimage and worship without disturbing the Muslim prayer service. The religious Zionists who first claimed ritual rights in Hebron have steadily expanded their presence in the mosque so that by 1990, they had a separate space for women, a Torah ark, a readers' platform, prayer books, and the right to hold regular services in the mosque even when this conflicts with the Islamic ritual calendar. In 1984, the Mufti of Jerusalem, Shaykh Sa'ad al-Din al-Alami, told us:

> In 1967 ... Moshe Dayan went to the Mayor of Hebron, Shaykh Jabbari, and he asked him to give him permission for the Jews to enter and visit the mosque. Shaykh Jabbari ... said that our mosques are open to any visitor who wants to visit, Jew, Christian, to any visitor ... The Mayor gave him permission. What has happened after that? First of all, they began to enter and visit after they took their shoes off. Then after a few days or a few weeks, they began to enter with their shoes on. Then they began to enter and pray. Then they brought their material for praying, benches and tables and so on. Then they began to pray most of the time and they don't let the Muslims enter to pray inside. If you go to see the mosque, you don't know whether it is a synagogue or a mosque. That's what has happened to our mosque in Hebron.

So, when Gershon Salomon and the Faithful of the Temple Mount threatened to march on the *haram* and set the cornerstone of the third Jewish Temple, many Muslims took the threat seriously. They likened Gershom Salomon, the leader of "The Faithful of the Temple Mount," to Rabbi Moshe Levinger. Had not Rabbi Levinger, a Gush Emunim rabbi, done the same thing in Hebron twenty years earlier?[17]

Sacred Space as Nationalist Battleground

In both episodes, the struggle between Muslims and Jews over this sacred center was an integral part of the national struggle between the Arabs or Palestinians, on the one hand, and the Zionists on the other. In both cases, groups within the nationalist movement used the sacred site and claims to it as a symbolic resource to mobilize a constituency, to assert their mandate to lead, and to defend the primacy of their definition of the conflict.

In the early twentieth century, Jerusalem was not nearly as central to the Zionist community as it is today. The bulk of early Jewish settlement was concentrated along the coastal plain, in the cities of Tel-Aviv and Haifa, and in the agrarian communities of the north. Jerusalem was dominated by non-Zionist and anti-Zionist Jews of the Old Yishuv who saw a predominantly secular Zionism as an anathema, a profane pre-emption of the messianic function.

Within the Zionist community, Jerusalem was a stronghold for the Revisionist movement, which was opposed to what was seen as the traitorous accomodation and gradualism of the Labour Zionists. The Revisionists were determined to make all of Palestine – Western and Eastern Palestine on both banks of the River Jordan – into a Jewish state.

In 1930, the Shaw Commission would find that Revisionist Zionist demonstrations on August 15, 1929 – a week before the Arab rioting which began on the 23rd – had set in motion a movement of reciprocal symbolic sacrilege. On that day, the Revisionists' youth movement, Betar, assembled at the Wall, shouting "The Wall is ours," raised the Jewish national flag and sang Ha-Tiqvah, the Zionist anthem. The unsubstantiated rumor that they had attacked Muslim residents of the immediate area and had cursed the name of the Prophet Muhammad only fanned the flames. The following day, some 2,000 Muslims marched to the Western Wall and destroyed a Torah scroll and prayer books. While some have argued that Hajj Amin attempted to manage the demonstration, the atmosphere was now so charged that there was no way to avert the explosion of violence which was unleashed a week later.[18]

The Palestinian population, in contrast to the Jewish, was concentrated in the central highlands, the towns and villages that dot the mountain range that today constitutes the spine of the "West Bank." While the Arabs of the coast had developed a coastal commercial bourgeoisie, Jerusalem remained their political center. The Arab political elites centered in Jerusalem had used the sacrality of the center to build the Palestinian nation and to assert their dominance. The Husayni family, descendants of the original custodians of the holy places of Mecca and Medina, had traditionally held municipal office in the city, as well as custodianship of the important Jerusalem-based Islamic *waqf* and its sacred Islamic sites. In 1921, one of their own, Hajj Amin al-Husayni, was appointed to a new position created by the British, the Grand Mufti, the highest Islamic post in Palestine. The Mufti built his own political base against the rival Jerusalem-based Nashishibi family, who were more supportive of a territorial accomodation with the Zionists, by emphasizing the sanctity of Jerusalem and exploiting the ritual conflict at the center with the Jews.

Almost immediately after his appointment to the position of Grand Mufti, Hajj Amin began an extensive restoration project on the *haram al-sharif*. Al-Aqsa Mosque and many of the religious schools and foundations located near it had deteriorated under the Ottoman administration of the city or had been damaged as a result of earthquakes in the previous centuries. Although the Mufti raised almost 105,000 British pounds, in order to complete his project he was forced to borrow heavily from other Arab regimes. The project was completed in August, 1928 and earned him the title of "Restorer of the *al-Haram al-Sharif* and Defender of the Holy Places."

Before the British Mandate, expressions of Muslim piety were regionally fragmented. Jerusalem's religious elites had long visited and made pilgrimage to the tomb of Moses – at least as Palestinian Islam understood it – on the road from Jerusalem to Jericho. Unlike the major festivals in the Muslim religious calendar this pilgrimage to the tomb of Moses was correlated with the Eastern Orthodox calendar. The pilgrims traditionally arrived at the tomb of Moses on Monday of Holy Week and spent two days there, after which they marched in procession to Jerusalem, ending their pilgrimage at the Dome of the Rock.

The pilgrimage to the tomb of Moses became a vehicle through which Hajj Amin al-Husayni forged a distinctive Palestinian religious and political identity.[19] Because the Nebi Musa pilgrimage was timed to coincide with Greek Orthodox Easter and hence frequently coincided with Passover as well, it periodically provided a context for conflict with the Jews who assembled in Jerusalem for their own nationalistic pilgrimage festival. Passover, after all, is the ritual re-enactment of national liberation.

This pilgrimage had been a site of conflict between Husayni's movement and the Revisionists. In April, 1920, Hajj Amin played an important role in violent demonstrations which broke out in Jerusalem in conjuction with the Nebi Musa pilgrimage. That year the festivals of Passover, Easter and Nebi Musa all took place at the same time in April. The procession that year wound its way up from Jericho and the tomb of Moses and arrived in Jerusalem, circling the Old City and halting in front of the Municipality building on Jaffe Road. There were a number of anti-Zionist speeches. When Hajj Amin, whose nationalism initially pushed him toward unity with King Faysal's Greater Syria, rose to speak he held up a portrait of the King and told the crowd that "This is your King!" The crowd roared back, "God save the King."

Meanwhile, Ze'ev Jabotinsky, the radical Zionist who would ultimately become the leader of the Revisionist movement and break with the Zionists, had organized a counter-demonstration in the Jewish Quarter of the Old City. This provoked the Muslim pilgrims, who rioted, killing three Jews and injuring scores of others. Jabotinsky's followers then counter-attacked the Muslim rioters. When the British finally were able to separate the two groups, the death toll was five Jews and four Palestinians and nearly a hundred injured.

In 1990, conflict over the uses of the *haram* remained a central issue between Israelis and Palestinians. Israel's victory against the attacking armies of Jordan, Egypt, Iraq and Syria in 1967 had given it control over the remaining parts of the West Bank of the Jordan River. Israel had constructed a new "unified" municipality of Jerusalem, including the entire Old City in which the *haram* was located. The Muslims may have been granted *de facto* control over the *haram*, but they operated under authority derived from a Jewish state. The conflict over Jewish and Muslim ritual rights on the *haram* now took on meaning as the extension or repudiation of Jewish sovereignty in the "unified" city of Jerusalem.

There were many Israeli activists who saw the demand for Jewish ritual rights on the *haram* as the necessary culmination of the Zionist revolution. There have been more than two dozen separate violent assaults on the *haram* since 1967. While we cannot offer a complete chronology of all the plots – individual and collective – against the *haram*,[20] the most dangerous was that planned by members of "the Jewish Underground" which was uncovered in 1984. In the wake of the murder in 1980 of six settlers in Hebron by Palestinians, a small number of Gush Emunim settlers, religious national- ists, organized an underground cell which targeted for revenge members of the Palestinian National Guidance Committee which had been formed in 1978. These settlers believed that Menachem Begin's signing of the Camp David Accords granting Palestinian "autonomy" would jeopardize Israel's claim to sovereignty over the West Bank and Gaza. After the brutal murder of another Hebron *yeshivah* student in 1983, they struck at the Islamic College in

Hebron and had planned an attack against Beir Zeit University. However, their plan to detonate bombs on five Palestinian buses was uncovered leading to their arrest and imprisonment, shortly before hundreds of Palestinians riding those buses would have been killed and injured.

The members of the cell were tried and found guilty, but in their early confessions, some admitted plotting to blow up the Dome of the Rock. Their plan was initiated after the Hebron attack in 1980. Its motivation, however, was not as simple as revenge. The plotters believed that the destruction of the Dome of the Rock would inaugurate a national redemption movement within Israel based on the writings of an obscure ultra-religious nationalist, Shabtai Ben-Dov. Human action to purify the Temple Mount of the Muslim "abominations" would lead them and the nation toward Israel's transcendent goal.

The plotters broke into a munititions depot and stole an Israeli device used to clear minefields. This provided them with the high explosives they would need for their carefully planned attack. They spent hours on reconnaisance missions, observing the Temple Mount through telescopes and binoculars from several locations. Every movement was logged and studied. One group observed the Temple Mount from a location between Mount Scopus and the Mount of Olives while another group watched from the roof of Yishivat Ha-Kotel in the Jewish Quarter of the Old City. A third group watched the Temple Mount from the belfry of the Church of the Redeemer in the Christian Quarter. Some members disguised themselves as tourists and entered the Temple Mount itself. They also planned to deliver a tape recording explaining their reasons for destroying the Dome of the Rock just minutes before the timers were set to explode and planned to have a photographer stationed on the Mount of Olives to commemorate the historic event.

The evacuation of Jewish settlers from Yamit, in connection with the peace settlement with Egypt in the Sinai, in 1982 accelerated the momentum to carry out the plot. The destruction of the Dome of the Rock would put an end to the Camp David Accords and Egypt would quickly back out of its new treaty relationship with Israel under Arab pressure. It was only the illness of one of the plot's three leaders and the diversion of their attention to the struggle for Yamit that forced the mission to be postponed.

Shortly after the withdrawal from Yamit, Allen Goodman, who had nothing to do with the plotters, attacked the Dome of the Rock. Security was intensified around the Temple Mount and a new series of lights placed on the eastern wall meant that the plotters could not scale the wall without being seen. It was decided to shelve the plan until some indefinite time in the future. The explosive charges were sealed in water-tight packages and hidden in a bomb shelter, its door sealed with cement. When the members of the cell were arrested over a year later, the news that they had carried out the attack on the Mayors and upon the students at the Islamic College, as well as planned to destroy the buses, shook the settlement movement to its very core.

Nevertheless, throughout the 1980s Israeli voices for a repeal of the Knesset's Law for the Protection of the Holy Places became more strident and their actions more provocative. In 1982, the maximalist party Tehiyah's Member of the Knesset Geula Cohen raised the issue of the Temple Mount's status as a civil matter. The Muslims, she argued, were building outdoor prayer platforms in clear violation of the *Status Quo*, which she believed was part of the Knesset's law, and were destroying archaeological sites.

A year later, Tehiyah made the status of the Temple Mount a key plank in its platform.

> The Temple Mount is not in our hands. Legally the Temple Mount is under Israeli sovereignty. In practice, however, it is ruled by the Muslim *waqf* and they do whatever they like there. They prevent Jews from praying there. They forbid entrance to Jews wearing *kippot* [head-coverings]. They build Muslim prayer altars on every site without building permits. Tehiyah will fight for actual Jewish sovereignty on the Temple Mount.

In the meantime, Cohen's charges in the Knesset had been tabled and they did not come before the Knesset's Interior Committee until early January, 1986. When a ten-person panel sought to investigate through a visit to the Temple Mount; they were confronted by a huge Muslim demonstration which blocked their entrance to the *haram*. A few days later the panel returned with more of the committee's membership. When Tehiyah's Rabbi Eliezer Waldman and another Tehiya party member took out prayer books and began the recitation of the Kaddish, a full-scale riot broke out. Over 600 Border Police were required to end the rioting and tear gas had to be used to disperse the mob.[21]

During the early 1980s the issue of the Temple Mount's status also found its way into the politics of other groups. In 1981, "The Faithful of the Temple Mount" was founded in Jerusalem with the explicit purpose of forcing the issue of Jewish prayer on the Temple Mount and restoring it to Israeli sovereignty.[22] At least five times a year, usually on the three pilgrimage festivals of Sukkot, Passover, and Shavu'ot when the Hebrew Bible commands Jews to appear before God at the Temple, and during Hanukkah and on Tisha be-Av, members of the Faithful of the Temple Mount attempt to enter the *haram* and pray. Each of these festivals is freighted with messianic and nationalistic symbolism; it was this calendar which brought the group to the Temple Mount on October 8, 1990.

Since the completion of the Israeli withdrawal from Sinai in 1982, the Temple Mount has become increasingly important as a rallying point for right-wing Israeli groups of all kinds who seek to prevent territorial compromise, who reject co-existence with the Palestinians, who seek to polarize the political situation so that another negotiated withdrawal is impossible. The attempts to pray on the Temple Mount and the conventions of The Faithful of the Temple Mount have provided a natural meeting ground for the extreme right to mobilize and make common cause with more centrist religious nationalists who simply seek to complete Jewish sovereignty in Jerusalem. So, in the group's first national convention in 1982, members of Rabbi Meir Kahane's far-right Kach party were present. Rabbi Kahane himself arrived at the convention to thunderous applause.

Like Tehiyah, Kach made the Temple Mount a central issue in its politics. Their activists plastered the walls of the Jewish Quarter of the Old City with posters showing a photomontage in which the Temple Mount has been cleared of the Dome of the Rock and al-Aqsa mosque. In their place stands the Temple of Solomon. Kach also distributed handbills which show Muslims at prayer with their backs to the Dome of the Rock and the location of the Temple on the same spot. These handbills usually carried a portion of the text of Numbers 1:51 (or 3:10, 10:38, or 18:7) where the biblical text describes the construction of the Tabernacle as the Israelites wandered in the desert and the punishment, death, for any non-Jew who encroaches upon the sanctity of this precursor to the Temple. This suggests that the Muslims have little or no real interest in the Temple Mount and that their mere presence on the Mount is punishable by death. The handbills also request support for Kach's efforts to push a bill through the Knesset which would remove the "foreigners from our Temple Mount." While there were tensions between Kach and the Faithful of the Temple Mount over strategy, Rabbi Kahane regularly participated in the prayer demonstrations organized by The Faithful of the Temple Mount.[23]

Since the mid-1980s the Temple Mount has also become a central issue for the Gush Emunim. In the early years of the decade, the movement's journal *Nekudah* hardly ever printed articles on the Temple Mount. Beginning in 1982, dozens of articles advocating the takeover of the Temple Mount appeared.[24]

By 1986 the issue of the Temple Mount had been fully integrated into Gush Emunim's political agenda. On Jerusalem Day in June of 1986, over 12,000 Temple Mount activists, many drawn from the ranks of the Gush Emunim, marched from the movement's seminary, Merkaz Ha-Rav, to the Mount of Olives to view a sound-and-light presentation entitled "The Temple Mount is the Heart of the People." A large detachment of soldiers and police was required to keep approximately 100 of these activists from forcing their way onto the Temple Mount.[25] The September, 1986 *Nekudah* editorial read: "What is proper regarding the whole Land of Israel must also be proper regarding the Temple Mount. ... If for returning to the whole Land of Israel, and for the establishment of the state, we have pushed [to] the end, by the same token we must now build the Temple."[26]

The following year, for the festival of Sukkot, the Gush Emunim and The Faithful of the Temple Mount together attempted to pray at the Mughrabian Gate. It caused a major riot in which an estimated 2,000 Muslims fought a pitched battle with police and border troops for over three hours. Tear gas and live ammunition were used to bring the rioters under control and more than 50 Palestinians were injured. Salomon told the press that "No power can stop us. We have the will of God."[27]

In the spring of 1987, for the first time since the early years of Jordanian rule in Jerusalem, an estimated 50,000 Palestinians drove in buses and cars to Nebi Musa for the pilgrimage. In July of 1988, more than 1,500 police were required to separate Muslims who wished to pray on the *haram al-sharif* on 'Id al-Adha, marking the end of the yearly pilgrimage to Mecca and Medina, and Jews who wished to pray at the Mughrabian Gate for Tisha be-Av. Approximately 100 Jews prayed at the gate, but police barred the group from entering the Muslim Quarter. Nevertheless, about 20 members of Tehiyah and Kach were able to slip through the police barricades and marched through the area waving Israeli flags.[28]

Both journalists and high-ranking military officers warned that it was now only a matter of time before very serious damage was done to the Dome of the Rock and al-Aqsa, and a plan to defend the Temple Mount from Jewish extremists must be implemented immediately.[29] Morris Zilka, Mayor Teddy Kollek's former Advisor for Arab Affairs, believed that the government had created ambiguity by seeming to waffle on the original 1967 decision to allow the Muslims to control the *haram*. The government, he told us, must once and for all determine who will rule the Temple Mount. "I can't live," he told us in 1983, "with the feeling that each day another group will come along and take the law into their own hands. That creates a problem and a mishmash in the town. If the government decides, bless you. That's their decision for the good or for the bad. They can do it. Let them decide, but they can't leave it to all kinds of hoodlums."

Just as militant religious nationalist Israelis used the Temple Mount as a symbolic battlefield on which to mobilize the Israeli public against territorial compromise, so militant religious Muslims have done likewise. The 1990 explosion on the *haram* took place during the *intifada*, a rising against the Israeli occupation whose public political leadership – as in 1929 – was concentrated in Jerusalem. The *intifada* had an organized political leadership, the Unified Leadership of the Intifada, which reflected and spoke in the name of the PLO. That "internal" leadership had been instrumental in pushing the PLO outside to declare finally in 1988 for an independent state, and to ground the legitimacy of that state in United Nations Resolution 181, the same resolution which had legitimated the partition of Palestine into a Jewish and an Arab state in 1947.

However, the PLO was being challenged by ever-growing militant Islamic movements. Over the years, the PLO had migrated towards the idea of an independent Palestinian state, thereby separating their local nationalism from the larger Arab nationalism, for which it had always presented itself as the most progressive vanguard. But Arab nationalism – whether radical or conservative, local or global – was being challenged everywhere by the rise of militant Islam. In the West Bank and Gaza, it was no different.

Supported by Israel and Jordan as an antidote to the PLO, for years the Muslim Brotherhood, a pan-Islamic movement seeking to ground state authority in Islamic law, had largely been content to spread the word, to build a Muslim society on top of which they would eventually build a Muslim state. The emergence of first, Islamic Jihad and then, after the *intifada,* HAMAS, an acronym for Islamic Resistance Movement, out of the Muslim Brotherhood changed all that. These militant movements, which put the priority back on expelling the infidel, represented a profound challenge to the PLO. Lacking cross-local mechanisms of representation, the network of mosques and Islamic schools was an indispensable political infrastructure.

The Islamic challenge was integral to the Palestinian revolt. In November, 1987, an Arab summit was called in Amman to discuss the Iran–Iraq war. In the face of Islam's rapid rise everywhere in the Arab world, Egypt – which had made peace with Israel eight years earlier – was finally allowed to return honorably to the Arab camp. Almost nothing was said about the Palestinian question. Arafat was treated shabbily. Apparently, militant Islam was more threatening than a Jewish state. Israel, likewise, had decided to crush Islamic Jihad in Gaza. It was against the backdrop of this combustible combination that the *intifada* exploded a month later.

HAMAS refused offers to become an integral part of the Unified Leadership of the *intifada*. Within the PLO too, they refused Arafat's efforts to incorporate and co-opt their movement. HAMAS has its own leaflets, its own "strike forces," its own conditions. Its slogan was "Allah is its target, the Prophet is its model, the Qur'an is its constitution, Jihad is its path, and death for the sake of Allah is the loftiest of its wishes." Its "covenant" defines all of historic Palestine, both Israel and the occupied territories as "an Islamic *waqf* for all the generations of Muslims until the resurrection." Partition was treasonous. Palestine was an Islamic trust, a *waqf*, that could not be bartered away at international conferences. "Giving up part of Palestine is like giving up part of religion," read the charter. "Such conferences are nothing but a form of judgment passed by infidels on the land of the Muslims."[30]

In the first year of the *intifada*, the PLO pointedly called for the Palestinians *not* to strike on Partition Day, a day which had always been mourned as an ignominious moment in Palestinian history. At last, the PLO was signalling its willingness to accept partition. In 1988, PLO activists had to use force to keep at bay HAMAS activists who demanded that the Palestinian shopkeepers shutter their stores as usual. But, already in the second year of the *intifada*, Palestinians obeyed HAMAS' call to strike on Partition day.

The Islamic militants have consistently attempted to escalate the *intifada*. Islamic militants were the first to open fire on Israeli troops in Gaza, a tactic explicitly foresworn by all streams of the Unified Leadership. Islamic militants have repeatedly stabbed innocent Jews to death in Jerusalem and elsewhere. It was an Islamic militant who seized the wheel of a Jerusalem bus and forced it off the road where it crashed in a ravine, killing a large number of passengers.

With such a strong Palestinian consensus against the escalation of material violence against Israelis, the followers of HAMAS naturally gravitated towards symbolic violence as an alternative. The *haram* was their natural battleground. It was significant then that HAMAS' first independent strike was held to commemorate the Australian Christian tourist Dennis Rohan's arson attack on al-Aqsa Mosque.

In April of 1989, at the beginning of Ramadan, there were massive disturbances on the *haram* which were widely believed to have been organized by members of HAMAS who had come to Jerusalem from the Gaza Strip. Huge boulders and stones which had been stored on the *haram* were hurled down onto the Jews praying at the Western Wall. Police retaliated with tear gas and rubber bullets.[31]

The following Friday, the Interior Ministry restricted entrance to the *haram* to those Muslims who were from Jerusalem. The Israelis set up roadblocks on the highways leading from the West Bank and Gaza to Jerusalem and stopped many who wanted to pray in al-Aqsa. Soldiers and Border Police, who manned check-points in the Old City and at the entrances to the *haram*, scrutinized every person's identity card so that only Muslims from Jerusalem could enter.[32] The Israeli police had previously estimated that 35,000 Muslims would want to pray at the *haram*; in the event, only 7,000 actually made it. The Mufti of Jerusalem, Shaykh Sa'ad al-Din al-Alami called for all Muslims to pray in al-Aqsa. If the Israelis "prevent them from entering the mosque," he said, "they are to pray in the Old City of Jerusalem. If they are barred from entering the city, they are to pray on the roads leading to Jerusalem."[33]

In 1990, Islamic militants were critical in galvanizing the Palestinian population to confront any attempt by Israelis to assemble or pray on the *haram*. While the PLO mobilized its nationalist forces to demonstrate their stead-fastness against the possible intrusion of The Faithful of the Temple Mount, HAMAS brought in its militants from Gaza spoiling for a confrontation. They were abetted in this objective by the growing power of the Muslem Brotherhood in Jordan.

As a result of the *intifada* and the riots that took place in Jordan, the Jordanian regime held its first elections since democracy was suspended in 1956. The Muslim Brotherhood immediately took 32 of the 80 seats, forcing King Hussein to cede them five ministerial portfolios. In addition, the Islamic militants gained greater influence over the *waqf* controlling the *haram*, thereby undercutting the *modus vivendi* that the Jordanians had worked out with the Israelis to prevent politicization of the *haram*.[34] Just as Islamic militants had sparked the *intifada* from Gaza in 1987, from Jerusalem they would now push the confrontation to a new level and gain authority over it.

On the other hand, the threat of the Jewish underground compelled the Israelis to strengthen their security on the *haram*. After the April, 1989 disturbances on the *haram*, the Israeli presence there was further augmented with the addition of the police post which would be the catalyst – as described in the initial reports – for the killings of October, 1990.

The Zamir Commission, which was appointed by Prime Minister Shamir to investigate the violence, recommended in its report of October 26, 1990 that "the police should consider limiting events on the Temple Mount, the Western Wall and in the Old City concourses which have high probability of resulting in severe disturbances." Further, the commission underscored that the state of Israel bears responsibility for maintaining the security of the Temple Mount and that it was of the opinion that the police have the "authority to close the Temple Mount gates and to prevent entry and assembly whose intent was unrest." The commission also recommended a complete ban upon any demonstrations on the *haram*, at the Western Wall and throughout the Old City. Only official state events should be permitted in the vicinity of the Western Wall.[35] In its report, therefore, the commission urged the Israeli state to implement a series of recommendations similar to those proposed by the Shaw Commission. However, the commission's recommendation that the police have the authority to close the *haram* is an extension of state power over the *waqf's* autonomy as suggested by the Law for the Protection of the Holy Places.

Sovereignty

In both cases of violent conflict, political sovereignty was at issue. At one level the issue of sovereignty defines the nature of the violence. In 1929, the violence was inter-communal; Arabs killed Jews outside the structure of governmental authority. In 1990, Jews killed Arabs as agents of the state within the structure of governmental authority. In 1929, neither community could claim sovereignty over the Temple Mount and *al-haram al-sharif*. The British had sanctioned custom in the holy places and then later the *Status Quo*, but they remained its arbiter. The Arabs keenly experienced British rule as a loss of sovereignty.

The 1990 killings were the result of a gradual process which revealed the inherent tensions within Jewish sovereignty both within Israeli society and over the Palestinians ruled by the Israeli state. The Knesset's Law for the Protection of the Holy Places gave each of the non-Jewish religious communities of the newly united city exclusive control over its holy places. This created both administrative and theological problems for each religious tradition which was now subordinated to Israeli sovereignty.

For the Muslim community of Jerusalem and the Middle East, Jewish sovereignty over the *haram al-sharif* posed both a historical and a theological problem. How could one of the subordinated minorities of traditional Muslim society now exercise political power and control over the Muslims? But the unification of Jerusalem as a result of the Six Day War was equally problematic for the Jews. Menachem Friedman, who has studied the anti-Zionist and non-Zionist Orthodox Jewish communities which constitute today the "Old Yishuv" of Jerusalem, has noted that "the boundaries delineated after the 1948 war severed the State of Israel not only from the Western Wall but also from the historic Land of Israel, the Land of the Patriarchs, cherished as a living thing by generations upon generations of Bible-reading Jews. The State was bereft of many and perhaps most of the paths, lands and tombs of Jewish *Eretz Israel*. Jews had always expressed affinity for their homeland through direct contact with these sites. This situation – and especially severance from the site of the Temple – effectively 'neutralized' the State of Israel from the more deeply religious and substantive dimension of the concept of 'Redemption.' It freed the various factions of the religious public from the need to cope with the religious, practical and concrete ramifications of Jewish sovereignty over the entire Land of Israel and especially the Temple Mount."[36] With the extension of Israeli

sovereignty over Jerusalem, the anti-Zionist and non-Zionist Orthodox
would either have to find new strategies to delegitimate the Jewish state
or reinterpret its theological significance.

But, Jewish sovereignty over the Old City of Jerusalem set other powerful
forces in motion within both the Israeli state and the Palestinian Muslim
community of East Jerualem and the West Bank and Gaza. The Western Wall,
an essentially religious space, penetrates to the very core of Israeli civil religion.
Israel's elite military units are initiated in ceremonies in the plaza in front
of the Wall and the state's new memorial festivals, Holocaust Memorial Day,
the Memorial Day for Israel's soldiers who have fallen in war, Independence
Day and Jerusalem Day, all involve important rituals at the Western Wall.
This has caused some Israelis like the late Professor Yeshayahu Leibowitz
to argue that this fusion of religion and state, transforming the Western Wall
into a national symbol, is idolatry.

The extension of Israeli sovereignty to the eastern side of the city and
conquest of the West Bank and Gaza triggered a redefiniton of Zionism itself,
or at least a *kulturkampf* over the content of the state's legitimation. While
it is beyond the scope of this discussion to explore this redefinition in great
detail, a word or two is necessary. Rabbi Avraham Yitzhak ha-Kohen Kuk
(1865–1935) accomplished a major re-interpretation of the relationship of
Zionism and Judaism, allowing for the possibility that secular Zionism
established the foundations for the religious redemption of the Jews. His
thought allowed religious Zionism in the form of the Mizrachi movement
to not only participate in nation-building, but also to reduce tensions between
secularists and the religious. His son Rabbi Zvi Yehudah ha-Kohen Kuk
exercised considerable influence over an entire generation of young religious
Zionists who were educated in his *yeshivah*, Yeshivat Mirkaz Ha-Rav in
Jerusalem, and was able to translate much of his father's intellectual world
into political action.[37]

While the father spoke of the idealized state of Israel, the son spoke of
the "real Israel" which was fully embodied in the state. In a collection of
sermons and lectures published in 1969 he wrote that the "real Israel is the
Israel which is redeemed; the kingdom of Israel and the army of Israel, a
whole nation and not an exilic Diaspora."[38] The political manifestation of
Zvi Yehudah's interpretation of his father's work is seen in the emergence
of the Gush Emunim and the settlement movement which emerged shortly
after the Six Day War.[39] The members of the Gush Emunim believe that the
political history of Israel is divinely guided, that the growing power and territorial extent of state authority is nothing short of the realization of God's
original promises to Abraham and his descendents. Many viewed the Six
Day War as the stirrings of the messianic era and their settlement of the

conquered lands of Judea, Samaria and Gaza as the sign and mechanism of movement toward the endtime.[40]

The Structure of Politicization

In both 1929 and 1990, the politicization of this sacred site had a defined partisan structure. At stake in both cases was the possibility of territorial partition, of dividing western Palestine into a Jewish and an Arab state. In both cases, those who sought to politicize the center were "rejectionists," those opposing any territorial settlement. In both cases, the groups which led the conflicts were relatively new movements trying to create a space for themselves in their nation's political culture and to transform its goals.

In 1929, the Arabs were led from Jerusalem by the dominant Palestinian leadership which sought to fuse Palestinian nationalism and Islam. Hajj Amin al-Husayni, who had assumed leadership of the Supreme Muslim Council eight years before, portrayed the Jewish threat as an attempt to control the *haram* and rebuild the Temple. While the Labour Zionist community was relatively weak in Jerusalem, the Jewish challenge was organized by an equally secular but marginal Zionist movement. The British, the governing Christian regime, attempted to regulate the conflict with reference to the *Status Quo* and defined the problem as one of maintaining order.

In 1990, although the parties to the conflict were again "rejectionists," the political terms of the conflict were partially reversed. This time the Palestinians were galvanized by an Islamic leadership which put primacy on transnational Islam and opposed any compromise with Zionism. Unlike 1929, HAMAS – like the Jewish Rejectionists in 1929 – was outside the central organizing body of the Palestinians, the PLO and the Unified Leadership of the Uprising. And this time the Islamic militants were led not from Jerusalem, but from Gaza.

As in 1929, the Jewish challenge was led by a marginal organization, The Faithful of the Temple Mount, created eight years earlier. They again defined the challenge of Jewish ritual rights as a nationalist, as opposed to a religious, issue. However, unlike 1929, their aims were no longer marginal to the dominant Israeli political culture. Their ultimate objectives and orientations were shared by the majority of the then Likud-led governing coalition, by the bulk of the Jewish settlement movement, Gush Emunim, and by significant segments of the state rabbinate. And this time, the conflict was adjudicated by a sovereign Jewish state controlled by the ideological heirs to those forces who challenged the Mufti at the Wall in 1929. Unlike the Labour Zionists who define the issue primarily in terms of religious pluralism and civil rights, the Likud defines it in terms of incomplete sovereignty.

The Conflicts in the Arena of International Politics

Both conflicts were set in a particular geo-political context. Indeed, Hajj Amin al-Husayni, in part used this site to help transform a local conflict into a pan-Islamic and pan-Arab struggle against the Zionists. The transformation of this conflict over ritual rights allowed him to secure his position as the unrivalled defender of the *haram al-sharif*'s sanctity and garner extensive support from all segments of the Muslim world.

The conflict over Jewish ritual rights at the Western Wall had intensified the year before. On September 23, 1928, the eve of Yom Ha-Kippur, an Ashkenazic attendant at the Western Wall began making preparations for religious services the next day. He brought a larger than usual ark, spread mats and set up lamps. But, he also attached a dividing screen to the pavement. This was brought to the attention of the *mutawalli* or guardian of the Abu Madyan *waqf,* who immediately notified the Mufti, who in turn sent a formal complaint to the Deputy District Commissioner of Jerusalem.

The Commissioner ordered the screen removed and was assured by the Jews that it would be gone by the following morning. However, when the Commissioner visited the area the next day, the screen was still there. When he again ordered the screen taken down, the Orthodox Jews who were at prayer refused to desecrate *Yom Ha-Kippur* by performing what they considered an act of labor. When the police started to remove the screen a fight began in which a number of Jews were injured.

In October 1928, the Mufti wrote a memorandum claiming that "having realized by bitter experience the unlimited greedy aspirations of the Jews in this respect, Moslems believe that the Jews' aim is to take possession of the Mosque of al-Aqsa gradually on the pretence that it is the temple, by starting with the Western Wall of this place, which is an inseparable part of the Mosque of al-Aqsa."[41] In November, 1928 he assembled an Islamic conference in Jerusalem to discuss the question of the Wailing Wall. The Mufti suggested that if the Jews continued to violate the *Status Quo* that the Muslims would be compelled to initiate an uprising. Some of the delegates were from India and the implied threat to the British was that if they did not restrain the Jews, the insurrection might even spread to India, then a British colony facing very severe communal conflict between Hindus and Muslims. This conference was the opening salvo of what became known as the *al-buraq* campaign in which Hajj Amin hoped to mobilize not only Palestinians, but Muslims throughout the world. His campaign was designed to challenge the British government to adhere to the *Status Quo* which he understood was a potent political stake and battleground with the Zionists.

The Zionists had few allies and therefore were vulnerable to how international politics might retard their national cause. Their response to this vulnerabilty was to try to avoid coercive tactics in such a sensitive site. They attempted to extend their ritual rights by buying them. They did not want confrontation with their lukewarm patron, the British, if it could be avoided. Many Zionists believed that Jerusalem, given its international sensitivity, might be beyond national reach. And any needless provocation in the city was sure to jeopardize international support.

Hajj Amin was well aware that the Jews had attempted to purchase sections of the Wall immediately after the First World War and again just two years before. In 1918, Chaim Weizmann had attempted to purchase the Wall for 70,000 Palestine pounds as a way to stimulate enthusiasm for Zionism. The deal was cancelled only when Palestinian nationalists discovered that the *waqf's* administrators had agreed to the transaction. In 1926, the Zionists raised the offer to 100,000 Palestine pounds for property in the Abu Madyan trusteeship. They were able to buy one large parcel only 50 meters from the Mughrabian gate to the *haram* and were beginning negotiations for additional property directly in front of the Wall. Immediately after the disturbances in 1928, Weizmann offered 61,000 Palestine pounds for the Wall itself, but the District Commissioner dissuaded him, suggesting he should postpone further attempts to purchase these properties until things had quieted down.[42] The whole affair of Jews attempting to purchase *al-buraq* and Palestinians wanting to sell it must have come as a great embarrassment to the Mufti who resided in the same neighborhood. The Revisionists wanted to undercut Weizmann, who supported partition, and to negate the rapprochement he had reached with the British.

But, Hajj Amin also took a number of steps to make the Jewish situation at the Western Wall even more untenable. He ordered that a *mu'azzin* take a position on top of the roof of a house immediately adjacent to the Wall, to call Muslims to prayer. The house became a *zawiya,* a small Sufi mosque, and hospice. Sufi Muslims would gather there for the ritual *dhikr* which would be accompanied by cymbals, gongs and the shouting of *Allahu akbar*. While the cacophonous sounds that emerged from the *zawiya* interfered with Jewish prayer, in Hajj Amin's strategy it was also intended to underscore the sanctity of *al-buraq* for Muslims. But, just as the Muslims had appealed to the British that the Jews had violated the *Status Quo*, the Jews now argued that the Mufti's actions were not sanctioned by the *Status Quo*.[43]

The following year, Hajj Amin's activities to demonstrate that the Jews intended to use the Western Wall as a platform to regain the Temple Mount culminated in the rioting which spread from Jerusalem to Hebron. The British ultimately took the issue of the Western Wall to the League of

Nations where they proposed that the League establish a commission to "study, define, and determine the rights and claims of the Jews and Muslims ..." The Mufti protested and argued that decisions concerning the holy places of Muslims could only be established by Shari'a law.

The British attempted to move both Jews and Muslims toward some compromise, but the Mufti steadfastly refused to meet with the Jews saying that "if he were to meet with the Jews, this would give them rights to the Wailing Wall."[44] The British came to see the Mufti as the chief obstacle to any resolution between the contending parties at the Western Wall. Al-Husayni's intransigence in the wake of the 1929 violence convinced the British that the Mufti endangered the continuation of the Mandate. They stripped him of any control over the revenue of *waqf* property by returning control to the central government as it had been under the Ottomans. Further, they barred the Mufti from heading the Shari'a courts.

Politicization of ritual space preceded collective nationalist struggle. The conflict over the Western Wall-Temple Mount and *haram al-sharif* continued to simmer throughout the 1930s and early 1940s. However, during the Palestinian revolt itself, between 1936 and 1939, the *haram* was not used to mobilize against either the British or the Zionists. During the first six months of the revolt, with as many as 150 demonstrations, strikes and acts of violence being reported each day by the *Palestine Post*, only one small demonstration was held on the *haram*. This is not to say that the *haram* was not of supreme symbolic importance during the revolt. Walid Khalidi's photographic documentation of Palestinian life before 1948 contains a guerrilla stamp issued in 1938 which shows both the Dome of the Rock and the Church of the Holy Sepulchre superimposed on the map of Palestine. While this stamp might have been intended to iconographically demonstrate the united cause of Palestinian Muslims and Christians against common enemies, it also reveals the continued intersection between this sacred center and politics.[45]

After the 1948 war which resulted in the division of Jerusalem and the annexation of the West Bank and the eastern sectors of the city by the Jordanians, both King Abdullah and then later King Hussein saw the *haram al-sharif* as a potential source of resistance to Jordanian sovereignty over Palestinian political affairs. King Abdullah was in fact assassinated on the *haram* in 1951 by a Palestinian associated with the Mufti's family who belonged to a militant Muslim movement called the Holy Jihad. Hussein tried to control the symbolic power of the *haram* by making the entire religious infrastructure of the West Bank and Jerusalem economically dependent on Amman as well as to use the Muslim Brothers to undercut Palestinian nationalists, the Communists, Baathists and Nasserites.[46] The Muslim Brothers were given prominent positions in Jerusalem's religious institutions.

For Muslims and Christians both Abdullah and Hussein kept the *Status Quo* as the regulatory regime for conflicts over the holy places. Jewish rights at the Western Wall-Temple Mount and *haram al-sharif* were completely abrogated. Despite the guarantees provided by Article 8 of the Armistice Agreement of 1949 which allowed Jews daily passage to the eastern sections of the city for purposes of prayer at the Western Wall, visitation of their cemetery on the Mount of Olives and the Tomb of Rachel, the Jordanian regime prohibited Jews from crossing at the Mandelbaum Gate and tourists visiting Jordanian Jerusalem were periodically required to show baptismal certificates when requesting tourist visas.[47] The Hashemite *haram* became one of the major centers of Jordanian influence on the West Bank. While Hussein relinquished sovereignty over the West Bank and Jerusalem in Summer, 1988 which included the termination of salaries for teachers and civil servants, he continued to fund the *waqf* of the *haram al-sharif* and to pay the salaries of its staff.

The international context for the violence of 1990 had two very important dimensions. First, Islamic movements had been on the rise throughout the Middle East since the late 1970s. Second, since the PLO's recognition of Israel and acceptance of partition in 1988, there was growing international support to find a territorial solution to the Palestinian problem. Saddam Hussein's invasion of Kuwait in August, 1990 only encouraged this trend. For the first time Jerusalem was seriously in play diplomatically. Exclusive Israeli sovereignty in the city had been called into question with President Bush's off-the-cuff remark in March, 1990 that East Jerusalem was occupied territory. This was one of the factors which led to the collapse of the Likud-led Unity Government. Israel had taken special pride in its ability to govern unified Jerusalem. The Palestinian uprising, which began in December 1987 redivided the city. The barbed wire, minefields, and sniper walls which had cut the city in two from 1948 to 1967 re-emerged as a geography of fear. Fewer and fewer Israelis visited Jerusalem and the Old City. Fewer tourists came each season.

Communal acts of Palestinian violence in Jerusalem were less intense than elsewhere in the West Bank and Gaza. There were important reasons for this, not the least of which is that Jerusalem was the center of the *intifada*'s leadership which enjoyed a freer political atmosphere in Jerualem than anywhere else. It was to the advantage of the Unified Leadership to keep violence to a minimum in Jerusalem so that their activities would not be curtailed.

The Palestinian rejectionists, however, concentrated their murders of Jews in and around the city. Yet the Israelis acted with great restraint in Jerusalem relative to the West Bank and Gaza. As a result, while a significant number of Jews died in Jerusalem during the *intifada* up until the *haram* conflict in October 1990, few Palestinians had been killed in the city. When Israel refused to respond to the PLO's gesture of recognition and the Americans appeared unwilling to press the Israelis for concessions, HAMAS was able to force the battle for the *haram*. The Islamic militants had brought the intifada to the center of Palestine.

The Political Consequences of the Conflicts

There is consensus that the inter-communal violence of August, 1929 marked a fundamental change in the relationships between Palestinian Arabs, Zionists, and the British. This confrontation also had internal consequences for the Palestinians and the Zionists.

It provided pro-Zionist opinion within the British Government with a powerful argument against a Palestinian legislative council, delaying the adoption of such a program until 1936, when the ever-growing Zionist Yishuv was able to counter it. More importantly it marked the beginning of the transformation of the Palestine question into a pan-Islamic issue. The Supreme Muslim Council led by Hajj Amin al-Husayni was able to translate its conflict with the Zionists into a conflict which commanded the attention of Muslim public opinion throughout the Middle East. Muslims everywhere, Porath writes, "now faced concrete demands by the Muslims of Palestine to come to their aid in defending the Islamic Holy Places in Palestine, which were entrusted to the care of Palestinian Muslims by the Muslims of the entire world." Large sums of money were raised within the world Muslim community on behalf of the Arab victims of the riots. But the crowning achievement took place in 1931 when a world-wide Muslim congress in defence of the Islamic Holy Places in Palestine was convened in Jerusalem under the presidency of Hajj Amin al-Husayni. Despite the fact that Zionist land acqui- sition, which was galvanizing Palestinian discontent, was minimal in Jerusalem, Husayni's utilization of the *haram* and its pan-Islamic signifi- cance helped him consolidate his claims to lead the Palestinian community and to define Palestinian political identity against rival formulations.[48]

Others have suggested that the level of conflict at the *haram* was a harbinger of the revolt which would shake Palestine in 1936–9. Militant Muslim clandestine groups like the "Green Hand," the very first Palestinian groups to engage in guerilla warfare, which appeared in Winter 1929–30, were formed by individuals implicated in the August rioting. Most important of these groups was that formed by Shaykh Izz al-Din al-Qassam (1871–1935) which operated against Jews and Jewish settlements in the Galilee. In 1930, al-Qassam was able to obtain a fatwa from the Mufti of Damascus which authorized violence against the British and the Jews and it appears that the August riots were instrumental in crystallizing his decision to adopt a revolutionary strategy. Killed in a shootout with the British in the hills outside of Jenin, al-Qassam was proclaimed a martyr who had sacrificed himself for the fatherland. His grave became a place of pilgrimage and he was extolled in religious circles as the paradigm of human behavior. [49]

The riots also altered the relationship between the "Old Yishuv" composed of Orthodox communities opposed to Zionism and the "New Yishuv," Zionists who were predominantly secularized and modernized traditional Jews. The great majority of Jewish victims in Jerusalem, Hebron and Safed were members of the Old Yishuv. Menachem Friedman has argued that the violence was one of the major factors which drove the Old Yishuv's central political organization, Agudat-Yisrael, toward greater and greater dependency on the New Yishuv.[50]

The violence on the Temple Mount/*al-haram al-sharif* in 1990 significantly altered the conflict, not only between the Israelis and the Palestinians but also in the geo-political arena. The Islamicists were seen among the Palestinian population as willing to sacrifice themselves to protect the *haram*'s sanctity. While HAMAS had been pivotal in the emergence of the *intifada* and had steadily grown in the early years of the revolt, the violence allowed them to capture much wider support for their position as leaders of the Palestinians. Some have suggested that the killings worsened US–Israeli relations. The United States voted to support the UN Security Council resolution which condemned Israel for using excessive force. However, some have suggested that American–Israeli relations had begun to deteriorate long before Saddam Hussein invaded Kuwait and long before the events of October 8. The most salient factors in the tension between the US and Israel during the Bush administration were the end of the Cold War, the end of the Iran–Iraq war, and the Iraqi crisis. Steven L. Spiegel writes that these factors brought "American policy-makers back to making uneasy calculations between Arabs and Israelis – much as they did before Reagan and Shultz tilted firmly toward Israel."[51] The victories of both Yitzhak Rabin and Labor in 1992 and Bill Clinton again shifted the balance and prepared the environment for the "Olso process."

THE DISCURSIVE POLITICS OF CENTERING

Paul Brass' introductory chapter for this volume reminds us of the importance of discourse in the formulation of meanings for collective and inter-communal violence. Acts of violence, in particular, must be interpreted by a community

within particular cultural frames or discursive fields. These frames are
always tied to the nature and identity of political authority given its claim
to monopolize legitimate violence. Every report, every narrative, every
description of violence reflects a specific community's self-understanding
and the way it legitimates state power. Given that all states are centered,
violence at the center is particularly powerful.

The political violence of 1929 and 1990 was appropriated through two
dominant discourses. First, discourses of sovereignty grounded the right of
the state to assert order. The governing formulation in this discourse was that
the violence reflects a breakdown in state control which can be avoided by
changing the organization and deployment of the state's coercive instruments.
The second discourse structures the violence in sacrificial symbolism. The
conflict is a natural expression of a cosmological struggle in which the
sacred center is a primordial signifier of the collectivity. In this discourse,
the victims are martyrs, whose willingness to shed their blood, to give their
bodies for the center, confirms the validity of the center as the primary representation of the body, the identity of the collectivity, and the status of its
defenders as the true patriots or believers.

In 1929, the discursive frame of sovereignty was promulgated by a
Christian colonial power attempting to arbitrate inter-ethnic violence, to
reduce the potential for additional outbreaks and to defuse the potential for
the escalation of political violence. The government sought to minimize the
significance of the outbreak as a Palestinian challenge to its governing
authority. The Shaw Commission found that the August, 1929 rioting was
not premeditated in that the disturbances "did not occur simultaneously
throughout Palestine but spread from the capital through a period of days to
most outlying centres of population and to some rural districts."[52] The root
cause of the violence, the Commission argued, was the government's inability
to curb Zionist activity in the country.[53] Howard Snell, the only member of
the Commission who had reservations about its findings, suggested that
Hajj Amin al-Husayni must bear "a greater share in responsibility for the
disturbance than is attributed to him in the report ... for his failure to make
any effort to control the character of an agitation conducted in the name of
religion of which in Palestine he was the head."[54] The logic of the discourse
points to the ordering capacities of the central state and revolves around the
issue of premeditation as opposed to spontaneous combustion.

Even the opponents stayed within the frame. Leonard Stein, who drafted
the Jewish Agency for Palestine's official response, was of the opinion that
the commission had not given significant attention to the systematic agitation
which had taken place after September, 1928. He wrote, for example:

In spite of the drastic action of the Government in the matter of the Jewish screen, and in spite of the Jews' emphatic repudiation of the suggestion that they had designs on the Moslem Holy Places, the cry was immediately raised by the Moslem leaders and their organs that the Holy Places were in danger. This was the cry that was reiterated with growing emphasis throughout the months that followed, and this was the cry that eventually brought the fanatical mob swarming out of the Haram to attack Jews.[55]

Even the Executive Committee of Zionist–Revisionists published a pamphlet which pointed to "the failure of Arabs to attend their work at Petach Tikvah before the outbreak, the arrival in Jerusalem of Fellahin armed with clubs and sticks, and the suprisingly large motor traffic on the roads carrying Arabs from the country districts to the various Jewish areas."[56] For the Revisionists too, the issue was premeditation. They further argued that their demonstration had been quiet, orderly and with the permission of the police, while the subsequent demonstration by the Arabs had been a violation of Jewish ritual space, noisy, accompanied by inflammatory speeches, the burning of Jewish prayerbooks and the physical attack upon the Jewish "beadle" or *shamas*.[57]

In 1990, the discourse of sovereignty was that of the Jewish state. On the brink of war with Iraq, then Prime Minister Shamir charged that the riot was planned and fueled by a "fanatical hysteria" whipped up by Baghdad. He praised the Border Police who "were vigilant and performed their duty."[58] The reaction of Knesset members to the shootings followed party lines. Tehiya's Yuval Ne'eman, the Minister of Science and Energy, told the press that "the Temple Mount was an arsenal of rocks, bottles and nails ... and the riots erupted simultaneously at various points. The truth of the matter is that for decades there has been no real Jewish control on the Temple Mount. The shame of it is that anyone – Christian, Buddhist or Hindu – is allowed up there, but not a Jew. This injustice must be done away with immediately." Labor Knesset members interpreted the shootings as a consequence of the basic fact that the *intifada* had not been put down. And, Yossi Sarid of the left-wing Citizens Rights Movement strongly encouraged the police to launch a thorough investigation of "that most dangerous band of provocateurs – the Temple Mount Faithful."[59] Then Jerusalem mayor, Teddy Kollek, went even further arguing that the "ideological government" had created conditions where such conflagrations were more likely.[60] The Zamir Commission's report, while it supported the government's contention that the police were justified in the shooting deaths of seventeen Palestinians, was critical of the police and the General Security Services for failing to anticipate events or to deploy sufficient strength, and not heeding the warning signs before the riot. The report supported the original sequence of events presented in media accounts. They recounted the sequence in this way:

> At 10:45 approximately 2,000–3,000 people stormed toward 44 Border Patrol policemen who were standing above the Western Wall. An order was given to shoot tear gas and rubber bullets, but the storming was not halted. Border Patrol policemen, some of whom were injured, retreated to beyond the Moghrabi Gate and toward the Mahkameh. The evacuation of worshippers from the Western Wall Plaza was begun immediately.
>
> At 10:55, hundreds of youths charged the police station on the Temple Mount, in which two policemen who were shouting for help were trapped. Contact with them was broken and the two policemen, who managed to escape, did not succeed in relaying word of their escape. Weapons and ammunition were left in the police station. While worshippers and Border Policemen were being evacuated, no live fire was directed at the rioters. At 11:05, policemen began breaking through to the Temple Mount via the Moghrabi Gate. The policemen met a barrage of stones and iron, and gas canisters which they fired were thrown back at them. The incited mob prevented the policemen from progressing toward the police post. Masked assailants stormed the policemen and, since they were not halted by rubber bullets, live ammunition was fired, first in the air, and subsequently toward the rioters.[61]

The Zamir Commission also charged that violent and threatening calls were given over the loudspeakers on the *haram* including *allahu akbar* ("God is great"), calls for *jihad* or holy war, and *itbah al-yahud*, "slaughter the Jews."

As in the 1929 violence, this official interpretation was challenged. Al-Haq, the Ramallah-based Palestinian affiliate of the International Commission of Jurists in Geneva issued its own reconstruction of the events of the morning of October 8th. They reported that there was no evidence to support the claim of the Zamir Report that there were inflammatory calls for the slaughter of the Jews over the loudspeaker system on the *haram*. Their sequence of events was diametrically opposed to the sequence reconstructed by the Zamir Commission members.

> The incident began when tear gas cansisters exploded in the midst of the crowd gather[ed] at al-Haram. This was followed by stone-throwing by the crowd gathered there, and by shooting by the police and Border Guards present.
>
> Contrary to official open-fire regulations, the Border Guards issued no verbal warnings to the crowd at al-Haram, and failed to fire warning shots into the air.

Once Border Guards started firing, they did so without restraint and, at times used automatic gun-fire. Several of the wounded were shot more than once.[62]

Al-Haq's interpretation, which reconstructed the sequence of events leading to the shootings, was given authority by three separate videotapes taken by private individuals as the events on the *haram* unfolded. The first tape was shown on the CBS Evening News several days after the events and shows rocks being thrown over the top of the Western Wall, but it does not show whether there was anyone in the plaza below at the time. The second tape, which shows both the Western Wall and the plaza, was obtained by *The Village Voice* and, according to Michael Emery, makes it clear that "the Palestinians did not rain stones into the Wailing Wall plaza until after the Border Police had fatally shot several Palestinians and wounded scores of others. By then, the plaza had been cleared of worshippers. In other words, that hail of stones that cause[d] you to sit up and take notice – that scene shown repeatedly by the networks – came about five to 10 minutes after a Border Police officer had squeezed off a long burst of automatic weapons fire into a crowd of angry Palestinians inside the Moroccan Gate." The third videotape was taken by a tourist standing on the Mount of Olives and suggests that there was not one but two periods of sustained, heavy gunfire on the *haram*.[63]

The Israeli human rights group, BeTzelem, also reported on the events at the *haram*. BeTzelem's report concluded that the Border Police fired indiscriminately into the crowd, that the small number of casualties among the security forces and Jewish civilians suggests that the justification for the extreme reaction was inappropriate, that at the point early in the event when mortal danger existed, live fire was not used, that the police used automatic fire, which is clearly an act of criminal negligence as defined by the Israeli Supreme Court, that the firing continued after the crowd had begun to disperse as well as at the point when ambulances and medical teams arrived to treat the wounded, that there was no gradual use of alternatives to live ammunition, that there was no effective overall command over the situation, that the shooting at ambulances and medical teams constituted a very serious violation of humanitarian and legal principles, and that the information given to the public about the events was incomplete and imprecise, raising the suspicion that attempts were made to hide the facts, mislead the public, give support to the security forces and evade responsibility.[64] As in 1929, the issues were about premeditation and the deployment of state authority.

In contrast to the discourse of sovereignty, the sacrificial discourse transforms the victims of the violence into religious or nationalist symbols in the struggle between Jews and Arabs or between Israelis and Palestinians. Yehoshua Porath has suggested that immediately after the 1929 violence, the Palestinian leadership and press initially attempted to disclaim all responsibility for it, even claiming that what had really taken place was a Jewish attack upon the Arabs. Porath notes, however, that a year or two later, attitudes toward the riots changed. On July 26, 1930, the fortieth day after the hanging of three of the Palestinian murderers who had taken part in the slaughter in Hebron and Safed, the Arab Executive Committee issued a manifesto entitled "Announcement to the Honorable Palestinian People" which stated that these men were "innocent saints ... prisoners of feedom and independence." Later on September 7, 1931, *Al-Jami'ah al-'Arabiyyah*, the official journal of Hajj Amin al-Husayni's Supreme Muslim Council, showered the riots with praise. In the wake of the riots "momentum was restored, will-power grew stronger, and those souls whose owners had been overcome by slumber awoke to life."[65]

On the fourth anniversary of the outbreaks, Amil al-Ghuri wrote as follows in "The Red Uprising of August," published in *Al-Jami'ah al-'Arabiyyah* of August 23, 1933.

> Today is the anniversary of the August uprising (*thawrah*), the flames of which were borne high on this day in 1929. That day was a day of brilliance and glory in the annals of Palestinian-Arab history. This is a day of honour, splendour and sacrifice. We attacked Western conquest and the Mandate and the Zionist upon our land. The Jews had coveted our endowments and yearned to take over our holy places. In our silence they had seen a sign of weakness, therefore there was no more room in our hearts for patience or peace; no sooner had the Jews begun marching along this shameful road than the Arabs stood up, checked the oppression, and sacrificed their pure and noble souls on the sacred altar of nationalism.[66]

On the Jewish side, the sacrificial discourse is typified by Menachem Begin's reflection on the Revisionist's attempt throughout the 1930s and 1940s to extend Jewish ritual rights at the Western Wall by violating the *Status Quo*. Begin saw the issue of the Western Wall as a microcosm for the entire struggle for the ownership of the Land of Israel. And, for Begin, the British policy which had restricted Jewish rights at the Western Wall, especially the Shaw Commission's finding that the Muslims had the sole right of ownership to the Wall and that Jews could not sound the *shofar* there, was a symbolic blow against the Jewish people. This is not simply Begin's rhetorical excess. For Begin, the Western Wall is the very center of the Jewish nation; people and nation are completely assimilated to one another. He writes:

But the ancient stones themselves refute the nonsense of those pathetic "progressives" who try to impress the foreigners with their "freedom from old fashioned prejudice." These stones are not silent. They do not cry out. They whisper. They speak softly of the house that once stood here, of kings who knelt here once in prayer, of prophets and seers who here declaimed their message, of heroes who fell here, dying; and of how the great flame, at once destructive and illuminating, was here kindled. This was the house, and this the country which, with its seers and kings and fighters, was ours before the British were a nation. [This is the] testimony of these stones, sending out their light across the generations."[67]

For Begin, the Jewish nation's attachment to the wall is not a matter of mysticism. It is rather the voice of history, which both the British and the Arabs have tried to silence. When the "young disciples of Jabotinsky" attempted to blow the *shofar* for 13 consecutive years after the British "Order in Council" robbed them of the right to be Jews, "an ugly spectacle, humiliating and infuriating always followed." He then describes how, in 1942 as one of the Revisionist youth attempted to blow the *shofar* at the end of the Yom ha-Kippur service, British police waded into the worshippers with their clubs flying. From the midst of chaos, the "real" Jews, the Revisionists, began to sing Ha-Tikvah. He and his colleagues went home that evening and made the decision quoted below:

[This] is the real slavery. What the Roman proconsuls did not dare do, Britain's Commissioners are doing. What our ancestors refused to tolerate from their ancient oppressors, even at the cost of their lives and freedom – is tolerated by the generation of Jewish people which describes itself as the last of oppression and the first of redemption. A people that does not defend its holy places – that does not even try to defend them – is not free, however much it may babble about freedom. People that permit the holiest spot in their country and their most sacred feelings to be trampled underfoot – are slaves in spirit. And we determined there and then that when the time came we would cleanse our people of this shame, and if we should have the strength we would not permit the oppressor's myrmidons to violate our Holy Place, disturb our prayers and desecrate our Festival.[68]

Begin and the Irgun then planned to continue their campaign to blow the *shofar*. Begin understood the inability of the Jews as a nation to celebrate their nationhood at the Western Wall as a stain upon the Jewish people. This stain of guilt, of passivity, could only be removed by the act of martyrs who transformed the "illegal" act of blowing the *shofar* into the trumpet of political revolt.[69]

In 1990, the Faithful of the Temple Mount, which figured so prominently in the attempt to repeal the Israeli Law for the Protection of the Holy Places and the violence of October, 1990, was pressing on with the Revisionist campaign. Members of the Gush Emunim have actively supported the demonstrations of the Faithful of the Temple and the Knesset initiatives of Tehiyah to repeal the law giving exclusive control of the Temple Mount to the Muslim *waqf*. The leader of the group, Gershom Salomon, is not a religious Jew, but he is every Muslim Palestinian's worst nightmare. In 1983 and 1984, he explained to us that the aim of his group was "to pray on the Temple Mount. Then the whole of the Mount should be restored to Jewish hands. Later, the Temple should be erected on the spot where the mosques stand. And ultimately, the Mount should become the center for official state events." As long as the Temple Mount was ruled by "an alien power," the group argued, redemption of the land and people of Israel was incomplete. That Jews cannot pray on the Temple Mount, reflects a Zionism that is afraid to assert its inviolable claim to Jerusalem as a Jewish city, a national center. Likewise Salomon is contemptuous of the Orthodox Jews who refuse to go up to the Temple Mount and follow the directive of the Chief Rabbinate. "If," he told us, "there are rabbis who believe that it is halakhically forbidden according to the Torah to pray on the Temple Mount they are living in Lodz or Plonsk in the 1500s. They don't feel the revolution that has taken place in the history of the Jewish people. This is the tragedy of religious Jewry." Muslim control of the Temple Mount is a yawning hole in the Jewishness of Jerusalem, in the materialization of Zionism.

In 1990, Jerusalem's Mufti, Shaykh Sa'ad al-Din al-Alami, likewise struck a sacrificial tone. Only by protecting the sanctity of the *haram* can there be true nationhood for the Palestinians. Almost immediately after the shootings of October, 1990 HAMAS offered its interpretation of the violence through a short allegorical story published in *Al-Shaab*. According to this story, white doves had always nested at the Kaaba in Mecca and Prophet's mosque in Medina. But recently they had been driven off by black crows. The doves flew to Amman and then came to rest in Jerusalem at the Dome of the Rock. The crows represented the American and European forces massed to attack Saddam Hussein. They had penetrated the sacred lands of Islam. But the doves, the defenders of Islam, had come to Jerusalem, suggesting that the Palestinians were the only ones protecting the sacred cities of Islam.[70] Their martyrs were the real Muslims and the Saudis were only pretenders. HAMAS has clearly been behind the wave of knife attacks which were spawned by the violence on the *haram*. HAMAS also left its iconographic marks throughout Gaza and the West Bank. In one drawing, a clenched fist breaks through the Dome of the Rock above the slogan, "HAMAS is stronger than bullets."

VIOLENT PLACES, SACRED SPACES

Since the end of the 1960s social theory about the nature of collective and inter-communal violence in politics has changed markedly. It was often assumed that acts of violence such as the riots of 1929 or the shootings of 1990 were aberrations. More recent theory suggests that violence is a part of the political process which, like many other social processes, can be organized and used to accomplish political goals. In part, this change in the interpretation of collective violence is the result of the debate between E.P. Thompson and Natalie Zemon Davis at the beginning of the 1970s.

Thompson's article on the English crowd in the eighteenth century was primarily interested in understanding how power operated between classes, between the gentry and the crowd. Thompson argued that the crowd used the riot to limit and curtail the hegemony of the gentry. His critics pointed out that his crowd remained an undifferentiated social group and that he paid little or no attention to what motivated them to select the riot as the primary mechanism to limit the power of the gentry.[71]

Natalie Zemon Davis, who studied the Catholic–Huegenot riots in France analyzed them not as instruments of popular control, but as expressions of communal beliefs. Not only did communal values determine the nature of the riot and the identity of its victims, but communal activities also influenced the riot's timing, legitimacy and ritualized quality. Davis suggested that religious riots frequently became an extension of religious ritual: violence often stemmed from moments of worship. Culture and community, not economics and class, were the critical forces that motivated religious rioters. The religious rioters went beyond defending a shared concept of justice; they turned to violence to purge or purify the community itself and to define its boundaries against threats both foreign and internal. She treated riot as a cultural phenomenon that, though violent, essentially had order and communal purity at its heart. For Davis, riot became a form of ritual activity which had as its goal communal unity.[72]

The violence of August, 1929 and October, 1990 would suggest that Davis was correct. Indeed, it is precisely the sacrality of the Western Wall and *al-buraq*, the Temple Mount and *al-haram al-sharif* which structures the nature of the violence, the contest over the extension of ritual rights, the structure of opposition, its political consequences, and how it will be understood within larger geo-political contexts.

The spatial context of this inter-ethnic conflict, the sacrality of the Western Wall and Temple Mount for the Jews and *al-buraq* and *al-haram al-sharif* for the Muslims, will also determine the strategies of symbolic violence used by the two communities. Acts of desecration are the most extreme form of symbolic violence.[73] Bruce Lincoln has recently published a penetrating analysis of one of the most bizarre events of the Spanish Civil War in which the bodies of hundreds, if not thousands of Spanish priests and nuns were exhumed by anarchists in Barcelona and Republican forces in other cities in Spain. The mummified remains of priests, bishops and nuns were ritually desecrated in the streets. Churches were burned, ritual images and statues were disfigured and decapitated. Ecclesiastical paraphernalia were expropriated in parodies of church ritual. Francisco Franco's Nationalists immediately seized upon these acts of anti-clericalism as demonstrations of the character of the opposition. The anarchists, communists and Republicans were innately inhuman, barbaric and bestial.

But, Lincoln describes these symbolic acts as "prophanophanies," the "revelation of the profanity, temporality and corruption inherent in someone or something."[74] These prophanophanies were intended "to demonstrate dramatically and in public, the powerlessness of the image and thereby to inflict a double disgrace on its champions, first by exposing the bankruptcy of their vaunted symbols and, second, their impotence in the face of attack."[75] He concludes by stating:

> Although the exhumations have consistently been presented as an aberrant and impious act of violence, such a simplistic analysis is untenable. Like all anticlerical violence throughout Spanish history, they were not an assault on religion per se, but rather on one specific religious institution: an institution closely aligned with, and subservient to, the traditionally dominant segment of society. At the same time that the exhumations were a ferocious assault on and mockery of that institution, they were also an assault on the segment of society with which it was symbiotically entangled, and what is more – they were a ritual in which the traditionally subordinated segment of Spanish society sought by means of a highly charged discourse of gestures and deeds to deconstruct the old social order and construct a new radically different order in its place.[76]

Symbolic violence, prophanophany, is an adjunct to material violence and sometimes the most efficacious alternative form of violence to those with inadequate material means of violence. Symbolic violence is used by members of one community or movement in order to mobilize their own community, to make their definition of reality the dominant one, to demonstrate the ultimate powerlessness of the other and to redefine the other as radically alien, as profane. By profaning the other's sacred place, the other is made profane, an alien with no claim to possession of that space. It is an alternative dramaturgy of power.

NOTES

1   This essay is the fourth in a series of studies examining the relationship of religion and politics in Jerusalem. The first, "Rocks, Roads and Ramot Control: The Other War for Jerusalem," *Soundings*, vol. 7.2–3 (Summer–Fall, 1989), pp. 227–74 explores *haredi* politics in the city through the struggle over the neighborhood of Ramot. The second, "The Politics of Sacred Space: Jerusalem's Temple Mount/*al-haram al-sharif*," in J.S. Scott and P. Simpson-Housley, eds, *Sacred Spaces and Profane Places* (Westport: Greenwood Press, 1991), pp. 21–61 examines the conflict between Israelis and Palestinians over Jerusalem's *har ha-bayit* or *al-haram al-sharif*. The third, "The Nebi Musa Prilgrimage: Symbolic Power and the Origins of Palestinian Nationalism," *Religion*, XVI, No. 2 (forthcoming April, 1996) explores the relationship between the annual pilgrimage to the tomb and sanctuary of Moses outside Jericho in the 1920s and 1930s and emergence of Palestinian political identity and nationalism.

2   Hugh Foot, later Lord Caradon, in Yigal Lossin, *Pillar of Fire: The Rebirth of Israel – A Visual History* (Jerusalem: Shikmona Publishing Company, 1983), p. 165.

3   Maurice Samuel, *What Happened in Palestine: The Events of August, 1929: Their Background and Their Significance* (Boston: Stratford, 1929), p. 120.

4   See for example, Sabra Chartrand, "19 Arabs Killed in Battle With Jerusalem Police," *New York Times*, October 9, 1990; Ron Kampeas, "21 Arabs die as the police quell Temple Mount riot," *Jerusalem Post*, October 9, 1990; Daniel Williams, "Israelis Slay 19 Arabs in Clash in Jerusalem," *Los Angeles Times*, October 9, 1990; and Peter Arnett, Cable News Network, October 9, 1990.

5   The initial accounts of the conflict placed the dead at between 19 and 21. At the press conference of the Jerusalem based Palestine Human Rights Information Center on October 15, this original number was reduced to 17. Of those who were initially reported to have been killed at *al-haram al-sharif* one died of a heart attack, two individuals who were initially reported to have died were injured and survived, and the fourth had been shot by an Israeli civilian in another part of the city and had died. See "Special File", pp. 134–59.

6   "Jewish family saved by Arab villagers," *Jerusalem Post*, October 9, 1990.

7   Daniel Williams, "How the Fuse of Jerusalem's Religious Rivalry Was Lit at Temple Mount," *Los Angeles Times*, October 15, 1990.

8   R. J. Zwi Werblowsky, *Jerusalem: Holy City of Three Religions* (Jerusalem: Israel Universities Study Group for Middle Eastern Affairs, 1977), p. 3.

9   The term *waqf* literally means a "pious foundation" of either real estate or buildings set aside by specific families or government officials. *Waqf* property cannot be taxed and its entire income must be devoted to charitable uses.

10   The most comprehensive history of this *waqf* is A.L. Tibawi, *The Islamic Pious Foundations in Jerusalem: Origins, History and Usurpation by Israel* (London: The Islamic Cultural Centre, 1978), esp. pp. 10–15.

11   See the comprehensive study of Shmuel Berkovicz, The Legal Status of the Holy Places in Israel, Unpublished PhD dissertation from the Hebrew University of Jerusalem, 1978 [Hebrew].

12   The British knew for example that in the winter of 1918, Syrian and Palestinian Cairenes came together, fearing the establishment in Palestine of a Jewish administration or state. On their mind was the expected large-scale Zionist purchases of Arab-owned land, and the possibility that the Jews would rebuild the Temple and thus cause sectarian strife in the country. See, Muhammad Y. Muslih, *The Origins of Palestinian Nationalism* (New York: Columbia University Press, 1988), p. 185.

13   *Ibid.*, p. 79.

14   The pertinent section of "The Proclamation of the State of Israel" of May 15, 1948 reads that the state will "safeguard the sanctity and inviolability of the shrines and Holy Places of all religions." The complete text of the Proclamation is found in Itamar Rabinovich and Jehuda Reinharz, eds, *Israel in the Middle East: Documents and Readings on Society, Politics and Foreign Relations, 1948–Present* (New York: Oxford University Press, 1984), pp. 13–15. For the text of the Law for the Protection of the Holy Places" see Walter Zander, *Israel and the Holy Places of Christendom* (New York: Praeger Publishers, 1971), pp. 102–3.

15   For a description of Rabbi Goren's activity immediately after the Six Day War, see Meron Benvenisti, *Jerusalem: The Torn City*, (Jerusalem: Isratypset, 1976), pp. 287–90.

16   Cited in Benvenisti, *Jerusalem*, pp. 290–1.

17   Jon Immanuel, "A clash of perceptions," *The Jerusalem Post: International Edition*, 27 October, 1990.

18   Philip Mattar, *The Mufti of Jerusalem and the Palestinian National Movement* (New York: Columbia University Press, 1988), p. 46.

19   Roger Friedland and Richard D. Hecht, "The Nebi Musa Pilgrimage."

20   See our *Jerusalem: The Profane Politics of a Sacred Place* (forthcoming Cambridge University Press, 1996), chapter 8, "The Very Best Battleground" for a complete discussion of each of the major attacks from 1967 to 1990.

21   See *Los Angeles Times*, January 9, 1986, *New York Times*, January 15, 1986 and *Jerusalem Post: International Edition*, January 25, 1986.

22   On the early years of this group and its first national conventions see Janet Aviad, "Israel: New Fanatics and Old – The Temple Mount Becomes a Political Issue," *Dissent* (Summer, 1984), especially p. 342.

23   *Jerusalem Post*, 29 July, 1985.

24   See for example, Motti Nachmani, "What is going on with the Temple Mount," *Nekudah*, no. 47 (September 3, 1989), p. 7 [Hebrew], Yigal Ariel, "The Temple Mount as *waqf* property," *Nekudah*, no. 58 (May 17, 1983), pp. 18–19 [Hebrew], Shabbatai Ben-Dov, "Fasts of the Temple Destruction," *Nekudah*, no. 61 (July 18, 1983), pp. 8–9, Yisrael Eldad, "In the Den of Numerologists," *Nekudah*, no. 78 (September 21, 1984), p. 14, Baruch Lior, "To Prepare the Generations for Prayer and War," *Nekudah*, no. 85 (April 5, 1985), pp. 12–13, Yisrael Medad, "Battle on the Temple Mount," *Counterpoint*, vol 3, no. 3 (February, 1986), pp. 8–9, Moshe Ben-Yosef, "Prelude to the Mount," *Nekudah*, no. 96 (February 21, 1986), p. 19 and Moshe Levinger, "We must not discard the old banners," *Nekudah*, no. 97 (March 25, 1986), p. 8 as well as the the following editorials, "The Temple Mount is not in Our Hands," *Nekudah*, no. 87 (May 24, 1985), p. 4, "The Fuse," *Nekudah*, no. 95 (January 21, 1986), p. 4 and "Messiah Now," *Nekudah*, no. 105 (September 5, 1986), p. 5.

25 Lustick, *For The Land and the Lord*, pp. 170–1.
26 Cited in Lustick, *For the Land and the Lord*, p. 172.
27 *Los Angeles Times*, October 12, 1987.
28 *Los Angeles Times*, July 25, 1988.
29 See Lustick, *For the Land and the Lord*, pp. 172–3 and Brigadier General Yoel Ben-Porat stated in *Ma'ariv*, May 10, 1987 and translated in *Israel Press Briefs*, no. 53, (May–June, 1987), pp. 14–15.
30 On HAMAS see, Don Peretz, *Intifada: The Palestinian Uprising* (Boulder: Westview Press, 1990), pp. 104–6 and Lisa Taraki, "The Islamic Resistance Movement in the Palestinian Uprising," *Intifada: The Palestinian Uprising against Israeli Occupation*, ed. by Zachary Lockman and Joel Beinin (Boston: South End Press, 1989), pp. 171–7 although we do not agree with her conclusion that "Hamas' active participation in the uprising, then, should best be seen as part of the campaign of a prospective opposition Islamist party in the future Palestinian state" (p. 177). See also the comprehensive history and analysis of Ziad Abu-Amr, *Islamic Fundamentalism in the West Bank and Gaza: Muslim Brotherhood and Islamic Jihad* (Bloomington: Indiana University Press, 1994) and Jean-François Legrain, "Palestinian Islamisms: Patriotism as a Condition of Their Expansion," *Accounting for Fundamentalisms: The Dynamic Character of Movements*, ed. by Martin E. Marty and R. Scott Appleby (Chicago: University of Chicago Press, 1994), pp. 413–27.
31 *Los Angeles Times*, April 8, 1989.
32 *New York Times*, April 15, 1989.
33 *Jerusalem Post*, April 21, 1989.
34 *Jerusalem Post: International Edition*, November 17, 1990.
35 Extensive excerpts from the Zamir Report were published in *Jerusalem Post: International Edition*, November 3, 1990, pp. 14–15.
36 Menachem Friedman, "The State of Israel as a Theological Dilemma," in Baruch Kimmerling (ed.), *The Israeli State and Society: Boundaries and Frontiers* (Albany: State University of New York Press, 1989), pp. 203–4.
37 Charles S. Liebman and Eliezer Don-Yehiya, *Religion and Politics in Israel* (Bloomington: Indiana University Press, 1984), p.74.
38 Zvi Yehudah ha-Cohen Kuk, *On the Paths of Israel* (Jerusalem: Menorah, 1969), p. 160.
39 On the history of Gush Emunim see, Tsvi Raanan, *Gush Emunim* (Tel Aviv: Sifrit Po'alim, 1980) [Hebrew], Danny Rubenstein, *On the Lord's Side: Gush Emunim* (Tel Aviv: Ha-Kibbutz Ha-Meuchad Publishing House Ltd., 1982) [Hebrew], David Biale, "Mysticism and Politics in Modern Israel: The Messianic Ideology of Abraham Isaac Ha-Cohen Kook," *Religion and Politics in the Modern World*, ed. by Peter Merkl and Ninian Smart (New York and London: New York University Press, 1983), pp. 191–204, Janet Aviad, "The Contemporary Israeli Pursuit of the Millennium," *Religion*, vol. 14 (1984), pp. 199–222, David Newman, ed., *The Impact of the Gush Emunim: Politics and Settlement in the West Bank* (London: Croom Helm, 1985), David J. Schnall, "Religion and Political Dissent in Israel: The Case of Gush Emunim," *Religious Resurgence: Contemporary Cases in Islam, Christianity and Judaism*, ed. by R.T. Antoun and M.E. Hegland (Syracuse: Syracuse University Press, 1987), pp. 169–93, and Gideon Aran, "From Religious Zionism to Zionist Religion: The Roots of Gush Emunim," *Studies in Contemporary Jewry*, vol.

2, ed. by Peter Y. Medding (Jerusalem and Bloomington: Institute of Contemporary Jewry of the Hebrew University of Jerusalem and Indiana University Press, 1986), pp. 116–43.

40 Gideon Aran, "A Mystic-Messianic Interpretation of Modern Israeli History: The Six Day War as a Key Event in the Development of the Original Religious Culture of Gush Emunim," *Studies in Contemporary Jewry*, vol. 4, ed. by Jonathan Frankel (Jerusalem and Oxford: Institute of Contemporary Jewry of the Hebrew University of Jerusalem and Oxford University Press, 1988), pp. 263–75. See also, Uriel Tal, "Contemporary Hermeneutics and Self-Views on the Relationship between State and Land," *The Land of Israel: Jewish Perspectives*, ed. by Lawrence A. Hoffman (Notre Dame: University of Notre Dame Press, 1986), pp. 316–38.

41 Jabara, *Hajj Amin al-Husayni*, p. 81.

42 Mattar, *The Mufti of Jerusalem*, p. 40

43 Mattar, *The Mufti of Jerusalem*, p. 40.

44 Jabara, *Hajj Amin al-Husayni*, p. 95.

45 Walid Khalidi, *Before their Diaspora: A Photographic History of the Palestinians 1876–1948* (Washington: Institute for Palestine Studies, 1984), p. 221.

46 Mohammed K. Shadid, "The Muslim Brotherhood Movement in the West Bank and Gaza," *Third World Quarterly*, vol. 10, no. 2 (April, 1988), pp. 658–82. But see also, Thomas Mayer, "The Military Force of Islam: The Society of the Muslim Brethern and the Palestine Question, 1945–1948," *Zionism and Arabism in Palestine and Israel*, ed. by Elie Kedourie and Sylvia G. Haim (London: Frank Cass, 1982), pp. 100–17.

47 See Walter Zander, *Israel and the Holy Places of Christendom* (New York: Praeger, 1971), p. 88 and Gabriel Padon, "The Divided City, 1948–1967," *Jerusalem City of Ages*, ed. by Alice L. Eckardt (New York: University Press of America, 1987), esp. pp. 134–42.

48 *The Emergence of the Palestinian–Arab National Movement 1918–1929* (London: Frank Cass and Company Limited, 1974), p. 272.

49 Fadwa Tuqan, *A Mountainous Journey: A Poet's Autobiography*, trans. by O. Kenny (St. Paul: Graywolf Press, 1990), p. 82.

50 Menachem Friedman, *Society and Religion: The Non-Zionist Orthodox in Eretz-Yisrael – 1918–1936* (Jerusalem: Yad Izhak Ben-Zvi Publications, 1977), pp. 315–33.

51 "America and Israel: How Bad Is It? Will It Get Worse?" *The National Interest*, Winter, 1990/91, p. 16.

52 "Official Report of the Shaw Commission on the Palestine Disturbances of August 1929," in Klieman, *The Turn Toward Violence 1920–1929*, p. 342.

53 *Ibid.*, pp. 347–8.

54 *Ibid.*, p. 356.

55 Leonard Stein, "Memorandum on the 'Report of the Commission on the Palestine Disturbances of August 1929," in Klieman, *The Turn Toward Violence*, p. 419. See also Porath, *The Emergence of the Palestinian–Arab National Movement*, p. 270.

56 "Examination and Critique by the Executive Committee of the World Union and Zionist Revisionists of the Shaw Commission Report – The Events of 1929

from the Perspective of the More Militant Zionist Wing," in Klieman, *The Turn Toward Violence*, pp. 532–3.

57 *Ibid.*, p. 532.
58 *Jerusalem Post*, October 9, 1990.
59 *Jerusalem Post*, October 9, 1990.
60 *Los Angeles Times*, February 17, 1991.
61 Excerpts from the Zamir Report as published in *Jerusalem Post: International Edition*, November 3, 1990.
62 "Reconstruction of Events, *al-Haram al-Sharif*, Jerusalem, Monday, 8 October, 1990," A Report by *Al-Haq*, Ramallah, October 12, 1990 (Revised October 28, 1990); excerpts reprinted in "Special File," pp. 138–9.
63 *Village Voice*, November 13, 1990, pp. 25–9.
64 "Loss of Control: The Temple Mount Events – Preliminary Investigation" by BeTzelem (October 14, 1990) excerpts reprinted in "Special File," pp. 139–42.
65 Porath, *The Emergence of the Palestinian–Arab National Movement*, p. 270.
66 *Ibid.*, p. 270.
67 Menachem Begin, *The Revolt* (1948; reprint, Los Angeles: Nash Publishing, 1972), p. 88.
68 *Ibid.*, p. 89.
69 *Ibid.*, p. 91.
70 The story and its interpretation by Yehuda Litani is summarized in Meron Benvenisti, *Fatal Embrace* (Jerusalem: Maxwell-Macmillan-Keter Publishing, Ltd., 1992), pp. 15–17.
71 E.P. Thompson, "The Moral Economy of the English Crowd in the Eighteenth Century," *Past and Present*, 50 (1971), pp. 76–136.
72 Natalie Zemon Davis, "The Rites of Violence: Religious Riot in Sixteenth-Century France," *Past and Present*, 59 (1973), pp. 51–91; reprinted in Natalie Zemon Davis, *Society and Culture in Early Modern France* (Palo Alto: Stanford University Press, 1975), pp. 152–87.
73 See for example, Pierre Bourdieu, "The Force of Law: Toward a Sociology of the Juridical Field," *The Hastings Law Journal*, 38 (July, 1987), pp. 805–53.
74 Bruce Lincoln, *Discourse and the Construction of Society: Comparative Studies of Myth, Ritual and Classification* (New York: Oxford University Press, 1989), p. 125.
75 *Ibid.*, p. 120.
76 *Ibid.*, p. 127.

5. Riots and Rituals: The Construction of Violence and Public Space in Hindu Nationalism

Peter van der Veer

INTRODUCTION

Riots and rituals are both often seen as instances of behavior without meaning or purpose. They are portrayed as closed universes in which every move relates to another move, but not rationally and purposefully to a world outside of them.[1] In this respect they look like games. There is also quite an opposite interpretation which tends to emphasize the spontaneity of riots and unpredictability of ritual performances which distinguishes them from rule oriented behavior like games.

However, riots in India I have witnessed or read about were more often than not well-planned and had well-defined targets and rules. In some cases you know exactly when and where to expect them to begin and end, as if they were rituals. Similarly, rituals I have studied in India showed intentional, rational behavior which was moulded and interpreted in the ritual process itself. We might suggest that both riots and rituals are meaningful and purposeful sets of actions. They are comparable in their organization of symbolic space, in their temporal structure and in their symbolic repertoire.[2]

Riots and rituals both appear to play a significant role in the construction of social identities. Since Durkheim anthropologists have been concerned with the ritual construction of social (group-) identity. Often a classification of rituals is made which reflects levels of social integration. Rituals like ancestor worship relate to community in a narrow sense (household, lineage, clan), while rituals like pilgrimage relate to community in a wider sense (nation, community of believers).[3] In an important book on the emergence of communalism in colonial North India Sandria Freitag emphasizes the importance of collective, symbolic activities in what she calls "public arenas." She shows that riots and rituals were actually linked in the construction of "communal" identities in public space.[4] There is indeed a strong association of identity and public space in both riots and rituals. Thus, for example, the importance of spatial interpenetration of "Hindu" and "Muslim" groups (or lack of such interpenetration) has been clearly shown in the dynamics of rioting in a number of places.

A direct connection between ritual performances in public space and riots seems also obvious in contemporary India. Ritual processions through "troubled" areas often end in full-scale riots. What we seem to have here are "rituals of provocation."[5] A whole symbolic repertoire, derived from the ritual realm of animal sacrifice, is often used to start a riot: a slaughtered cow in a Hindu sacred space or a slaughtered pig in a Muslim sacred space. Of course, the "troubles" relate to all kinds of contextual circumstances of an economic and political nature, such as competition between shopkeepers, the power of bootleggers, the communal activities of the police, the active leadership of politicians in riots. They may, indeed, on a higher level of abstraction be fundamentally related to changing projects of a centralizing state. Without in the least discounting such elements in the genesis, development and outcome of riots, I want to suggest that riots provide a ritual space in which subjectivity, and its relation to state power, is discursively constructed. Public space does not only pattern ideas of community, but is itself, to an important extent, constructed through ritual and rioting. The spatial factor is as much a result as a basis of conceptions of community.

Freitag shows a connection between riots and rituals in modern India, but focuses on the local community, while nationalism is the phenomenon in which she is interested. It is therefore important to look beyond the rituals of the local community to pilgrimage, which bridges the local and the wider community (the nation). Pilgrimage is often seen to reflect a supra-local level of integration. It reinforces "the larger moral community of the civilization."[6] A classic statement of this function is made in an article by Wolf on the Virgin of Guadelupe in Mexico, which "links together family, politics and religion; colonial past and independent present; Indian and Mexican ... It is, ultimately, a way of talking about Mexico: a collective representation of Mexican society."[7] In a similar vein, Srinivas writes about Hindu sacred centers as the places in which the Great Sanskritic Tradition is transmitted to the peasants of the region: "Every great temple and pilgrim centre was a source of Sanskritization, and the periodic festivals or other occasions when pilgrims gathered together at the centre provided opportunities for the spread of Sanskritic ideas and beliefs."[8] While Srinivas' analysis refers to civilizational integration, Mandelbaum makes a somewhat different, but related analytical move by arguing that pilgrimage acts to create national identification and thus plays a role in nation-building:

There is a traditional basis for the larger national identification. It is the idea, mainly engendered by Hindu religion but shared by those of other religions as well, that there is an entity of India to which all inhabitants belong. The Hindu epics and legends, in their manifold versions, teach that the stage for the gods was nothing less than the entire land and that the land remains one religious setting for those who dwell in it. That sense was and is continually confirmed through the common practice of pilgrimage.[9]

That pilgrimage is always a ritual of the wider community is in some sense a truism. By definition, it involves a journey from one's village or town to a sacred center and back and its performance seems to reinforce the notion of a wider community of believers. This ritual seems then to lend itself eminently for linkage to the discourses and ritual practices of religious nationalism (communalism). What we might consider is the possibility that pilgrimage in India, based on linkages between distant regions, provided notions of religious community long before the British entered the scene. Information and ideas went from one part of India to another and, in case of the Muslims, even from Mecca to India and vice versa.

There is no doubt that the nineteenth century brought great transformations to Indian society which were reflected in the public arena of pilgrimage. Especially the improvement of infrastructure enabled more and more people to perform pilgrimage. Also, the emergence of a relatively secure class of landowners and bureaucrats resulted in a greatly expanded patronage of religious institutions, such as pilgrimage centers. Finally, Western discourse on the nation as a territorially based community colluded with religious discourse on sacred space.

The importance of pilgrimage and sacred centers in the (re)definition of community in India becomes clear when we consider the various struggles for control in these arenas. In some cases these are struggles primarily within a religious community, such as the Gurdwara Reform movement among the Sikhs in the 1920s which tried to reallocate control over Sikh temples. In other cases these are struggles between the state and religious elites, such as the struggle for control over Hindu temples in South India.[10] And again there are struggles between communities over the control over sacred space, such as between Hindus and Muslims in the case of Ayodhya.

What theories of pilgrimage which emphasize integration[11] tend to neglect is that violent antagonism may be an important mechanism of integration. It is through the construction and maintenance of boundaries between "us" and "them" that group identities are shaped. While the ritual process integrates individuals in a community of worshippers, it sets it apart from those who do not worship. Moreover, in a number of cases, it tends to portray "the other" as "demonic," "threatening" and "impure." Such conceptualizations can imply ritual action to exorcize, subjugate or conquer the "alien presence." Moreover, the "alien" elements may be understood to be both "within" the self and "outside" of it, so that violence is directed simultaneously to discipline the self and conquer the "other." In that sense antagonistic violence can be an integral part of the ritual process.

As Maurice Bloch has shown in his study of circumcision rituals among the Merina in Madagascar, the powers of nature which are present in the "self" are not replaced by the ancestral powers of the elders, but violently conquered and appropriated by the elders who perform the circumcision on new members of the society. In this way the cultural conquest of natural powers establishes the authority of elders which can in turn be appropriated by the state. Bloch suggests that the violence of the ritual conquest of nature is directly connected to the legitimation and motivation in warfare against "others," outside of society.[12]

When we turn our attention to the phenomenon of nationalism it is important to consider Bruce Kapferer's notion that nationalist discourse feeds upon the cultural logic of everyday practice.[13] The "demonization" of another ethnic group by portraying it as a threat to the integrity of one's cultural identity and thus as a matter of life and death can only be understood in its cultural specifics by relating it to particular orientations to the world. The ritual nature of riots and the riotous nature of ritual are thus connected through discursive traditions on the nature of the "self" and the "other." These traditions are not homogeneous or monolithic, but are subject to constant debate (sometimes of a violent nature) in cultural arenas.

The above discussion leads to the following arguments about the connection between riots and rituals. The first is that an important function of ritual is to construct the identity of the participants as a religious community. In the modern period, religious discourse on the community is directly linked to the discourse of nationalism. The second is that the ritual construction of identity often implies actual violence and antagonism. It does so by providing an arena in which the "self" is constructed by opposition to an "other" that is demonized and violently conquered. While some of this violence is directed inward to discipline the members of a community, part of it may be directed outward to members of other communities in the form of riots. Instead of being spontaneous outbursts of passions, riots can thus be seen as a form of ritual antagonism through which a community expresses its identity. Rather than being meaningless and irrational, I would propose that

riots and rituals are both forms of behavior through which people communicate their identity and their understanding of the world.

Finally, I want to suggest that both riots and rituals derive their meaning
from the way they relate identities to public space. That is to say that although
the actual occurrences of communal riots, separated in time and place,
resemble each other in form and contextual explanation[14] – as do indeed ritual
performances – their meaning has to be historically understood in terms of
discursive shifts.[15] As far as I am able to see now, there has been a major
discursive shift in the nineteenth century through the linkage of sacred space
and national territory.

In the pre-colonial period, Hindu notions of sacred space were connected
to pilgrimage and centers of regional devotion. These notions connected certain
groups of Hindus to certain places and involved violent struggles between
groups of specialists for control over scarce resources. However, they refered
to discontinuity between sacred spots and secular routes to reach them and
to discontinuity among the people who go to visit them. The notion of
continuous territory which is sacralized as the "motherland" is clearly
different from these earlier understandings and belongs to the modern
discourse of nationalism which reaches India in the nineteenth century.
What seems to have happened in the nineteenth and twentieth centuries is
that the discourse on nation and territory was discursively linked to the
ritual construction of sacred space. Riots and rituals become then performances
which derive their meaning from a discourse on communal identity. As we
will see, this is not only a matter of interpretation, but also of innovative
practice. It seems obvious that the rituals of Hindu nationalism are innovations which are consciously designed to have riotous consequences.

I want to illustrate the above arguments by looking somewhat closely at
a few selected religious conflicts over the past three centuries in Ayodhya,
a Hindu pilgrimage centre in North India. This place has gained considerable notoriety over the last decade, since it has become the main source of
conflict between Hindus and Muslims in India. In 1984, the Vishva Hindu
Parishad, a Hindu nationalist movement, started a campaign to remove a
mosque, built in the sixteenth century, from a place which it considered the
birthplace of the God Rama. The issue was made central in the national political
arena by the Bharatiya Janata Party (BJP), a party with a long history in Hindu
nationalism. In the general elections in May and June, 1991 the BJP gained
again considerably and has become the second party in India after the
Congress party.[16]

I want to place the current issue in the context of a series of historical confrontations in Ayodhya. In this way I can demonstrate how changing historical configurations have led to shifting notions of violence, space and identity.

VIOLENCE IN SACRED SPACE[17]

There is a strong tendency among both outsiders and Hindus to present Hinduism as an exception to the general picture of religious violence. Hinduism is often characterized as "tolerant." I would suggest that this characterization has a specific orientalist history. "Religious tolerance" as an ideal in the West derives from an abstraction and universalization of religion which is part of a Western discourse on "modernity." The move in seventeenth-century Europe to produce a universal definition of Natural Religion as existing in all societies shows a fragmentation of the unity and authority of the Roman Church, but also the rise of new discourses and practices connected to modern nation-states.[18] A growing emphasis on religious tolerance as a positive value is thus related to the marginalization of religious institutions in Europe. This discourse is brought to bear on the Muslim and Hindu populations incorporated in the modern world-system. Muslims are labeled as "fanatic" and "bigoted," while Hindus are seen in a more positive light as "tolerant." At the same time, this labelling explains why Muslims have ruled Hindu India and why Hindus have to be "protected" by the British. The attribution of "tolerance" to Hinduism has come to dominate Hindu discourse on Hinduism to the extent that tolerance is now one of the most important characteristics of Hinduism, while as a doctrinal notion it had no specific place in Hindu discursive traditions before the nineteenth century.

Much of what I have just said about "tolerance" could also be applied to concepts like Gandhi's "non-violence" or the social egalitarianism of Hindu devotional groups. It is sometimes difficult for westerners to grasp violence perpetrated by Hindu monks[19] (*sadhus*) who speak and act militantly, since there is the persistent notion of "non-violent" other-worldliness attributed to Hindu "spirituality." Again, while "non-violence" had a place in Hindu discursive traditions as a rejection of the violence of animal sacrifice, which has resulted in vegetarianism among some groups, the idea that Hindus would be religiously prevented from pursuing their interests by violent means is Gandhi's construction of Hindu spirituality. Especially Hindu monks have a long and interesting history of warfare related to trading which continues to the present day.[20] It is modern Hinduism which ignores these traditions in its self-presentation through the mirror of the West while, at the same time, manifesting a behavior which is not "non-violent" or "tolerant" by any stretch of the imagination.

The symbolism of antagonism and violent conquest is also very clearly present in the case of the devotional worship of Rama, with which I am concerned in this paper. Gods wage a continuous war with demons, the powers of evil. The *Ramayana*, the central text of the Rama devotion and Hinduism's most important religious saga tells the story of Rama's struggle with the demons and his ultimate victory. This story is continuously told by story-tellers, enacted in religious dramas, such as the Ram Lila, and has recently been the subject of a most successful soap-opera on Indian television. The places connected to the Rama story are important centers of pilgrimage.

Vishnu takes the incarnation (*avatara*) of Rama, the son of Ayodhya's king, to save the world from the growing power of demons. He travels throughout India to Lanka in a tour of royal conquest. It is this freedom of movement – by removing every obstacle to it – which symbolizes Hindu notions of sovereignty. Finally, he launches with his army of monkeys an attack on Lanka and slays all the demons. Returning to Ayodhya he becomes the paradigmatic just king (*dharmaraja*) who preserves the purity of the caste order and the chastity of women. It is his rule (*Ramraj*) which serves as a political ideal in Hindu political thought.

The devotional worship of Rama is one of the most important strands in contemporary Hinduism, at least from the sixteenth century. The most important element in the spread of a particular kind of Rama devotion in North India has undoubtedly been the sixteenth-century Hindi rendition of the *Ramayana* by Tulsi Das. This text has become the basis for both popular and theological interpretation of Rama devotion. Although Tulsi Das was probably not a Ramanandi himself, his story has been much promoted by the Ramanandis, who spread from Rajasthan to other parts of North India during the sixteenth century. In the seventeenth and eighteenth centuries, the Ramanandis had established themselves in holy places connected with episodes in the Rama story, such as Janakpur in the Nepalese Tarai, and Ayodhya and Chitrakut in Uttar Pradesh. Although the monks settled in Ayodhya at the beginning of the eighteenth century, Ayodhya became the main center of the order only in the nineteenth century. Ramanandis now form the majority of Ayodhya's population.

The establishment of the Ramanandis in Ayodhya did not happen without a great deal of conflict. The Ramanandis are known for their organization in military bands (*jamat, khalsa*). In the eighteenth century, they were further organised in armies (*ani*) and regiments (*akhara*). Their main competitors were not Muslims, as modern Hindu writing often has it, but followers of the other great Hindu god, Shiva. Together, these monks controlled much of the trade routes of North India – which doubled as pilgrimage routes – and they became organized in armies to fight against each other. Ramanandi oral history has it that Ayodhya was in the hands of their rivals, the Shaivas, before they had established themselves. The first written account about a conflict in Ayodhya indeed concerns a violent confrontation between Shaivas and Ramanandis. *Shrimaharajacaritra*, a hagiography of the important abbot Ramprasad (1703–1804), written by Ragunathprasad in 1804–5, describes a violent confrontation in the early eighteenth century in which Shaiva monks still prevailed over Ramanandis.

It should be clear that this kind of conflict involved religious specialists seeking to expand their control over religious centers and pilgrimage/trading networks. It did not involve clashes between religious communities, between "Hindus" and "Muslims." The rivals were Ramanandi and Shaiva monks, both "Hindu" groups, though occasionally other monks may also have joined the fray. The conflicts had certainly a "religious" aspect. Often, they are described as involving not only weaponry and fighting, but spiritual powers, derived from ascetic practices. The curse of an ascetic was considered a weapon perhaps more dangerous than a matchlock. Control over sacred space had clearly economic and political consequences, but it also showed spiritual superiority.

In the case of Ayodhya, the Ramanandis succeeded in establishing their dominance. However, it is important to note that they could build temples in Ayodhya only with the explicit permission of the Muslim rulers of the area. Ayodhya certainly constituted sacred space, eulogized in pilgrimage manuals and ritually established by annual circumambulation. At the same time, however, Ayodhya was the capital of a province (*suba*) in the Mughal empire. The struggle between Hindu ascetics for control over sacred space did not in the least challenge the sovereignty of the Shi'a Nawabs of Awadh. Ultimately, it was only through tax-free land grants that the ascetics could settle in Ayodhya and start to build temples. For example, Safdar Jang (r. 1739–54) gave land to Abhayaramdas, abbot of the Nirwani *akhara*, for building Hanumangarhi, which is now the most important temple in Ayodhya. The removal of the Nawabi administration first from Ayodhya to Faizabad and then to Lucknow is often interpreted as the liberation of a Hindu sacred place from Muslim oppression in Hindu historical writing. Clearly, the contrary is the case, since Ayodhya rose as a Hindu pilgrimage center in direct relation with the expansion of the Nawabi realm and with direct support from the Nawabi court.[21]

The complexities of the relationship between the Nawabi court and the Ramanandis in Ayodhya is shown in the next important instance of violence between religious groups, of which we have written evidence. There was a dispute about a mosque before the British took over the realm of the Nawabs of Awadh in 1856, but this mosque was not the Babari Masjid, the current bone of contention, but a mosque which was allegedly in the most important Hindu temple in Ayodhya, Hanumangarhi. The conflict led, however, to a Hindu assault on what must have been the most important mosque near Hanumangarhi, which is now universally known as the Babari Masjid, but might then have been simply known as the Jama Masjid.[22]

The 1855 dispute is confusing for those interested in the current Babri Masjid conflict. Most commentators today take it for granted that the 1855 dispute had been about the Babari Masjid in the first place. One can understand the confusion. While now all attention is given to a conflict about a mosque which occupied the place of a temple, the conflict in 1855 was about a temple occupying the place of a mosque. Indeed, no party in the conflict nowadays even mentions a disputed site in Hanumangarhi and from today's perspective it seems difficult to imagine that a bunch of Muslim militants would launch an attack on Hanumangarhi, a huge fortified temple, with the belief that they should repossess their sacred space. Nevertheless, this was indeed the case in the mid-nineteenth century.

The god worshipped in Hanumangarhi is, of course, now unequivocally incorporated within Ramanandi ritual practice, but this has not always been so. Local tradition has it that the god worshipped on the hill on which the Ramanandis built Hanumangarhi was indeed Hanuman, who was worshipped by both Shaivite *sanyasis* and Sufi *faqirs* under the name Hathile.[23] The Ramanandis had to chase these competitors first before they could claim the place and the worshipped aniconic stone as their own. This struggle is recounted in local tradition. I would suggest that it was such a tradition in the nineteenth century on which the belief of Muslims was based that within the precincts of Hanumangarhi a sacred place could be located which belonged to them.

That Muslim militants could launch an attack on such a well-entrenched Hindu bulwark as Hanumangarhi has to be understood in its broader political context. The attackers were Sunnis under the leadership of Shah Ghulam Husayn, a religious scholar (*maulvi*). Ayodhya belonged to Awadh, a regional realm governed by Shi'ite rulers since the beginning of the eighteenth century. The defeat and massacre of the Muslim militants by Hindu *sadhus* (and their supporters, local landowners) compromised the Islamic legitimacy of Shi'ite rule which was always under threat of rejection by Sunnis, the majority among the Muslim population. In an interesting move, the chief religious official among the Shi'ite population of Awadh argued that a Muslim state had to put an end to the wickedness of the infidels.[24]

This instance shows clearly the predicament of a Muslim ruler confronted with communal violence. The predicament of Vajid Ali Shah, the ruler of Awadh, was, however, worsened by the fact that he had not only to avoid hurting Muslim feelings, but also was effectively dependent on the political support and consent of the British resident in Lucknow who took to the defense of the Hindus. A government commission was formed, which concluded that no mosque existed in Hanumangarhi. This led to violent demonstrations among Muslims. Maulvi Amir Ali Amethavi called for a holy war and organized an army to march on Ayodhya. Now the chief Shi'ite religious official declared this a forbidden act when it was not supported by the state. In effect, he ruled against popular action of Sunnis in a Shi'ite state. The Shi'ite ruler had the prerogative to protect the Islamic Law. When the holy warriors decided to ignore the warnings of the Shi'ite government and marched on Ayodhya, they were confronted by government troops and massacred. Soon after these events the British decided to take over the administration of Awadh by making it a province of British India.

The 1855 dispute throws light on a complex configuration. No doubt, there was a communal conflict between Hindus and Muslims about sacred space. However, this conflict also involved conflictual interactions between Shi'as and Sunnis in their relations with the Hindu population. Disenfranchised Sunnis wanted to take political action against Hindus when they felt that the Shi'ite state was not protecting Muslims or advancing Islam. The capability of the Shi'ite state to do so was, however, limited by its dependence on the British. Moreover, the Shi'a rulers of Awadh had also always depended on support from Hindu elites whom they wished not to alienate. In fact, as we have seen, many of Ayodhya's temples – Hanumangarhi is one of them – had been built with donations from Hindu officials in Awadh's Shi'ite government.

In a way, the British interference caused the collapse of the delicate balance the Shi'ite rulers had to keep. When they finally took formal control in 1856, the British understood that it was their foremost task to police and control communal relations. Since the Hanumangarhi issue had effectively dissolved, they focused on the other potential site of conflict, the Babari Masjid. By placing a railing, they materially and symbolically divided the worshippers in the Babari Masjid compound.

The Babari Masjid became now a sacred space symbolizing the antagonism between two "nations," "Hindus" and "Muslims," rather than one of the elements in a complex configuration of power, in which Shi'a rulers and Sunni and Ramanandi religious specialists found themselves in a delicate balance. While till the nineteenth century Rama devotion had to be violently defended against Shaivite Hindus, after the British annexation of Awadh it came to be linked to the discourse of Hindu nationalism which defined Muslims as the eternal enemy.

RITUALS OF NATIONALISM

While there can be no doubt that the religious history of India, prior to the establishment of British colonial rule, had been as violent as religious histories elsewhere in the world, it is also true that the scope and the nature of violence, related to religious beliefs and practices, changed when they came to be related to the discourse of nationalism. There are at least two notions of crucial importance in this shift. The first is the notion of "territory". The second is the notion of "representation". A polity characterized by hierarchical relations between elites and subjects was transformed by the notion of the nation-state, in which the state is the instrument of the political will of the majority of equal citizens. While the earlier polity was characterized by discontinuity in the hierarchical relations between centers and peripheries, the modern nation-state is characterized by territory, a continuous tract of land. As Dumont argues, the modern nation is the collection of individuals and their properties.[25] The sovereignty of the nation depends on the sacrality of its territory, marked by its borders. As Anderson shows,[26] this notion of territory, marked by borders, imagined as continuous map-lines, is modern, introduced into nineteenth century Asia by colonialism.

When we see the importance of the notion of "territory" for the definition of the nation, it should not surprise us that it is grafted on earlier notions of "sacred space." This linkage is brought out with admirable clarity in an oft-cited passage in Veer Savarkar's *Hindutva*: "A Hindu means a person who regards this land of Bharat Varsha, from the Indus to the Seas as his Fatherland as well as his Holy-Land that is the cradle of his religion."[27] However, it was only through political ritual that this sense of territory could be made real in people's imagination of national belonging.

The first important supra-local movement to succeed in creating a sense of a Hindu nation as opposed to Muslims and the British was the Cow Protection Movement in the last decades of the nineteenth century. As Anand Yang (1980) has shown, large numbers of people were mobilized through the networks of local marketing systems. In the case of Saran District in Bihar, on which Yang focuses,[28] it was the transit of cattle intended for slaughter which led to widespread rioting. Not only cattle was on the move, but Hindu monks travelled the countryside as well to organize people against the slaughter of the Cow-Goddess. Circular letters (*patias*) were used to spread the message of the Hindu nation.[29] While the movement to protect Mother

Cow from Muslim butchers and British barbarians concentrated on the Punjab, Uttar Pradesh and Bihar, riots also took place elsewhere, notably in Calcutta and Bombay. The great "success" of the Bombay cow protection riot of 1893 led Bal Gangadhar Tilak, the Maharashtrian Hindu leader, to continue to develop new ritual strategies for mass mobilization.[30] The most striking among those was the reinvention of the festival for Ganapati, the elephant-headed Hindu God, and a series of rituals connected to the all-but-forgotten founder of the Maratha empire, Shivaji (1627–80). The direct connection between these rituals and communal riots is perfectly clear from Douglas Haynes' work on colonial Surat.

The first series of communal riots in Surat took place in 1927 as a result of processions held to commemorate the birthday of Shivaji, who symbolized "the common heritage of the Hindus." A second series of riots followed the next year after processions celebrating the Hindu god Ganapati.[31] The "catchment area" of these ritual innovations, however, was more limited than that of the Cow Protection Movement. It remained largely restricted to Western India, what is now known as the states of Maharashtra and Gujarat.

It is probably fair to say that it was Gandhi's political genius which allowed the Independence Movement to gain "nationwide" attention in his celebrated Salt March. In March 1929, Gandhi set off on his month-long, 240-mile pilgrimage to the coastal town of Dandi, where he would make salt from the sea. Seventy-eight carefully selected male supporters accompanied him, representing different regions, religions and castes. By ritually attacking the salt tax and the colonial salt monopoly, he challenged Britain's right to rule over India. He went on foot and stayed overnight in villages, asking only for simple rural food. In this way he symbolized the perpetual moving around of the Hindu monk who embodied the higher values of the Hindu nation in the face of colonial oppression. While Gandhi undoubtedly preached a tolerant, pluralistic nationalism, his political style derived from the nationalist interpretation of Hindu discourses and practices. His use of a whole range of forms of protest, such as fasting and marching in what he did not call "political action," but "experiments with Truth," have become part of the modern political instrumentarium in India, used by any politician who wants to engage in extra-parliamentary action to press his issues.

Ayodhya and the Babari Masjid did not play significant roles in the Indian struggle for Independence. No doubt, like other places, Ayodhya was affected by the political turmoil, but it did not gain center stage in attempts to define Hindu–Muslim relations. Also, after Independence, when the Muslim presence in the area was much weakened by migration to Pakistan, the mosque–temple issue came up only briefly. After Independence, the mosque was protected by a police picket. Despite this precaution, Hindus entered the mosque in the night of December 22, 1949 and converted it to a temple by installing an idol of Rama in it. The following morning large crowds assembled in front of the mosque and tried to force entry, led by the idea that Rama had appeared. The gate was locked and the police force strengthened. However, the District Magistrate, K.K.K. Nayar, refused to remove the idols. Nayar's position was supported by the Divisional Commissioner, who proposed to keep the site under police control, but allow a priest to do the necessary worship till the excitement would wear off and a plan could be made with leaders of both the Hindu and Muslim communities. Something similar was indeed done. A committee of respectable Hindus of Ayodhya was allowed to enter the temple and worship the idol every year at December 22, while the site remained closed for the general public. In the meantime civil suits were filed by both Hindus and Muslims concerning the exclusive right to worship.

A forceful conversion of Babar's mosque into Rama's temple was succesfully stopped by the police who closed the gate. Nevertheless, the idols were not removed nor Hindu worship completely stopped. This meant that the mosque had *de facto* been converted into a temple, since Hindu worship had replaced Muslim worship. On the higher levels of the administration there had been a strong feeling that the idols had to be moved, but District Magistrate Nayar, under whose responsibility the idols had been surreptitiously installed, had been totally uncooperative.[32] Letting the courts decide implied a political strategy of pacification by infinite delay and indecision.

The very fact of Hindu worship in the mosque left the issue wide open for further action. However, it is striking that, after the frenzy of the post-Partition years, no further initiative was taken on the local level. This can be explained by the fear felt by local religious leaders that a temple on Rama's birthplace would provide strong competition with existing religious attractions in Ayodhya. The action had to come from outside and it did come in 1984, when the Vishva Hindu Parishad (VHP) or World Hindu Council began a campaign to liberate Rama's birthplace.

The Vishva Hindu Parishad is a Hindu nationalist movement, which was founded in Bombay in 1964. Its main objective is "to take steps to arouse consciousness, to consolidate and strengthen the Hindu Society." It organizes religious leaders of various Hindu communities in one overarching body which holds meetings at important Hindu festivals. In the 1960s and 1970s, the VHP focused on missionary work in tribal areas and on organizing Hindus overseas. Although it had not been unsuccessful in these activities, it was only in the eighties that it gained prominence on the Indian political scene. This was achieved by creative use of political ritual on a grand scale. In 1983, the VHP staged the *Ekatmatayajna*, a procession for national unity, which reached, according to its own estimate, some 60 million people. In 1984 it started the *Ramjanmabhumi-muktiyajna*, a procession to liberate the birthplace of Lord Rama. This action aimed at the removal of the Babari Masjid and the building of a temple at this site.

The VHP's mass rituals effected at least two important things. They constructed a homogenized national Hindu identity by using a ritual repertoire, derived from various traditions, which excluded non-Hindus. To be a non-Hindu was to be an anti-national person, a demonic threat to the unity of Hindu India. Secondly, this Hindu identity was linked to a sense of sacred territory.

The first successful ritual of Hindu nationalism organized by the VHP, was the "Sacrifice for Unity" (*Ekatmatayajna*) in 1983. Three large processions (*yatra*) traversed India in November and December, 1983. One went from Hardwar to Kanyakumari, the second from Gangasagar to Somnath, and the third from Kathmandu (Nepal) to Rameshwaram, inaugurated by the king of Nepal, the world's only independent Hindu kingdom. At least 47 smaller processions (*upayatra*) of five days traversed other parts of the country and connected at appointed meeting-points with one of the three large processions. The routes taken by the processions were well-known pilgrimage routes connecting major religious centers and suggesting a geographical unity of India (*Bharatvarsha*) as a sacred area (*kshetra*) of Hindus. In this respect, pilgrimage was indeed quite consciously perceived and used as a ritual of national integration.

Processions of "temple-chariots" (*rathas*) are an important part of temple festivals in India. An image of the god is taken for a ride in his domain, confirming his territorial sovereignty and extending his blessings. The processions of the VHP made use of two "chariots," *rathas* in the modern form of brand-new trucks. The symbolism of the temple-chariot was perpetuated, but also the militant symbolism of the "war-chariot" of Arjuna in the Bhagavad Gita. The story of the Bhagavad Gita, which was made into the fundamental text of Hinduism in the nineteenth century, emphasizes the duty of the warrior to fight when war is inevitable. In the pamphlets of the VHP, Arjuna's chariot is a recurring symbol. On one of the two chariots of the VHP, an image of Bharat Mata, Mother India, was carried.

The Mother Goddess is worshiped in many forms in India. Some of those are new. Santoshi Mata, "Satisfying Mother," for example, conquered India in the 1960s under the influence of a very successful movie. The political use of Mother symbolism is also widespread in India. In Andhra Pradesh, the regional party, Telugu Desam, has introduced a Telugu Mother Goddess and the late prime minister Mrs Indira Gandhi tried to use the Goddess symbolism for her own glorification. The connection between the worship of the Mother Goddess and Mother India has been most forcefully laid in

Bengal where the worship of the Goddess is exceptionally strong. The Indian National Congress has chosen Bande Mataram (Hail Mother), a poem by the Bengali nationalist Bankim Chandra Chatterjee as the national anthem despite its strong Hindu emphasis. The making of an image representing Bharat Mata is the VHP's reference to this nationalist tradition.

The other chariot carried an enormous water pot (*kalasha*) filled with water from the Ganges and a smaller water pot filled with local sacred water. This chariot was followed by a truck which sold Ganges water in small bottles. The Ganges is seen as a deity and her water contains the power to purify from sin and to grant salvation. All the sacred water in the rest of India is a secondary derivation of the Ganges. In this way, all rivers and temple-tanks are symbolically connected with the Ganges as the unifying symbol of Hindu India.

The waterpot (*kalasha*) is one of the most important objects in Hindu ritual. It symbolizes power and auspiciousness. The processions of the "Sacrifice for Unity" made a very effective use of an existing ritual repertoire on the Mother Goddess, the sacredness of Ganges water, and on Lord Ram and transformed this repertoire to communicate the message of Hindu unity. This could only be done by using a ritual repertoire which engages generally accepted Hindu conceptions without running into conflict with specific doctrines espoused by one of the many religious movements represented in the VHP. It is also perfectly clear that those who did not participate in this Hindu ritual could not be seen as part of the nation. In effect, the message was as much about Hindu unity as about the Muslim Other.

The processions gained an enormous publicity and enabled the VHP to start local branches in all parts of the country. It formed the basis for the VHP to subsequently organize a "sacrifice to liberate the birthplace of Lord Ram" (*Ramjanmabhumimuktiyajna*) in 1984.[33] A procession, starting in Sitamarhi (the birthplace of Sita, Ram's wife) reached Ayodhya on Saturday, October 6, 1984. The procession did not consist of much more than a few private cars with monks and a truck with the large statues of Ram and his wife, Sita under a banner with the slogan: *Bharat Mata ki Jay*, Hail to Mother India. On the next day, speeches were held in Ayodhya by VHP leaders and local abbots. All this was not very impressive. When the procession moved on to the state capital Lucknow, however, it gained considerably more attention. Later, the procession moved on from Lucknow to Delhi where the VHP intended to stage a huge rally, but it was caught in the aftermath of the murder of Mrs Gandhi by her Sikh bodyguards which had turned national attention away from the Ayodhya issue. Nevertheless, in the following years, the VHP continued to put pressure on politicians, which resulted in a decision of the

District and Session Judge of Faizabad on February 14, 1986 that the disputed site should be opened immediately to the public.

The VHP continued to agitate for the demolition of the mosque and the building of a temple. From September 1989, the VHP engaged in the consecration of "bricks of Lord Ram" (*ramshila*) in villages in North India and the organization of processions to bring these sacred bricks to Ayodhya for building a temple on Ram's birthplace in place of the mosque of Babar on November 9. Riots connected to these processions broke out in Gujarat, Madhya Pradesh, Bihar and Uttar Pradesh. They were most serious in Bhagalpur, Bihar, where hundreds of Muslims were killed in October 1989. In the midst of this, the Government of India announced parliamentary elections to be held in November. As a reaction to that announcement, the VHP decided to call off its plan for a march on Ayodhya, but to continue with their foundation plans. Ultimately, the VHP was allowed to lay its foundation stones in a pit outside the mosque on so-called undisputed lands. It is remarkable that some of the stones prominently exhibited came from the US, Canada, the Caribbean, South Africa, as if to emphasize the transnational character of this nationalist enterprise.

The BJP gained considerably in the national elections of November 1989, taking its strength in Parliament from two seats to 86. While remaining outside the National Front government of former opposition parties, its parliamentary support was indispensable for the central government's survival. Since the BJP's electoral gain was clearly related to its direct support of the VHP's Ayodhya program, the temple–mosque controversy was kept alive as one of the most important political issues. Especially in the second part of 1990 there were two major political developments which affected the course of action regarding Ayodhya. In the first place, the Kashmir issue flared up with an unprecedented flow of Hindu refugees trying to leave that part of the country. The BJP took a strong anti-Pakistan stance here and this is always related in India to an anti-Muslim stance.

Secondly, in September, V.P. Singh's government decided to implement an earlier report of the so-called Mandal Commission which proposed a considerable increase of reservations for the Backward Classes in educational institutions and government service. This resulted in wide-spread anti-reservation riots in which a large number of students immolated themselves in a new form of protest for India. Since the agitation around reservation imperiled the Hindu agenda of the VHP/BJP, L. K. Advani, the leader of the BJP, decided to start a procession from Somnath in Gujarat to Ayodhya, another *rath yatra*, through ten states, with its declared goal the construction of the temple on October 30, 1990.[34] This initiative met with great enthusiasm all over the country. Members of the Youth Branch of the VHP, the Bajrang Dal, offered a cup of their blood to their leader to show their determination. All this set a kind of time bomb which ticked with every mile taken in the direction of Ayodhya. Mulayam Singh Yadav, the chief minister of Uttar Pradesh (UP), in which state Ayodhya is located, took a vow that he would not allow Advani to enter Ayodhya. However, before he reached UP, on October 30, Advani was arrested on the orders of Laloo Prasad Yadav, the chief minister of neighboring Bihar. This did not prevent Advani's followers from marching to the mosque, but they were stopped by police firing. To appreciate the firm stance taken by Mulayam Singh Yadav and his caste-fellow Laloo Prasad Yadav, backed by V.P. Singh's central government, one has to take into account that they are leaders of an upwardly mobile backward caste which would benefit considerably from the implementation of the Mandal Report. Partly for this reason, the action by the government resulted in its loss of the BJP's support in Parliament and its subsequent fall on November 16, 1990.

The VHP continued its agitation with a highly effective video and audio casette campaign on the happenings in Ayodhya on October 30, 1990. It claimed that thousands were killed by the police and that the evidence was suppressed. Martyrs (*amar kar sewaks*) were cremated and their bones and ashes taken in ritual pots (*asthi-kalashas*) through the country before immersion in sacred water. In Ayodhya, sacrificial rituals and marches to the Babari Masjid continued to be staged intermittently.

In May and June 1991, new national elections were held, in which 511 seats were contested. The BJP won 119 seats and 20 percent of the votes. This meant that it had nearly doubled its share of national votes and that it emerged as, by far, India's largest opposition party.[35] Perhaps even more significantly, it won the state elections of UP, India's most populous state of more than 100 million people, in which Ayodhya is located. This success, however, placed the BJP in the difficult position of having to placate the VHP, which continued to press for the demolition of the mosque, while trying to prevent the Congress (I) from finding any legitimation for replacing the BJP goverment of UP with Governor's rule.

A deliberate attempt to place the Ayodhya issue on the backburner was made, again by starting a procession. An *Ekta Yatra*, (Procession for Unity), was performed by Murli Manohar Joshi, the president of the BJP, starting in Kanyakumari, India's southernmost tip on December 11, 1991, destined to reach Srinagar, the capital of Kashmir in the North, on January 26, 1992. The difference between the 1983 *Ekatmata Yajna* and the 1991–2 *Ekta Yatra* was a shift from a focus on religious ritual, symbolizing Hindu unity, to a more unembellished secular ritual, symbolizing the unity of India as a nation-state. It was the BJP's aim to draw attention away from the Ayodhya issue to the Kashmir issue and Joshi's ultimate ritual action was a specifi-

cally nationalist one, the unfurling of the Indian flag in Srinagar. In an interesting way, this ritual act was made possible only by support from the
Congress (I) Union government, which ordered the Indian military in Kashmir
to protect Joshi and his comrades from assaults by Kashmiri Independence
fighters.

The failure of the *Ekta Yatra* has been one of the factors leading the BJP
to focus its attention again on the Ayodhya issue. Another element has been
that the VHP did not allow the BJP to sidetrack it after its electoral gain. In
the course of 1992 the Congress (I) government continued its attempts to
resolve the issue by organizing direct negotiations between the VHP and the
Muslim Babari Masjid Action Committee, but these negotiations proved
fruitless. Then, on December 6, 1992, a rally in Ayodhya, organized by the
VHP and the BJP, resulted in an attack on the mosque and its subsequent
demolition. Although BJP leader Lal Kishan Advani, who was present at this
occasion, immediately tried to distance himself from the act of demolition,
there can be little doubt that the entire event had been well planned in
advance. At the same time there can be no doubt that the paramilitary forces,
present at the site, could have prevented the demolition. However, Congress
(I) stood to gain from this illegal act of its political opponents, since it
provided the legitimation for dismissing the BJP governments of the states
of Uttar Pradesh, Madhya Pradesh, Himachal Pradesh and Rajasthan. Very
serious riots broke out in several parts of the country, notably in Bombay,
Ahmedabad, Surat and Calcutta. More than a thousand people, mostly
Muslims, were killed in Bombay alone. Muslim gang leaders retaliated
months later with bomb attacks on several official buildings in Bombay. All
this has caused an enduring crisis in Hindu-Muslim relations, but also a decline
of Muslim confidence in the Indian secular state's capacity to protect
minorities. For the BJP the demolition of the mosque has caused a considerable set-back in Uttar Pradesh, but, on the whole the party has continued
to be strong in other parts of the country, notably in Maharashtra and Gujarat,
two of the more industrialized states in Western India.

CONCLUSION

We have discussed three instances of religious conflict in Ayodhya. The first
written record we have of such a conflict concerns a battle between two groups
of Hindu monks. This conflict concerned the control over sacred space as
well as over networks of pilgrimage and long distance trading. Its violence
was religious in the sense that the results of it showed not only the physical
strength (*bal*) of one party as compared to the other, but also the

superiority of its ascetic discipline (*sadhana*). There was no sense of gaining leadership over the Hindu population in order to overthrow Muslim rule. Rather there was a competition to gain the patronage of Muslim rulers. There was also, surely, no sense of territory in the modern sense. These monks probably operated with a kind of sacred geography which connected the main religious centers through their annual cycle of pilgrimage.

The second recorded conflict did show some concerns of a communal nature. The conflict was about sacred space, a Muslim mosque, allegedly in the principal Ramanandi temple. In a superficial reading, it almost looks like the current situation in reverse. A major difference, however, is that the conflict showed the fragmented nature of Muslim identity, just as the first incident showed the fragmented nature of Hindu identity. This conflict concerned, more than anything else, a lower-middle-class Sunni challenge to the religious authority of the Shi'a Nawabs to define correct Islamic politics towards Hindu idolaters. The violent confrontation which ultimately ensued was not between Hindus and Muslims, but between Sunni 'holy warriors' and a Shi'a army. That it came to such a confrontation had to do with the erosion of Nawabi authority by the already formidable British presence in Awadh. The notion of space operative in this context was one in which the ruler governs an – in principle – unbounded, universal realm in the name of Islam. The relation with non-Muslims in such a realm is a challenge which would, ultimately, be solved by conversion. (In Islamic discourse, non-Muslims are comparable to permanent 'guests' who have to be protected by Muslim rulers).[36] It was the status of Hindus and their religious practices in a realm governed by Muslims that was at issue in the debate between Shi'as and Sunnis which turned violent. In the end, this was a debate about the power to define orthodoxy. It should be clear that we are far removed from the politics of representation here, in which the political will of the majority counts, not the orthodoxy of the 'true believers'.

To understand the current mosque–temple issue one has to take the discourse of modern nationalism into account. Although the VHP consists largely of Hindu monks, they do not discuss doctrinal orthodoxy. Rather it is the opinion of the majority of the people which they seek to express. This homogenized opinion is created by mass ritual which is a combination of heterogeneous elements. Again, there is a notion of space involved here, but it is the modern one of territorial nationalism articulated with the sacred geography of Hindu pilgrimage. The movement "to liberate Rama's birthplace" implies a "nationalization" of Rama devotion. It shows the linkage between the ritual discourse of Rama devotion and the discourse of Hindu nationalism.

As we have seen, Rama is an incarnation of the god Vishnu and, at the same time, he is the king of Ayodhya who rules according to the Religious

Law (*dharma*). He is therefore a god-king. This discourse lends itself, of course, for appropriation in Hindu kingdoms of the pre-Independence period. For dynasties such as that of the Bhumihar Rajas of Banaras, investment in the pageantry of the Ram Lila was an important aspect of their legitimacy. Much of this, however, collapses in the 1920s and 1930s. The role of patrons of religion was taken over by business groups, such as the Marwaris. Both ex-aristocrats and Marwaris have come to play a significant role in supporting the nationalization of Rama devotion.

The notion that the kingdom of Rama provided one with an ideal model for the nation-state was taken to some extreme length in a marginal Hindu party, the Rama Rajya Parishad, founded by Swami Karpatri (1907–82). In a 1952 party manifesto, Rama's glorious reign is invoked: "Every citizen of Ramraj was contented, happy, gifted with learning, and religious-minded ... All were truthful. None was close-fisted, none was rude; none lacked prudence; and above all, none was atheist. All followed the path of dharma."[37] While Karpatri did not have much success with his adventure, it is important to note that the notion of Ramraj was also important in the political philosophy of Mahatma Gandhi. In Gandhi's view, based on his reading of Tulsi Das, Ramraj was "not only the political Home Rule but also dharmaraj ... which was something higher than ordinary political emancipation."[38]

It is indeed fairly typical for Hindu nationalism that it allows for a wide divergence of political interpretations of religious concepts. There is a vast gap between Karpatri and Gandhi, but still they are operating within the same discourse which cannot be very appealing to those who are outside the Hindu fold. It is the particular strength of the VHP that it articulates aspects of the state-religion rhetoric of Karpatri and Gandhi at a conjuncture in which the "secular multiculturalism" of Nehru's Congress appears to be failing.

Finally, what do these three incidents show us in general about the relation between riots and rituals? While there can be little doubt that, firstly, ritual performance plays an important role in the construction of religious identity (and difference) and, secondly, that we are dealing with riots between groups with a religious identity here, it is more difficult to demonstrate a direct causal relation between rituals and violence outside those rituals. Pilgrimage to Ayodhya and participation in the worship of Rama have taken place for centuries without leading directly to the large scale riots we have seen in the last few years. Besides, riots between Hindus and Muslims have taken place for centuries without any relation to Rama devotion. A straightforward approach would be to say that riots have all kinds of contextual explanations and that in some cases they are discursively linked to the performance of ritual. However, it is hardly feasible to make sharp distinctions between events and their interpretations, between practices and their discursive context. Indeed, the interpretation is part of the event.

The discourse of modernity, introduced in Indian society in the nineteenth century, has changed considerably the discursive context in which religious violence is interpreted. While in the first two instances of religious violence we have discussed there would not have been any notion of a distinction between religion and politics, such a distinction dominates the discursive context of the current violence. This distinction belongs to a discourse of secularization, developed in the European Enlightenment, which assigns religious faith to the private domain as a matter of personal beliefs without political consequences. The political aspect of religion is often seen as a transgression of what religion is supposed to be.[39] A widespread idea is that religious people should not fight each other, but live in harmony. When confronted with violent conflict between religious communities, outsiders often deplore the "politicization" of religion. A version of this view is the argument that violence between religious communities has nothing to do with religion, since it is *really* economical and political competition which fuels it. This discourse which makes a sharp dichotomy between *real* religion and "politicized" religion can be located, by-and-large, among the well-meaning, well-educated, "responsible" individuals in society as well as among social scientists. Those who perpetrate the violence are often characterized as "fanatic" members of mobs led astray by their "irresponsible" leaders. It is this discourse which obfuscates the important connections between riots and rituals in the modern world.

NOTES

1 For rituals, see J.F. Staal, "The Meaninglessness of Ritual", *Numen*, XXVI (1970), 2–22. The description of the "insane" violence of "senseless" mobs is very common in newspaper descriptions and in the discourse of the state. Riots are seen as spontaneous explosions of pent-up feelings. This interpretation emphasizes their irrationality and lack of purpose. It becomes the acting out of "narcissistic needs" in psychoanalytic discourse; see Sudhir Kakar, "Some Unconscious Aspects of Ethnic Violence in India", in Veena Das (ed.) *Mirrors of Violence* (Delhi: Oxford University Press, 1990), 135–45.
2 See Das, *Mirrors of Violence*, 1–36.
3 Victor Turner, *Dramas, Fields, and Metaphors* (Ithaca: Cornell University Press, 1974).
4 Sandria Freitag, *Collective Action and Community* (Berkeley: University of California Press, 1989).

5   Marc Gaborieau, "From Al-Beruni to Jinnah: Idiom, ritual and ideology of the Hindu–Muslim confrontation in South Asia," *Anthropology Today*, I, No. 3, (1985), 7–14.

6   Gananath Obeyesekere, "The Buddhist Pantheon in Ceylon and its Extensions," in Manning Nash (ed.), *Anthropological Studies in Theravada Buddhism* (New Haven: Yale University Press, 1966).

7   Eric Wolf, "The Virgin of Guadeloupe: A Mexican National Symbol," *Journal of American Folklore*, LXXI, No.1 (1958), 38.

8   M. N. Srinivas, "The Cohesive Role of Sanskritization," in Philip Mason (ed.), *India and Ceylon: Unity and Diversity* (London: Oxford University Press, 1967), p. 74.

9   David Mandelbaum, *Society in India* (Bombay: Popular Prakashan, 1972), p. 401.

10 Chris Fuller, *Servants of the Goddess* (Cambridge: Cambridge University Press, 1984).

11 Turner, *Dramas, Fields, and Metaphors*.

12 Maurice Bloch, *From Blessing to Violence* (Cambridge: Cambridge University Press, 1985).

13 Bruce Kapferer, *Legends of People, Myths of State: Violence, Intolerance, and Political Culture in Sri Lanka and Australia* (Washington, DC: Smithsonian Institution Press, 1988).

14 C. A. Bayly, "The Pre-history of 'Communalism'? Religious Conflict in India, 1700–1860," *Modern Asian Studies*, XIX, No. 2 (1985), 177–203.

15 Gyanendra Pandey, *The Construction of Communalism in Colonial North India* (Delhi: Oxford University Press, 1990).

16 See Peter van der Veer, "Hindu 'Nationalism' and the discourse of 'Modernity': the Vishva Hindu Parishad," in Martin Marty and Scott Appleby (eds) *Accounting for Fundamentalisms* (Chicago: University of Chicago Press, 1994).

17 Some of my arguments in this section can be found in greater detail in my recent book, *Religious Nationalism: Hindus and Muslims in India* (Berkeley: University of California Press, 1994).

18 Talal Asad, "Anthropological conceptions of Religion," *Man (NS)*, XVIII (1983), 237–59.

19 I use the term "monk" to refer to *sadhus* who live apart from the world under religious vows and according to a rule.

20 Peter van der Veer, *Gods on Earth* (London: Athlone [LSE Monographs 59], 1988).

21 See Van der Veer, *Gods on Earth*.

22 G.D. Bhatnagar does not even mention the Babari Mosque in his account, but calls it the Jama' Masjid, in *Awadh under Wajid 'ali Shah* (Varanasi: Bharatiya Vidya Prakashan, 1968).

23 This may look like 'syncretism', but the shared worship of a slab of stone may not mean a shared understanding of what that worship means. I would suggest that the place in question is contested terrain and that, at some point, Ramanandi militant ascetics were able to get it under their control.

24 See Juan Cole, *Roots of North Indian Shi'ism in Iran and Iraq* (Berkeley: University of California Press, 1988), p. 245. My account of these events is based on Bhatnagar, *Awadh*, and on Cole's careful description.

25   Louis Dumont, *Homo Hierarchicus* (Chicago: University of Chicago Press, 1980), p. 333.

26   Benedict Anderson, *Imagined Communities* (London: Verso, 1990), p. 172.

27   V. D. Savarkar, *Hindutva* (Poona: S.R., 1942; originally published in 1922), p. 1.

28   AnandYang, "Sacred Symbol and Sacred Space in Rural India: Community Mobilization in the 'Anti-Cow Killing' Riot of 1893," *Comparative Studies in Society and History*, XXII, No. 4 (1980), 576–96.

29   Pandey, *Construction of Communalism.*

30   Richard Cashman, *The Myth of the Lokamanya* (Berkeley: University of California Press, 1975).

31   Douglas Haynes, *Rhetoric and Ritual in Colonial India* (Berkeley: University of California Press, 1991), pp. 277–81.

32   Nayar was forced to resign over this case, but his attitude made him a local hero; see Harold A. Gould, "Religion and Politics in a UP Constituency," in Donald E.. Smith (ed.), *South Asian Politics and Religion* (Princeton: Princeton University Press, 1966), pp. 51–74. His portrait was enshrined in a pavillion, built by the VHP on the grounds of the mosque, to show the pictorial history of the Hindu struggle for Rama's birthplace.

33   This part is based partly on Peter Van der Veer, "God Must be Liberated," *Modern Asian Studies,* XXI, No.2 (1987), 283–301.

34   Somnath was chosen as a starting-point for this procession since the VHP/BJP regards it as a precedent for the Mosque/Temple dispute in Ayodhya. The Somnath temple was destroyed by Mahmud of Ghazni in 1024 and rebuilt by Hindu nationalists, including Congress ministers, such as Vallabhbhai Patel and K.M. Munshi, in 1950–1. The then President of India, Dr Rajendra Prasad, performed the installation ceremony on May 11, 1951. The VHP/BJP argument is that, when the state could support the rebuilding of the Somnath temple even in the "secular" Nehru years, it should certainly be supportive of the rebuilding of Rama's temple in Ayodhya (see about this issue, my "Ayodhya and Somnath: Eternal Shrines, Contested Histories," *Social Research*, LIX, No. 1 (Spring 1992), 85–109.

35   The Congress (I) party which suffered in May the loss of its leader, Rajiv Gandhi, who was murdered by Sri Lankan Tamil extremists, won 225 seats and 37 percent of the votes which allowed it to form the government.

36   Farzana Shaikh, *Community and Consensus in Islam* (Cambridge: Cambridge University Press, 1989), p. 41.

37   Quoted in Philip Lutgendorf, *The Life of a Text* (Berkeley: University of California Press, 1991), p. 385.

38   Quoted in Lutgendorf, *The Life of a Text,* p. 380.

39   My analysis here has been informed by Talal Asad's introduction to "Religion and Politics," a special number of *Social Research*, LIX, No. 1 (1992), 3–17.

6. *Dharma Yudh*: Communal Violence, Riots and Public Space in Ayodhya and Agra City, 1990 and 1992

Jayati Chaturvedi and
Gyaneshwar Chaturvedi

On December 7, 1992, following the demolition of the Babari Masjid in the northern Indian town of Ayodhya the previous day by enthusiastic bands of *kar sevaks*, drawn from all parts of the country, the Republic of India erupted in communal riots, the initial round of which took almost a week to subside, leaving in its trail a toll of over one thousand dead and four thousand injured.[1] Hindu tradition held that the three-domed mosque was built in the sixteenth century by Mir Baqi, a general of Babur, after razing to the ground a previous temple that stood on the birth place (*janmasthan*) of the Hindu god Rama, a central figure in Hindu mythology and folk culture. The Vishwa Hindu Parishad (VHP) in conjunction with other militant Hindu organizations like the Bharatiya Janata Party (BJP) and the Rashtriya Swayam Sevak Sangh (RSS) had been spearheading an energetic campaign for the mosque to be relocated and a temple to be built in its place. The above incident was seen as one culmination point of its pro-Hindu activities.

According to Hindu perception, the reclamation of the site from the control of the Muslim "other" was a *Dharma Yudh* (crusade). This paper presents a case study of Agra City in the context of the countrywide riots and communal violence sparked by the attempt to regain control of that public space in Ayodhya. It also proposes to survey the events of December, 1992 when riots did not occur in Agra in the light of similar happenings in October–November, 1990 when riots did take place.

THE QUESTION OF IDENTITY

The contesting claims of the two communities to the disputed site in the past few years had resulted in the marshalling of a considerable body of literature by the contending parties. This literature and archaeological excavations at the site proved inconclusive. The issue snowballed and *mandir nirman* (construction of the temple) became an attempt by the Hindu community to define its identity and assert its community rights through concerted actions. Affirmation of this identity involved the practice of symbolic rituals and a struggle for control of public space which, in a chain sequence, generated a confrontational situation with the Muslims.[2] The symbolic use of Hindu rituals will be discussed in the following pages.

The initial Muslim response (also discussed at greater length below) was that the mosque represented a part of their glorious past and threatened future. Muslims at first denied even that there had been any temple demolition on the site. In the face of mounting evidence and Hindu mobilization, there came about a grudging acceptance that a Hindu temple, though not necessarily a Ram temple, had been demolished, but it came to be bracketed with the plea that one historical sledge-hammer act does not justify another. Even if a temple had been destroyed, it did not justify another act of demolition by Hindus, which would have adverse effects psychologically and tactically upon Muslim feelings and Hindu–Muslim relations.

Meanwhile, the VHP had drawn up a list of Hindu temples allegedly razed, whose sites were occupied by mosques. Topping the list were two additional mosques, one in Mathura and another in Varanasi.

The VHP (established in 1964), which barely existed at the beginning of the last decade, has experienced truly amazing growth by presenting itself as the militant defender of Hindu interests and identity. The grass roots workers for this movement, however, were the RSS *swayamsevaks* (volunteers). The RSS, for the greater part, draws its sustenance from that section of Indian society which keenly feels the crisis of identity precipitated by the alienation and insecurity brought on partly by the breakdown of social, moral, and political norms in present-day India and partly by the accelerated rate of change related to modernizing and Westernizing influences.

After Independence, the twin processes of modernization and Westernization created an identity crisis for middle class Hindus, pushing them to search for new forms of self-definition. The individual's thrust towards explicit self-identity became a matter of greater concern. The quest of the middle class Hindu for his new self-image became increasingly urgent, giving birth to a greater self-assertion and competitiveness. The RSS, with its tradition-oriented, Hindu nationalism was able to fill the vacuum amongst large segments of the Hindu urban petty bourgeoisie as well as among the Hindu rural populace.[3]

The Sangh believes in the "catch-em-young" theory and these young indoctrinated storm troopers were the driving force of the *mandir-andolan* (temple movement) and active participants as defenders of the Hindu community in riot situations. This task of organizing the Hindus at the grass roots levels, undertaken by the RSS, was made difficult by the fact that Hinduism is an all-embracing religion, with no prescribed rules for membership, no insistence on adherence to specified customs, rituals and code of conduct, with no mechanisms for purging of non-believers. In addition, the amorphousness of flexible religious sects in classical Hinduism led to diversities within the Hindu fold and created organizational problems for the RSS as well. The Sangh succeeded largely in filling up the vacuum. This is borne out by the fact that large sections of the Hindu populace not participating in the riots showed open sympathy for the rioters in December, 1992. *Sadhus* and itinerant holy men lent legitimacy to the movement under the combined BJP-VHP-RSS banner and lowly Hindu castes teamed up with upper castes in the process. Clearly, it was a case of Ram bridging the gap between urban and rural India, between the elite and popular levels of consciousness.[4]

THE SETTING

The people of Agra waited with bated breath on the morning of December 6, 1992. The BJP Chief Minister of Uttar Pradesh (UP), Kalyan Singh, had assured the central government under Prime Minister Narasimha Rao that, barring opening fire on *kar sevaks*, he would do all in his power to stop them from demolishing the Babari Masjid. The winter session of Parliament had commenced from November 25, and ever since the Ayodhya issue had figured prominently. Fearing dismissal by the central government, the BJP government of UP had dug in before November 25 by massing *kar sevaks* at Ayodhya. One prominent feature this time, as opposed to the previous confrontation of October–November, 1990, was the overwhelming response of people from the southern states and Maharashtra. The choice of the southern states had been arrived upon with the motive of pulling the carpet from under the feet of Mr Narasimha Rao and demonstrating to him the hold of the BJP-RSS in the southern states as well now that the BJP was firmly in the saddle in the northern states of UP, Rajasthan, Madhya Pradesh, and Himachal Pradesh. The volunteers from these BJP-ruled northern states had received instructions to wait till further call.

The services of the *mahants*, *sadhus*, and *mathadhishas* (monastic heads) had been requisitioned for this purpose: they had been instructed to marshall volunteers from the southern states and bring them along to Ayodhya. One hundred thousand Shiv Sena volunteers also were to participate in the *kar seva*,[5] raising apprehensions in all quarters. The Supreme Court had been petitioned by two Muslim citizens, Achan Rizvi and Mohammad Aslam, to restrain the BJP-RSS from any construction activity in the 2.77 acres of land acquired by the UP government until the High Court of the state decided upon the validity of the acquisition. On November 29, the UP government assured the Supreme Court that there would be no construction at the disputed site, that the *kar seva* would be of token value and would be limited to the singing of *bhajans* (hymns). The Bajrang Dal chief and MP from Faizabad constituency (which includes Ayodhya), Vinay Katiyar, issued a statement saying that he and the Bajrang Dal did not consider themselves bound by the decision of the provincial BJP government. The *sadhus*, incensed at having their thunder stolen, insisted that they would have to break the law for, without that, *mandir nirman* was impossible. The Muslims, normally quick on the organizational front, particularly after the congregational Friday *namaz* at the Jama Masjid in Delhi, just seemed to stand by with a naive faith in the central government.

AGRA

Agra, the historic city on the banks of the Yamuna River, the city of the Taj, has gradually evolved into an economic epicenter in contemporary western UP. The population of the city comprises Hindus, Muslims and Jatavs (some of whom are Buddhists). The Hindus can be further split up into numerous castes. The city is the home of a thriving leather industry in which the economy is controlled by the Hindus (the Punjabis to be precise). The Jatavs, traditionally leather workers, constitute the work force. The Punjabis, mostly refugees from the post-partition days, displaced the traditional Muslim elite as controllers of the economy of the leather industry. The new terms and conditions forged by the Punjabis vis-à-vis the Jatav work force, placed the latter in a more disadvantageous position in comparison to the pre-partition days, when the leather economy was controlled by the Muslim elites. Besides, the entrepreneur-laborer relationship between the Punjabi Hindus and the Jatavs accounted for some degree of strain in their mutual relationship. In addition, Agra houses the stone industry (marble, red sandstone, inlay work, and so on), some small scale industries like the manufacture of plastic goods, household detergents, and so on, and some medium industries like the manufacture of generators and foundries. In the hinterlands, manufacturing of carpets and *kalins*, for which the city becomes the marketing point, flourishes. All other industries, except the leather industry, are to a large extent controlled by the Banias (a Hindu trading caste).

The economic dominance of the Hindus, the impoverishment of the Muslims, and the deplorable economic status of the Jatavs contrasted with their near belligerent political stance constitute the social realities of the city. For the Jatavs, the process of Sanskritization within the Hindu fold has proved far too strong, despite some conversions to Buddhism, a newfound identity. Consequently, many of them live with dual identities – Buddhist as well as Hindu. The Jatav vote has been pursued as a consolidated vote bank for which local political leaders bid and also as cannon-fodder for the Hindutva forces at times of communal clashes. Shahganj and Lohamandi constitute the most prominent Jatav habitation tracts while Tajganj, Nai ki Mandi, Namner, Mantola, Pai Chowki, Gudri Mansur Khan, Ghatia Azam Khan, and Ghatia Mamu Bhanja constitute Muslim *mohallas* (neighborhoods). Needless to say that these latter areas also contain upper caste Hindu pockets too, making the situation explosive in riot conditions.

From pre-Independence times to 1977, Agra remained an exclusive Congress bastion. In the 1977 elections, in the aftermath of the Emergency, the Congress stalwart, Seth Achal Singh (a Jain) lost to the Janata party candidate, Shambhunath Chaturvedi. Thereafter, Seth Achal Singh's successor, Nihal Singh, managed to barely cling to the Agra seat until 1989, by which time, at the city level, the BJP had emerged as a force to reckon with.

Despite a history of communal amity, Agra had become a BJP-RSS-VHP stronghold. Three out of four MLAs – Hardwar Dubey, a Brahman from Agra Cantonment, Satya Prakash Vikal, a Bania from Agra (East), and Kishan Gopal, a Harijan from Agra Reserved constituency were former RSS men and all men of the BJP. The fourth, Vijay Singh Rana from Dayalbagh was a Janata Dal MLA. The MP (Member of Parliament) from Agra, Bhagwan Shankar Rawat, a Brahman, was a former RSS man. The municipal corporation had a BJP majority and the Mayor, Ramesh Kanta Lavaniya also was a Brahman and a former RSS *swayamsevak*.

Agra, at the beginning of the winter of 1992, was in an apprehensive mood. What would the month of December, 1992 bring? Compromise? Violence? Curfew? Riots? The petty-bourgeois trading classes, forming the bulwark of the BJP-RSS support base, conservative in nature and numerous in the city, identifying strongly with the temple reconstruction demand, looked forward to a limited amount of excitement, but detested the idea of long-drawn curfews and closure of markets as unsettled conditions in the city would mean a crippling blow to their economic interests.

On December 2, the BJP President, Dr Murli Manohar Joshi, and the leader of the opposition in Parliament, Mr L. K. Advani, visited Agra in the course of a campaign to rouse public opinion for the proposed *kar seva*. At their mammoth public meetings, they made statements designed to arouse Hindu sentiments like, "One more partition of Hindustan will not be acceptable to the BJP" (Joshi) and "For the sake of the temple we will sacrifice not one but many governments" (Advani). The success of these mammoth public meetings far exceeded the expectations of the local organizers.[6] Prior to this, all leave sanctioned to policemen had been cancelled.[7] By November 26, the entire administrative division of Agra was humming with various kinds of preparatory activities. The governmental intelligence network was active and the Commissioner for Agra division was closeted with his officers in official meetings. The local VHP men, fearing preventive arrest, had gone under ground, while 200 *kar sevaks* and ten specially trained assault squads, galvanized by a "do or die slogan," comprising 50 Bajrang Dal volunteers left for Ayodhya with five days of self-sustaining rations and woolens.[8] Panic buying and hoarding of foodstuffs was on the increase as the inhabitants of the city began to prepare for long stretches of violence and curfews.

Following the assurance given by the UP government to the Supreme Court on November 29 that there would be no construction activity at the disputed site but only token *kar seva*, the local RSS cadres were temporarily thrown in a dismal state of disarray and confusion, but recovered speedily saying that this was the hour of trial when they must show faith in their leadership. Meanwhile, within the city, small Hindu shrines and temples were being found in a state of demolition in the wee hours of the mornings, the jobs having been accomplished in the darkness and anonymity of the night. One such notable incident was the demolition of a Shiv *mandir* in the residential area of the backward castes of Kolis in *thana* Chatta, the area known as Johns Mill Line in Agra. The administration lay the blame at the doors of anti-social elements and hurriedly repaired them, but communal tensions were on the rise.

The VHP organized a country-wide *lalkar saptah* (challenge week) consisting of street corner meetings, the blowing of *shankh* (conch-shell), clanging of *ghanta-gharial* (ringing of prayer bells and striking at a plate of alloyed metals), hoisting saffron flags in the daytime and *mashals* (flaming torches) at night on terraces, and organizing *mashal jaloos* (processions bearing lighted torches). These audio-visual symbols of communal solidarity went a long way toward polarizing the communities, organizing the Hindus and striking fear among Muslims. On the same day, November 29, another batch of 410 *kar sevaks* left for Ayodhya from the rural hinterland of Agra. The grass roots workers within the RSS, troubled by the loss of face on account of the compromise formula, had been pressing for a hard line approach. They were supported by the *sadhus*, the VHP, and the Bajrang Dal.[9] After various phases of waxing and waning, the stage was now set for the final Armageddon.

Like all the previous movements and dates chosen, the choice of December 6 too had a covert Hindu connotation.[10] It was the day on which the eighteen-day *Mahabharata* war had begun in which Lord Krishna had exhorted Arjun to do his duty and not count the cost. Once again, as on many previous occasions, the VHP had used Hindu ritual symbolism to bring home a strong message of Hindu nationalism and Hindu identity to its great advantage.

The choice of the date, December 6, however, presented one difficulty for Agra. It marked the death anniversary of the depressed class leader, Bhim Rao Ambedkar. Agra has a sizable Jatav community and the choice of this date was becoming a cause of contention for the Harijans. Perhaps this can be linked to the fact that a number of small Hindu shrines and temples were found damaged in the dead of the night in localities inhabited by these depressed classes – the *malin bastis* (slums) – as mentioned earlier. One opinion holds that this might have been the handiwork of Hindutva troublemakers, attempting to rally the depressed classes to the larger Hindutva cause, while another opinion holds that this might have been the doing of non-Hindutva *agents provocateurs* for the purpose of weaning away some of the Harijans associated with the temple movement.

When the Central Minister for the Department of Human Resources, Arjun Singh, decided to lead the *Ram-Rahim Rath* peace march, a team of Congress workers from Agra left for Ayodhya under the leadership of District Congress (I) President Azad Kumar Kardam (a Harijan) to join Arjun Singh, but their peace march was aborted after a telephonic conversation with the Prime Minister. The choice of Mr Azad Kumar Kardam was a significant one. Agra's large Jatav population is also politically conscious. Some of the Jatavs are also relatively prosperous since, as noted above, Agra is a prominent center for leather work. Having realized the value of their collective vote, the Jatavs of Agra often play hard-to-get on the political front vis-à-vis the various political parties, more so because Agra has a constituency reserved for Scheduled Castes for the state legislative assembly.

The Jatavs had been wooed most assiduously by the Hindutva forces to join the temple movement. *Sewa Bharati*, an organizational arm of the RSS, designed to work in the *malin bastis* mostly inhabited by the Jatavs, had for long been working overtime with the aim of integration of the Jatavs in the temple movement. Their efforts were paying dividends, as many Jatavs were enrolling themselves as volunteers for the *kar seva*. Kardam, though a Jatav, was a Congressman. The choice of Kardam to lead the protest march of the Agra contingent against the temple movement was designed to prove that while some Jatavs might be supporting the BJP on the issue, there were other Jatavs who were against the BJP and with the Congress (I). The Congress (I) wished to prove that the BJP victory regarding the successful integration of the Jatavs into the temple movements, could at best be regarded as partial only.

Following the demolition of the mosque a red alert was sounded all over UP in which nine towns including Agra were put under curfew. Seven police stations in Agra were put under tight curfew and these included Chatta, Lohamandi, Shahganj, Tajganj, Kotwali, Mantola, and Nai ki Mandi. An uncanny quiet prevailed in the Muslim areas. Secret meetings were held in these areas and in certain areas of the Lohamandi Police Station: Bagh Ram Sahai, Tolipara, Gali Rangrejan, Rajnagar and Sir ki Mandi. Both Hindus and Muslims had evacuated their houses, anticipating a sudden upsurge of violence.

The demographic configuration of Agra City is such that it is possible to identify four sensitive areas where Hindus and Muslims are cloistered in juxta-posing pockets: Tajganj, where the 1990 riots began, Nai ki Mandi, Namner, and Lohamandi. The Tajganj area, near the Taj Mahal, has an almost even distribution of Hindus and Muslims. This was a continuous trouble-spot for the police in the 1990 riots in which the police had conducted house-to-house searches and recovered a large cache of arms (bombs in particular) from Muslim homes. In spite of this recovery, regular bomb bursts had plagued the police force in the Tajganj area in 1990.

The Nai ki Mandi area joins with other Muslim-predominant areas in its neighborhood – Mantola, Sadar Bhatti, Pai Chowki, Gudri Mansur Khan, and Ghatia Mamu Bhanjua – to form a large Muslim habitation tract. This forms the congested heart of the city marked by narrow *galis* (alleys) known to the local residents like the lines of their palms, conveniently structured for the conduct of riotous activity. It is easy enough to throw bricks and acid concentrates or to lob crude country-made bombs from the terraces of houses to people or police passing below. Escape routes, which can be resorted to by jumping from terrace to terrace, are not very difficult to negotiate. In inter-ethnic conflagrations, the Muslims find themselves in an advantageous position in the above-mentioned areas. The majority of Agra Muslims who migrated to Pakistan in 1947 were from this tract. Their houses were allotted to refugee Hindus by the custodians, creating pockets of Hindus within the general Muslim-predominant residential areas. These refugee Hindus, for whom the spectre of partition comes alive every time there is a communal riot, are willing to stake all in confrontationist situations.

The Namner area houses the *Idgah*. It is ringed on one side by the main road in the city, the Mahatma Gandhi Marg which, being a trunk route, is constantly and heavily patrolled in riot conditions. This main road also has government buildings like the Public Works Department Inspection House and commercial establishments which deploy their own *chowkidars* (guards, sometimes even armed guards from the Central Industrial Security Force) as well. The other end of the Namner area is fringed by Hindu houses. This

area has, by and large, these two exit points and the Muslims here are practically sandwiched between the main road patrolled by security men and the
Hindus. In case of riot, escape routes in this area are at best difficult, at worst
impossible to negotiate.

The Lohamandi area, apart from the usual Hindu–Muslim sprinkling, has
large concentrations of backward and low castes – Kolis and Jatavs – who
generally tilt the scales. They are wooed assiduously by the Hindutva forces
and often play hard-to-get. For the last two years, the Jatavs had not been
very forthcoming or vocal in their statements, attitudes, or support of the
Hindutva cause, seen to be dominated by upper caste Hindus. Their displeasure
with the upper caste Hindus could be attributed to two incidents: the Panwari
Outrage and the Kumher Outrage. Panwari and Kumher villages in the
vicinity of Agra had been scenes of massacre of local Jatavs by Thakurs in
caste confrontations and the Panwari incident had even brought Rajiv Gandhi,
then out of power and in the Opposition, to that village. The Jatavs, being
traditionally leather workers, working on carcasses, were generally regarded
by the Hindus as a community possessing nerves of steel and therefore more
capable of dealing with the Muslims, some of whom were Kasais (butchers).

The sound of *ghanta-ghariyal* (Hindu bells and alloy plates) and *shankh*
(conch shells), continued to rend the evening air along with cries of Jai Shri
Ram from terrace tops. Saffron flags distributed by the RSS-VHP-BJP were
hoisted atop many Hindu homes in silent empathy and support, demonstrating
that large sections of the Hindu population not actually participating in the
near-riot activities were openly sympathetic to the Hindutva cause. When
Muslim homes hoisted black flags as a token of their opposition to the
demolition of the mosque, the Hindutva forces changed their saffron-flags
for black ones, as a token of their own protest against the large scale arrest
of Hindu workers and leaders. When the Muslims pulled down the black flags
from their homes for fear of being interpreted as supporting the Hindu cause,
the saffron ones went up atop Hindu homes again!

The mobilization tactics of the Hindutva forces seemed to be working
successfully. In the city itself, Hindu sentiment seemed to be on the upswing,
as indicated by the fact that, in a number of residential areas (*mohalla*s), loud
hailers were put up to play seemingly innocuous *bhajans* (devotional songs)
in the mornings with occasional inflammatory banned songs lacing the
bhajans. When the arrests of RSS-VHP workers began after the imposition
of a central government ban on these organizations on the night of December
10, their grass roots workers assumed pseudonyms, shed their Sangh uniforms,
and collected at the temples of their *mohalla*s at eventide for *Hanuman
Chalisa Path* (recitation of verses from the religious book commemorating
an ode to *Hanuman*, the bachelor monkey-god devotee of Lord Ram). This

religious activity would be followed by loud and long clanging of temple bells and sustained calls of *Jai Shri Ram* rending the evening air. After all, that was no illegal activity!

Needless to say that these gatherings were utilized as substitutes for the banned *shakhas* (morning and evening meetings of the RSS) to keep in touch with members and orient them about the developing situation. Here we witnessed once again the ingenuity of the RSS-VHP in the determination of its mobilization tactics. Temples in India have been the traditional meeting place of members of the community and, by converting the temple into substitute *shakhas*, using them as venues for their meetings and utilizing the evening *aartis* (evening prayers involving the burning of lamps and the chanting of hymns) for the exchange of information and orientation of members in particular and the Hindu community in general, the RSS-VHP once again used an existing Hindu custom to reinforce Hindu ritual and Hindu identity. It would certainly not be far fetched to view it as an attempt to collectivize the Hindu community, which is really a flexible mingling of religious sects. The polymorphousness of classical Hinduism and its heterodox nature, the prevalence of many deities and internal diversities, the concept of the *sadhak* ploughing his lonely furrow, were regarded by the dynamic Hindutva forces as detracting from the potency of the religion vis-à-vis its capacity to take up the challenge of exclusive (so-called "Semitic") religions, which had the advantage of congregational worship. They viewed the use of evening prayer meetings in neighborhood temples for religio-political purposes of mobilization as a corrective step in this regard.

By December 11, the countrywide violence toll crossed 900 dead, yet Agra remained ominously peaceful. There were scattered and sporadic incidents of violence, but they were contained locally. For instance, on December 11 at 9:00 p.m., after an incident of sloganeering, firing, and bomb bursts near the *karbala* adjoining the Kamlanagar area, where Muslims and Hindus lived cheek by jowl, strict curfew was imposed in the *karbala* area of *thana* New Agra for 70 hours. It was enforced with such extreme strictness that the 10,000 residents, mostly poor Muslims, were not allowed out of their houses for toilet purposes or for drawing water. Police personnel patrolling the area yelled at old women and told them, "When you will produce so many children then this will be your plight." Some of the residents allege that the constables suggested that they leave for Pakistan if they desired a better life style.[11] In the predominantly BJP-RSS city of Agra, the residents of the *Karbala* area lodged a protest with Mr Vijay Singh Rana, the Janata Dal MLA from Dayalbagh. Earlier in the day, trouble had erupted in the Lohamandi *thana* of the city but had been brought under control. In the Naubasta *mohalla* of *thana* Lohamandi, a Hindu youth engaged in the manufacture of crude

Molotov Cocktails got his hands blown off. On the same day, in Alamganj, a predominantly Muslim area, a country made bomb was lobbed at a *masjid* when the faithful were preparing for their Friday prayers at 6:45 p.m. The bomb landed on the tin roof of a section of the mosque, creating more din than damage. Nobody was killed. December 14 witnessed more bomb blasts in Alamganj, which led to the arrest of twelve more youths, one of whom was a Muslim. On the night of December 13–14 at 9:15 p.m., a bomb exploded in a dump heap at Nala Kanskhar in the Nai ki Mandi locality. Nobody was hurt. Police reinforcements from Nai ki Mandi police station and Madan Mohan Gata *thana* reached the spot and helped bring the situation under control. Border Security Force (BSF) pickets were posted on 24 crossings and a total of 39 police pickets were set up in the entire city. By December 13, the national death toll crossed the 1,000 mark as the country began to limp back to normalcy. Of course, the city was often rife with rumors, spreading on the grapevine as a consequence of the attempts of the city administration to conceal the facts.

For eight days, from at least December 6 to December 14, while the country was engulfed in communal riots, Agra remained a simmering cauldron of communal mistrust, rumors, occasional police atrocities, and sporadic violent incidents, yet the city did not erupt in riots. This was in sharp contrast to the widespread riots that occurred in the city in October–November, 1990 in the course of the Ram Janmabhumi Movement at that time. On the basis of what we ourselves witnessed, it seems not unreasonable to assert that riots do not happen, they are caused. They are not spontaneous uprisings but rather constitute organized activities.

In October–November, 1990, the provincial government was controlled by the Samajwadi Janata Party and was headed by Chief Minister Mulayam Singh Yadav, whose style of leadership betrayed a marked degree of clumsiness, certainly lacking the finesse required for administering the most populous state of the Republic with its concomitant diversities and complexities. At the Center was Mr V. P. Singh, who had displayed an equal degree of ham-handedness in dealing with the Mandal (anti-reservation) riots. Both did their political arithmetic with an eye on the Muslim votes. It is commonly, though falsely, believed that Muslims always vote *en bloc* and that this is done after receiving directives from their clergy through the congregational services on Friday, which accounts for the prominence gained by the Shahi Imam Abdul Bukhari of the Jama Masjid of Delhi at that time. In 1990, while on the national level the Congress (out of power) and the Janata Dal (in power) vied with each other in securing the Imam's support, the Samajwadi Janata Party, headed by Mulayam Singh Yadav in Lucknow too sought to gain Muslim votes in UP. Many observers blame him for police

firings on unarmed groups of *kar sevaks* in Ayodhya, for encouraging the
Muslims to adopt a belligerent posture, and for polarizing the Hindus under
the militant Hindu banner with its consequences in the organization of riots.
In contrast, in December, 1992, the inaction displayed by the Rao government
in the initial stages, the firm control of the BJP at the state level in UP, and
the complete control of the BJP at the city level in Agra, placed the police
and paramilitary forces in a pro-Hindu stance and precluded the possibility
of riots at the city level.

Another basis for the organization of riots are as a chain response to
incidents that are local or have taken place close by. In the 1990 riots, first
the grapevine had it and the vernacular press reports (wrongfully) confirmed
in Hindu minds the commission of Muslim excesses against minority Hindus
in Aligarh. The Aligarh Medical College housed in the Aligarh Muslim
University campus was said to have been attacked by Muslim rioters who
slaughtered the helpless victims and their attendants, which set off a vengeful
Hindu reaction against Muslims in Agra. In the 1992 situation, Aligarh, which
M. J. Akbar in his book *Riot after Riot*, certifies as "a city where tension in
any case hardly ever comes down," was clamped under a severe continuous
curfew for a week, which was relaxed only for two hours on the eighth day.

Agra and Aligarh are often linked in a cyclic chain of mutual action and
reaction so far as inter-ethnic riots are concerned. The Hindu community in
Aligarh largely consists of two Bania sects, the Agarwals and the Barasainis.
These groups in Aligarh deviate from the Bania stereotype, according to which
its members are regarded as being very shrewd, even foxy, but not particularly heroic. With years of experience of and exposure to riot conditions in
Aligarh, these groups now feel quite at home in dealing with riots. While
the Agarwals make available the material resources, particularly financial
donations, in bolstering the Hindutva forces in Aligarh, the Barasainis
provide the muscle power and are derisively referred to as "worse than
butchers" by the local Muslims.

It was reported to the authors that, in the beginning of December, but before
the 6th, the local administration held parleys with the RSS-VHP office
bearers soliciting their support and discussing ways and means to work out
a preventive plan of action in case of possible riots in Aligarh. Similar
parleys were held with Muslim leaders and workers as well. These confidence
building discussions by the district authorities with prominent leaders of the
two communities were confirmed both by the Mufti of Uperkot, Aligarh, as
well as Mr Navman, ex-MLA (BJP) from Aligarh.[12] The Mufti seemed
highly appreciative of this step taken by the district administration. The Hindu
leaders and local level workers assured the local administration that peace
in the Hindu *mohallas* would be their responsibility and that the adminis-

tration should rather focus upon the deployment of forces in the Muslim localities. The Muslims did likewise. This, coupled with the partial vacation of Aligarh Muslim University hostels before December 6 and the clamping of curfew in the city after December 6, precluded inter-ethnic eruptions in Aligarh and prevented the development of a chain reaction response in Agra.

The foregoing would tend to confirm that riots are often caused by elite manipulations on either side involving not only the manipulation of the general masses but also a slick manipulation of the dynamics of the empirical situations. The religiosity of the masses only serves to further elite game plans.[13] Moreover, there is a deliberate purpose behind the killings and violence of riots which, in essence, reflects an imbalance amongst groups. Their contending claims to the control of public space disrupt the political equilibrium of a particular time and place. The opportunities for riots and violence develop when a previous balance between contending groups is altered.[14]

A case in point would be the Kamlanagar Temple, which was constructed within the wink of an eye during a curfew relaxation hour in October, 1990. The Temple straddles a road tri-junction and has since been considerably embellished. While on the one hand the authorities were most unhappy at the construction of the temple in a communally tense situation, the cultural values of the people would not allow the desecration of the rudimentary temple structure and there it stands to this day. The fate of the small temple constructed at the site of the demolished Babari Mosque at Ayodhya is likely to be the same.

Thus, riots occur in a given set of conditions. Effective management of the factors that produce riots would preclude the possibility of riots while mismanagement of them would enhance the possibilities of their occurrence. Riot control, in essence, is the management of the potential for conflict. The BJP had promised "a riot-free administration" if it was voted to power in UP and, in the 18-month tenure of the BJP government, UP experienced only a single riot, in Varanasi.[15]

Brass has held that riots are "a continuation and extension of communal politics by other means."[16] The evidence from Agra city as well as from UP as a whole supports his argument. In Agra, after the defeat of the Congress stalwart Seth Achal Singh in 1982, who had been the sitting MP from Agra without a break from 1952 to 1977, the Congress under his successor Nihal Singh (1980–9) found itself increasingly unable to incorporate the groups it had previously mobilized: the Muslims, the Jatavs in the city, and other intermediary and elite castes (Ahirs, Thakurs, and so on) in the rural hinterlands of Agra. These groups were thus left available for mobilization by other parties. Agra being a prominent trading center where Bania groups abound and constitute the traditional support base of the BJP, the latter, supported by the grass roots RSS workers, witnessed a phenomenal success in the city such that by December, 1992, Agra had emerged as a total BJP citadel. The courting of the Jatav groups by the BJP-RSS, its anti-Muslim mobilization and pro-Hindu appeals can be viewed as attempts by the BJP to alter the established patterns of political alliances in its own favor. The occurrence of the riots in October–November, 1990 signified the struggle of the Hindutva forces to gain ascendancy in the city while the non-occurrence of riots in December, 1992 denoted their consolidated position in the city and the state.

THE PRESS AND THE POLICE

The English language press has largely internalized the value system of the over-interventionist state. This explains not only its serious inability to comprehend the meaning and power of the Hindutva resurgence but also its almost total alienation from popular sentiment in reporting the demolition of the "disputed structure."[17] Even Western media persons are often amazed at the hiatus between the ground reality and the reporting/prognoses of the English language press.[18]

It is almost as if, cocooned in their plush offices in metropolitan centers, editors and news reporters are writing in a state of alienation from mass sentiment. It is rather the press photographers and the cartoonists who give an objective account of events. Reporting on riots, which inevitably have a component of police-people confrontation, the English language press often assigns to itself the role of the nation's conscience-keeper without being in touch with the nature of national consciousness. Their orientation regarding the Ram Janmabhoomi/Babari Masjid issue has been no different. *India Today* did a cover story on the security failure titled "Spineless Spectators," targeting the police for its inaction. Elsewhere, it reported, "Policemen sat among *karsevaks* watching and grinning, smoking lazily, and occasionally cheering." That bit of slick reporting, though true, did not take into account the dangerous portents inherent in the situation. Nor did it attempt to analyze the causes of that ennui. A mere indictment was enough for the conscience keepers. The fact of the matter is that, be it the beat constable in a riot situation, the DM Faizabad or SSP Faizabad, an increasing number of Hindu agents of the interventionist state are finding it more and more difficult to stifle what they see as their own conscience and render unquestioning obedience to the dictates of an increasingly alien state.[19]

Let us now look at the charges concerning trigger happy policemen victimizing the Muslims. The volume as well as the frequency of such charges is not insignificant.[20] In UP, this charge is particularly directed against the Provincial Armed Constabulary (PAC). The politicization of the police force in UP, leading to its criminalization and subsequent communalization, has been a subject of much recent comment. What begins as an ethnic riot often develops into a direct confrontation between the PAC and the Muslims, leading to the charge that the PAC is a communal force working in conjunction with the Hindutva forces.

During the November, 1990 riots in Agra, it was discovered that the PAC constables on duty in the Muslim-dominated Nai ki Mandi area could not be supplied with food for almost 36 hours. The operational exigencies of the curfew-bound areas did not permit the supply of food to the constables on field duty. The authors were informed that they would not accept food from Muslims for fear of being poisoned. There was a minor sensation in the city when Mrs Kamla Pande, dynamic wife of the BJP MLA, Hardwar Dube, organized mass feeding of the PAC force in Nai ki Mandi locality.

The authors have been told by police officials that, outside his uniform, the PAC constable is a Hindu first and last. He belongs squarely in the traditional, folk culture of rural India. The constable's training seeks to instill in him some degree of professionalism, but it leaves untouched his hard-core Hindu identity. In times of crisis, his Hindu identity has the better of his professional identity as an impersonal instrument of the secular state. As the Rudolphs have noted, at a time when conflict and violence of all types have been on the increase in India, an "undereducated, undertrained and underpaid" constabulary force, which is also overworked and politically manipulated, "must mediate sporadic class and community conflicts in which its own cadres have divided loyalties."[21] Even K. F. Rustamji, a senior police administrator and member of the National Police Commission sadly reflected, "I have watched with dismay during the year 1982 the conversion of the UP PAC from a model force I worked with in the fifties to a unit which is fêted by the Hindus and hated by the Muslims."[22]

Yet, there is another side to the story. The politicization of criminals leaves the police with little option but to crack down heavily when a crisis of law and order seems just round the corner. The authors learnt during a field study in June, 1992[23] from reliable official circles that the immediate impetus to communal riots in December, 1992 in Khatauli, a bazaar town 22 kilometers from Muzaffarnagar, were incidents of stabbing undertaken by Muslims. Likewise, official sources confirmed that, in December, 1992 in Khatauli, the Muslims tried to organize themselves around known criminals and that 80 percent of riots are the handiwork of criminals (in the Muzaffarnagar area, mostly from the Gujar caste), who move from district to district. Another official source in Muzaffarnagar confirmed that, on the morning of December 8, 1992, when curfew had been in force in the city from the previous day, a gang of Muslims in Khatauli attacked Hindu colonies close by, stabbing one Muslim in a case of mistaken identity. This official believed that mass killings of Hindus was the objective of the Muslim gang, but they were taken by surprise at the immediate response of the police, the army, and the BSF, which had been mobilized to prevent riots. He disclosed that local rivalry and competition between two prominent politicians was the root cause of riots in this area, leaving the police with little option but to crack down, perhaps even indiscriminately once in a while. Frequently, what began as a criminal activity took on the hues of a communal riot, fanned by the personal ambitions of local politicians, placing the police in a "damned if you do and damned if you don't" situation.

At least two political notables amongst those interviewed in western UP commented upon the role of criminals in riots in Muzzafarnagar. They had a lot to say about police brutalities in general but when asked pointedly if he thought the PAC was a communal force, a Muslim leader replied that was the general Muslim perception but the PAC had saved Muslims also. Nevertheless, Parliament has witnessed repeated demands for changing the community composition of the PAC in UP, even for its total disbandment. On the whole, it nevertheless appears to us that the situation on the ground in UP in riot situations which we have witnessed or discussed with local authorities confirms that the PAC are often involved, acting in a partial manner in situations which turn from apparent riots into pogroms.

CONFLICTING DISCOURSES

Nationalism in India has been double-faced as a result of an interaction between two idioms: one being the "modern," "secular" idiom of the occidental culture which is very much alive in the urban centers among the English-educated and the other being the Bharatiya elite cultural identity based on folk culture, drawing strength from traditional values, forms and structures of large sections of society, both rural and urban. The former is largely represented by the Congress and the English language press, the latter by the forces of Hindutva.

The inconsistencies of the nationalist discourse in India can be explained as a consequence of the coalescence and divergence of these two idioms.[24] Sometimes these discourses can overlap too. Although India gained freedom in 1947, it appears that the political system, state structure, and the mental orientation of the English-educated ruling elite remained much the same. Even prior to Independence, Hindu reconstruction movements were raising basic questions about the content and quality of Hindu identity and Hindu traditions. Congress leaders may have deplored the tendency of these movements to define the allegiance of the community in a sectarian manner, but they were powerless to prevent it.[25] In the viewpoint of Hindu populists, Congress stood for the ascendancy of Western values and the displacement of traditional elites by English-speaking graduates.[26] Minor cleavages between colonialist-nationalist discourses apart,[27] the more basic divergence is between the colonialist/nationalist discourse on one side and the authentically indigenous traditionalist discourse on the other, represented by the forces of Hindutva.

Gandhi is credited with the transformation of the national movement into a mass movement by substantial exploitation of Hindu religious symbols. Nehru took to Western values lock, stock, and barrel and used the entire power of his charismatic personality to legitimize the Western world-view, so much so that large sections of the Hindu community internalized the Nehruvian perception to the point where "Hindu tradition" became synonymous with obscurantism and communalism, if not worse. After the war of 1971, Mrs Gandhi approvingly donned the image of a "Durga astride a tiger." Thereafter, she also exploited to the hilt other Hindu symbols and publicized her many visits to saints and godmen, to famous temples and heads of monastic orders, and her consultation with astrologers. The symbols of the "Hindu Right" were being legitimized by the "secular" Congress itself and, in 1980, Mrs Gandhi was making another shift from socialist populism to a more pronounced Hindu appeal, eliciting positive RSS responses of co-operation even when she was lambasting the BJP as a political rival.

Rajiv Gandhi could not even speak proper Hindi when he assumed office, had an extremely weak Hindu identity, and could not understand the power of traditional Hindu India. His handling of the Hindu–Muslim contentions (the Shah Bano case and the *Shilanyas*) were wanting in political deftness and further stoked the communal fires. Mrs Gandhi had ushered in the "de-institutionalization" of the Indian political system with much élan. This was part of her political legacy to Rajiv Gandhi.[28] Along with Rajiv Gandhi's own amateurishness, it contributed significantly to the resurgence of the "saffron brigade." The age of Hindu confessional politics had come into its own. "Religious performances, celebrations and demonstrations began to transcend localities and to acquire national dimensions. As they did so, they became more strident and militant. The agitations and *yatras* (pilgrimages) of the Hindu solidarity and unity movements such as the Vishwa Hindu Parishad were no longer the local phenomena they had been."[29]

The Hindu discourse regarding the Ayodhya dispute rests upon a certain kind of self-image, an interpretation of history, and a definite world view.

It held that centuries of political subjugation and domination had caused grave damage to the Hindu psyche, leading to timidity and loss of confidence. What has been worse is that the Hindu has internalized these negatives and glorified them in his own self image, as "the gentle Hindu, the patient Hindu" (Swami Vivekananda). The Hindu and the Hindu community present the pathetic spectacle of a people living an apologetic life in its own land, unsure of its own identity, and uprooted from its traditions. According to the new militant Hindu discourse, the Congress denied them the right to interpret their history.[30]

Militant Hindus view iconoclasm as an integral part of Islam and cite the instance of the Prophet destroying the pagan idols in the Ka'bah[31] as a precedent for the alleged demolition of a Ram Temple and the subsequent construction of the Babari Masjid at the same site with the debris thereof. This latter belief is largely drawn from the works of two prominent Indian historians.[32] The Babari Mosque is viewed by BJP ideologues "as an assault on the Hindu identity and Hindu culture."[33]

The Muslim discourse presents a more complicated mixture. It includes the attitudes and interpretations of Muslim politicians and intellectuals, including nationalist, communal, and Marxist Muslims. Nationalist Muslims in India have acknowledged the country as their place of birth and their only home. Most of them had grown up watching *Ram leelas* (annual folk enactments of the life of Lord Ram), reading about *Ram Rajya* (Ram's rule of perfect justice and tolerance), and playing with Hindu friends. A few had even reached a point in their personal inner evolution at which they felt no contradiction between their own identity and the BJP-RSS stance and felt emboldened enough to join the party. Sikandar Bakht, leader of the opposition in the Rajya Sabha, Sayed Naqvi, who fought the election on a BJP ticket from Bihar and lost, Muzzaffar Hussain, who presided over intellectual sessions of the RSS, Mohammed Arif Khan, BJP MP from Rajasthan, Ammar Rizvi, Minister for Jails in the Kalyan Singh government, Jaffar Sharif, Railway Minister in the Narasimha Rao government, who had been an RSS *swayamsevak* in his youth,[34] were amongst those whom the BJP-RSS chose to call Hindu Muslims, the term "Hindu" here being used to denote a resident of Hindustan.[35] They were the ones who in private argued with their own people that they should give up their claims to the mosque as no *namaz* (prayers) had been offered in it for the last four decades and also because the installation of the idol of Ram-Lala (infant Ram) there had rendered the mosque *na-pak* (impure) according to Qranic injunctions. They were the ones who had sat back in complacency in the belief that the storm in the tea cup had blown over. They had reposed faith in the Hindu spirit of tolerance. Finally, some of them felt conned by a central government which failed to protect the mosque, hiding behind a veneer of constitutional technicalities.

The political leadership of the Muslims asserted that neither Babar nor any other Muslim would ever have erected a mosque by displacing a temple. Syed Shahabuddin proclaimed that if it was shown independently of British sources that the Babari Mosque had displaced a temple he would pull it down with his own hands and hand it over to the Hindus. The fall of the "disputed structure" generated a deep sense of shock in the Muslim leadership who failed to translate that shock into any coherent action or strategy. It was the Muslim leadership who, by their determined opposition to the BJP-VHP had transformed an obscure mosque into a highly volatile issue.

The intellectual Muslim's discourse admits the tradition of Muslim demolition of infidel places of worship and the accompanying theological injunctions to that effect. Though the Shariat lays down that no mosque can be built on land grabbed or illegally acquired, yet it does not apply to land acquired in *jihad* (religious war). The Prophet clearly laid down that all land belongs to God, the Prophet and, through him, to the Muslims. Other Muslim writers have admitted that Muslim rulers demolished Hindu temples.[36]

These different perspectives constituted the chief cornerstones of the national debate on the Ram Janmabhumi–Babari Masjid issue. While one view has it that communalism (majority or minority) develops in opposition to nationalism, we believe that what we are witnessing on the Indian scene is a form of nationalism driven into religious channels.

CONCLUSION

One conclusion which flows out of this study concerns the role of the highly interventionist present-day state in India. Its interventionist nature is reinforced by its powerful centralized features. It is also self-professedly "neutral," standing away from and above the conflicts of society, not a part of it. The validity of such a claim is, of course, doubtful and may be viewed as a remnant of the colonial regime's basic premise that the state should not tolerate the outrages of communal strife and should, therefore, remain an arbiter/law enforcer. This view of the state has, in the past, however, been repeatedly challenged in India, at least in so far as two of the coercive arms of the Indian state are conerned, namely the police and the PAC: in the communal strife at Bombay, Ahmedabad, Meerut, Moradabad, Bareilly, Delhi and elsewhere where they have played infamous roles.

It is the thesis of this essay that, in the absence of an excessively interventionist and dominant state, the various communities would work out their own equations and equilibrium, with adaptations where necessary. This is not tantamount to a plea for Social Darwinism in the Indian context. Rather, the study of inter-communal violence in India is so replete with instances of adaptations for mutual self-preservation that one cannot but feel that this thesis reflects no more than the empirical realities.

Our study of the occurrence of the riots in Agra in 1990[37] and their non-occurrence in 1992 has led us to the conclusion that everywhere the ordinary and poor people dislike violence. For them, very often the control of riots is worse than the riot itself because of the treatment meted out by the police force. In the April, 1990 riots of Ahmedabad, Hasina, a young Muslim woman told Mark Tully, the BBC correspondent, "It is not so much the *toofan* (riot) itself we suffer from as the curfew. We don't have the sort of homes or shops that mobs will loot, and if we stay inside we normally won't be harmed during the riot. But we suffer very badly from the curfews. We are relying on daily work and so if we can't go out to work, where do we get the money? If a man goes out to work he may get killed, and his family won't even know where he is." When Tully presumed that the Muslims were being targeted by the police, an elderly woman called Jetun Appa put him right on that when she said, "They treat the poor Hindus just as badly. It's always the poor who are killed in riots and it's always the poor who suffer the police *zulum* (atrocities). If a Muslim is killed, they go for the innocent Hindus. If a Hindu is killed, they go for the innocent Muslims.[38]

In the 1990 riots in Agra city, in the Patel Nagar area near Langre-ki-Chowki, a not-so-well-off locality, where Hindus and Muslims are relatively evenly distributed and intermingled as well, a Muslim, the lone proud owner of a generator, would switch it on during power failures in the area at night not only to light up his own home and protect his own property, but rather he had it connected to a string of bulbs in the *galli* to light up the entire area around in an effort to keep away miscreants and trouble-makers, thereby providing security to Hindu houses as well. The 1990 riots threw up another instance of mutual agreement for self-preservation. In the Bagh Anta area of Lohamandi where there are just a handful of Hindu (Bania) houses in a predominantly Muslim locality, the Hindus worked out an agreement with their Muslim neighbors that they would not allow the agents of violence on either side the use of their terraces for the lobbing of bombs, and so on in return for a guarantee of the safety of their families and property from the Muslims. In addition, they paid a *chautha* (fee) to the Muslims which was utilized by them for the purchase of firearms for use in the riots. This area witnessed pitched battles in the riots of 1990, but these Hindu houses were spared.

Harry Eckstein, in a variation of the political culture theory, enunciated the thesis that harmony in authority patterns between state structure and society made for stability and prosperity of democratic institutions in a country, whereas its incongruence accounted for breakdown.[39] If the demolition of the Babari Mosque and the scores of minor or major riots that have affected the body politic in India in recent years may be viewed as a challenge to the state structure and its institutions, is it not then time to take a fresh look at the traditions of hierarchy and authority prevalent in India, at its political culture, at the question of identity plaguing the vast body of its citizens both Hindus and Muslims? This study seeks to suggest that the Nehruvian model of socialism, secularism, and democracy is on the brink of collapse due to its alien origins and superimposition on the mass folk culture of the land. Further, it suggests that, unless modified substantially in view of the dominant culture patterns, the Nehruvian values would soon risk total collapse in the face of an emerging, authentically indigenous *Bharatiya* culture symbolized by the force of Hindutva.

The resurgence of a self-conscious Hindu identity really denotes a process of a Hindu community-in-the-making. The positive implications of the current saffron advance could be to enhance national integration and to provide the much-needed legitimacy to a crisis-ridden system. The problem of overload on the state is a real problem in contemporary India. Hindu nationalism could seek to cope with this problem by urging greater sacrifice in the name of patriotism. Its pro-Hindu approach could also help cement some of the basic divisions in society: of caste, class, ethnicity, and so on. On the other hand, wolf-pack Hindu nationalism could elicit resistance from southern and eastern India and generate a strong backlash against Hindi-belt dominance. It would further exacerbate the sentiments of the Indian Muslims who are too numerous to be wished away. It could also feed minority fundamentalism which, of course, is not merely a reaction to Hindutva but has its own independent dynamics.

In the final analysis, this paper holds that political nationalism and Hindu cultural nationalism are compatible and that the latter deserves to be freed of the odious notions associated with it in the last 45 years of Congress domination. No party or organization can bring about such widespread changes in the mental make-up of a country unless the people are willing. One can conclude that democracy, socialism and secularism are not enough, nor incidentally is economic growth. What is also relevant today is how to create a legitimate political system – the VHP and Swami Muktanand have been questioning the legitimacy of the Constitution – in harmony with India's past traditions as well as the present. India's ancient culture sits heavy on her, slowing down any pace of change, yet investing her with social stability despite a not-so-stable political system. It is attempting to beget a new order which is not just an illegitimate offspring of the Raj, but is authentic and indigenous, with little need for external legitimacy.

NOTES

1   These figures are derived from the reputed English language national daily, the *Times of India*, December 12, 1992. However, they are at best conservative estimates.

2   See Peter van der Veer's contribution to this volume.

3   Walter K. Andersen and Shridhar D. Damle, *The Brotherhood in Saffron:The Rashtriya Swayamsevak Sangh and Hindu Revivalism* (New Delhi: Vistaar, 1987), "Introduction." See also Lloyd I. Rudolph and Susanne H. Rudolph, *In Pursuit of Lakshmi : The Political Economy of the Indian State* (Bombay: Orient Longman, 1987), pp. 41–3.

4   For two historical parallels, see John McLane, "The Early Congress, Hindu Populism and the Wider Society," in Richard Sisson and Stanley Wolpert (eds), *Congress and Indian Nationalism* (Delhi: Oxford University Press, 1988), p. 49 and Sandria Freitag, "Sacred Symbol as Mobilizing Ideology: The North Indian Search for a 'Hindu community'," in *Comparative Studies in Society and History*, XXII, No. 4 (October, 1980).

5   *Amar Ujala*, Hindi daily, Agra edition, December 2, 1992.

6   *Amar Ujala*, December 2, 1992.

7   *Amar Ujala*, November 25, 1992.

8   *Amar Ujala*, November 26, 1992. At about this time, the authors came across a circular issued by the RSS to their workers which laid down that they must take only as much luggage as they can carry themselves, a blanket, a *lota* (small water pot for drinking, washing, etc.), *chana* (roasted gram, both filling and of well-established high nutritional value), *sattu* (cereal flour of roasted mixed grains used as an instant meal by the poor) and *gur* (jaggery).

9   *Times of India*, December 2, 1992.

10 Participants in the *Ekatmata Yatra* of 1983 carried all over the country pots of sacred Ganges water, held to be potent enough to wash away all sins, forging a link of unity amongst Hindus; the *Ram-Janki Rath Yatra* or *Ram Janmabhoomi Mukti Yajna* of 1984 was charted on the ancient pilgrim routes; the *Ram Shilas Pujan* (rites consecrating bricks in honor of Lord Rama to be used to rebuild the temple) of 1989 coincided with Hedgewar's birth centenary; the use of *kalash* (urns) for Ganges water as well as for the *asthi* (remnants) of *amar kar sevaks* (martyred *kar sevaks*) also had great ritual-emotional significance.

11 *Ujala*, December 15, 1992.

12 This information comes from interviews conducted in a field trip with Paul R. Brass in June, 1993.

13   Arun Shourie, *Religion in Politics* (New Delhi: Roli Books, 1989), pp. 15–51, 288, 298.

14   For a scholarly analysis of the same phenomenon in nineteenth century colonial India, see Gyanendra Pandey, *The Construction of Communalism in Colonial North India* (Delhi: Oxford University Press, 1990).

15   While the relative freedom of UP from riots was a case of violence restrained politically, instances of politically sponsored violence in India are more frequent; see Arun Shourie, *Religion in Politics*, pp. 137–44.

16   Paul R. Brass, *Language, Religion, and Politics in North India* (Cambridge: Cambridge University Press, 1974), p. 265.

17   The very term used to describe the Babari Masjid became a controversial matter, with Muslims naturally continuing to refer to it as a mosque and militant Hindus and many other Hindus as well referring to it as a "disputed structure."

18   See Mark Tully, *No Full Stops in India* (New Delhi: Viking Penguin, 1991), p. 124.

19   A number of police officials have confessed to us in private that they regard themselves as Hindus first, but that while in uniform they are helpless where acquiescence to state directives is concerned. It is also worth remembering that the wives of Faizabad officials, unable to witness silently the strains of the inner conflict upon their husbands, marched in a procession to the DM Faizabad after the firing on *kar sevaks* in October–November, 1990, and pleaded with him to allow their menfolk to remain human beings first. See VHP cassette, *Pran Jaye Par Vachan Na Jaye*, Jain Colour Lab Pvt. Ltd, Delhi.

20   *India Today*, December 31, 1992, pp. 58–9 and M. J. Akbar, *Riot after Riot: Reports on Caste and Communal Violence in India* (New Delhi: Penguin, 1991), pp. 132–3. See also Paul R. Brass, *The Politics of India Since Independence* (Cambridge: Cambridge University Press, 1990), p. 200.

21   Rudolph and Rudolph, *In Pursuit of Lakshmi*, p. 94.

22   Cited Henry C. Hart, "Political Leadership in India: Dimensions and Limits," in Atul Kohli (ed.), *India's Democracy: An Analysis of Changing State–Society Relations* (New Delhi: Orient Longman, 1991), p. 25.

23   The information in this paragraph comes from interviews carried out with Paul R. Brass in Muzaffarnagar district and Khatauli town in June, 1993.

24   For an application of this theory in a study of pre-independent India, see C. A. Bayly, *The Local Roots of Indian Politics: Allahabad, 1880–1920* (Delhi: Oxford University Press, 1975), pp. 109 ff. and for a study of post-independent India, see S. Gopal (ed.), *Anatomy of a Confrontation* (New Delhi: Penguin, 1991), pp. 15–16.

25   Gopal, *Anatomy of a Confrontation*, pp. 15–16.

26   McLane, "The Early Congress," pp. 52–5.

27   Pandey, *The Construction of Communalism*, p. 11.

28   Lloyd I. Rudolph and Susanne H. Rudolph, "Organizational Adaptation of the Congress under Rajiv Gandhi's Leadership," in Richard Sisson and Ramashray Roy (eds), *Diversity and Dominance in Indian Politics*, Vol. I: *Changing Bases of Congress Support* (New Delhi: Sage, 1990), pp. 95–6, 98–101.

29   Rudolph and Rudolph, *In Pursuit of Lakshmi*, p. 41.

30   The Hindu version of history finds reflection in a number of pamphlets and booklets published and sold in connection with the Ramjanmabhoomi movement, prominent amongst which were *Kya Kahati Saryu Ki Dhara* (What

the Currents of the Saryu River Tell Us) and *Sri Ram Janmabhoomi ki Rakt Rajit Itihas* (The Blood-smeared History of Sri Ramjanmabhoomi).

31   See *The New Encyclopaedia Britannica, Micropaedia*, Vol. V (1976), p. 649.
32   Sir Jadunath Sarkar's *History of Aurangzeb* (Calcutta: M. C. Sarkar and Sons, 1925) and Sri Ram Sharma's *Religious Policy of the Mughal Emperors* (Bombay: Asia Publishing House, 1962).
33   Jay Dubashi in the *Organizer*, November 19, 1989.
34   *Panchjanya*, official Hindi language weekly of the RSS, November 8, 1992. This report was not contradicted by Jaffar Sharif.
35   Syed Ahmad Khan also used the term "Hindu" for the inhabitants of Hindustan, including Muslims. See Gyanendra Pandey, *The Construction of Communalism*, p. 216; also Andersen and Damle, *The Brotherhood in Saffron*, p. 222. After the demolition of the Babari Mosque, Sikandar Bakht, in the course of a visit to Agra to meet the BJP national leaders interned in the Agra Jail, gave an interview to the local press which was totally on the lines of Hindu nationalism; *Amar Ujala*, December 16, 1992.
36   Rais Ahmad Jafri, *Wajid Ali Shah Aur Unka Ahd* (Lucknow: Kitab Manzil, 1957), p. 247; cited in letter of Harsh Narain to the *Indian Express*, February 26, 1990.
37   Gyaneshwar Chaturvedi and Jayati Chaturvedi, "Hindutva: The Aggressive Face of Hinduism: Tactics of Mobilization Adopted by the RSS-VHP in the Ram Janmabhoomi Movement, a Case Study of Agra City, October–November, 1990," unpublished paper presented at the Seminar on Religion, Identity, and Politics at the University of Hull, England, November, 1991.
38   Tully, *No Full Stops*, pp. 241–3.
39   Harry Eckstein, *Division and Cohesion in Democracy: A Study of Norway* (Princeton, NJ: Princeton University Press, 1966).

7. The Anti-Sikh Riots of 1984 in Delhi: Politicians, Criminals, and the Discourse of Communalism

Virginia Van Dyke

On the evening of Rajiv Gandhi's assassination, Jim Lehrer asked the India experts who were guests on his McNeil-Lehrer News Hour if the Gandhi family had been the glue that held India together. Without a strong figure in the center, he wondered, what would keep India's diverse ethnic and religious groups from killing each other? This conventional wisdom that some strong force is necessary to hold ethnic animosity in check is echoed in scholarly literature. Horowitz, for examples, argues that the "fear of extinction" or subordination is characteristic of unranked multi-ethnic societies, and that this "anxiety-laden perception" leads inevitably to a state of discomfort and uncertainty. The latter state in turn often produces a desire to assimilate or eliminate the opposing group, particularly in the case of backward groups who may experience a sense of hostility towards groups perceived as forward at a level of intensity quite disproportionate to any actual threat.[1]

This type of explanation has been given to explain the mob violence perpetrated against the Sikhs in 1984 following Mrs Gandhi's assassination by two of her Sikh bodyguards. Although the official figures on the numbers killed in Delhi are 325, they have been described by the People's Union for Democratic Rights and the People's Union for Civil Liberties in Delhi as "ridiculously low."[2] Most unofficial estimates range above 2,000. The victims were caught totally unprepared and uncomprehending by four days of murder, rape, torture, looting and destruction. The murders and atrocities occurred primarily in Delhi, but a similar pattern of violence prevailed in the Hindi-speaking heartland states of Bihar, Madhya Pradesh, Uttar Pradesh and Haryana, where "criminally led hoodlums" looted and killed "while the police twiddled their thumbs."[3]

In spite of the best efforts of the Congress (I) officials and state leaders to portray this as a spilling over of mass sentiments of grief and anger, a conflict between ethnic groups instead of a pogrom, the blatantly planned and well directed nature of the violence was impossible to conceal. While animosity such as Horowitz describes could explain why most of the majority community stood aside and some spoke approvingly of the riots after the fact, it does not explain the actions of most of the participants—backward and scheduled caste ("untouchable" or low caste) men who were organized, provided with liquor, paid and led by Congress recruits drawn from the underworld. Although, as Tambiah points out, the case is not so simple to support the contention that only marginalized elements were involved in the riots, that in fact men from a wide variety of occupational niches participated,[4] still the leadership provided and the preplanning necessary points to the "terrorist state" as the perpetrator.[5] The victims themselves cannot be seen as comprising one camp in a situation of mutual hostility and suspicion; instead, many of the murdered had been Congress supporters, few of the victims had any links with militant, Punjab politics. "The victims of engineered riots are always substitutable. ... The *goonda*s [toughs] who did the killing and looting were not doing so because they believed in a particular ideology. ... They did so because the political bosses ... had ordered them to attack."[6]

There has never been a similar type of large scale attack on Sikhs, or any other type of Hindu–Sikh communal riot, either before or subsequent to this event. There were, however, at the time of Mrs Gandhi's assassination, heightened tensions between the two communities because of the development of a militant, and even secessionist movement in Punjab, the state where Sikhs hold a bare majority. But rather than the unrest in Punjab having its roots in Hindu/Sikh animosity, it began with a violent encounter in 1978 between orthodox Sikhs – led by Sant Jarnail Singh Bhindranwale, the head of a fundamentalist center of Sikh learning – and a breakaway Sikh sect. This sectarian conflict then merged with state political conflicts as the Congress sought to use Bhindranwale in order to split the Sikh vote to Congress' advantage.

Bhindranwale, a messianic and charismatic leader who clearly had his own agenda apart from that of his sponsors, became increasingly popular in Punjab as a consequence of which none of the political leaders of the Sikh political party, the Akali Dal, were willing to take a strong position against his brand of aggressive, Sikh nationalism. Instead, other Sikh leaders launched their own mass movement against the central government, framing their demands in terms of greater regional autonomy for Punjab. While violence initially was confined within the Sikh community, it escalated into attacks on Hindus who were opposed to the Sikh cause and then spread to attacks on innocent Hindus. Bhindranwale and his followers ultimately moved into the Golden Temple complex in Amritsar, the most sacred of sites to the Sikhs, from which he allegedly directed a campaign of terror against those who opposed him, immune from the police or other agencies of the government.

Operation Bluestar, the 1984 army action to remove the militants from the temple complex, ended in the death of Bhindranwale, the alienation of Sikhs all over the world because of the violation of their holiest site, and the growth of Sikh militancy. Mrs Gandhi's assassination was in retaliation for this assault.

The responsibility for this debacle lies with Mrs Gandhi and the Congress (I), but it is not limited to a failure to choose the best alternative in dealing with militants. When Mrs Gándhi returned to power in 1980, after the brief interlude when India was ruled by a coalition of opposition parties, many of the members of Congress (I)'s traditional support groups had become disenchanted. In search of some new electoral equation with which to bolster her position, Mrs Gandhi is widely thought to have utilized the "Hindu card" by patronizing Hindu religious leaders and places of worship, forging new links with Hindu nationalist groups such as the Rashtriya Swayamsewak Sangh, and fostering anti-Sikh and anti-Muslim policies. In Punjab she supported the rise of Bhindranwale as a tool with which to divide the more moderate Sikh leadership. She then allowed the growing tension to simmer rather than dealing decisively with the issues in contention in order to cultivate the Hindu vote. At the same time, police terrorism in Punjab, including "false encounters" in which young Sikh men were killed and incidents such as the harassment of Sikhs coming to Delhi for the Asiad Games, further alienated the Sikhs while creating an image of them as anti-national. The riots against the Sikhs in November, 1984, can be seen as a continuation of this policy of creating a national nemesis in the Sikhs from which the Congress party had to save the nation.

Mainstream journals and newspapers along with citizen's groups have published reports of the organized savagery and given the names of those believed to be involved from ministers in the Prime Minister's Cabinet to local police and *pradhans* (village headmen). Yet, those few arrested were quickly released at the behest of Congress (I) party workers, a reluctantly conceded and much hindered official inquiry known as the Mishra Commission gave a blanket exoneration to Congress (I) leaders, and those politicians implicated in the violence continued to hold important party posts and to be elected to local positions. It is generally believed that the government is still actively shielding Congress (I) party functionaries from prosecution, most notably former Union Minister and current president of the Delhi Pradesh Congress (I) Committee H. K. L. Bhagat and Delhi MP Sajjan Kumar. Congress party leaders have repeatedly and vehemently denied any involvement in the rioting.

Three dominant narratives crop up in explanations and descriptions of the 1984 riots, arguing either that they reflected: (1) mass sentiment, that is, resentment against the Sikhs for political or economic reasons coupled with anger and grief over the assassination; (2) a law and order problem, as lower castes looted better off neighborhoods with the complicity of the police–*goonda*–politician nexus; and (3) a search for political gain. This last narrative is less well developed, but explains the attacks on the Sikhs in terms of electoral advantage for the Congress either because Congress must prove itself the protector of the Hindus or because it must take revenge for its leader's death. All of these may become mingled in the telling, or one may be used as a cover or explanation for another, or all three may even emerge from one source.

India Today, for example, mixed all three types of explanation when it reported that "The bubble had to burst. It had been filling through nine months of extremist violence against the Hindus in Punjab. ...The resentment simmered, and the inevitable denouement came." Still, "the signs already were ominous that this was the handiwork of marauders from outside, not a spontaneous outpouring of grief." The law and order explanation also shows up in this account as police disappear from the scene, whereupon "the reaction against the Sikhs was to provide a justification for letting out of all the pent-up envy and anger of the poorer neighbors," whose "motive was mainly looting."[7]

These three interpretations each lead to different philosophical and political conclusions. If one accepts the first thesis concerning mass sentiment, one is led to deduce a need to direct more resources toward the instruments of coercion in terms of a larger police force to protect the minorities[8] and to argue for the necessity of the minority groups to mend their ways so as not to antagonize the majority, to make them realize "how vulnerable they are."[9] Ultimately, this type of account contributes to a larger argument in which a strong centralized state, existing of course above society's conflicts, is required to protect ethnic groups from each other.[10] "It is popular among those who hover in the corridors of power in Delhi to believe that brutality, disorder, chaos and anarchy are the hallmarks of regionalism; that in contrast, the centre symbolized by Delhi, stands for civilized government, liberal and humanitarian values."[11]

From within the law and order discourse emanated demands to break up the nexus between less than impartial police, criminals, and those criminal politicians who were incorporated into the Congress party when Sanjay Gandhi shared power with his mother, and for those involved in the riots to stand trial. As one article stated, asserting that the riots were "a dress rehearsal" for holding the entire populace for ransom, "We have been warned – and we still have the vote."[12] Along with this idea is the contention on another level that something must be done to remedy the sub-human conditions under which those groups live who were actually responsible for carrying out the violence.[13] In this version, riots are a social problem.

The instrumentalist explanation, that the riots were engineered for political gain, is clearly enunciated by a group called the Citizens for Democracy, who claim the Congress party's reasoning was as follows:

> Sikhs as a community must be taught a lesson and demonstratively so. ...The Hindu community's confidence in the ability of the ruling party to give protection against 'militant' Sikhs would have been shattered, the Hindu votes would have swung toward the opposition, if nothing whatsoever was done to suggest immediate retribution or *badla* for her assassination.[14]

This type of interpretation may be linked to a broader argument concerning the "deinstitutionalization" of India's political system, namely, that normal channels of grass roots politics and responsiveness to the populace and the autonomy of political institutions were eroded as a consequence of Mrs Gandhi's personalistic style of governing during her long years in power. Those in authority became mainly sycophants characterized by their personal loyalty to the Gandhi family, "a peculiar breed of operators who today pervade the whole country like the smell of rotten fish," who firmly believe "that anyone opposing them deserves elimination."[15] Therefore, such a political vacuum exists, the system of governance has so degenerated, that those in authority are incapable of responding in other than a narrow interest-based manner and the entire fabric of the state needs to be rewoven.[16]

This paper will first discuss the actual events that occurred during the four days of the riots. It will then discuss the how and the why of the riots in an attempt to shed some light on the various interpretations of the causes, interpretations which are not neutral but political statements as well. This discussion will also tell us something about the development of Hindu/Sikh communalism which, such as it exists at all, has only emerged over the last ten years or so. In the end, no simple explanation – from communal riot to conspiracy – is possible, in that all these versions interpenetrate and all illustrate factors which contribute to the system that allows such riots to go on. Large scale institutional changes had to have occurred within Delhi – the criminalization and personalization of the organs of the state, the political demography of Delhi which freed up segments of the population for amoral action, and the fostering of antipathy toward a minority community.[17] Rather than arguing that the government, that is, Rajiv Gandhi and his cabinet, ordered the killings as part of a conspiracy, it seems more likely that the riots were organized for the government by forces which the government itself had created.[18]

THE RIOT BEGINS

Indira Gandhi was shot by two of her Sikh body guards at 9:15 a.m. on October 31, 1984. The news spread throughout the day through radio and newspaper reports as a crowd gathered outside the All India Institute of Medical Sciences (AIIMS) waiting for news. Sikhs, many of whom were Congress supporters and were "as shocked and grieved as anyone else,"[19] mingled with the rest of the onlookers evidently not in any fear for their safety.

Between 1:00 and 5:00 p.m. ever more ominous events began to occur. According to one eye witness cited in Madhu Kishwar's report, two truckloads of men from nearby villages arrived at the site along with a tempo (outsized auto rickshaw) well stocked to provied them with *lathis* and iron rods. The men reportedly got off the truck and stood around as if waiting for orders. Soon after, a Congress corporator, who was later implicated in organizing the riots in the trans-Yamuna area, aroused the crowd with a speech and raised the slogan, "Khun ka badla, khun se lenge" (blood for blood). The crowd followed suit, raising this slogan and also "Indira Gandhi Amar Rahe" (may Indira Gandhi remain immortal/eternal). Kishwar argues that it was at the instigation of this Congressman that the crowd first attacked a Sikh motorcycle policeman who was then rescued by the police. Then the mob fanned out toward Naoroji Nagar, INA market, Yusuf Sarai and South Extension, pulling Sikhs out of vehicles, beating them and setting their turbans on fire, burning the vehicles, and looting and burning Sikh shops.[20] Two *gurdwara*s (Sikh temples) were also set on fire while the police watched passively. When President Giani Zail Singh, who is a Sikh, arrived at 5:00 p.m. at the AIIMS, his motorcade was stoned by the angry crowd.

At 5:30, "Rajiv Gandhi came out ... after having seen his mother's ... body," followed by Minister of State for Information and Broadcasting, H. K. L. Bhagat. The latter, who has been accused of master-minding the riots, reportedly "scolded the crowd" saying: "What is the point of assembling here?"[21] This reported statement could obviously have alternate meanings, suggesting either that the crowd had no purpose in assembling there or that it might have a more useful purpose elsewhere. After Mrs Gandhi's body was taken from the AIIMS, the "police disappeared" as if by an "unseen signal," clearly indicating to eye witnesses their sanctioning of the violence already underway.[22]

The general consensus is that Wednesday's random violence could be ascribed to outrage and anger, while the more organized and directed violence began on Thursday, November 1. It seems clear, however, that the direction and encouragement of the violent actions by those in authority coupled with the clear intent of the police not to intervene moved the violence out of the random category from its inception.

It is reported that meetings were held on the night of October 31 by Congress officials, pulling together their previously made plans to "exterminate the Sikhs."[23] At the same time Rajiv Gandhi, who had been sworn in as Prime Minister at 6:50 p.m., appeared on television appealing for calm.[24] There are instances of Sikhs being disarmed at this time by men in their neighborhood who convinced them to turn over their arms and to stay in their homes. These same weapons were used on them the following day.[25]

On November 1, organized and systematic killing of Sikhs began, done with remarkable precision and consistency. The attacks began at approximately the same time all over Delhi as groups of young men, mainly from the resettlement colonies and the urban villages, were delivered to various areas along with *lathi*s (bamboo sticks), iron rods, and buckets of phosphorous mixed with kerosene. Worst affected were the resettlement communities of East, West and North Delhi such as Trilokpuri, Kalyanpur, and Mangalpuri. But, all day long tempos brought in thousands of people from these colonies and from the satellite villages "to pay homage to Indira Gandhi. Once in town they ran amuck."[26] These marauders from outside brought the violence to the middle class neighborhoods of Connaught Place, Vasant Vihar, Maharani Bagh, New Friends Colony and Hauz Khas. In Chandni Chowk and Janpath shops were destroyed and vehicles set on fire.

The crowds of mostly illiterate men who would have been unable to read the names on the shops and houses and who, being from outside the neighborhood, would not have been able to identify the Sikh establishments, were reportedly led by Congress Party officials carrying voter lists, ration cards and school registers pointing out the Sikh shops and houses or marking them with paint Nazi style prior to the arrival of the crowds.[27] There was a method to the madness. Men would be called out of their homes, often by name, stunned with *lathi* blows to incapacitate them or hacked to pieces, then they would be burnt alive. Their homes were looted and then set on fire. Women and children were usually, although not always, spared. The crowds would come in waves, particularly if there was any resistance, retreating, regrouping and then returning to search the houses of neighbors for any Sikhs they may have missed on the first round. Reportedly, the gangs acted at their leisure, certain of no interference, and their demeanor was that of people at a festival, not of people full of anger and sorrow. Neighbors and peace marchers who called on them to desist were met with derisive laughter and threats.[28]

The perpetrators had not only been liberally supplied with liquor, but many had actually been paid. Sajjan Kumar, Congress (I) MP from Mangolpuri and Lalit Makan, Congress (I) Trade Union Leader and Metropolitan Councillor, are identified in *Who are the Guilty?* as having paid each man involved Rs. 100 and a bottle of liquor.[29] These men were transported on DTC buses in south Delhi, as well as, in some cases, police vehicles. Organization extended to the point where, when warned of the possible danger of fire reaching the overhead wires, one arsonist said: "Don't worry we have switched this section off from the main. We are not fools." Other evidence of coordination occurred in Sunlight Colony where a train arrived, let loose its load of rioters, and then waited for them until they returned. Someone with authority was controlling the electricity and the trains. [30]

By November 2, the second full day of the rioting, the orgy of killing and destruction was on the increase. Trains were "forcibly stopped by crowds" in order that Sikh passengers could be murdered.[31] In just one instance, 17 Sikhs "were taken out of the Pink City Express ... in Haryana and killed."[32] November 3 showed some signs of abatement particularly in the more central areas, while violence continued in the resettlement communities. By November 4, although violence continued, the trend of a return to normalcy was in evidence. [33]

There were instances of women being gang-raped and abducted, but the crowds were largely interested in exterminating the men, thereby depriving the families of their means of support and eliminating the possibilities of reprisals. Or, if one believes that looting was the main motive, as some of the survivors did, the argument then is that the killing was done to prevent identification of the looters.[34] One wonders, however, why women could not identify criminals as well as men. Another interpretation is that the men thought it would reflect badly on them if they killed women.

THE ROLE OF RUMOR

Many reports suggest that there was a deliberate floating of rumors designed to arouse and incite different emotions at different stages during the four days of violence. On October 31, a variety of rumors were spread. It was said that the Sikhs were dancing the Bhangra, setting off firecrackers, and distributing sweets, a rumor designed to incite a "spirit of revenge."[35] It was also said that terrorists were gathering in Delhi, Sikhs were forming gangs to attack Hindus, and "the city was without police" protection. Some neighborhoods formed self defense committees to defend themselves against Sikhs, while in a smaller number of communities, mutual defense groups were formed by Hindus and Sikhs.[36] At this same time, the inflammatory slogan "Khun ka badla, Khun se lenge" raised by the crowd paying homage to Indira Gandhi could clearly be heard over the State-controlled television's continual display of Mrs Gandhi lying in state, while the ethnic origin of her assassins was also repeatedly broadcast, implicating the media in unsettling the situation.

On November 1, the rumor was spread by telephone calls from police officials, as well as by touring police vans with loudspeakers, that the Sikhs had poisoned the water supply and that a train from Punjab had arrived full of dead Hindus.[37] In fact, Hindu residents of a colony in which Sikhs were massacred "looked disbelieving" when they were told that the trains were carrying dead Sikhs not Hindus. They had believed that the Sikhs in their neighborhood were killed in retaliation for an attack on Hindus.[38]

After the violence had begun, other rumors were spread in order to "prevent or remove any kind of sympathy or compassion" that every burnt "*gurdwara* was an arsenal," that the Sikhs were gathering and would "attack at night" or would kidnap children.[39] This rumor of Sikh revenge was kept alive by the newspapers, which reported that gangs of Sikhs were "out to create panic"[40] and that the number of Sikhs and Hindus admitted to the hospitals were equal, as if pitched battles between equally matched sides were occurring.[41] In reality, those Hindus admitted to the hospitals with sword or gunshot wounds were very "reluctant to give their names," even as they insisted they had not provoked an attack "in any way."[42] One hospital worker stated that the Hindus admitted came in "shrieking" with very inconsequential wounds calling to the crowds outside to look what the Sardars (another term for Sikhs) had done: "They are attacking, the Sikhs are attacking." After being questioned, of course, it became clear that they had been part of a mob attacking a *gurdwara* and the Sikhs had fired in self-defense.[43]

Rumors were also spread to prevent Hindus from helping their neighbors. In Trilokpuri, Hindu women who had given refuge to Sikh women told "unbelievable stories" about Sikhs who had killed their "benefactors."[44] Rumors were used to justify and perpetuate the carnage. One eye-witness told of some Jawaharlal Nehru University students "spreading the rumor that ... Sikhs with ... guns were on the rampage" and one of them claimed to have actually seen Hindus gunned down. When onlookers offered to go with him to see these bodies to verify his story, he walked away. A Congress (I) car was seen "making the rounds of the campus" and its occupants were conversing at length with the student rumor spreaders.[45]

The only incidents of violence on the part of Sikhs were the small number of cases where Sikhs were able to put up a credible defense. These are the few instances in which the police intervened to "maintain law and order" by disarming the Sikhs, thereby increasing the death toll above what it would have been if the police had simply stood aside.

ROLE OF THE STATE'S INSTRUMENTS OF VIOLENCE: THE POLICE, SPECIAL FORCES AND THE ARMY

Brass has described the relationship of the police to the populace living in the Indian countryside in the following manner. "It is a Hobbesian world in which security and safety are not provided by the state, but are in themselves values – that is, valued objects – integral to and inseparable from the struggle for power and influence." He argues that control over the police is part of the political struggle.[46] Given this descriptive analysis of the biased nature of the police, it should be no surprise that the police were actively involved in the carnage perpetrated against the Sikhs. The police "were reported to have said" to the mobs: "We gave you 36 hours. Had we given the Sikhs that much time they would have killed every Hindu."[47]

The police had three different methods of dealing with the riots: they were either "conspicuous by their absence," passive observers, or acting in complicity by encouraging or actually participating in the violence.[48] The police force was reduced at the beginning of the riots – the 13 to 20 percent of the force who were Sikh were disarmed and taken off duty or confined to their barracks.[49] This was ostensibly done to prevent them from acting as a red flag to the mobs. Another possible explanation was to prevent any police sympathy for the victims.

Also, a large proportion of the police were stationed around Teen Murti House protecting dignitaries and guarding a dead body,[50] and later lining the route of Mrs Gandhi's funeral procession. A dearth of manpower was, in fact, the defense the police used to justify their lack of action during the riots. However, the way in which the police conducted themselves during the four-day riot illustrates clearly that more instruments of state coercion would not have been the answer.

There was a large gap between the announced official policy and what was actually happening on the streets. According to the *Indian Express*, Delhi was a city without a police force. "Although shoot on sight orders were issued to the security forces on Thursday night and the entire city ... was placed under curfew, there seems to be no one around to enforce these orders."[51] Telephone calls to emergency numbers were "either not answered or callers were given the stock reply that no help could be proferred."[52] In some instances Hindu callers seeking assistance for Sikhs were told to turn them "over to the mob." Many of the smoldering bodies were in close proximity to a police station.[53] The army was in evidence, after being deployed at 2:00 p.m. on November 1, but was given no authority to open fire without the express permission of an executive magistrate, who "could be a police officer". This procedure proved useless since the units were often unaccompanied by an executive magistrate.[54] The army was in many cases "deliberately misled." They were seen wandering around Delhi out of touch with their headquarters or formations, in one case with a map predating the creation of the resettlement communities where the worst violence was occurring. At no time was the usual policy followed of setting up a joint command post to coordinate the police and army actions. In some cases, the army was sent to areas of carnage after the damage had been done. A "deliberate design" seems to have been in place "to keep the army ineffective" even after the delay in deployment.[55] The para-military forces of the Central Reserve Police Force (CRPF) and the Border Security Force (BSF) were supposedly deployed on October 31. They were not in evidence on the streets either.[56]

Most horrifying are the reports of case after case of police assistance to the mobs. The rioters were heard openly bragging that, "Police hamare saath hai" (The police are with us).[57] One SHO, a Mr Batti, killed a few Sikhs himself and "helped the mob" disarm their victims in Sultanpuri.[58] A Sikh survivor told of seeking refuge on a police jeep to escape a pursuing mob, only to be pushed off and left at the mercy of the crowd. In other cases police were seen directing the mobs to Sikh houses, giving matches to a crowd "to burn a pile of bodies," participating in looting,[59] and providing arsonists with fuel "from their jeeps."[60] The police did spring into action to defend the rights of the marauding mobs. Peace marchers who had taken out a procession to Lajpat Nagar were stopped and sternly warned by police "that the city was under curfew and Section 144," limiting the number of people who can congregate. When the marchers wanted to know why the police did nothing to control those young people who were patrolling the roads "armed with swords, daggers, spears, steel *trishul*s (tridents) and iron rods" he replied only that the marchers could expect no protection from the police.[61]

In another incident, Sikhs who were defending themselves from the mobs were taken down to the police station, disarmed and released. All of these defenceless men were then butchered on their way back home from the station.[62] Numerous incidents were cited where Sikh men had gathered together and beaten back the mobs. The police would then come and convince them all to go back into their homes, assuring them of protection. Then when the mobs returned, they were dragged out one by one and killed.[63]

Police complicity continued after the riots, as they refused to record people's complaints and FIRs (First Information Reports). Hindu complainants were berated by the police for coming to the aid of Sikhs and "advised ... to look after the safety of Hindus."[64] FIRs registered by the police do not mention "the names of suspects or criminals" as would be expected and were probably filed much after the fact, an attempt, it could be argued, to cover up "gross negligence."[65]

How can this role of the police be explained? One way is to assert that the police suffer from the same communal hatred as the rest of the populace; one common argument is that much of the police force was drawn from Hindus from the state of Haryana (adjacent to the Sikh-majority state of Punjab), who were anti-Sikh. Another way is to say that they were interested in the loot; it is alleged that much of the plunder found its way into the homes of the police. A third argument is that they were either ordered from above to allow the riots to proceed unhindered or they deduced any interference would incur the wrath of their superiors since Congress officials were clearly in charge. All the above arguments in fact contribute to an understanding of the system; within the criminalized political culture, politicians aid the police in making a living while the police aid politicians in their quest to stay in power.

What was the role of the civil administration during the riots? The procedure for calling out the army is established by law. The Lt Governor, who was Mr Gavai, can request the Home Minister, a position then held by Narasimha Rao, who then can request the Defence Minister, a portfolio held by Rajiv Gandhi, to call in the army. "It is known" that Gandhi wanted to call out the army on October 31, but Mr Rao convinced him to wait.[66] When the army was finally called out on Thursday afternoon, it was only as a token force. The army was deployed in stages[67] and only established its control on November 3 after the cremation.[68] *Who are the Guilty,* taking note of the removal of a few officials like Gavai, and a few police officers like the former Delhi Police Commissioner, Mr Subhash Tandon, after the riots, suggests that these actions hardly exonerate the administration for its total failure to maintain law and order. The inquiry rather suggests that the unavailability of anyone in the administration or Cabinet during the days of the riots, in spite of numerous attempts to contact them by people from the media and opposition leaders, indicates that extra-administrative forces were controlling the deployment of troops.[69]

The treatment of the survivors makes clear the intention of the government to play down the extent of the damage and to minimize the possibility that the perpetrators would be successfully identified and brought to justice. While Congress officials were at police headquarters demanding that those arrested not be considered criminals, victims of the riots were being cared for by voluntary organizations. When politicians made grandstanding visits to refugee camps bearing food and blankets, those who were identified by victims as having been involved in the violence were driven out of the camp.[70] People were forcibly evicted from the refugee camps with undue haste,[71] and sent back to the scene of past horror where survivors were threatened by those who had killed their families. M.M.K. Wali, the new Lt. Governor, claimed he did not want to start a precedent by being too generous with the victims.

SOCIO-ECONOMIC DESCRIPTION OF THE ASSAILANTS AND THE POLITICAL DEMOGRAPHY OF DELHI

The speed with which these riots were organized following the assassination leads to two inescapable conclusions: they were prearranged and preplanned and an institutional riot structure was already in place, a pre-existing "technology of terror."[72] In support of the first conclusion, evidence exists that plans of retaliation against the Sikhs were formulated before the assassination, following Operation Bluestar (the army assault on the Golden Temple in Amritsar to remove from it the arms and armed men who had taken refuge there) and the magnitude of the response to this army action from the Sikh community.[73] Insofar as the existence of an institutional riot structure is concerned, Brass argues in general that communal riots are undertaken mostly by "specialists" who operate within an institutionalized riot system in which known actors are "ready to be called out on such occasions, [who] profit from it, and [whose] activities benefit others who may or may not be actually paying for the violence carried out."[74] The organization in the resettlement communities, where the most intense violence occurred, epitomizes this type of pre-existing structure of potential violence.

The resettlement colonies, originally know as J.J. (*jhuggi-jhonpri,* that is, huts and shacks) colonies, were a creation of the Congress (I) and the Emergency, the two-year period of authoritarian rule inaugurated by Mrs Gandhi in June, 1975 during which her young son, Sanjay Gandhi became especially promiment. Sanjay Gandhi's plans to beautify Delhi included relocating squatters who lived in illegal huts or on the pavement to communities outside the city. Slums and squatter areas were bulldozed and residents of those areas, along with street dwellers, were moved, under coercion, "in trucks accompanied by police vans" and dumped on plots of bare land.[75] Even though this was widely decried at the time as cruel and inhumane, Congress was able to transform these communities into a solid vote bank. Recipients of plots of land, including many who ultimately became riot victims, came to feel their position had been improved by their new land owning status and were grateful to the party.[76] In addition, forcing these people outside the city, far from job opportunities, providing no social services and lumping all lower classes together outside of social organization and normal patron-client relationships, freed them up for all sorts of duties including criminal activities.

Local gang leaders called *dadas* have political clout within the colonies; they have close ties with local politicians and the police and control portions of the land. These *dadas* extort money through their ability to evict residents who threaten their control. Since the Congress (I) has been in power the longest and set up these colonies, they have a well-developed network of gang leaders through whom they can organize violence.[77]

This system had been used previously for political rallies, for "storm trooping into courts and commissions of inquiry," for posing threats and intimidation, in actual acts of violence against an opposing group,[78] and for any occasion in which a demonstration of Congress (I)'s ostensible popular support was deemed necessary.[79] These "professional processionists" regularly rented out their presence and their leaders were kept on the "payroll of the party."[80] In return for their services, irregular constructions are legalized, liberal loans are given, and they are protected from prosecution.[81] It is "these *goonda* leaders and their mercenaries," then, who perpetrated most of the carnage, making these riots not communal, but a "criminal hatchet job."[82]

Besides these individuals, backward castes of Jats (farmers) and Gujars (milk venders) from the urban villages were identified over and over as major participants in the riots. These villagers were previously very marginal farmers who supplemented their livelihood with brigandage and so had a history of living outside the law. They were given a trifling amount of money to make room for posh new colonies, as well as for the resettlement communities, whose residents they greatly resented.[83] Of those Scheduled Castes whose agricultural livelihood was also disrupted by Delhi expansion, many utilized the reservation system to get jobs. Of these the Bhangis were "solid supporters of Congress (I)," worked as sweepers for the Corporation and were also involved in the violence.[84]

THE COMMUNAL DISCOURSE AND ITS PERPETUATION

The discourse of mass sentiment is very useful in diverting blame from politicians who are instigating violence, while removing responsibility from individuals who actually commit violence as well. The religiosity of the people, or popular values, then are seen as the root cause of the violence. Clearly, Congress Party officials prefer the interpretation that the 1984 carnage against the Sikhs was a communal riot, based in popular sentiments. The Centre blames the inaction of the police on the fact that the police are largely drawn from the ranks of Jat Hindus from Haryana "whose traditional dislike of the Sikhs, . . . was indulged in with a vengeance."[85] H. K. L. Bhagat blames the victims, "It seems the Sikhs distributed sweets on hearing of Mrs Gandhi's death."[86] Government officials consistently not only underplayed the extent of the damage, but attempted to make it seem as if a battle between two forces had occurred. On November 1, after hundreds of people had been killed, then Union Home Secretary Mr M. M. K. Wali announced that ten people had died, five of these in Delhi: one as a result of "police firing, three in exchange of fire between two groups," and one in a stabbing.[87] Such a report conceals the true nature of the violence which is revealed by the organization involved, the many instances where Hindus sheltered their Sikh neighbors in their homes, and the absence of any Sikh–Hindu riots either before or since. "These were not Hindu–Sikh riots," said one elderly survivor from Kalyanpuri. "These were *goonda*–Sikh riots."[88]

The communal explanation is accepted, though, by many who consider the riots the fault of the Sikhs. They pushed people too far, this viewpoint holds, they roused the anger and hostility of the common man beyond the containment point by not criticizing the terrorists in Punjab, by not loudly condemning the assassination.[89] There was a certain sense of satisfaction among Hindus that the Sikhs got what was coming to them, that they were too arrogant and needed to be brought down a peg. Many also continue to believe and to write that the riots were a spontaneous expression of anger and grief. According to one account, the type of violence itself, including the mutilation of men in the presence of their families who were spared, points to the degree to which "Sikhs as a community are hated" and perceived as national enemies.[90]

So what do we make of the strength of the communal discourse among people trying to understand the riots? First, it was deliberately used as a cover for politically motivated and criminally motivated action. But, second, an atmosphere of fear and resentment must exist in order for the communal explanation to be accepted.

Sikh victims of the carnage interviewed by Chakravarti identified different events in history which for them represented a cut-off point from a pre-communal golden era: the Arya Samaj *shuddhi* (or reconversion) movement which was countered by Singh Sabhas designed to strengthen Sikh identity in the late nineteenth century, the declaration of Hindi by Punjabi-speaking Hindus as their mother tongue during the agitation for a Punjabi-speaking state in the 1960s, the manipulation of religious symbols and "intertwining of religion and politics" by Akali Dal politicians, and the communal politics which the nationalist elite pursued for electoral ends.[91] This very effort to date the emergence of mistrust between the two communities is evidence for the contention that genuine communalism, that is, the hatred of one community for the other purely on religious or ethnic grounds, does not exist between the Sikh and Hindu communities. It has been cultivated and per-petuated at least partially through the policies of the Congress Party as it attempted to maintain power, and by Sikhs in Punjab striving to consolidate their community. The riots of 1984 can only be understood in this context.

It is clear that the crisis in Punjab in the early 1980s was exacerbated, if not created, by short sighted, electoral calculations designed to split the Sikh vote while consolidating the Hindu vote. The encouragement of extremist elements like Bhindranwale, the discrediting of more moderate influences in Punjab, the acts of omission which allowed the Punjab situation to fester while more and more Hindus associated Sikhs with terrorists and sepa-ratists, and finally the invasion of the Golden Temple in Punjab all served to isolate the Sikhs as a community, a result without which these riots could not have been so successful. One does not have to argue, as does Fera, that some grand, sinister design was in place to set the Sikhs up as victims in order to create inter-community animosity. Rather, as Mrs Gandhi refused to make any concession to the moderate leaders in Punjab, her intransigence was justified as resistance to secessionist elements, thereby protecting the unity of India. Sikhs gradually became perceived as threatening that unity. "Officially violated to this extent, the Sikhs were now common fodder for everyone,"[92] and perceived more as enemies than as friends.

Proof of this contention lies in the fact that many of the common citizens of Delhi seemed to feel that the killings were somehow justifiable: Not only for revenge, but because "they have been convinced by years of vicious chauvinist propaganda that a purging operation was necessary in order to "save the nation" and "keep the country united."[93] Comments made by Hindus who did not themselves participate in the riots are telling; the perpetrators of the violence could not have accomplished their aims if the climate did not condone such acts. One of those interviewed by Chakravarti tells of "normal, nice people" on the bus immediately after the assassina-tion, surprising her with "extremely venomous, hate spewing kind of talk about the Sardars."[94] Even some of those Hindus who sheltered Sikhs, who were personal friends, in their homes felt that Sikhs as an abstract unit had to be taught a lesson. Kishwar cites a curious blend of pride in the mob actions done in the name of Hindus, that "Hindus have finally put fear into the hearts" of an "aggressive" community, and an unwillingness to take responsibility

for the actions.[95] Evidence exists "of ordinary middle class youth" participating in the "looting and arson" or merely looking on, taking vicarious pleasure
out of "the fact that the Sikhs had finally been given their due."[96]

In discussing these different interpretations of the riots, I have tried to show
how particular explanations of the riots in themselves help to perpetuate the
violence. Labeling politically engineered riots spontaneous outburts of hatred
contributes to the widening of the gulf between Hindu and Sikh communities. Pandey argues that the history of communalism in India is itself a
construct, as British administrators of the time, and later historians, filed any
kind of disturbance, including those opposing the state, under this communal
heading, an essentializing view which saw religious bigotry and conflict
between religious communities as a distinguishing feature of "the Orient."[97]
It is of course always possible that this construct could become a reality; the
effort to create a division between the two communities has certainly been
partially successful. Human rights abuses in Punjab, the enactment of martial
law in that state, false encounters in which Sikh youths are killed, the
mistreatment of Sikhs coming into Delhi for the Asiad games, all served to
legitimate violence against this community in the eyes of Hindus, while creating
estrangement among the Sikhs.

The common interpretation of any inter-ethnic violence in India as
stemming from communalism contributes to the perpetuation of riot systems.
The massacres of the Sikhs in 1984 were not an anomaly, although they stand
out in the degree of direction and orchestration involved. They were part of
a construction of communalism which heretofore had been limited mainly
to Hindus and Muslims and which has a number of functional uses. By exon-
erating those responsible, it provides a cover for competing elites and a
diversion from the inability of the Indian government to address the basic
needs of its populace. It also operates as a guise under which the secular nationalists can pursue their goal of a strong centralized state, which they can then
justify as essential in keeping ethnic groups from killing each other.[98]
Ironically the worst violence is done by the agents of the state themselves.

NOTES

1 Donald L. Horowitz, *Ethnic Groups in Conflict* (Berkeley: University of
   California Press, 1985), pp. 179–80.
2 People's Union for Democratic Rights and the People's Union for Civil
   Liberties, *Who Are the Guilty? Report of a Joint Inquiry into the Causes and*

Impact of the Riots in Delhi from 31 October to 10 November, 1984 (New Delhi: PUDR and PUCL, 1984), p. 1.

3   *India Today*, November 30, 1984, p. 38. Violence broke out but was contained in West Bengal, where the state government moved quickly to stop the violence even as the local Congress party was taking out processions carrying pictures of Mrs Gandhi and shouting, "death to the killers."

4   Stanley Tambiah, "Presidential Address: Reflections on Communal Violence in South Asia," *Journal of Asian Studies*, XLIX, No. 4 (November, 1990), 746–8.

5   Rajni Kothari, *Politics and the People: In Search of a Humane India*, Vol. II (Delhi: Ajanta Publications, 1989), pp. 445–6.

6   Veena Das *et al.*, "The Weekly Special," *The Illustrated Weekly of India*, December 23, 1984, p. 22.

7   *India Today*, November 30, 1984, pp. 40-5.

8   Madhu Kishwar discusses how the central government proposed the addition of "more police stations" in Delhi in the aftermath of the riots, but argues that, in the context of a criminalized police force, this would be "like rubbing salt into our wounds," in "Gangster Rule: The Massacre of the Sikhs," *Manushi* 5 (1984), 27.

9   *Hindustan Times*, November 1, 1984.

10   See the remarks by Paul R. Brass in the introduction to this volume, pp. 54.

11   Baljit Malik, "The Cry for Justice," *The Illustrated Weekly of India*, February 16, 1986, p. 47.

12   Romesh Thapar, "When the State Collapses," *The Illustrated Weekly of India*," December 23, 1984, p. 13.

13   Ivan Fera, "The Enemy Within," *The Illustrated Weekly of India*, December 23, 1984, p. 16 and Inder Mohan, "Resettlement: The Other Delhi," in Smitu Kothari and Harsh Sethi (eds), *Voices from a Scarred City: The Delhi Carnage in Perspective* (Delhi: Lokayan, 1985), p. 58.

14   Amiya Rao *et al.*, *Report to the Nation: Truth about Delhi Violence* (New Delhi: Citizens for Democracy, 1985), p. 4.

15   Sumanta Banerjee, "Contradictions with a Purpose," *Economic and Political Weekly*, XIX, No. 48 (December 1, 1984), 2,028–30.

16   Rajni Kothari, "The Aftermath," *The Illustrated Weekly of India*, December 23, 1984, p. 9.

17   Rajni Kothari, "The How and Why of it All," *The Sikh Review*, XXXIII, No. 376 (April, 1985), 17-19.

18   As in the 1983 riots in Sri Lanka and the killing of Tamils by organized Sinhalese thugs; see Gananath Obeyesekere, "The Origins and Institutionalization of Political Violence," in James Manor (ed.), *Sri Lanka in Change and Crisis* (New York: St. Martin's Press, 1984), p. 174.

19   Rao, *Report to the Nation*, p. 2.

20   Kishwar, "Gangster Rule," p. 20.

21   Rao, *Report to the Nation*, pp. 2–3.

22   *Indian Express*, November 9, 1984.

23   Rao, *Report to the Nation*, pp. x and 17–18.

24   *Indian Express*, October 31, 1984.

25   Rao, *Report to the Nation*, pp. x and 46.

26   *Indian Express*, November 8, 1984.

27   Rao, *Report to the Nation*, pp. 20–1.

28 Kishwar, "Gangster Rule," p. 19.
29 PUDR and PUCL, *Who are the Guilty?*, pp. 20 and 43.
30 Raj Thapar, "How do You Do It?" in Kothari and Sethi, *Voices from a Scarred City*, p. 20.
31 *Delhi, 31 October to 4 November, 1984: Report of the Citizens Commission* (Delhi: Tata Press, 1984), pp. 14–15.
32 *Times of India,* November 2, 1984.
33 *Who are the Guilty?*, pp. 28–30 and *Report of the Citizen's Commission,* pp. 12–15.
34 *Indian Express,* November 8, 1984.
35 *Who Are the Guilty?*, pp. 1–2. The authors of this report concluded from numerous interviews that such incidents of Sikhs celebrating were "few and isolated." Many people whom they interviewed spoke authoritatively about the Sikhs celebrating and gave this as a justification for the violence, yet hardly anyone actually saw this, they heard about it "from someone else." See also Rao, *Report to the Nation*, pp. 23–4.
36 "One Hundred Hours in the Life of a City," in Kothari and Sethi, *Voices from a Scarred City*, p. 8.
37 *Who Are the Guilty?*, p. 2.
38 *Telegraph,* November 3, 1984.
39 Rao, *Report to the Nation*, p. 24.
40 *Indian Express,* November 2, 1984.
41 *Indian Express,* November 1, 1984.
42 *Indian Express,* November 3, 1984.
43 Chakravarti, *The Delhi Riots*, pp. 636–7.
44 Kishwar, "Gangster Rule," p. 23.
45 *Who Are the Guilty?*, p. 31.
46 Paul R. Brass, *Theft of an Idol* (Princeton, N.J.: Princeton University Press).
47 *Who Are the Guilty?*, p. 5.
48 *Who Are the Guilty?*, p. 4.
49 Vinod Sharma and G. K. Singh, "Massacre: Madness with a Method," *The Week,* November 18–24, 1984, p. 20 and Rao, *Report to the Nation*, p. 39.
50 Banerjee, "Contradictions," p. 2,028.
51 *Indian Express,* November 2, 1984.
52 *Indian Express,* November 1, 1984.
53 *Indian Express,* November 9, 1984.
54 *Indian Express,* November 9, 1984.
55 *Who Are the Guilty?*, pp. 9-10.
56 Rao, *Report to the Nation*, pp. 38–9.
57 Rao, *Report to the Nation*, p. 38.
58 *Who are the Guilty?*, p. 4.
59 *Indian Express,* November 9, 1984.
60 *Who are the Guilty?*, p. 4.
61 *Who are the Guilty?*, p. 4.
62 Rao, *Report to the Nation*, p. 46.
63 Kishwar, "Gangster Rule," p. 12; Rao, *Report to the Nation*, p. 8.
64 *Who are the Guilty?*, p. 5.
65 Rao, *Report to the Nation*, pp. 34–5.
66 *India Today,* November 30, 1984.

67 *Who are the Guilty?*, pp. 9–10.
68 *India Today*, November 30, 1984.
69 *Who are the Guilty?*, pp. 10-11.
70 *Indian Express*, November 10, 1984.
71 *Indian Express*, November 9, 1984; *Report of the Citizens Commission*, p. 34.
72 Kothari, "The How and Why," p. 18.
73 Kothari, "The How and Why," p. 20.
74 Brass chapter, this volume, p. 12.
75 Mohan, "Resettlement," p. 55.
76 Kishwar, "Gangster Rule," p. 11.
77 Mohan, "Resettlement," pp. 56-7.
78 Kothari, "The How and Why," p. 18.
79 Fera, "The Enemy Within," p. 14.
80 Kishwar, "Gangster Rule," p. 20.
81 *India Today*, November 30, 1984.
82 Kothari, "The How and Why," p. 18.
83 *Indian Express*, November 8, 1984; Fera, "The Enemy Within," p. 16; Mohan, "Resettlement," p. 55; and *Who are the Guilty?*, p. 3.
84 *Who are the Guilty?*, p. 3.
85 Fera, "The Enemy Within," p. 15.
86 Sharma and Singh, "Massacre," p. 19.
87 *Hindustan Times*, November 1, 1984.
88 *Indian Express*, November 10, 1984.
89 *Hindustan Times*, November 1, 1984.
90 Fera, "The Enemy Within," p. 16.
91 Chakravarti and Haksar, *Delhi Riots*, p. 19.
92 Fera, "The Enemy Within," p. 16.
93 Kishwar, "Gangster Rule," pp. 22–3.
94 Chakravarti and Haksar, *Delhi Riots*, pp. 569–70.
95 Kishwar, "Gangster Rule," pp. 22–3.
96 Kothari, "The How and Why," pp. 22–3.
97 Gyandendra Pandey, *The Construction of Communalism in North India* (Delhi: Oxford University Press, 1990), pp. 23 and 64–5.
98 Brass chapter, p. 35.

8. Racial Killing or Barroom Brawl? Multiple Explanations of the Killing of Vincent Chin

Yen Le Espiritu

In the late 1970s, Asian American leaders began to call attention to what they termed "rising anti-Asian activities." At a congressional hearing on the impact of the new Asian immigration, an Asian American attorney contended that "today we are witnessing a resurgence of anti-Asian sentiment manifest by growing problems of vandalism, physical attack, and on occasion murder."[1] In a statement submitted to the US Commission on Civil Rights, US Representative Robert Matsui[2] alerted the commission to the danger of rising anti-Asianism. In a 1988 keynote speech, the founding president of the Asian/Pacific Bar of California similarly warned, "The danger I see in the next decade is the revitalization of anti-Asian hostility".[3]

Because no systematic data exist on incidents of violence against Asians, it is difficult to substantiate the claim of rising anti-Asianism. As the US Commission on Civil Rights[4] reported, "There is currently no way to determine accurately the level of activity against persons of Asian descent, or whether the number of incidents has increased, decreased, or stayed the same in recent years." But there is another difficulty: how to give an etiology of any specific incident. Short of an admission by the perpetrator, it is often impossible to establish that incidents of violence are indeed racial. What we have instead are competing interpretations of motives espoused by interested participants. While these competing discourses complicate the search for actual motives, they are important sources of information. Beyond mirroring the particular stakes that the participants have in the case, these discourses reflect their knowledge of and experience with racism in US society.

This chapter analyzes the multiple interpretations of the 1982 killing of Vincent Chin, a Chinese American who was beaten to death in Detroit by two white men, Ronald Ebens and Michael Nitz. On the night of the murder, Chin was celebrating his upcoming wedding with several friends at a nightclub. While there, Chin became involved in a fist fight with two white men, Ronald Ebens and Michael Nitz. The quarrel continued into the parking lot, where Ebens pulled a baseball bat from Nitz's car. Chin and his friends fled. Half an hour later, Ebens and Nitz located Chin outside a fast food restaurant. There, while Nitz grabbed Chin in a bear hug from behind, Ebens struck at least four blows to Chin's head. Chin died four days later from severe head injuries.[5]

The ensuing controversy surrounding Chin's murder was not over the physical facts of the slaying, but over the prosecution of Chin's killers and over motives, with Chin's supporters charging that the killing was racially motivated and Ebens' and Nitz's allies claiming that it was simply a barroom brawl that ended in violence. The purpose of this chapter is not to determine the racial aspect of the case, but rather to analyze the discourses that were used by the participants to "explain" the incident; and in so doing, to discern why the racial implications of the case were so readily understood by Asian Americans and other people of color but not by those of the majority culture.

THE SENTENCING

Shocked by Chin's brutal death, Asian Americans were further outraged by the lenient sentences meted out to Chin's killers. In filing charges, the Wayne County prosecutor opted for second-degree murder, that is, homicide with no premeditation. After lengthy plea-bargaining with the prosecutor's office, Ebens consented to plead guilty to the reduced charge of manslaughter; Nitz did not contest his charge. Although a manslaughter conviction in Michigan carries a maximum sentence of 15 years in prison, Wayne County Judge Charles Kaufman imposed no prison time on Ebens and Nitz. Instead, he sentenced both to three years' probation and fined each man a mere $3,700, payable at $125 per month with no interest.[6] In explaining his sentence, Judge Kaufman cited the defendants' stable working backgrounds and lack of criminal records: "You don't make the punishment fit the crime; you make the punishment fit the criminal."[7]

Seeking prosecution of Chin's killers, the outraged Asian American community in Detroit formed American Citizens for Justice (ACJ) to publicize the killing, the mishandling of the case by the prosecutor's office, and the light sentencing of Ebens and Nitz in the state court. This publicity led to an extensive and bitter media coverage of the case. Condemning the miscarriage of justice, a barrage of editorials and columns blasted Judge Kaufman's ruling. In the Detroit Free Press, columnist Nickie McWhirter penned, "In Wayne County having a job and a good work record, or being a student, is a license to kill, at least once. In Wayne County the value of a life wrongly taken in anger is $3,000 per person, or less than the cost of a used car."[8] Along the same line, the *Detroit News* published a cartoon showing a judge wearing a baseball cap and a goofy grin. In it, the judge tells two men: "You killed a man with a baseball bat, eh? Gee, I used to play a lot of ball myself when I was younger."[9]

After the public excoriation, the explanations began. Judge Kaufman admitted that he had overlooked a probation officer's report recommending imprisonment for Ebens for the murder of Chin. Prosecutors conceded that they had agreed to the manslaughter pleas with slight attention to the facts. Police granted that they had neglected to question the key witnesses. All three parties blamed their negligence on the crushing workload, the overcrowded jails, and the underfunded criminal justice system. As a Wayne County Circuit Judge stated in a television interview:

> This state can't even find enough money to house those people who go through the process, who get convicted of serious crimes, who get out of jail much too soon for the crime that they've committed, let alone trying to get the resources necessary to have longer and more complicated procedures to get more information.[10]

In other words, the legal community and the larger public (however sympathetic) approached the case from the legal angle, ignoring the racial element. As an Asian American leader complained, "No one even thought to ask if race might have been a factor."[11] In contrast, for Asian Americans, the Chin case meant more than a failure of the criminal justice system, it meant racial discrimination, "a very real discrimination that Asian Americans of all our diverse nationalities have been forced to endure since our forebears set foot on this land."[12] Thus, to reduce the case to a legal discussion, dismissing its racial aspect, is to "sweep it under the rug."[13]

For Asian Americans, the historically-derived racial stratification of White-Asian racialized the case from the beginning. They cited as an example court proceedings that highlighted the defendants' stable working background and lack of criminal records but omitted comparable information on Chin's character and the details of his brutal death.[14] This setup, they argued, privileged the defendants' side of the story, leading to Judge Kaufman's sentence which appeared to place more value on the lives of the killers than the life of the slain victim. Like many Asian Americans, Chin's mother attributed this privileging to the racial ordering of Ebens/Nitz–Chin, "All through the courts no one talked to me. They just listened to the defendants' story. I said it's because those two are white. If they were Chinese it'd be so different!"[15] In other words, it was this racial hierarchy – and not the overburdened criminal system – that made it possible for two *white* men to receive probation and a small fine for the killing of a *Chinese* man.[16] As the "mayor" of Detroit's Chinatown lamented, "In Detroit, for $3,000, you can get a license to kill a Chinaman."[17]

The purpose here is not to argue that the legal handling of the Chin case was racially biased, but rather to point out that for people of color, the experience of racism is a cumulative process – as contemporary incidents are interpreted and evaluated against the background of earlier experiences and general knowledge of racism in society.[18] As an Asian American writer relates, "in my talks with whites about race, I very quickly find myself referring to history."[19] Similarly, in a study of the daily racial experiences of Black women, Philomena Essed reports that "in accounts of their own experiences of racism, the women are able to effectively use the history of Blacks in the United States as a frame of reference."[20] In the Asian American case, the history of anti-Asian legislation – from immigration exclusion to economic discrimination, social segregation, and incarceration – is the frame of reference within which these Americans place contemporary incidents. Invoking this knowledge of anti-Asianism, one angry Chinese American said of Judge Kaufman's ruling, "It has aroused the anger of the Asian community by recalling the days of 'frontier justice' when massacres of Chinese workers were commonplace."[21] Another activist similarly charged that "it is turning back the calendar to the days when Chinese could be lynched and Chinatown could be burned down."[22] This historical orientation – of viewing history as experience – became even more prevalent as Asian Americans sought to "explain" the killing of Vincent Chin.

EXPLAINING THE KILLING

Responding to heavy public pressure and petition from the Asian American community, the US Justice Department ordered an FBI investigation of Chin's death for possible civil rights violation. This investigation was also prompted by eyewitness claims that Ebens directed racial slurs at Chin, calling him a "Chink" and a "Nip." One witness stated that Nitz offered him $20 to "help catch those Chinese guys," thereby suggesting that the defendants singled out for pursuit only Chin and his other Chinese friend, and not their white companions.[23] Another witness, a dancer in the bar, testified, "All I heard him [Ebens] say when I turned around is, 'It's because of you little mother fucker that we're out of work.' Mr Chin replied, 'I am not a little mother fucker.'" [24] It was this testimony that gripped the nation. At a time when the American automobile industry was facing stiff competition from

Japanese imports, this statement implied that Ebens, a foreman at an automobile plant, mistook Chin for a Japanese and blamed him for the layoffs in the automobile industry.

In November 1983, a federal grand jury indicted Ebens and Nitz on two counts of civil rights violations: Count I charges them with conspiracy to deprive Chin of his civil rights, and count II with interfering with Chin's right to enjoy a place of public accommodation by "willfully injuring, intimidating, and interfering with Chin on account of his race or national origin."[25] Since the physical facts of the assaults were essentially undisputed, the entire civil rights case rested on the racial overtones of the slaying. Given their respective interests in the case, it is not surprising that the Asian American community charged racism while the defendants insisted that the fight was not racially motivated. However, what is of interest here is the construction of these competing interpretations – the discourses that were used to claim and disclaim racism – for they reveal the participants' experience with, knowledge of, and interpretation of racism in the United States.

The Defendants' Response

To establish that the slaying was not racially motivated, the defendants and their supporters first characterized the murder as an unfortunate but *isolated* incident in a local bar which "could happen to anybody. It's just one of those things."[26] Disclaiming the racial nature of the remarks attributed to him, Ebens contended that "the fight arose over Chin's insulting treatment" of one of the dancers.[27] In other words, what transpired was simply a barroom incident between two intoxicated men that ended in the death of one of the participants, and not a deliberate racial attack. In the documentary *Who Killed Vincent Chin?* the defense attorney for Ebens outlined this argument:

> Ron Ebens is guilty of having too much to drink, being a macho man who wouldn't back down from a fight, ... and he is guilty of letting himself go too far and killing somebody with a baseball bat. A serious crime, no doubt. But he is not guilty of doing this because of racial animus or racial feelings or racial bias or racial prejudice. It so happened that the person he was involved with was Chinese.[28]

The defense's contention that the fight arose over one of the dancers was corroborated by this dancer's testimony:

> He [Chin] wanted to give me a tip which was cool with me, ya know. I went to get the tip but when I went to accept the tip, ya know, he didn't want to give it to me the way I wanted to receive it, ya know, he wanted

to put it in my G-string . . . So I refused . . . and went to the other end of the stage . . . And then Ebens comes in . . . He was boosting me up and encouraging me and it made me feel good, ya know. . . . Then Chin and his friends, ya know, . . . they were like, "She is not, ya know, you don't know what you're talking about." Ebens was at the end of the stage, going, he called him boy, "Boy, you don't know a good thing when you see one." And Chin goes, "I am not a boy."[29]

In this same documentary, Ebens' and Nitz's supporters further dismissed the racial aspect of the case by characterizing the two defendants as "the most unprejudiced people." Ebens himself declared emphatically, "I am no racist. I've never been a racist. I've never had anything against anybody in this whole world. With God as my witness, that is the truth." A long-time friend insists that Ebens "is just not the type of person that is outward prejudiced. You know, you might have some little comments or something when you are alone, but he wouldn't go into a public bar, a public place and call names and really make the type of gestures and things that was said during that time."[30]

To support the contention that Ebens is not a racist, a friend cited as evidence the fact that "Ron owned a bar in a pretty crummy neighborhood and had every walk of life as a customer." The same reasoning was employed by an auto worker who claimed that "this is not a prejudice situation" because "we've got Japs, Chinese, any goddamn guy in the world working on our line and it don't bother us one bit."[31] This logic seems to suggest that if one associates or works with people of color, then one is not a racist. Regardless of its validity (in general or in this particular case), this reasoning stems from the position that racism means individual prejudice – unconnected to larger economic trends and historical conditions. As such, it reflects the prevalent neoconservative belief that the gains of the civil rights movement have made discrimination a thing of the past, so that racism now largely means individual prejudice.[32]

When confronted with evidence of racism, these dominant group members deny their own responsibility and blame others for calling undue attention to race, thereby marginalizing these oppositional views.[33] In this case, some of Ebens' and Nitz's supporters blamed the media: "I think that somehow the media found out that Ron worked for Chrysler and jumped off on that and made it a racial thing" and "the person who made a documentary about the Chin case exploited those pictures of people smashing Japanese imports."[34] Others, like Ebens, blamed the Asian American activists: "I personally think that a lot of them used it for their own vehicle just to get ahead. Secondly, they used it to, ya know, promote the Asian America[ns] and their alleged plight in this country which I am not aware of that they have a plight because

I know very few Asians, very few."[35] This statement is instructive because it reveals that unlike people of color, dominant group members have limited understanding of the problem of racism in US society. According to Essed,[36] this is the case because dominant group members are not regularly confronted with critical views of race and ethnic relations and thus do not gain knowledge of social reality from the point of view of the dominated. Along the same line, Mary Waters[37] suggests that the way white Americans think about their own ethnicity – the symbolic, flexible, and voluntary aspects of it – makes it difficult for them to "understand the everyday influence and importance of skin color and racial minority status for members of minority groups in the United States."

The Asian American Response

For Asian American activists, the racial statements attributed to Ebens confirm that the slaying was racially motivated. As a former ACJ president stated, "The one thing that has pulled together, through sheer concern, all Asian Americans in this country and brought press and so forth from overseas and concern from overseas is the belief that Vincent Chin would be alive today if he were not Asian and there is no question about that in any of our minds."[38] However, it is important to note that this conclusion is not based solely on their knowledge of the Chin case itself, but also on their awareness of violence against Asians in the US. In other words, Chin's killing is not viewed as an isolated incident (as maintained by Ebens and Nitz) but as part of a larger racial victimization of Asian Americans. Speaking to a group of community activists in San Francisco, a Chinese American insisted that Chin's killing was part of a "very, very disturbing trend of racially-motivated violence."[39] Another called the Chin case a "symbol of anti-Asian violence in the 80s," which included the attacks on Vietnamese fishermen in Texas, the stabbing death of a Vietnamese youth in northern California, and the beating death of an Indo-American in New Jersey.[40] Regardless of the diversity of incidents and the actual motives behind them, these Asian Americans view them as part of a single pattern and explain them in terms of racial and ethnic domination. While this view may reflect a deliberate strategy to racialize the Chin case, this racialization is based on the experienced reality of racism in their lives. In the following account, an Asian American police officer in Detroit cites his own encounter with racism as a starting point from which to explain Chin's murder:

> I've been followed down the road by hostile people screaming out of the windows of their cars, brandishing weapons in their windows and

everything else. I've come very close on several occasions to having a serious confrontation where someone probably would have got hurt ... I just mind my own business but in light of how many people who go out of their way to antagonize people who look different than them, at least in this part of the country, it is surprising that there hasn't been more than one Vincent Chin case.[41]

Although the Chin case started out as a Chinese American issue, it quickly became an Asian American cause. While this pan-Asian strategy is a reaction to the allegation that Ebens mistook Chin for a Japanese, it is also a response to the history of Asian lumping in the United States. This history indicates that because outsiders do not or cannot distinguish among Asian subgroups, they target all Asians for their "message of hate," punish one group for another's behavior, fail to distinguish recent immigrants from later-generation citizens, and seldom distinguish Asian Americans from Asian nationals.[42] For example, this misconception is reflected in the recurrent blaming of Japanese Americans for the bombing of Pearl Harbor and for the trade imbalance with Japan.

More than any other incident, the beating death of Vincent Chin epitomizes for many Asian Americans the racism of racial lumping: blamed for Japan's economic advantage, a Chinese American, mistaken for Japanese, was murdered. As a key organizer of the case explained, "People understood that it involved more than Chinese, more than one nationality. Anybody who looked Asian could be attacked. It just happened that Chin was Chinese. He could have been Korean or any other Asian nationality."[43] Another Asian American expressed the community's fear and rage when he wrote, "[Asian Americans] know Vincent Chin was killed because of his racial membership; they realize it could happen to any one of them – to anyone with black hair and slanted eyes."[44]

Cognizant of the racism of Asian lumping, Asian Americans across the country also came together to demand the prosecution of Chin's killers. Demonstrations and support activities took place in San Francisco, Oakland, Los Angeles, Denver, Chicago, Toronto and New York.[45] In addition to the long-established Japanese American Citizens League, Organization of Chinese Americans, and National Chinese Welfare Association, Asian Americans also formed new pan-Asian organizations to seek justice for Chin's death.[46] To subsidize the legal expenses of the Detroit-based American Citizens for Justice (ACJ), many organizations and businesses around the nation collected money for the case and forwarded the sum to ACJ. During the period from March 1983 to December 1984, ACJ received close to $83,000 from supporters across the country.[47] Supporters of the Chin case also participated in ACJ's nationwide letter-writing campaign to government officials and the press. The Justice Department reportedly received more than 15,000 letters, "They got more mail from the Chin case than from any other case in the department's recent history."[48] Indeed, the indictment of Chin's killers came only as a result of this massive campaign.

The recognition of the centrality of race – and racism – in American society also led to critical support of the Chin case from the African American and Jewish American communities. According to a former ACJ executive director, "Experienced hands from the NAACP, the Anti-Defamation League of B'nai B'rith and the Detroit Association of Black Organizations provided invaluable contacts and information."[49] For both communities, their own history of racial oppression forms an important frame of reference within which they place the Chin case. As an African American supporter stated,

> it was such a brutal murder that it really hits the conscience of everyone else. But I guess even more so was the fact that so many of us have experienced that kind of thing for so long. I think it has had a tremendous impact because it demonstrated that this whole question of injustice was endemic to the system in America.[50]

Similarly, in a letter to the *Los Angeles Times* in support of the Chin case, the Jewish Federation Council reminded the reader that "the Jewish community has suffered from economic scapegoating in many lands for many years."[51] Explaining this interracial kinship, writer David Mura states, "It is a kinship that comes from our histories as victims of injustice" and "is reinforced by our current position as minorities in a white-dominated culture."[52]

LEGACY OF THE CHIN CASE

The above discussion suggests that the Asian American response to the Chin killing is not based just on the actual facts of the case but also on their collective memory of and personal experiences with racism. Although Chin's killers were ultimately acquitted of federal civil rights charges, the Chin case has "taken on mythic proportions" in the Asian American community and has become yet another point of reference in the community's knowledge and comprehension of racism.[53] Speaking in Detroit on the tenth anniversary of Chin's death, a community leader articulated the legacy of the Chin case:

> For Asian Americans everywhere, that event [the murder of Vincent Chin] seared itself on our psyche and still burns with immediacy today, whether we are Chinese, Japanese, Korean, Filipino, or Vietnamese, . . .

we know that violent racial hatred can leap out at any of us from the dark recesses of this country, whether we are students, shopkeepers, professionals climbing the corporate ladder, or litigants in a court of justice, ... we realize that racism can flare up in our faces in the most unexpected ways. Since the murder of Vincent Chin, we most keenly feel the challenge of being an Asian in America.[54]

As a result of the Chin case, Asian Americans today are much more willing to speak out on the issue of anti-Asianism; they are also much better organized than they were at the time of Chin's death. Across the country, Asian Americans have formed new organizations to monitor, report, and protest anti-Asian incidents.[55] Because no systematic data exist on anti-Asian violence, Asian Americans have also pushed for the collection and reporting of statistics on anti-Asian crimes at the local, state, and national levels.[56]

The legacy of the Chin case is most evident in the Asian American response to another tragic case of mistaken racial identification. In late July 1989, two white men, Robert and Lloyd Piche, pistol-whipped a Chinese American man, Jim Loo, in a North Carolina pool hall after allegedly mistaking him for Vietnamese. Jim Loo died two days later from severe head injuries. According to eyewitnesses, the Piche brothers directed racial slurs at Vietnamese while attacking Loo and his Asian American friends. The two men were quoted as saying that they did not like Vietnamese because they had lost a brother in the Vietnam war. Of the five Asian Americans present that night, only one was in fact Vietnamese.[57]

Fearing a repeat of the Chin case, Asian Americans responded immediately to the Loo killing. Less than a month after Loo's death, Asian Americans in Raleigh formed the Jim Loo American Justice Coalition to ensure the prosecution of Loo's killers. The coalition's chairman explained the group's strategy: "We know that in the Chin case, there was no Asian representation in the early stage. No one paid attention until the judge announced the sentence. In this case, we tried to get involved early in the game."[58] Asian American organizations across the country also acted quickly, offering their assistance to the Jim Loo Coalition and later the Jim Loo Memorial Fund Committee.[59] In an open letter to Asian Americans, the president of the Organization of Chinese Americans in San Francisco urged Asian Americans to unite behind the Loo case: "What we can do is to mobilize a letter-writing campaign to let the governmental authorities and agencies know that we have learned our lessons from the Vincent Chin case and will not stand by and suffer another incident of mock justice and ridicule."[60]

Although poised to wage a nationwide protest on behalf of Loo, Asian Americans in this instance did not have to do so because, for the most part, the legal system was responsive and responsible. In March 1990, the Wake County Court found Robert Piche guilty of second-degree murder and sentenced him to 37 years in prison. In July 1991, Lloyd Piche, who received only a six-month sentence for disorderly conduct and assault, was tried and convicted by a federal jury for violating the civil rights of Loo and his six Asian American friends. Piche's conviction was the first successful federal prosecution of a civil rights violation case in which the victim was an Asian American.[61]

In sum, not only did the Chin case provide a background against which to explain the motives of Loo's killers, it also supplied a blueprint for how to proceed. In the Chin case, Asian Americans did not act until after the local courts had issued the lenient sentences – eight months after Chin's murder. In the Loo case, Asian Americans (in Raleigh as well as across the country) mobilized *before* any verdict had been reached. This early mobilization was instrumental in forcing the legal system to be more responsive to anti-Asian crimes.

CONCLUSION

Unlike the legal and the larger community, Asian Americans did not approach the Chin case from a legal, but from a racial angle. And unlike the defendants and their supporters, Asian Americans did not depict the killing as an isolated, local incident in which the victim happens to be a Chinese, but rather as part of a trend of racially-motivated violence nationwide. This "reading" of the Chin case suggests that racism is experienced in multidimensional ways – not only in personal encounters, but also through history, and vicariously through the experiences of other group members.[62] Thus an individual incident, like the killing of Vincent Chin, is understood in the context of the historical experience of the group and explained in terms of racial and ethnic domination.

NOTES

1   WilliamWong, in "Bill Wong" column, *Asian Week*, October 6, 1985.
2   Robert Matsui, Testimony submitted to the US Commission on Civil Rights, October 31, 1984 in U S Commission on Civil Rights, *Recent Activities Against Citizens and Residents of Asian Descent* (Washington, DC: US Government Printing Office, 1986), pp. 63–5.

3   Asian Pacific American Coalition USA, "AACI Celebrates 15th Anniversary," *APAC Alert*, February, 1989.
4   US Commission on Civil Rights, *Recent Activities Against Citizens and Residents of Asian Descent* (Washington, DC: US Government Printing Office, 1986), p. 5.
5   Paul Weingarten, "Deadly Encounter: Did Vincent Chin's Assailants Get Away with Murder?" *Chicago Tribune Magazine*, July 13, 1983.
6   Helen Zia, "The New Violence," *Bridge* IX, No. 2 (1984), pp. 18–23.
7   American Citizens for Justice, "The Case for Vincent Chin: A Tragedy in American Justice (the Official Position of American Citizens for Justice)," press release, May 4, 1983.
8   Nickie McWhirter, "A lesson – and a License – that Kids Should Never Get," *Detroit Free Press,* March 25, 1983.
9   Cited in Paul Weingarten, "Deadly Encounter: Did Vincent Chin's Assailants Get Away with Murder?" *Chicago Tribune Magazine*, July 13, 1983.
10 Renee Tajima and Christine Choy, *Who Killed Vincent Chin?* (New York: Third World Newsreel, 1988).
11 Zia, "The New Violence," 19–20.
12 Zia, "The New Violence," p. 18.
13 Paul Justi, "Bay Area AAs Protest Racial Violence in US," *East West*, May 18, 1983.
14 Chinese On Leong Association, press release, March 23, 1983.
15 Tajima and Choi, *Who Killed Vincent Chin?* (Video spoken in Chinese with an English voice-over translation).
16 Zia, "The New Violence," p. 23.
17 Cited in Wong, *Asian Week*, October 6, 1985.
18 Philomena Essed, *Understanding Everyday Racism: An Interdisciplinary Theory* (Newbury Park, CA: Sage, 1991), p. 8.
19 David Mura, " Strangers in the Village," in R. Simonson and S. Walker (eds), *Graywolf Annual Five: Multi-Cultural Literacy* (St. Paul, MN: Graywolf Press 1988), p. 138.
20 Essed, *Understanding Everyday Racism*, p. 90.
21 Cecil Suzuko, "Detroit's Asian Americans Outraged by Lenient Sentencing of Chinese American Man's Killer," *Rafu Shimpo*, May 5, 1983.
22 Justi, "Bay Area AAs Protest Racial Violence."
23 US Court of Appeals, Sixth Circuit, "United States of America, Plaintiff-Appellee, *v.* Ronald Ebens, Defendant-Appellant," *Federal Reporter* 800 (2) (1986), p. 1440.
24 US Court of Appeals, "U.S.A. *v.* Ebens," p. 1427.
25 US Court of Appeals, "U.S.A. *v.* Ebens," p. 1427.
26 Tajima and Choi, *Who Killed Vincent Chin?*
27 US Court of Appeals, "U.S.A. *v.* Ebens," pp. 1428–9.
28 Tajima and Choi, *Who Killed Vincent Chin?*
29 Tajima and Choi, *Who Killed Vincent Chin?*
30 Tajima and Choi, *Who Killed Vincent Chin?*
31 Tajima and Choi, *Who Killed Vincent Chin?*
32 J. B. McConahay, "Modern racism, Ambivalence, and the Modern Racism Scale," in J.F. Dovidio & S.L. Gaertner (eds), *Prejudice, Discrimination, and Racism,* (Orlando, FL: Academic Press, 1986), pp. 91–125.

33 David Mura, "Strangers in the Village," p. 137 and Essed, *Understanding Everyday Racism,* p. 7.
34 Tajima and Choi, *Who Killed Vincent Chin?*
35 Tajima and Choi, *Who Killed Vincent Chin?*
36 Essed, *Understanding Everyday Racism,* p. 280.
37 Mary C. Waters, *Ethnic Options: Choosing Identies in America* (Berkeley: University of California Press, 1990), p. 158.
38 Tajima and Choi, *Who Killed Vincent Chin?*
39 Justi, "Bay Area AAs Protest Racial Violence."
40 Justi, "Bay Area AAs Protest Racial Violence" and Max Millard, "Ohio Jury Acquits Ebens in Vincent Chin Killing," *East/West News*, May 7, 1987.
41 Tajima and Choi, *Who Killed Vincent Chin?*
42 Irving L. Allen, *The Language of Ethnic Conflict* (New York: Columbia University Press, 1983), p. 162; US Commission on Civil Rights, *Recent Activities Against Citizens and Residents of Asian Descent,* pp. 2–3; and Laird Harrison, "White Supremacist Group Targets Asians," *Asian Week*, December 4, 1987, p. 69.
43 Helen Zia, telephone interview, October 10, 1989.
44 Ronald Takaki, "Who Really Killed Vincent Chin?" *Asian Week*, November 29, 1983.
45 Zia, "The New Violence."
46 *Asian Week,* "National Day of Mourning Slated for Vincent Chin" June 2, 1983 and Paul Feldman, "Asian Groups Stage Protest on Slaying," *Los Angeles Times,* June 19, 1983.
47 Helen Zia, *1983 Yearbook* (Royal Oak, Mich.: American Citizens for Justice, 1984), p. 15.
48 Telephone interview with Jim Shimoura on October 23, 1989.
49 David Fukuzawa, "The Vincent Chin Case and the Detroit Asian American Community," *EWGAPA (Ecumenical Working Group of Asian and Pacific Americans) News,* Winter 1989.
50 Tajima and Choi, *Who Killed Vincent Chin?*
51 Martin Glenn and Ferry F. Habush, Letter from the Jewish Federation Council of Greater Los Angeles to the *Los Angeles Times,* June 13, 1983.
52 Mura, "Strangers in the Village," pp. 138–9.
53 Wong, *Asian Week,* October 6, 1989 and George Kagiwada, "The Killing of Thong Hy Huynh: Implications of a *Rashomon* Perspective," in Gail M. Nomura *et al.* (eds), *Frontiers of Asian American Studies* (Pullman, WA: Washington State University Press, 1989), pp. 253–65.
54 George Takei, "Our Challenge After Vincent Chin," *Justice Update,* IX, No. 2 (Spring–Summer, 1992), p. 3.
55 Eric Mar, "Vincent Chin's Killers Go Free," *People's Monitor/Third World Forum,* May 28, 1987 and Anonymous, "Vincent Chin Memorial Grant Recipients Named," *Rafu Shimpo,* January 6, 1989.
56 Rose Ochi, "Statement of Rose Ochi of the Office of the Mayor of the City of Los Angeles," in US House, Committee on Post Office and Civil Service, *Demographic Impact of Immigration on the U.S., Hearings,* 99th Congress, 1st session, July 19, 1985, p. 177.

57 Ned Glascock, "Chinese Slain in Raleigh Pool Hall Attack," *News and Observer*, August 1, 1989 and Grace Wai-Tse Siao, "Chinese Man Beaten to Death in North Carolina," *Asian Week*, January 27, 1989.
58 Po Chan, telephone interview, November 2, 1989.
59 Po Chan, interview.
60 Claudine Cheng, "Let Your Voices Be Heard," *Asian Week*, September 8, 1989.
61 Helen Zia, "Loo Slaying Trial Witnesses Say Piche Taunted Asians," *Asian Week*, July 12, 1991.
62 Essed, *Understanding Everyday Racism*.

9. African American Boycotts of Korean-Owned Stores in New York and Los Angeles
Edward T. Chang

INTRODUCTION

The Los Angeles riots of 1992 were America's first multi-ethnic riots in which African Americans, whites, Latinos and Asian Americans participated as both victims and assailants. According to the records of the Los Angeles County Sheriff's Department, 12,545 arrests were made between 6:00 p.m. April 29 and 5:00 a.m. May 5, 1992 – the period of the civil disorder. The racial breakdown of those arrested is as follows: Latinos 45.2 percent, African Americans 41 percent, and whites 11.5 percent. "The fixation on black versus white is outdated and misleading – the Rodney King verdict was merely the match that lit the fuse of the first multiracial class riot in America."[1]

Unfortunately, many businesses that were looted and burned down were owned by Korean Americans. Approximately 2,300 Korean-owned businesses suffered an estimated $400 million in property damage – about one-half of the total loss from the riots. In the aftermath of the riots, indications are that Korean-owned businesses were targeted for destruction by rioters. It is important to note, however, the FBI investigation found no hard evidence to support the existence of pre-riot planning, but they did not rule out the possibility of such pre-planning. Korean Americans were outraged and saddened by the loss of life and property damages they suffered during the riots. Many Korean Americans felt that they had been unfairly scapegoated for America's racial and economic problems.

Although nearly half the looters arrested were Latinos, the media portrayed the 1992 Los Angeles riots more in terms of the on-going conflicts between Korean Americans and African Americans. Since the outbreak of several boycotts against Korean-owned stores by African American residents during the 1980s and 1990s, tensions have been high in inner cities throughout the United States. More recently, two highly publicized boycotts in New York (Red Apple boycott) and Los Angeles (Latasha Harlins shooting) exacerbated tensions between the two minority groups.

The purpose of this chapter is to compare and contrast the Red Apple boycotts (1990) in New York and the Latasha Harlins shooting case (1991) in Los Angeles. The controversies surrounding the two cases have raised many important questions about how inter-ethnic conflict is interpreted by the parties involved: the media, the police, politicians and courts. This paper focuses especially on the roles played by the media, with some attention also to the politicians, the police and the courts. Specifically I ask how did the politicization of the boycotts and the coverage in the *Los Angeles Times* and *New York Times* shape and influence the nature of Korean-African American relations? A closer examination of these two similar, and yet different cases can provide a valuable insight into the nature of conflicts, the agents of escalation, and the mediation processes.

Proliferation of Korean-owned Businesses in African American Neighborhoods

Race riots in America have a long history.[2] During the urban riots of the 1960s, "Jewish-owned stores were targeted by protesters, and many white-owned stores were destroyed."[3] Most white and Jewish store owners moved out of African American neighborhoods after the riots. During the 1980s, Korean-owned stores proliferated in African American neighborhoods to fill the vacuum created by the departure of white and Jewish merchants and large chain stores from African American communities.[4] With the increase of Korean-owned businesses in African American communities, complaints, disputes and boycotts against Korean merchants have intensified. African Americans complain that Korean merchants are "rude and disrespectful, do not hire African American workers, overcharge for inferior products, and do not contribute profits back into the community."

Many observers described the volatility of Korean-African American relations in many cities as "a keg of dynamite ready to explode." Numerous altercations between Korean American merchants and African American customers in Philadelphia, Atlanta, Chicago, Washington DC, and Baltimore were reported during the 1980s. Sometimes the proliferation of Korean-owned businesses in African American neighborhoods is portrayed as a conspiracy against the African American community by government and the Korean American community. In Chicago, the *Metro News*, an African American newspaper, claimed that "Koreans are planning to take over Southern Chicago 47th District, and are buying buildings from Jewish owners which usually are run down buildings."[5]

In Los Angeles, tensions between Korean Americans and African Americans was first reported in a series of articles and editorials published by the

Sentinel, the largest African American newspaper in the Los Angeles area in August and September 1983. It was charged that "the African American community had literally been taken over by Asian businesses in the last five years."[6] In April 1986, four Korean American merchants were shot to death during separate robberies by African Americans. Responding to the concerns of Korean American business owners, the Los Angeles County Human Relations Commission helped to establish the Black–Korean Alliance.[7] Despite efforts to improve relations between the two communities, Korean-African American tensions continued to deteriorate during the late 1980s and the early 1990s.

Accounts of the Red Apple and Latasha Harlins Cases

Although New York City is synonymous with the "Big Apple," the "Red Apple" became a symbol of New York in early 1990. Red Apple is a name of Korean-owned produce stores in Brooklyn, New York. The Red Apple boycotts began shortly after a dispute between a Haitian immigrant woman Gisleaine Felissainte, and a Korean American store manager, Pong Ok Jang, on January 18, 1990.

Facts are in dispute. What happened to Mrs Felissainte at the Red Apple? Was she assaulted by a store employee as she claimed? Or was she merely restrained by the Korean American employee shortly after a verbal argument? According to Mrs Felissainte, "Jang grabbed her, insinuated that she had been shoplifting and slapped her face three times. She said that two store employees punched and kicked her, knocking her to the floor and causing injuries that kept her out of work for months."[8]

On the other hand, the manager Pong Ok Jang, presented an entirely different story. Jang insisted that he and other employees did not assault the woman. Mrs Felissainte was accused by the manager of not paying the appropriate amount for the items she wanted to purchase. "While she looked in her bag for another dollar, the employee began to wait on the next customer in the long line. Mrs Felissainte became angry and threw a hot pepper at Mr Jang. The cashier responded by throwing a pepper back at her. As the argument grew more heated, Mr Jang tried to calm her down by placing his hand on her shoulder. She sat down on the floor. Police called an ambulance.[9] Initially, Bong Jae Jang, a store owner and brother of the manager Pong Ok Jang, who had just returned from getting his hair cut was arrested on an assault charge. Obviously, it was a case of mistaken identity that often victimizes Asian Americans.[10]

No one imagined that the Red Apple boycott which followed, marked by chants of "No Respect, No Business" and "We Will Not Be Moved," would last a year and five months. Neighborhood residents established the Flatbush Frontline Collective to take care of the day-to-day needs of getting people to the picket line. Sonny Carson and the December 12th Movement provided advice to the Flatbush Frontline Collective boycotts of the Red Apple store. Sonny Carson had previously led boycotts of Korean-owned stores in the New York area.[11] A jury acquitted Mr Jang of the assault charge on January 30, 1991. A doctor who examined Mrs Felissainte at the hospital testified that "her face had a red mark that looked like a fingerprint."[12] In late May 1991, Mr Jang sold his store to another Korean immigrant. Mr Jang said that he was "too stressed" from the confrontation with protesters and boycotters. The Red Apple boycott was finally over.

On March 16, 1991, a Korean American shopkeeper, Soon Ja Du, shot and killed a 15-year-old African American girl in South Central Los Angeles. This tragic incident generated anger, disbelief and shock waves within both communities. It is important to note that the Latasha Harlins shooting occurred less than two weeks after the beating of Rodney King by four white police officers. Both the Rodney King beating and the Latasha Harlins shooting incidents were captured by video camera and security camera, respectively. Racial tensions were already high in Los Angeles with repeated showings of the videotape that captured the scene of Rodney King being repeatedly beaten by four white police officers. In these circumstances, it is understandable that the African American reaction to the Latasha Harlins shooting was highly charged.

Emotions ran high. Several Korean-owned stores were reportedly attacked and vandalized by angry crowds shortly after the incident.[13] Korea Town Police confirmed that they received several telephone calls from Korean American merchants who were burglarized and vandalized in South Central Los Angeles. One Korean-owned store was shut down for six consecutive days to avoid violent confrontations with angry African American residents.[14]

The community crime prevention hot line was busy with telephone calls from Korean American merchants who expressed their fear of retaliation by African Americans. One Korean American merchant reported that an African American patron walked out of the store with a piece of candy without paying and said, "Are you going to shoot me, too?"[15] Tensions ran high in South Central Los Angeles. Many observers were praying that this incident would not trigger race riots such as occured during the 1960s. Although the Latasha Harlins shooting case did not trigger the 1992 riots, many observers believe that it played a major role in the destruction of Korean-owned businesses during the riots.[16] Many African Americans expressed a deep sense of anger and resentment. They felt that their rights had been violated twice, by police and a Korean American merchant.

Again, facts were disputed by supporters of the assailant and the victim. A security camera videotape showed that Soon Ja Du grabbed the knapsack, thinking that the girl was shoplifting. According to the initial police report, the teenager left the juice and the knapsack on the counter and was turning to leave the store when Soon Ja Du shot her once in the back of the head. Soon Ja Du, however, contended that the teenager, in addition to shoplifting, was trying to take money from the store's cash register. Before the shooting, Latasha Harlins hit Soon Ja Du several times and Mrs Du fell down. As soon as Mrs Du got up, she pulled the trigger.

Latasha Harlin's aunt insisted that "Harlins was shot in cold blood without provocation." She also disputed the police contention that the shooting was not racially motivated. On the other hand, the son of Soon Ja Du argued that "the shooting was an accident."[17] Joseph Du, a son of Soon Ja Du, believes his mother is being used as a scapegoat by authorities to appease the African American community in the wake of the Rodney King beating scandal. In the Korean American community, the shooting is known as the Soon Ja Du case.

There are many similarities and differences between the Red Apple and Latasha Harlins cases. Both incidents were triggered by disputes involving little more than a dollar and a bottle of orange juice. Unlike many incidents prior to these two cases, Korean merchants were the assailants and African American customers were the victims. In many everyday encounters, Korean American merchants are the victims of robbery, burglary, and murder. According to the Korean American Grocery Association of Southern California (KAGRO), 38 Korean American merchants were murdered during the past 10 years in Los Angeles.[18]

These two incidents occurred in the midst of heightened tensions between the African American and white communities. In New York, the tensions had been escalating for several years. In December 1984, Bernard Goetz shot and wounded four African American youths who asked for a few dollars in a half-empty subway car. Goetz claimed that he fired in self-defense. He was found not guilty of all charges, except the charge of "carrying an unauthorized fire-arm."[19] Racial tensions continued to increase following the highly publicized Howard Beach murder (1986) and the Bensonhurst murder (1989). White mobs attacked and murdered African American youths because they were in the wrong neighborhoods of mostly white Bensonhurst. "The incidents in the two New York neighborhoods reminded African Americans of how vulnerable they are in a country where they are a minority in numbers and power."[20]

In 1989, the "melting pot" of New York city turned into a "boiling pot" when a white woman executive was attacked and beaten by a large group

240 *Riots and Pogroms*

of African American youths in Central Park, of whom several were found
guilty of sexual assault and rape charges and received long prison sentences.
Taken together, these highly visible and publicized racial incidents have had
a profound impact on the lives of whites and African Americans in New York
city. By 1990, it appeared that the city was headed on a collision course toward
"racial war."

Los Angeles has been promoting itself as a shining example of a multi-
cultural city. In contrast with New York city, white liberal, Jewish and
African American coalitions seemed to be working well as they shared
political power in the city.[21] In Los Angeles, the "infamous" Rodney King
beating videotape intensified racial polarization between whites and African
Americans. The videotape showed King being struck at least 56 times by
four Los Angeles police officers. The Rodney King beating case exposed
police brutality and pervasive racism against minorities. Tension had often
flared up between police and African American residents in the streets of
South Central Los Angeles. It is relevant to recall that the Watts riot of 1965
was ignited by alleged police brutality against an African American motorist.
Before the Rodney King beating, however, race relations in Los Angeles
appeared to be better than in other major cities including New York.

THE ROLE OF THE *NEW YORK TIMES* AND *LOS ANGELES TIMES*

The media has the power to shape, influence and control public opinion. It
appears the media played a critical role of not only simply reporting, but also
shaping public perception of the nature of Korean-African American conflict.
A close examination of the *New York Times* and *Los Angeles Times* reports
of the Red Apple and Latasha Harlins incidents reveals that media coverage
of the conflict may have exacerbated the tension and possibly prolonged the
Red Apple boycott. In fact, I argue that both the *New York Times* and *Los
Angeles Times* played agitators' roles, far beyond that of simply printing facts
objectively, as they claim.

Most newspaper reporting of these two events was factually correct.
However, it often distorted or exaggerated the situation with a selective
reporting of incidents. Frequently, facts were distorted by leaving out critical
information from the stories.

There are striking differences in coverage of the incidents, use of editorials,
and portrayal of Korean Americans and African Americans between the *New
York Times* reports of the Red Apple boycotts and the *Los Angeles Times*
reports of the Latasha Harlins shooting incident. Mainstream media including
the *New York Times* either failed or refused to cover the boycott of the Red

Apple for several months. Although the incident occurred on January 18, 1990 and the boycott began immediately afterward, the *New York Times* did not report the incident and boycott until early May 1990. In fact, a *New York Post* editorial of April 23, 1990 criticized the *New York Times* for being "irresponsible in its failure to cover the boycott."[22]

How do we explain the delayed timing of the *New York Times* reporting of the Red Apple boycott? We do not exactly know who were the editors who decided not to report the boycott for four months nor why they so decided. It certainly raises question about when, how, and who decides what is a "newsworthy" story. We can only speculate about their motives based on the circumstances at that time. As mentioned earlier, New York City was in racial turmoil because of several highly publicized and charged incidents between whites and African Americans. In these circumstances, New Yorkers were more interested in the Bensonhurst trial and the Central Park rape cases than the boycott of Korean-owned stores by African American residents. Editors may have made a decision that it simply was not a "newsworthy" story.

Suddenly, this "not newsworthy" story became the headline news of the *New York Times*. From May 7, 1990, the paper ran articles and editorials on the Red Apple boycott for six consecutive days and 17 times during the month of May. Shortly before the extensive coverage of the Red Apple boycott, the Bensonhurst trial had ended. Racial tensions ran high as the jury failed to convict white assailants of first degree murder. Because of the extensive coverage of the Red Apple boycotts by the press, the focus of racial tensions shifted from white-African American tensions to Korean-African American conflict. It helped to defuse racial tensions between whites and African Americans. Instead, Korean Americans became the symbol and target of African American anger and resentment. In other words, Korean immigrants are serving the function of a middleman minority.[23] The theory of middleman minority predicts that middleman minorities are likely to face at least some antagonism from the societies in which they settle. Furthermore, Bonacich argues that "conflict becomes exaggerated when the buyers are poor and the sellers are foreign."[24]

The *New York Times* articles and editorials were sympathetic to Korean immigrant merchants. In the eyes of this paper, the Korean American merchant was a victim and African American boycotters were racist. Korean American merchants were presented as hard-working, possessing strong family values, frugal, and industrious members of a "model minority" who were struggling to make the American Dream come true. Despite language barriers and cultural differences, Korean immigrants were determined to succeed by working hard for long hours:

Kil Jin Kim's daily schedule: head for the Hunt's point market in the Bronx at midnight and spend the night buying produce he will then transport, unload and arrange on display shelves. He will be busy until 4 p.m. or so, when he will go home, eat and go to bed, to wake up six hours later, at 11 p.m.[25]

Korean immigrants were "moving up" the economic ladder on their own without assistance from the government.[26]

On the other hand, African American boycotters were presented as radicals and racists who were trying to take advantage of innocent Korean immigrant merchants. A minor incident had been blown up to justify boycotts. "The boycott rides on the tide of ugly, unmistakably racist rhetoric that warrants condemnation from every fair-minded New Yorker starting with Mayor David Dinkins."[27] A great deal of attention was focused on a leader of the boycott, Sonny Carson. The *New York Times* articles and editorials mentioned several times that Robert (Sonny) Carson was a convicted kidnapper and racial provocateur.[28] Indeed, Sonny Carson repeatedly proclaimed himself as "anti-white," and urged "boycott [of] all Korean-owned stores." By focusing on the issue of Sonny Carson's credibility, the *New York Times* tried to discredit the legitimacy of the Red Apple boycott.

The New York Times articles also introduced to its readers the Korean immigrants' *kye*, or rotating credit association.[29] A *kye* is based on mutual trust and ethnic and homeland ties among members. Each member contributes a fixed amount of money each month and each month one person receives a pool of money. The process continues until everyone has received the money. *Kye* has been one of the important social and financial institutions helping Korean immigrants raise necessary initial and operational capital for their business ventures in the United States. The "model minority" images of Korean immigrants are often reinforced by emphasizing self-help institutions such as *kye*.

By praising Korean immigrant merchants as "a shining example" for other minorities to emulate, it implies that African Americans have no one but themselves to blame for their own failures. The subtle message seems to be that African Americans who claim to be the victims of white racism are themselves racists against Korean immigrants. By pitting one group against another, it may have prolonged the stand-off between the parties involved. African American activists may not have wanted to leave the impression that they were giving in to the public pressure and attack from the media.

The coverage by the *Los Angeles Times* of the Latasha Harlins shooting case was quite different from the *New York Times* report of the Red Apple boycott. The *Los Angeles Times* reported the tragic shooting of Latasha Harlins as soon as it occurred. Interestingly, the perspective of the *Los Angeles Times* was opposite to that of the *New York Times*. The tone of the *Los Angeles Times* reports was more sympathetic to the African American community than to Korean immigrants. For example, the first report of the shooting featured the headline: "Slain Girl Was Not Stealing Juice, Police Say."[30] The headline of this article directly or indirectly portrayed the Korean merchant as "guilty" of murdering an innocent girl. Next day, the paper published an accusatory editorial against the Korean grocer, "A Senseless and Tragic Killing."[31]

Obviously, the *Los Angeles Times'* portrayal of Korean immigrant merchants was negative. Often the paper highlighted complaints by African American customers toward Korean immigrant merchants of being "rude" or "disrespectful." For example, one *Times* article pointed out that "many people who live and work near the Empire Liquor Market (owned by Soon Ja Du) had stopped patronizing the store because the owners often shouted insults at customers and frequently accused them of shoplifting."[32]

Unlike the *New York Times*, the *Los Angeles Times* never printed accusatory editorials against the leader of the boycott of Korean-owned markets, Danny Bakewell of the Brotherhood Crusade, who has served as its president for the last two decades. Instead, the *Los Angeles Times* identified Mr Bakewell as a "new voice" and a key spokesperson for the African American community in Los Angeles. Mr Bakewell appeared on numerous radio and television talk shows, and he was extensively quoted by the *Los Angeles Times*.

Mr Bakewell understood how to manipulate the media to get as much exposure as possible. In the midst of the increasing tensions between Korean Americans and African Americans, a nine-year-old Korean American girl was critically wounded by an armed African American robber. Mr Bakewell took quick action. A *Los Angeles Times* writer commented that "the media-savvy Bakewell beat the Korean American community to the punch, announcing that he will hold a news conference of his own today to condemn the shooting. Mr Bakewell said he was outraged by the shooting."[33] Although the *Los Angeles Times* knew that Mr Bakewell was a controversial and provocative leader, it continued to portray him as one of the most important leaders of the African American community by granting him continuous publicity.

By focusing on Korean-African American conflict, the white establishment can disguise the real issue of institutional racism and racial inequality in America. The white establishment in New York was able to dismiss the charge of racism by African Americans by accusing them of being "racists" themselves. On the other hand, the *Los Angeles Times* and the Los Angeles

District Attorney's Office, whose role is discussed below, may have used the Latasha Harlins shooting case to appease the anger of the African American community in the wake of the Rodney King videotape incident.

It is clear that both the *New York Times* and the *Los Angeles Times* played agitators' roles by pitting one group against another. As a third party to the conflicts, the media tended to sensationalize them by taking sides with Korean merchants or African American customers, depending upon the social and racial climate of each city. Biased reporting of the boycott by the *New York Times* and other mainstream media may have prolonged the boycotts because protesters had no other choice but to insist on their hardline positons.

Of course, there are other important reasons why the New York boycott lasted longer than anyone had expected. Sonny Carson and his December 12th Movement used the Red Apple boycott to politicize the African American community in the Flatbush neighborhood of Brooklyn. Flatbush is a predominantly immigrant community with many residents from the Carribean countries of Haiti, Jamaica, Guyana, and Trinidad and Tobago. Therefore, there was no established political leadership in Flatbush. This political vacuum allowed a politically motivated outsider such as Sonny Carson to enter the scene and use the local boycott to organize the immigrant community and advance his own cause.

However, it is also important to acknowledge that the boycotts received considerable support within the African American community of Flatbush. Without community support, it would have been impossible to sustain the boycott for such a duration. One of Mayor David Dinkins' closest advisers said:

> You could say that we blew it, that we totally misread and misunderstood the boycott ... The protesters hung on and now they know that they don't need us. They have enough support in the community to stand up to the police, the courts, and the mayor.[34]

There are several reasons why the boycott generated considerable support from the African American community in Flatbush. In the African American community, the boycott is seen as an "appropriate" and "effective" response to racism and injustice. During the civil rights struggle, African Americans effectively mobilized their community to stage boycotts, marches, and other non-violent peaceful protests to end segregation and racial discrimination. For these reasons, it is rare for African Americans to publicly criticize a boycott unless there is concrete proof that it is an illegitimate action. The code of silence among African American leadership with regard to boycotts is interpreted as endorsement of them.

Second, Korean-African American tensions had been simmering since the early 1980s in the New York area. Therefore, Korean immigrant merchants had become a convenient scapegoat for African American frustration and anger. Anti-Korean sentiment was widespread in the African American community as rumors spread quickly. For example, many African Americans believe that Korean immigrants receive special government support to establish businesses in African American neighborhoods.[35] In recent years, Southeast Asian refugees have settled in African American neighborhoods in Oakland, Los Angeles and other parts of California cities. Southeast Asian refugees are entitled to receive special federal government supports because of the passage of the Refugee Acts. For example, Southeast Asian refugees are given special preference for public housing, jobs, and other government benefits. Many African American residents resent this practice. Rumors concerning preferential treatment for Korean immigrants may have started from this practice, although I have no proof of this. Sonny Carson and his December 12th movement exploited the anti-Korean sentiment and appealed to African Americans to boycott the Korean-owned stores. Frequently, fliers were distributed throughout the African American neighborhoods proclaiming slogans such as "Korean Merchants Must Go," and "Jail Koreans Who Assaulted Our Sister."

In addition, Sonny Carson and his followers were disappointed and angry over Mayor David Dinkins' refusal to support what they perceived as a "black" agenda.[36] Carson may have tried to use the boycott as a bargaining chip with the Mayor's office by refusing to negotiate to settle the boycott.

In contrast, a threatened boycott of the Empire Liquor Market in South Central Los Angeles did not occur because the store never tried to reopen. Since the tragic shooting incident, the store remained closed, and it probably will never open gain. There was no need to continue a boycott. Instead, Danny Bakewell and his supporters focused their attention on a second shooting incident that occurred three months after the Latasha Harlins shooting in South Central Los Angeles. It is known as the "John's Market" shooting incident. An African American customer, Lee Arthur Mitchell, was shot and killed by a Korean American merchant, Tae Sam Park, in South Central Los Angeles on June 2, 1991. Although it was ruled a justifiable homicide (self-defense), the shooting led to a four-month boycott. Several Korean-owned stores were boycotted and firebombed. Bakewell and his supporters demanded permanent closure of the store. Four months later, the boycott ended with an agreement between Bakewell of the Brotherhood Crusade and the Korean American Grocery Association (KAGRO). Under the agreement, protesters stopped boycott of the store, and the store will be closed and put up for sale, initially exclusively to African American buyers and then to others after 30 days.

Quick and decisive intervention by the Black-Korean Alliance (BKA) and the Mayor's Office helped to contain the anger and antagonism toward Korean merchants on the streets of South Central Los Angeles after the Latasha Harlins shooting incident. The BKA issued a statement: "We are shocked and appalled at the circumstances surrounding the death of Latasha Harlins. We are deeply concerned that this terrible incident of violence does not aggravate the relationship between African Americans and Korean Americans in our communities."[37] In addition, the Mayor's office played a major role in completing the negotiations between the two parties.

THE MAYOR'S OFFICE: QUIET NEGOTIATIONS

One of the most striking differences between the Red Apple and Latasha Harlins cases was the response of the respective Mayor's office toward each crisis. David Dinkins was elected as Mayor of New York City with a reputation of being a consensus builder who could heal the racial wounds of the city. However, Dinkins made it clear that "he was not prepared to take sides in what he said was a 'legitimate' dispute over what had occurred."[38] Mayor Dinkins believed that quiet or behind-the-scene negotiations were the best way to resolve the boycott. However, the Mayor suffered major political damage as he was unable to handle the Bensonhurst murder trial[39] and the Red Apple boycott.

The Korean American community in New York and the mainstream media were critical of Dinkins' indecisiveness and reluctance to intervene for a quick resolution of the crisis. He was criticized by a Brooklyn judge who expressed regret that "the Mayor had not intervened personally to help end the boycott."[40] Feeling the heat and pressure from all sectors of the community, Mayor Dinkins was finally forced to announce that he was "personally prepared to mediate." He also said that "he was against the boycotts on a racial basis."[41]

To defuse criticism against him, Mayor Dinkins established a Fact-Finding Committee to investigate the causes of the boycott in April 1990. Four months later, the committee published a report that "the boycott is not racial in nature, but it stems from cultural differences."[42] The report basically blamed everyone else except the Mayor and praised the Mayor's use of "moral authority" to encourage both sides to negotiate. The report was particularly critical of District Attorney Charles J. Hynes "for moving too slowly in the investigation of the events and the prosecution of pending cases."[43]

Still, Mayor Dinkins refused to take a public stand against the boycott. However, he was forced to do so when close to 10,000 Korean Americans rallied in front of City Hall to demand more active intervention by the Mayor's Office on September 18, 1990. Three days later, Mayor Dinkins visited the Red Apple store and bought about $10.00 worth of produce and declared that "the boycott should end."[44] The Mayor's visit appeared to intensify the tensions as 19 gasoline bombs were found on the roof of the Red Apple store shortly afterward.

Mayor Bradley was a highly visible figure in the Latasha Harlins and John's Market boycott. The Los Angeles Mayor was determined not to make the same mistakes as Mayor Dinkins had in New York City. He was quick to get involved in the Latasha Harlins shooting case as he promptly assembled leaders of the Korean American and African American communities to his office. The Mayor urged community leaders to issue a statement calling for unity and understanding between the two communities. Bradley's intention was to resolve this politically volatile situation as soon as possible. Proper credit should be given to the Mayor for mobilizing his staff to negotiate a truce between the Korean American merchants and African American activists.

However, it is equally important to note that Mayor Bradley did not do much to improve the deteriorating relationship between the two communities during his tenure in office. Although Bradley took credit for forming the Black-Korean Alliance in 1986, he did not do much to support the activities of the BKA.[45] For example, the BKA never received any financial support from the city although Mayor Bradley repeatedly praised the BKA as one of the most important organizations in the city.

Mayor Bradley also favored "quiet diplomacy" to resolve the crisis. He argued that it was his style and the most effective way to handle the boycotts. It appears that "quiet diplomacy" are ways for politicians to protect their own self-interests. In retrospect, both Mayor Dinkins of New York and Bradley of Los Angeles were more interested in protecting their own political careers than in resolving the crisis.

THE POLICE AND THE COURTS

In the beginning, the New York police and the District Attorney's Office were reluctant to get involved in the Red Apple boycott. The police refused to intervene, claiming that police usually do not get involved in a civil case. Although the court issued a preliminary injunction order against the boycotters to stay at least 50 feet from the Red Apple and Church Fruits stores, police refused to enforce the court order. As I mentioned earlier, the Mayor's Fact-Finding Committee report was particularly critical of the handling of the boycott by the District Attorney's Office. The report stated that "the District Attorney's efforts have contributed to the cynical attitude of the parties and the public toward the justice system, and given an opening to charges of selective prosecution based on race."[46] In response, Charles J. Hynes criticized the Committee's report as "flawed because of inaccuracy and an inaccurate review of the facts and circumstances."

In contrast, the police and the District Attorney's Office in Los Angeles took an "activist" approach in the Latasha Harlins trial. A day after the shooting, the police hastily called a press conference and issued a startling statement. Commander Michael J. Bosti said, "the videotape shows only a 'scuffle' begun by Du over the knapsack, not an attack mounted by the teen-ager. There was no attempt at shoplifting. There was no robbery. There was no crime at all."[47] The statement clearly implied that the shooting was "unjustifiable." Later, Deputy District Attorney Roxane Carvajal said, "it is clear and evident, Mrs Du is a danger to society. Mrs Du said she was under attack, but the evidence in this case doesn't bear that out."[48] It is difficult to comprehend the motives for the action of the District Attorney Office against Mrs Du. It created the atmosphere that anything less than the conviction of the first degree murder of Mrs Du would be seen as injustice in the African American community.

It remains a mystery why the DA's office decided to bring the first degree murder charge against Mrs Du when the police knew exactly what happened based on the security camera videotape. The videotape clearly showed the altercation between Mrs Du and Latasha Harlins. Contrary to the earlier statements by the DA's office, the videotape showed that the shooting took place in the heat of struggle. Objective observers would agree that the videotape did not show premeditation by Soon Ja Du against Latasha Harlins. During the trial, Superior Court Judge Joyce Karlins threw out the first degree murder charge against Mrs Du. Instead, Mrs Du was convicted of an involuntary manslaughter charge.

Superior Court Judge Joyce Karlins sentenced Soon Ja Du to five years' probation. Judge Karlins said that "Mrs Du was not a threat to society. It was not a time for revenge but for healing. It should serve as a catalyst for better relations."[49] She also expressed hope that the tragedy would be used to further understanding and tolerance. In retrospect, the sentencing of Mrs Du to probation created more controversy than the shooting incident itself. The African American community was shocked and outraged by the lenient sentence. "It was an outlandish injustice," declared Bakewell of the Brotherhood Crusade.[50]

The irresponsible sentencing by an inexperienced Superior Court judge and the sensational reporting of the anti-Karlins campaign by the local media, including the *Los Angeles Times*, increased tensions and polarized ethnic communities in Los Angeles.[51] Obviously, the Soon Ja Du ruling caused strains between the Korean American and African American communities. The sentencing became one of the most hotly debated issues in the legal community as well. It became increasingly difficult to take a neutral position on the Soon Ja Du ruling.

CONCLUSION

In recent years, we have witnessed a dramatic increase in racial tensions and violence in the United States. Demographic shifts, including "white flight" from urban centers and increasing Asian and Latino immigration have exacerbated conflicts between minority groups. During the 1980s, Korean-African American tension has emerged as one of the most visible and pressing racial issues in America. The media may have played an agitator's role by portraying Korean immigrant merchants and African American residents as adversaries fighting for their own interests. In New York City, African American boycotters were portrayed as racists and radicals. On the other hand, Korean immigrants were portrayed as hard-working and industrious merchants who were trying to make their American Dream come true with their own bootstraps.

In Los Angeles, boycotts against Korean-owned stores were legitimized by the *Los Angeles Times* articles and the police, who portrayed the shooting of Latasha Harlins as unprovoked and an unjustifiable act. Korean immigrant shop owners were portrayed as rude, disrespectful and money-chasers, implying that African American residents had legitimate reasons to boycott the Korean-owned stores. The leader of the boycott, Danny Bakewell, was praised as a new voice of the African American community who filled the leadership vacuum. Because African Americans have been an important part of the dominant biracial coalitions in Los Angeles politics, the *Los Angeles Times* articles may have been more sensitive and sympathetic toward African American issues. In addition, the Rodney King beating videotape probably generated more sympathy toward African American concerns.

Regardless, the media played a critical role in shaping public perception of the nature of the Korean-African American conflict. Depending upon the social and political circumstances, the media took sides with Korean Americans or African Americans. The reporting of the boycotts by the media became a political act of itself. By pitting Korean American merchants against African American residents, the media defused the potentially explosive white-African American tensions in New York and to a lesser extent in Los Angeles.

Public officials also contributed to intensifying the conflict. The District Attorney's Office brought a first degree murder charge against Soon Ja Du despite the existence of a videotape showing clearly that the shooting took place in the heat of a struggle. The District Attorney's Office and police may have attempted to deflect mounting criticism against them in the wake of the Rodney King police beating case. The first degree murder charge against Soon Ja Du can be interpreted as an attempt to appease the African American community by the District Attorney's Office.

As we have seen, the courts, politicians, activists, and the media manipulated Korean-African American disputes in New York and Los Angeles in an attempt to gain "legitimacy." In order to resolve their own "legitimacy crisis," these agents often construct the disputes with interpretations far removed from the facts.

NOTES

1   Peter Kwong, "The First Multicultural Riots." *Village Voice,* June 9, 1992.
2   See *Report of the National Advisory Commission on Civil Disorder.* March 1, 1968.
3   Shlomo Katz (ed.), *Negro and Jew: An Encounter in America* (New York: Macmillan, 1967), p. 76.
4   According to the *Los Angeles Times,* November 24, 1991, there are only two Vons Cos., which is the largest supermarket chain in Southland with more than 300 stores, left in South Central Los Angeles. In addition, there is not a single Target discount outlet left in South Central Los Angeles, although 73 new discount outlets opened during the last eight years in Southern California.
5   May 12, 1984.
6   *Los Angeles Sentinel,* August 11, 1983.
7   See Edward T. Chang, "Building Minority Coalitions: A Case Study of Korean and African Americans," *Korea Journal of Population and Development,* Vol. 21, No.1 (1992), 37–56. On November 1992, the BKA dissolved because it was unable to deal with the volatile issues facing Korean and African American communities. After the Latasha Harlins shooting case, the BKA found it increasingly difficult to promote understanding and coalitions between the two communities.
8   *New York Times,* January 31, 1991.

9   Interview with Mr Man-Ho Park (August 15, 1992), an owner of Church Fruit across the street from the Red Apple. The boycott spread to Church Fruit because the protesters insisted that the two stores were owned by the same person.

10   It is important to note that Asian American images are that of "all look alike." Police couldn't tell the difference between the store manager Pong Ok Jang and the owner and brother Bong Jae Jang. It is a problem that Asian Americans have constantly to confront in America.

11   Carson led a boycott in Bedford-Stuyvessant against a Korean-owned store where a 67-year old African American woman was beaten. He also led a boycott in Jamaica (1981) and Harlem (1984).

12   *New York Times*, January 31, 1991.

13   *Korea Times*, March 22, 24, and 26, 1991; see also *Korea Central Daily News*, March 22 and 28, 1991.

14   Rumor spread quickly that Chung Lee was related to Soon Ja Du. Chung Lee's store was burned down shortly after the Latasha Harlins shooting incident. He had to rebuild his store. However, his store was again burned down during the Los Angeles riots. Chung Lee served as a co-chair of the Black–Korean Alliance.

15   *Korea Times*, April 17, 1991.

16   For more details of the 1992 Los Angeles riots, see Edward T. Chang "America's First Multiethnic Riots," in Karin Augilar-San Juan (ed.), *The State of Asian America: Activism and Resistance in the 1990s* (Boston: South End Press, 1994), pp. 101–17.

17   *Los Angeles Times*, March 19, 1991.

18   *Korea Times*, April 17, 1991.

19   *New York Times*, October 20, 1987.

20   Andrew Hacker, *Two Nations: Black and White, Separate, Hostile, Unequal* (New York: Charles Scribner's Sons, 1992), p. 195.

21   See Raphael Sonenshein, *Politics in Black and White: Race and Power in Los Angeles* (Princeton: Princeton University Press, 1993).

22   *New York Post*, April 23, 1990.

23   Edna Bonacich, "A Theory of Middleman Minorities," *American Sociological Review*, Vol.38 (October 1973), 583–94; Hubert M. Blalock, Jr, *Towards a Theory of Minority Group Relations* (New York: John Wiley, 1967).

24   Edna Bonacich and Tae Hwan Jung, "A Portrait of Korean Small Business in Los Angeles: 1977," in Eui-Young Yu *et al.*, *Koreans in Los Angeles* (Los Angeles: Koryo Research Institute, 1982), p. 77.

25   *New York Times*, May 17, 1990.

26   *New York Times*, May 27, 1990.

27   *New York Times* editorial, May 8, 1990.

28   It was mentioned at least four times in articles on May 7, 8, 9, and 10, 1990.

29   For more detail see Ivan Light, *Ethnic Enterprise in America* (Berkeley: University of California Press, 1972).

30   *Los Angeles Times*, March 20, 1990.

31   *Los Angeles Times* editorial, March 20, 1990.

32   *Los Angeles Times*, March 20, 1990.

33   *Los Angeles Times*, October 23, 1991.

34   *Village Voice*, May 29, 1990, p. 31.

35 During the past seven years, I was able to speak with many African American leaders and residents of South Central Los Angeles. Most people, regardless of education level and ideology, believe that Korean immigrant merchants receive special help from government programs to purchase businesses in their own neighborhoods.

36 Elsa Chen, Black-led Boycotts of Korean-owned Grocery Stores: Background, Analysis, and Policy, Senior thesis, Woodrow Wilson School of Public and International Affairs, Princeton University, 1991.

37 *Korea Times*, March 27, 1991.

38 *New York Times*, May 9, 1990.

39 Bensonhurst murder trial refers to the murder trial of the African American youth, Yusuf Hawkins, who was killed by a white mob in the Brooklyn neighborhood of Bensonhurst in 1989.

40 *New York Times*, May 11, 1990.

41 *New York Times*, May 12, 1990.

42 *New York Times*, August 31, 1990.

43 *Ibid.*

44 *New York Times*, September 22, 1990.

45 For more detail, see Edward T. Chang, "Building Minority Coalitions: A Case Study of Korean and African Americans," *Korea Journal of Population and Development*, Vol.21, No.1 (1992).

46 *New York Times*, August 31, 1990.

47 *Los Angeles Times*, March 19, 1991.

48 *Los Angeles Times*, April 8, 1991.

49 *Los Angeles Times*, November 16, 1991.

50 *Ibid.*

51 See the *Los Angeles Times* articles on November 16, 20, 22 and December 13, 15, 16, 1991.

Index

criminals, role of, 12–3, 16–21, 42; in
anti-Sikh riots, 201–2, 204; 208,
212–14; in riots in Muzaffarnager,
191–2
criminalization, of the state, 28, 205,
212
criminalized population, created by the
"war on drugs, " 44
Czech people, 99
Czechoslovakia, 89, 96–7, 99

dadas (local gang leaders), 214
Davis, Natalie Zemon, 2, 3, 16, 19, 20,
22, 24, 147
Dayan, Moshe, 119, 120
December 12th Movement (in New
York), 238, 244
Delhi, 14, 17, 24, 28, 35, 168, 180,
187, 195; anti-Sikh riots in, 201–17
deportation, of *Ostjuden* (eastern Jews)
from Germany, 90, 101, 106
Detroit, murder of Vincent Chin in,
221–4, 227–9; riots in, 18, 29
Detroit Association of Black
Organizations, 229
dharma (religious Law), 173
Dharma Yudh (religious crusade), 177
Dinkins, David (former Mayor of New
York), and his role in the Black
boycotts of Korean-American estab-
lishments, 242, 244–7
Dnepropetrovsk, 81
dockworkers, 17, 61, 76–9
Du, Soon Ja, 238–9, 243, 248–50
Dubey, Hardwar, 181
Dubnov (Dubnow), S. M., 42, 70
Dumont, Louis, 164
Durkheim, Emile, 154

East St. Louis riot of 1917, 18
Ebens, Ronald, 221–8
Eckstein, Harry, 197
economic competition, as a factor in
riots, 9–11, 17, 20
economic domination, as a factor in
causing riots, 11
Ekaterinoslav, 57, 81–3
Ekatmatayajna (Sacrifice for Unity),
166–7

Ekta Yatra (Procession for Unity),
170–1
Emergency, (in India), 181, 213
Enabling Act (Germany), 95
Engineer, Ashgar Ali, 10
Essed, Philomena, 224
ethnic groups, 1, 26, 33, 40, 41, 43, 81,
201, 204, 217
ethnic movements, 40
ethnicity, 6, 40, 41, 89, 92, 108, 197,
227
eugenics, 92, 104
European, 8, 19, 38, 40, 108, 146, 174
exploitation, as explanation for riots,
11

Faithful of the Temple Mount, 115,
121, 125–7, 130, 133, 146
faqirs, 162
fatwa, 120, 138
FBI, 224, 235
Felissainte, Gisleaine, 237
firman, 117
Flatbush Frontline Collective, 238
Fogelson, Robert M., 19–21
Frankfurter, David, 95–6, 102
Freitag, Sandria, 154–5
Friedman, Menachem, 131, 139

Ganapati, 165
Gandhi, Indira, 14, 24, 168, 201–3,
206–7, 209–10, 213, 215–16,
Gandhi, Mahatma, 7, 159, 165, 173,
193
Gandhi, Rajiv, 24, 185, 193, 201,
205–7, 212
Gandhi, Sanjay, 204, 213
Ganges, River, 168
Gavai, P.G., 212
general strike, in Odessa in 1905, 60,
64–5; in Ekaterinoslav in 1905, 82
Germany, 13, 17, 30, 35, 89–108
Goebbels, Joseph, 35, 92, 102–3, 107
Goetz, Bernard, 239
Gopal, Kishan, 181
Goren, Rabbi Shlomo, 119–20
Göring, Herman Wilhelm, 98, 103, 107
government inquiry, into Odessa
pogrom, 70–5